RUN:
Computer Education

Brooks/Cole Series in Computer Science

Program Design with Pseudocode
T.E. Bailey and K.A. Lundgaard

BASIC: An Introduction to Computer Programming with the Apple
Robert J. Bent and George C. Sethares

BASIC: An Introduction to Computer Programming, Second Edition
Robert J. Bent and George C. Sethares

Business BASIC
Robert J. Bent and George C. Sethares

FORTRAN with Problem Solving: A Structured Approach
Robert J. Bent and George C. Sethares

Beginning BASIC
D.K. Carver

Beginning Structured COBOL
D.K. Carver

Structured COBOL for Microcomputers
D.K. Carver

Learning BASIC Programming: A Systematic Approach
Howard Dachslager, Masato Hayashi and Richard Zucker

Problem Solving and Structured Programming with ForTran 77
Martin O. Holoien and Ali Behforooz

Basic Business BASIC: Using Microcomputers
Peter Mears and Louis Raho

Brooks/Cole Series in Computer Education

An Apple for the Teacher: Fundamentals of Instructional Computing
George Culp and Herbert Nickles

RUN: Computer Education
Dennis O. Harper and James H. Stewart

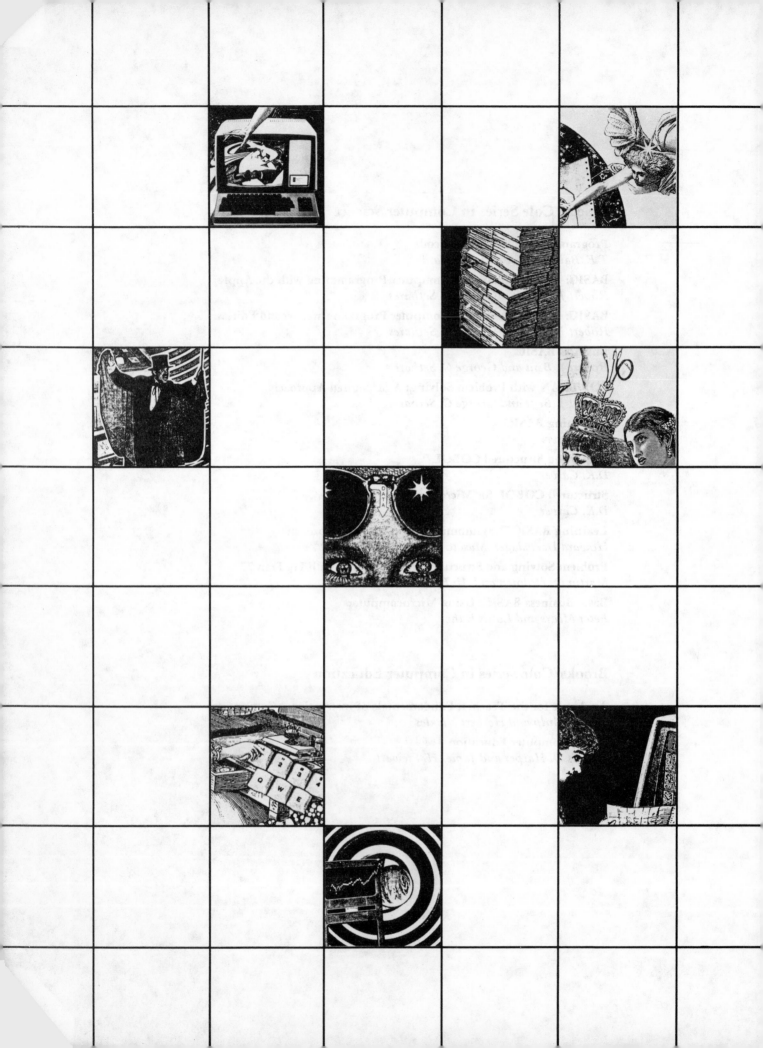

RUN:
Computer Education

Dennis O. Harper
University of California, Santa Barbara

James H. Stewart
London, Ontario, Canada

Brooks/Cole Publishing Company

Monterey, California

Brooks/Cole Publishing Company
A Division of Wadsworth, Inc.

Printed in the United States of America

10 9 8 7 6 5 4 3

Library of Congress Cataloging in Publication Data
Main entry under title:

RUN, computer education.

　　Includes index.
　　1. Education—Data processing—Addresses,
essays, lectures.　　2. Microcomputers—Addresses,
essays, lectures.　　3. Teachers—Training of—
Addresses, essays, lectures.　I. Harper,
Dennis O., date　　.　II. Stewart, James H.,
date
LB1028.43.R86　1982　　370'.28'54　　82-12933
ISBN 0-534-01265-5

Subject Editor: *James F. Leisy, Jr.*
Production Editor: *Suzanne Ewing*
Manuscript Editor: *Barbara Burton*
Interior and Cover Design: *Vicki Van Deventer*
Cover and Chapter Opening Art: *Therese Donath*
Illustrations: *Tim Keenan*
Typesetting: *Omegatype Typography, Inc., Champaign, Illinois*

Joan & Evelyn,
Jennifer & J

Preface

Teachers, parents, and even students are bringing personal computers into the classroom in an impressively growing grass roots movement. The benefits of having microcomputers in schools are obvious to anyone who has witnessed the enthusiastic response of students using them. A critical need exists, however, for information aimed at teachers of all grade levels and subject areas because so many teachers are inadequately prepared to understand the new technology fully. To fill this void we have selected and categorized pertinent articles about the use of microcomputers in precollege education. These articles reflect a sense of high excitement and optimism in the academic community regarding instructional computer use.

This book is designed as a text or reference book for educational colleges or school districts offering computer literacy to preservice or inservice elementary or secondary teachers; it can easily serve other audiences as well. The wide range of topics makes it a valuable starting point for anyone interested in exploring the rapidly expanding world of computing. Educators of any group from kindergarten to university level will find each chapter professionally rewarding and instructive. Computing and noncomputing teachers, professors, student teachers, and school administrators can all benefit from this text. In addition, the casual reader will find most chapters offer a wealth of interesting, fundamental information regarding educational computer use. The teacher's manual offers other sources of information to those who wish to pursue a particular theme, as well as many practical discussion topics and exercises intended to involve people in a teacher-training program.

The suggested activities are presented on two levels to take advantage of differences in teachers and teacher trainers. The "What's Your Opinion" section at the end of each chapter contains key points from the preceding articles. These statements can be used as the seeds for class or group discussions, homework assignments, summarizations, debates, and other uses as outlined in the teacher's manual.

The "Exercises," also found at the end of each chapter, provide topics for essay questions, assignments, projects, and similar activities requiring extra-curricula study or research by the student.

The articles are written by many of the leaders in instructional computing throughout the world. Names such as Papert, Bork, Taylor, Billings, Braun, Moursund, Poirot, Molnar, Jones, Luehrmann, Klassen, Watt, Dennis, and Chambers are very familiar to computer educators. These authors and others provide expert analyses of the major issues facing educators in this age of information. The diverse writing styles and opinions of the authors provide an excellent cross-section of the current, relevant literature.

We extend our sincere appreciation to Dr. R. Murray Thomas of the University of California, Santa Barbara, whose encouragement, support, and expertise were great aids to the fruition of this text. We thank the reviewers of the manuscript, whose thoughtful comments were also great aids: Cheryl A. Anderson, University of Texas; J. Richard Dennis, University of Illinois; Barbara Dubitsky, Bank Street College of Education; Dorothy H. Judd, Northern Illinois University; Jacqueline McMahon, University of Missouri; and Ted Sjoldsma, University of Iowa.

Dennis O. Harper

James H. Stewart

Contents

THREE Teacher Education 60

FOUR Computer Assisted Instruction 107

FIVE Software and Hardware Selection 144

RUN:
Computer Education

ONE

Teaching and Learning Theory

Examining the place of the microcomputer in the learning process, this chapter shows that educators are becoming increasingly aware of the machine's versatility, power, and potential for the classroom. The microcomputer offers a reason for analyzing and revising entire curricula as well as the impetus for devising totally new methods of instruction. Indeed, once introduced to microcomputers, teachers soon realize that their imagination is the only limiting factor in the creation of classroom applications.

With infectious enthusiasm Seymour Papert describes his application of Piagetian theory to the teaching of math and of programming concepts to young children; his successes with the LOGO environment are exciting. He demonstrates that children can learn about computing *by* computing. Drawing an analogy between the QWERTY typewriter keyboard and the popular BASIC language, he suggests that both fail to resolve their respective problems adequately and forecasts their long-range detrimental effects. Darlene Crawford offers both an intelligent assessment of future needs and suggestions for program implementation. She shows how the microcomputer can be used to solve the problems of the barriers between home and school as well as between teachers and computerization. John D'Angelo notes that the microprocessor offers a method of rethinking and restructuring current educational delivery systems. As George Miller suggests, however, though the computer culture may be inevitable, human nature will endure. Examining the value of the computer versus that of the human teacher, Miller concludes that each has its own particular role to play.

Computers and Computer Cultures

Seymour Papert

In most contemporary educational situations where children come into contact with computers the computer is used to put children through their paces, to provide exercises of an appropriate level of difficulty, to provide feedback, and to dispense information. The computer programming the child. In the LOGO environment the relationship is reversed: The child is in control: The child programs the computer. And in teaching the computer how to think, children embark on an exploration about how they themselves think. Thinking about thinking turns the child into an epistemologist, an experience not even shared by most adults.

After five years of study with Jean Piaget in Geneva, I came away impressed by his way of looking at children as the active builders of their own intellectual structures. To say that intellectual structures are built by the learner rather than taught by a teacher does not mean that they are built from nothing. Like other builders, children appropriate to their own use materials they find about them, most saliently the models and metaphors suggested by the surrounding culture.

Piaget writes about the order in which the child develops different intellectual abilities. I give more weight than he does to the influence of the materials

Condensed from Chapter 1 of MINDSTORMS by Seymour Papert. Copyright © 1980 by Basic Books, Inc. By permission of Basic Books, Inc., Publishers, New York. (British Commonwealth rights by permission of The Harvester Press Ltd., Sussex.)

a certain culture provides in determining that order. For example, our culture is very rich in materials useful for the child's construction of certain components of numerical and logical thinking. Children learn to count; they learn that the result of counting is independent of order and special arrangement; they extend this "conservation" to thinking about the properties of liquids as they are poured and of solids which change their shape. Children develop these components of thinking preconsciously and "spontaneously," that is to say without deliberate teaching. Other components of knowledge, such as the skills involved in doing permutations and combinations, develop more slowly, or do not develop at all without formal schooling.

The computer presence might have more fundamental effects than did other new technologies, including television and even printing. The metaphor of computer as a mathematics speaking entity puts the learner in a qualitatively new kind of relationship to an important domain of knowledge. Even the best of educational television is limited to offering quantitative improvements in the kinds of learning that existed without it. **Sesame Street** might offer better and more engaging explanations than a child can get from some parents or nursery school teachers, but the child is still in the business of listening to explanations. By contrast, when a child learns to program, the process of learning is transformed. It becomes more active and self directed. The knowledge is acquired for a recognizable personal purpose. The child does something with it. The new knowledge is a source of power and is experienced as such from the moment it begins to form in the child's mind.

I have spoken of mathematics being learned in a new way. But much more is affected than mathematics. Piaget distinguishes between "concrete" thinking and "formal" thinking. Concrete thinking is already well on its way by the time the child enters first grade at age 6 and is consolidated in the following several years. Formal thinking does not develop until the child is almost 12, give or take a year or two, and some researchers have even suggested that many people never achieve fully formal thinking. I do not fully accept Piaget's distinction, but I am sure that it is close enough to reality to help us make sense of the idea that the consequences for intellectual development of one innovation could be qualitatively greater than the cumulative quantitative effects of a thousand others. My conjecture is that the computer can concretize (and personalize) the formal. Seen in this light, it is not just another powerful educational tool. It is unique in providing us with the means for addressing what Piaget and many others see as the obstacle which is overcome in the passage from child to adult thinking. I believe that it can allow us to shift the boundary separating concrete and formal. Knowledge that was accessible only through formal processes can now be approached concretely. And the real magic comes from the fact that this knowledge includes those elements one needs to become a formal thinker.

This description of the role of the computer is rather abstract. I shall concretize it by looking at the effect of working with computers on two kinds of thinking Piaget associates with the formal stage of intellectual development: combinatorial thinking, where one has to reason in terms of the set of all possible states of a system, and self referential thinking about thinking itself.

In a typical experiment in combinatorial thinking, children are asked to form all the possible combinations (or "families") of beads of assorted colors. It really is quite remarkable that most children are unable to do this systematically and accurately until they are in the fifth or sixth grades. Why should this be? Why does the task seem to be so much more difficult than the intellectual feats accomplished by seven and eight year old children? Is its logical structure essentially more complex? Can it possibly require a neurological mechanism that does not mature until the approach of puberty? I think that a more likely explanation is provided by looking at the nature of the culture. The task of making the families of beads can be looked at as constructing and executing a program, a very common sort of program, in which two loops are nested: Fix a first color and run through all possible second colors, then repeat until all possible first colors have been run through. For someone who is thoroughly used to computers and programming there is nothing "formal" or abstract about this task. For a child in a computer culture it would be as concrete as matching up knives and forks at the dinner table. Even the common "bug" of including some families twice (for example, red-blue and blue-red) would be well known. Our culture is rich in pairs, couples, and one to one correspondences of all sorts, and it is rich in language for talking about such things. This richness provides both the incentive and a supply of models and tools for children to build ways to think about such issues as whether three large pieces of candy are more or less than four smaller pieces. For such problems our children acquire an excellent intuitive sense of quantity. But our culture is relatively poor in models of systematic procedures. Until recently there was not even a name in popular language for programming, let alone for the ideas needed to do so successfully. There is no word for "nested loops" and no word for the double counting bug. Indeed, there are no words for the powerful ideas computerists refer to as "bug" and "debugging."

Without the incentive or the materials to build powerful, concrete ways to think about problems involving systematicity, children are forced to approach such problems in a groping, abstract fashion. Thus cultural factors can explain the difference in age at which children build their intuitive knowledge of quantity and of systematicity.

While still working in Geneva I had become sensitive to the way in which materials from the then very young computer cultures were allowing psychologists to develop new ways to think about thinking. In fact, my entry into the world of computers was motivated largely by the idea that children could also benefit, perhaps even more than the psychologist, from the way in which computer models seemed to be able to give concrete form to areas of knowledge that had previously appeared so intangible and abstract.

I began to see how children who had learned to program computers could use very concrete computer models to think about thinking and to learn about learning and in doing so, enhance their powers as psychologists and as epistemologists. For example, many children are held back in their learning because they have a model of learning in which you have either "got it" or "got it wrong." But when you learn to program a computer you almost never get it right the first time. Learning to be a master programmer is learning to become highly skilled at isolating and correcting "bugs," the parts that keep the program from working. The question to ask about the program is not whether it is right or wrong, but if it is fixable. If this way of looking at intellectual products were generalized to how the larger culture thinks about knowledge and its acquisition, we might all be less intimidated by our fears of "being wrong." This potential influence of the computer on changing our notion of a black and white version of our successes and failures is an example of using the computer as an "object to think with." It is obviously not necessary to work with computers in order to acquire good strategies for learning. Surely "debugging" strategies were developed by successful learners long before computers existed. But thinking about learning by analogy with developing a program is a powerful and accessible way to get started on becoming more articulate about one's debugging strategies and more deliberate about improving them.

My discussion of a computer culture and its impact on thinking presupposes a massive penetration of powerful computers into people's lives. That this will happen there can be no doubt. The calculator, the electronic game, and the digital watch were brought to us by a technical revolution that rapidly lowered prices for electronics in a period when all others were rising with inflation. That same technological revolution, brought about by the integrated circuit, is now bringing us the personal computer.

There really is no disagreement among experts that the cost of computers will fall to a level where they will enter everyday life in vast numbers. Some will be there as computers proper, that is to say, programmable machines. Others might appear as games of ever increasing complexity and in automated supermarkets where the shelves, maybe even the cans, will talk. There is no doubt that the material surface of life will become very different for everyone, perhaps most of all for children. But there has been a significant difference of opinion about the effects this computer presence will produce. I would distinguish my thinking from two trends of thinking which I refer to here as the "skeptical" and the "critical."

Skeptics do not expect the computer presence to make much difference in how people learn and think. I have formulated a number of possible explanations for why they think as they do. In some cases I think the skeptics might conceive of education and the effect of computers on it too narrowly. Instead of considering general cultural effects, they focus attention on the use of the computer as a device for programmed instruction. Skeptics then conclude that while the computer might produce some improvements in school learning, it is not likely to lead to fundamental change. In a sense, too, I think the skeptical view derives from a failure to appreciate just how much Piagetian learning takes place as a child grows up. If a person conceives of children's intellectual development (or for that matter, moral or social development) as deriving chiefly from deliberate teaching, then such a person would be likely to underestimate the potential effect that a massive presence of computers and other interactive objects might have on children.

The critics, on the other hand, do think that the computer presence will make a difference and are apprehensive. For example, they fear that more communication via computers might lead to less human association and result in social fragmentation. As knowing how to use a computer becomes increasingly necessary to effective social and economic participation, the position of the underprivileged could worsen, and the computer could exacerbate existing class distinctions. As to the political effect computers will have, the critics' concerns resonate with Orwellian images of a 1984 where home computers will form part of a complex system of surveillance and thought control. Critics also draw attention to potential mental health hazards of computer penetration. Some of these hazards are magnified forms of problems already worrying many observers of contemporary life; others are problems of an essentially new kind. A typical example of the former kind is that our grave ignorance of the psychological impact of television becomes even more serious when we contemplate an epoch of super TV. The holding power and psychological impact of the television show could be increased by varying the content to suit the tastes of each individual viewer, and by the show becoming interactive, drawing the viewer into the action. Critics already cite cases of students spending sleepless nights riveted to the computer terminal, coming to neglect both studies and social contact.

In the category of new problems, critics have pointed to the influence of the allegedly mechanized thought processes on how people think. Marshall MacLuhan's dictum that "the medium is the message" might apply here: If the medium is an interactive system that takes in words and speaks back like a person, it is easy to get the message that machines are like people and that people are like machines. What this might do to the development of values and self image in growing children is hard to assess. But it is not hard to see reasons for worry.

Despite these concerns I am essentially optimistic —some might say utopian—about the effects of computers on society. I do not dismiss the arguments of the critics. On the contrary, I too see the computer presence as a potent influence on the human mind. I am very much aware of the holding power of an interactive computer and of how taking the computer as a model can influence the way we think about ourselves. In fact the work on LOGO to which I have devoted much of the past ten years consists precisely of developing such forces in positive directions. For example, the critic is horrified at the thought of a child hypnotically held by a futuristic, computerized super pinball machine. In the LOGO work we have invented versions of such machines in which powerful ideas from physics or mathematics or linguistics are imbedded in such a way that permits the player to learn them in a natural fashion, analogous to how a child learns to speak. The computer's "holding power," so feared by critics, becomes a useful educational tool. Or take another, more profound example. The critic is afraid that children will adopt the computer as model and eventually come to "think mechanically" themselves. Following the opposite tack, I have invented ways to take educational advantage of the opportunities to master the art of *deliberately* thinking like a computer, according, for example, to the stereotype of a computer program that proceeds in a step-by-step, literal, mechanical fashion. There are situations where this style of thinking is appropriate and useful. Some children's difficulties in learning formal subjects such as grammar or mathematics derive from their inability to see the point of such a style.

A second educational advantage is indirect but ultimately more important. By deliberately learning to imitate mechanical thinking, the learner becomes able to articulate what mechanical thinking is and what it is not. The exercise can lead to greater confidence about the ability to choose a cognitive style that suits the problem. Analysis of "mechanical thinking" and how it is different from other kinds and practice with problem analysis can result in a new degree of intellectual sophistication. By providing a very concrete, down to earth model of a particular style of thinking, work with the computer can make it easier to understand that there is such a thing as a "style of thinking." And giving children the opportunity to choose one style or another provides an opportunity to develop the skill necessary to choose between styles. Thus instead of inducing mechanical thinking, contact with computers could turn out to be the best conceivable antidote to it. And for me what is most important in this is that through these experiences these children would be serving their apprenticeship as epistemologists, that is to say learning to think articulately about thinking.

The intellectual environments offered to children by today's cultures are poor in opportunities to bring their thinking about thinking into the open, to learn to talk about it and test their ideas by externalizing them. Access to computers can dramatically change this situation. Even the simplest Turtle work can open new opportunities for sharpening one's thinking about thinking: Programming the Turtle begins by making one reflect on how one does oneself what one would like the Turtle to do. Thus teaching the Turtle to act or to "think" can lead one to reflect on one's own actions and thinking. And as children move on, they program the computer to make more complex decisions and find themselves engaged in reflecting on more complex aspects of their own thinking.

In short, while the critic and I share the belief that working with computers can have a powerful influence on how people think, I have turned my attention to exploring how this influence could be turned in positive directions.

The central open questions about the effect of computers on children in the 1980s are these: Which people will be attracted to the world of computers, what talents will they bring, and what tastes and ideologies will they impose on the growing computer culture? I have observed children in LOGO environments engaged in self-referential discussions about their own thinking. This could happen because the LOGO language and the Turtle were designed by people who enjoy such discussion and worked hard to design a medium that would encourage it. Other designers of computer systems have different tastes and different ideas about what kinds of activities are suitable for children. Which design will prevail, and in what subculture, will not be decided by a simple bureaucratic decision made, for example, in a government Department of Education or by a committee of experts. Trends in computer style will emerge from a complex web of decisions by foundations with resources to support one or another design, by corporations who may see a market, by schools, by individuals who decide to make their career in the new field of activity, and by children who will have their own say in what they pick up and what they make of it. People often ask whether in the future children will program computers or become absorbed in pre-programmed activities. The answer must be that some children will do the one, some the other, some both, and some neither. But which children, and most importantly, which social classes of children, will fall into each category will be influenced by the kind of computer activities and the kind of environments created around them.

As an example, we consider an activity which may not occur to most people when they think of computers and children: the use of the computer as a writing instrument. For me, writing means making a rough draft and refining it over a considerable period of time. My image of myself as a writer includes the expectation of an "unacceptable" first draft that will develop with successive editing into presentable form. But I would not be able to afford this image if I were a third grader. The physical act of writing would be slow and laborious. I would have no secretary. For most children rewriting a text is so laborious that the first draft is the final copy, and the skill of rereading with a critical eye is never developed. This changes dramatically when children have access to computers capable of manipulating text. The first draft is composed at the keyboard. Corrections are made easily. The current copy is always neat and tidy. I have seen children move from total rejection of writing to an intense involvement (accompanied by rapid improvement of quality) within a few weeks of beginning to write with a computer. Even more dramatic changes are seen when the child has physical handicaps that make writing by hand more than usually difficult or even impossible.

This use of computers is rapidly being adopted wherever adults write for a living. Most newspapers now provide their staff with "word processing" computer systems. Many writers who work at home are acquiring their own computers, and the computer terminal is steadily displacing the typewriter as the secretary's basic tool. The image of children using the computer as a writing instrument is a particularly good example of my thesis that what is good for professionals is good for children. But this image of how the computer might contribute to children's mastery of language is dramatically opposed to the one that is taking root in most elementary schools. There the computer is seen as a teaching instrument. It gives children practice in distinguishing between verbs and nouns, in spelling, and in answering multiple choice questions about the meaning of pieces of text. As I see it, this difference is not a matter of a small and technical choice between two teaching strategies. It reflects a fundamental difference in educational philosophies. More to the point, it reflects a difference in view on the nature of childhood. I believe that the computer as writing instrument offers children an opportunity to become more like adults, indeed like advanced professionals, in their relationship to their intellectual products and to themselves. In doing so, it comes into head-on collision with the many aspects of school whose effect, if not whose intention, is to "infantilize" the child.

Word processors *can* make a child's experience of writing more like that of a real writer. But this can be undermined if the adults surrounding the child fail to appreciate what it is like to be a writer. For example, it is only too easy to imagine adults, including teachers, expressing the view that editing and re-editing a text is a waste of time ("Why don't you get on to something new?" or "You aren't making it any better, why don't you fix your spelling?").

As with writing, so with music making, games of skill, complex graphics, whatever: The computer is not a culture unto itself but it can serve to advance very different cultural and philosophical outlooks. For example, one could think of the Turtle as a device to teach elements of the traditional curriculum, such as notions of angle, shape, and coordinate systems. And in fact, most teachers who consult me about its use are trying to use it in this way. Of course the Turtle can help in the teaching of traditional curriculum, but I have thought of it as a vehicle for Piagetian learning, which to me is learning without curriculum.

There are those who think about creating a "Piagetian curriculum" or "Piagetian teaching methods." But to my mind these phrases and the activities they represent are contradictions in terms. I see

Piaget as the theorist of learning without curriculum and the theorist of the kind of learning that happens without deliberate teaching. To turn him into the theorist of a new curriculum is to stand him on his head.

But "teaching without curriculum" does not mean spontaneous, free form classrooms or simply "leaving the child alone." It means supporting children as they build their own intellectual structures with materials drawn from the surrounding culture. In this model, educational intervention means changing the culture, planting new constructive elements in it and eliminating noxious ones. This is a more ambitious undertaking than introducing a curriculum change, but one which is feasible under conditions now emerging.

Suppose that thirty years ago an educator had decided that the way to solve the problem of mathematics education was to arrange for a significant fraction of the population to become fluent in (and enthusiastic about) a new mathematical language. The idea might have been good in principle, but in practice it would have been absurd. No one had the power to implement it. Now things are different. Many millions of people are learning programming languages for reasons that have nothing to do with the education of children. Therefore, it becomes a practical proposition to influence the form of the languages they learn and the likelihood that their children will pick up these languages.

Throughout the course of this chapter I have been talking about the ways in which choices made by educators, foundations, governments, and private individuals can affect the potentially revolutionary changes in how children learn. But making good choices is not always easy, in part because past choices can often haunt us. There is a tendency for the first usable, but still primitive, product of a new technology to dig itself in. I have called this phenomenon the QWERTY phenomenon.

The top row of alphabetic keys of the standard typewriter reads QWERTY. For me this symbolizes the way in which technology can all too often serve not as a force for progress but for keeping things stuck. The QWERTY arrangement has no rational explanation, only a historical one. It was introduced in response to a problem in the early days of the typewriter: The keys used to jam. The idea was to minimize the collision problem by separating those keys that followed one another frequently. Just a few years later, general improvements in the technology removed the jamming problem, but QWERTY stuck. Once adopted, it resulted in many millions of typewriters and a method (indeed a full blown curriculum) for learning typing. The social cost of change (for example, putting the most used keys

together on the keyboard) mounted with the vested interest created by the fact that so many fingers now knew how to follow the QWERTY keyboard. QWERTY has stayed on despite the existence of other, more "rational" systems. On the other hand, if you talk to people about the QWERTY arrangement they will justify it by "objective" criteria. They will tell you that it "optimizes this" or it "minimizes that." Although these justifications have no rational foundation, they illustrate a process, a social process, of myth construction that allows us to build a justification for primitivity into any system. I think we are well on the road to doing exactly the same thing with the computer. We are in the process of digging ourselves into an anachronism by preserving practices that have no rational basis beyond their historical roots in an earlier period of technological and theoretical development.

The use of computers for drill and practice is only one example of the QWERTY phenomenon in the computer domain. Another example occurs even when attempts are made to allow students to learn to program the computer. Learning to program a computer involves learning a "programming language." There are many such languages—for example, Fortran, Pascal, Basic, Smalltalk, and Lisp, and the lesser known language LOGO, which our group has used in most of our experiments with computers and children. A powerful QWERTY phenomenon is to be expected when we choose the language in which children are to learn to program computers. I shall argue in detail that the issue is consequential. A programming language is like a natural, human language in that it favors certain metaphors, images, and ways of thinking. It would seem to follow that educators interested in using computers and sensitive to cultural influences would pay particular attention to the choice of language. But nothing of the sort has happened. On the contrary, educators, too timid in technological matters or too ignorant to attempt to influence the languages offered by computer manufacturers, have accepted certain programming languages in much the same way as they accepted the QWERTY keyboard. An informative example is the way in which the programming language Basic has established itself as the obvious language to use in teaching American children how to program computers. The relevant technical information is this: A very small computer can be made to understand Basic, while other languages demand more from the computer. Thus, in the early days when computer power was extremely expensive, there was a genuine technical reason for the use of Basic, particularly in schools where budgets were always tight. Today, and in fact for several years now, the cost of computer memory has fallen to the point where any remaining economic advantages of using Basic are insignificant. Yet in most high schools, the language remains almost synonymous with programming, despite the existence of other computing languages that are demonstrably easier to learn and are richer in the intellectual benefits that can come from learning them. The situation is paradoxical. The computer revolution has scarcely begun, but it is already breeding its own conservatism. Looking more closely at Basic provides a window on how a conservative social system appropriates and tries to neutralize a potentially revolutionary instrument.

Basic is to computation what QWERTY is to typing. Many teachers have learned Basic, many books have been written about it, many computers have been built in such a way that Basic is "hardwired" into them. In the case of the typewriter, we noted how people invent "rationalizations to justify the status quo." In the case of Basic, the phenomenon has gone much further, to the point where it resembles ideology formation. Complex arguments are invented to justify features of Basic that were originally included because the primitive technology demanded them or because alternatives were not well enough known at the time the language was designed.

An example of Basic ideology is the argument that Basic is easy to learn because it has a very small vocabulary. Its small vocabulary can be learned quickly enough. But using it is a different matter. Programs in Basic acquire so labyrinthine a structure that only the most motivated and brilliant ("mathematical") children do learn to use it for more than trivial ends.

One might ask why the teachers do not notice the difficulty children have in learning Basic. The answer is simple: Most teachers do not expect high performance from most students, especially in a domain of work that appears to be as "mathematical" and "formal" as programming. Thus the culture's general perception of mathematics as inaccessible bolsters the maintenance of Basic, which in turn confirms these perceptions. Moreover, the teachers are not the only people whose assumptions and prejudices feed into the circuit that perpetuates Basic. There are also the computerists, the people in the computer world who make decisions about which languages their computers will speak. These people, generally engineers, find Basic quite easy to learn, partly because they are accustomed to learning such very technical systems and partly because Basic's sort of simplicity appeals to their system of values. Thus, a particular subculture, one dominated by computer engineers, is influencing the world of education to favor those school students who are most like that subculture. The process is tacit, unintentional: It has

never been publicly articulated, let alone evaluated. In all of these ways, the social embedding of Basic has far more serious consequences than the "digging in" of QWERTY.

There are many other ways in which the attributes of the subcultures involved with computers are being projected onto the world of education. For example, the idea of the computer as an instrument for drill and practice that appeals to teachers because it resembles traditional teaching methods also appeals to the engineers who design computer systems: Drill and practice applications are predictable, simple to describe, efficient in use of the machine's resources. So the best engineering talent goes into the development of computer systems that are biased to favor this kind of application. The bias operates subtly. The machine designers do not actually decide what will be done in the classrooms. That is done by teachers and occasionally even by carefully controlled research experiments. But there is an irony in these controlled experiments. They are very good at telling whether the small effects seen in best scores are real or due to chance. But they have no way to measure the undoubtedly real (and probably more massive) biases built into the machines.

We have already noted that the conservative bias being built into the use of computers in education has also been built into other new technologies. The first use of the new technology is quite naturally to do in a slightly different way what had been done before without it. It took years before designers of automobiles accepted the idea that they were cars, not "horseless carriages," and the precursors of modern motion pictures were plays acted as if before a live audience but actually in front of a camera. A whole generation was needed for the new art of motion pictures to emerge as something quite different from a linear mix of theater plus photography. Most of what has been done up to now in the name of "educational technology" or "computers in education" is still at the stage of the linear mix of old instructional methods with new technologies.

We are at a point in the history of education when radical change is possible, and the possibility for that change is directly tied to the impact of the computer. Today what is offered in the educational "market" is largely determined by what is acceptable to a sluggish and conservative system. But this is where the computer presence is in the process of creating an environment for change. Consider the conditions under which a new educational idea can be put into practice today and in the near future. Let us suppose that today I have an idea about how children could learn mathematics more effectively and more humanely. And let us suppose that I have been able to persuade a million people that the idea is a good one. For many products such a potential market would guarantee success. Yet in the world of education today this would have little clout: A million people across the nation would still mean a minority in every town's school system, so there might be no effective channel for the million voices to be expressed. Thus, not only do good educational ideas sit on the shelves, but the process of invention is itself stymied. This inhibition of invention in turn influences the selection of people who get involved in education. Very few with the imagination, creativity, and drive to make great new inventions enter the field. Most of those who do are soon driven out in frustration. Conservatism in the world of education has become a self-perpetuating *social* phenomenon.

Fortunately, there is a weak link in the vicious circle. Increasingly, the computers of the near future will be the private property of individuals, and this will gradually return to the individual the power to determine patterns of education. Education will become more of a private act, and people with good ideas, different ideas, exciting ideas will no longer be faced with a dilemma where they either have to "sell" their ideas to a conservative bureaucracy or shelve them. They will be able to offer them in an open marketplace directly to consumers. There will be new opportunities for imagination and originality. There might be a renaissance of thinking about education.

Breaking Down the Barriers: The Real Micro Miracle

Darlene E. Crawford

Fifty years ago the educational institution was perceived as the authority on education and parents backed the premise 100%. Twenty-five years ago parents had some questions and were invited to participate to a small degree in their child's educational process but there was not really an active impact. In the last ten years, the parental community has stood up and said it wanted to be counted as an integral part of their children's educational process. Citizens' committees and parental groups have sprung up in all areas of the educational field. Buildings no longer appear based on administrative or school board perception alone; curriculum changes constantly include teachers' and parent input; transportation of students has been impacted greatly by parents'

From "Breaking Down the Barriers: The Real Micro Miracle," by Darlene E. Crawford. In the *17th Annual AEDS Proceedings,* Association of Educational Data Systems, May, 1979. Reprinted by permission.

involvement. What is happening to the school's authority and credibility? Community action has challenged them to further accountability in every facet of education. Parents are demanding that their children read, that they have equal opportunity to participate in athletics, and other extra-curricular activities; that the curriculum be expanded to include daily living practices, i.e., family living courses and developmental psychology courses. This sounds as though parents really have a say in their students' educational goals and objectives but the fact remains that even though we have made tremendous strides in the past few years, a real barrier remains between school and home. This barrier needs to be broken down drastically in the near future if we as educators are sincere in preparing the student for every aspect of life as it will be in the twenty-first century!

Van Mueller of University of Minnesota speaks of Futures in Education regarding school finance and one of his statements was "families will choose their school and teachers in year 2000." Some school districts allow their families to choose the school and the teachers now, so why wait for 2000—let's start now and be ahead of the times. Howard Karlitz, in the October 1978 issue of *Kappa Delta Pi Record,* issues a challenge to parents to take an active role in the educational community. That role should not only dictate specific political behavior but behavior related to the process of education itself. He says "Do not surrender or delegate to the 'experts' one's educational decision-making authority as a parent." Hallelujah!

Before someone accuses me of heresy, let me say that no one values an education more than I do—but education can come in many ways. I remember when I sent my first child to school back in 1959. The teacher told me that I should have never taught him how to print because I had done it improperly and now he has to learn over. Ditto for numbers. Well, I wonder how a teacher may feel now when the student comes to kindergarten from his experience with something as simple as *Sesame Street* where he learns numbers and letters. What will the kindergarten teacher do when the child will learn how to read before he comes to school? What will the teacher do when the Little Professor or Dataman has already taught the 3 or 4 year old how to come up with the division, multiplication, addition, subtraction sets and Speak and Spell has taught them spelling. I suppose the teacher can feel useless—OR—educators can recognize the inevitable and plan now for a new mode of instruction. We must stop trying to justify the system, spot the ills and cure them. Technology can aid immensely in this task. Computers should calculate, bear pressure, help in decision making, stamp out pieces, pack and do all those menial tasks that they can possibly accomplish so people can participate in what is enjoyable. Our nation is born of the work ethic—in order to survive—in order to be worth anything—in order to succeed—in order to get powerful—in order to get money—you must work, work, work. WONDERFUL—as long as you are working at what you like, what is beneficial to you and yours as people—not work horses. Computers should be used to accomplish that end. If the instructional system does not meet the needs of the twenty-first century, our students will be growing up with an outdated method of instruction to live in a modern world of technology that will not only overwhelm them, but perhaps control them. If they are going to be effective leaders in our future society, then we had better start now to show them the way—to equip them with the tools necessary to make decisions based on this reality. *Family*

Another heavy impact on education will be the changing family structure. Sixty percent of the mothers in this nation will be members of the work force by 1985. The percentage of single parents is on the increase. I remember when our Census clerk in our Office could count on a couple of hands the number of students with last names different than the family. Now it takes cross-reference lists and a separate file to track this kind of student. This is another positive fact that the family structure is changing. These children will always come to school but now they'll need more personal care and babysitting than ever before. . .and it looks like these needs will far outrank their academic needs if the trend continues. Motivation, back patting, problem solving (the personal kind—not the math kind) will be teacher functions. The days are gone when we can insist that schools are not responsible for parenting. Parents may want to do it but find it impossible. The economic picture dictates that many mothers work today. Owning a home for the young people in the near future means both work and maybe two jobs. *Fear of Comp*

Another barrier that needs breaking is the barrier between the instructor and the computer. The perceived threat by teachers as computers are suggested to be instructional tools is a reality. They see it as a replacement—a loss of job and security—a taking over by the inhuman element. Education in this area has been minimal. We need to overcome this fear by showing the instructor that the computer is no more a threat than the slide projector. The computer is the greatest technological advance in years—particularly the micro computer. It can release the teacher from oppressing tasks so that time can be used to further humanize education. There has been such bad utilization of computerization that some teachers have had poor experiences—therefore their

perspective is cloudy. Teachers used to mark report cards manually in the teacher's lounge or had individual contact with each student as they graded them. Then along came the new time saving, up-to-date mark-reporting system! It was to save them time and effort. Unfortunately, instead of time-saving and efficiency, the teacher found a cumbersome, difficult to understand system that often times provided incorrect information. Of course, the standard answer came, "the computer made an error." Personal experience shows that the computer did what it was told to do by some programmer who wrote a mark-reporting program based on what he decided the needs were. Then a service bureau sold the system to a school district superintendent who enthused his principals by stating some record keeping advantages that may or may not be true. To the teacher there is no real advantage, the work load is new and increased, and suspicions relative to computers and their task capabilities grew. It is this mindset that needs altering if we are to help teachers fully realize the unending potential these micros have to assist them, relieve them, teach them, BUT NOT TO REPLACE THEM! They need to learn that teachers are the masters; they tell the computer what to do, when to do it, how to do it and that they have the power to shut them down when all else fails.

As I stated previously, the educational community went unchallenged for years thereby allowing a prevalence of complacency in all areas of administration. These attitudes sponsored the causes of the barrier we have today—academic minded instructors and administrators; untrained administrators; either fiscally trained or academically oriented. There were no managers, decision makers, trained executives that looked on the educational world as a big business; ran it as such and felt accountable to the taxpayers for the way in which they spent the dollars. There is some advancement in this area, but it is minimal. This kind of administration fosters barriers between home and school.

Increased levels of union activity on the part of organized teaching and administrative personnel is another large cause of barriers between home and school. Parents who are being asked for more money with less accountability and no active part in the decision-making do not see walls coming down, but getting higher. They feel frustrated by a situation that seems to have mushroomed into unhappy personnel strikes, shorter hours by teachers, and less and less cooperation from administration and instructors when they call the school.

Decreased levels of state and federal aid to school districts has created a monumental problem for administrators, school boards and staff as they face decreasing enrollment and school closings, in addition to cut-backs in many levels of support. The mis-management of funds by incompetent administrators and/or school boards fostered much of the cut-backs we are not experiencing as a result of untrained personnel.

Taxpayer revolts have pressured educators regarding more accountability. Taxpayers are demanding more for their money and the money is getting harder to come by.

The authoritarian attitude of administrators has propagated a decision making atmosphere that excludes not only parents and students but also instructors and often times board members from any participation. This kind of planning does not assist the instructor in dealing with new and innovative ideas in curriculum, let alone prepare them for the impact of the computer on their teaching experience.

The appearance on the scene of the micro computer seems to offer some beginnings to a solution to the problems stated above. It is available to school and home, to experienced user and novice, to industry and education. It comes in attractive outfits, is comparatively inexpensive, and poses less threat than ever before. It is wonderful, marvelous, challenging, frightening, overwhelming but it is not a fad. It is here to stay and if used properly, it can turn the educational community around in its approach to students, parents and teachers.

If handled properly, the micro has the potential to do all the following: evaluation and monitoring of student and staff, record keeping tasks too numerous to mention, lesson planning, menu planning, assist with energy saving, store and find information, provide data to assist in decision making, act as a catalyst to bring the teacher closer to the student and home, serve as a communication device between school and home, offer excellent video capabilities complete with color and graphics, add a sound dimension enabling musical outpouring, and heading toward voice recognition possibilities already in use but not refined.

Ultimately, all the tasks performed by the micro should free a teacher to involve himself with students and other teachers in a more personal and human way. Once the onus of menial tasks is reduced to a minimum, the instructor can then share with, listen to, and care about students in a personal way. It should free teachers and students to do what people should do—talk, listen, reach out, confide, grow, relax, smile and love. This will only come to fruition after extensive education and in-service training of the professional staff that their changing role can be met and conquered but certainly not dispensed with.

We have some of the best educational facilities in Minnesota—particularly in Rosemount. We have come a long way in administering to the special needs of students, but a miracle has happened—the micro miracle—and it has the ability to so drastically change the whole lifestyle of this country that it truly is mind boggling. It is here to stay, it is not a fad, it is a sweeping technological advance such as our society has not seen since the splitting of the atom. What was suppose to be the space age really turned out to be the computer age—and more specifically the micro computer age. It will have its impact on society as computers never have before. Computers in the past have always been that big machine somewhere out there that does an inconceivable job of messing up my phone bill or bank statement. It was perceived as a threat in most instances—but it came and it stayed. The micro miracle changes that picture drastically—people are shopping in the personal computer shops—they are becoming less frightened—they see fun, games and real aids to running their lives in these marvelous little pieces of equipment. They are bringing them home. Many of those kids will come to school with knowledge of what a micro can do in the next five years. Will we be ready for them? Will teachers overcome their fear in time to view the computer as a valuable aid?

Technology will force the educational structures to change in this society in the near future. By 1985, says Bob Albrecht, 10 million personal computers will be placed in the homes; by 1990, says Earl Joseph, anyone can carry a pocket computer around with an unbelievable wealth of information at their [sic] fingertips. Educators can be in on the ground floor and try to lead the revolution in learning processes or they can sit back and wait for technology to revolutionize the educational institution and then react to it. One thing is certain; the process by which students will learn is going to change. Picture a classroom where a group of students come to school to tell the teacher what they have learned on their micro last night. Envision a teacher who then acts as the catalyst for this group of students to pass the information between them. I am sure this seems frightening to many people—parents as well as teachers—but I do believe it will become reality. Why should a teacher spend hours formulating lesson plans, lecturing, grading, testing and forcing academic learning in a structured classroom when a student can sit down at home, access a library of information and find out anything he ever wanted to know about anything by pressing a few commands on a micro—or even better yet—a hand-held computer that has enough memory on a small chip to store a treasure of information.

The first cry that goes out from educators when you talk about computerization is "We can't afford it" and "Where do we get the money?" In our district, we did a couple of things—we started looking at how much money we were spending on other subject areas, i.e., biology—do you have any idea how much money has been spent on microscopes, lab manuals and last, but not least, live frogs and chickens for experimental purposes? Check it out in your district. How many math curriculums and reading curriculums has your district tried and discarded in the past 10 or 15 years? Now justify that in accordance with the dollars spent on computer literacy and impact on society. Investigate, educate, prod your board of education, your administration, your community to take another look. Don't just jump to the conclusion that its not affordable. Next we looked at how Title IV-B money is being spent. It is money federally granted and available to school districts throughout the nation. The administrator in charge of Federal Funds makes a proposal to your State Department of Education stating ways in which it proposes to spend the money. This is where we have received the majority of our funds for the TRS-80's and Commodore Pets.

In addition, we have been willing to designate consultant funds for specific assistance. We picked a consultant carefully. Teachers are not inspired by consultants that walk in and tell them that they have all the answers; nor are they inspired by a consultant that says to them "Write your own curriculum." We found a happy answer and a middle of the road attitude in the person of Norm Bell of Michigan State. He comes with expertise in the field of handling people problems, formulating ideas, putting them on paper and finally into action. He listens, writes, listens again, re-writes, pilots re-writes and constantly evaluates what kind of program is being offered. Teachers from all grade levels served on a computer committee to aid, assist and challenge Norm to produce what we feel are some soundly based lessons dealing with computer literacy and impact on society. It was not a simple task; it took months of planning, research, piloting, evaluating, and revamping before we introduced it as a part of the curriculum.

Scope and sequence is another area that needs addressing when a curriculum is impacted as heavily as this. Our pilot was conducted from first through seventh grade and was decided finally to be used in the fifth grade level. Immediately upon that decision, we began making plans for curricula that could be implemented at the first grade level all the way to twelfth grade. As the learning becomes more sophisticated the students become more aware at a younger level. As the students progress through grades it is imperative that they have opportunity to review but not repeat information.

It is extremely important to include teachers in placing curriculum at a grade level. They don't always

agree but if they feel a part of the decision, the way in which they handle the lessons is certainly more positive. It is vital to remember that no decision is cast in concrete, so if a move needs to be made in the future, the opportunity to do so should always be left openended.

Our district is just beginning to meet the challenges of breaking down the barriers I have defined above! We are looking forward to the time when our final goal is met—students, parents, teachers and administrators all working together to learn from each other. Our philosophy of education will be finally to prepare our students to gain the knowledge necessary to run this country in the twenty-first century.

Before you leave, consider this. Times are changing—education is changing! Technology is changing our educational scene in such a rapid manner it is mind-boggling! Will you be reacting to or leading the revolution?

THE MICROPROCESSOR AS PENCIL

John D'Angelo

The Microprocessor as Pencil!

Not too many years ago that indeed would have been a strange topic. However, we have progressed rapidly during the last few years. This item, the microprocessor, has become quite an ordinary thing.

Recently I had the occasion to revisit Marshall McLuhan, who surprisingly enough, has been all but forgotten, even in this time of increased use of technology. Although he was not specifically referring to education, McLuhan said,

> History is made up of three stages: (1) Preliterate or Tribal, in which men lived close together and communicated orally; (2) the Gutenberg or Individual Stage in which men communicated by the printed word and thinking was done in lineal-sequential patterns; and (3) the Neo-Tribal or Electric, in which computers, television and other electronic communication media have moved men back together ("implosion").

It is interesting to note that in education we have scarcely moved into the Neo-Tribal electric stage while society, at least according to McLuhan, has.

Books and books with pages and pages have been written relative to the whys and wherefores of the introduction of an innovation, technological or otherwise. Therefore, I will not belabor the point. Practically every study at some point or another

From "Microprocessor as Pencil," by John D'Angelo. In *AEDS Monitor,* November, 1979, Association of Educational Data Systems. Reprinted by permission.

in the study will place the success or failure of an innovation on whether or not the practitioner, i.e., the teachers were involved and participated in the decisions made before, during and after the innovation's introduction. The key to the involvement is in the decision-making process used in deciding on the innovation. The practitioners must be part of the process before the change is even considered, since they are the ones who will actually implement the innovations. The only way to logically accomplish this is to have a system in place for allowing teacher input into the school's decision-making process. However, that's a topic of another paper.

WHAT IS A MICROPROCESSOR?

Perhaps it is appropriate at this time to define the microprocessor. In the sense we are using it, the microprocessor is the central chip used to process the data supplied. Used in this way it might also be considered a computer-on-a-chip. Therefore, this whole paper could have been entitled "The Computer as Pencil." To be more specific, we might say that the microprocessor chip consists of an extremely miniaturized, reduced version of several integrated circuits which are capable of processing large amounts of data at rapid speeds. The integrated circuits are devices which consist of several hundreds of transistors. A large computer consists of many integrated circuits, whereas the microprocessor may consist of a single chip. The trade-off for size is speed and user capacity.

Without spending too much time investigating, one can very easily say that not a day goes by that each of us does not come into contact with an item which uses the microprocessor. The first of these was the hand-held calculator. Very few homes are without one, and many homes have several. The calculator is built around the microprocessor chip. The microwave oven's microprocessor provides you with the capability of cooking at more than one temperature, different times, or a combination of these. Cameras, TV sets, video tape recorders all have one or more such chips. Many of the newer cars have a microprocessor as part of the ignition system, the exhaust system, or the fuel system. In the latter case, its main purpose is to monitor the amount of fuel needed in relation to the particular driving conditions.

MODIFICATION OF THE TEACHING/LEARNING PROCESS

As was pointed out by McLuhan earlier, the delivery system of education has changed very little during the past 500 years. By the delivery system, we are referring to the process by which we teach, coupled to the process by which students learn. This combination becomes the process of education, i.e., the delivery system of education. With the advent of the printed word, the delivery system changed radically from the Socratic system of verbal transmission of "learning" based to a great extent on the personality of the instructor, to the more concise, formal, impersonal approach of the book. An excellent analogy is presented by Dustin Heuston of WICAT. He states,

> Educational leaders have found themselves trapped in a position similar to the one in which transportation experts might have been had they been forced to improve an old delivery system (the horse) without transitioning to new ones (the train, car, and plane). A horse can do only a limited amount of work, and experiments which attempted to improve breeding or dietary practices, or even use titanium shoes, were simply not going to produce adequate productivity gains.

For at least the past twenty years that I've been in education, we have pumped millions of dollars into the educational system of the United States, only to find that achievement scores have gone down! As our work force has increased and become much more sophisticated, the demands on the education system have proportionally increased. As a result of this awareness, we have made many attempts to "meet the needs of our students." But, like the transportation system of 100 years ago, the present delivery system of education is no more capable of the desired level of productivity than was the horse. We have made attempts to rectify this situation. We have added language labs, hundreds of overhead projectors, and even computers to duplicate the present delivery system, all to no avail. The scores are still going down! Again allow me to reiterate, there is the very real possibility that the education delivery system has reached its maximum productivity even with all the "innovations" which have been added. We might portray this graphically as in Figure 1.

It can be readily seen that the education delivery system has kept pace with its demand until only the

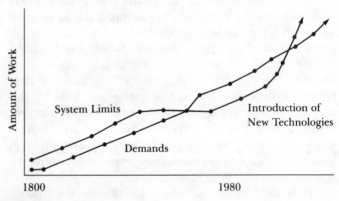

FIGURE 1

past thirty or forty years. It has also been during the last thirty or forty years that we have tried desperately to make modification without changing the basic delivery system.

I must be quick to point out that my comments regarding the present educational system are in no way intended to be critical of the many excellent projects and programs or of the valiant attempts which have been made to improve the system. It is simply that the system has reached maturity. We have infused the system with much "technology" in the form of audio-visual equipment and its accompanying software, but even this has not made a significant difference. Perhaps the reason for this has been that the instructional process has continued to be serial in nature. That is to say, the student has had little opportunity to branch to an alternative point in the instructional process. It is not that we educators have not had a sincere desire to do this, but desire and good intentions have not been enough. The technology has not been available prior to the last few years.

We have even had available to us the so-called Instructional Development Process, by which we can approach instruction in an orderly, systematic fashion. This process has not met with much favor by the teachers and administrators of the education establishment. What most instructional developers have not realized is that they have inadvertently been asking to replace, or at least change, the present delivery system. Anything else makes them extremely uncomfortable and rather insecure. Part of our failure, as instructional developers, and I include myself among their numbers, is that we have asked that, in order to meet the student's need, material be accessed randomly, while the technology to do so has not yet been available.

In their book, *Teaching Students through Their Individual Learning Styles: A Practical Approach*, Rita Dunn and Kenneth Dunn enumerate eighteen learning styles and nine elements of teaching style. They, along with most traditional curriculum developers (as opposed to instructional developers) fully expect the classroom teacher to cope with these many combinations. This becomes a management nightmare. Most educators usually dismiss this idea as "pie-in-the-sky", i.e., The Impossible Dream. This dream can be summed up in two words— Individualized Instruction! For educators this has become a sacred concept, like the flag, apple pie, and motherhood.

It might well be that, like trying to improve on the horse instead of moving on to the airplane, we are trying to improve on the pencil. Rather than attempting to make pencil lead so that it will not break quite so easily, why not use something else as pencil? Then will the impossible dream become not quite so impossible? Are we, in all our wisdom, so bent on improving that pencil, that we have lost sight of the possibility that there may be another way of accomplishing the same end? It's the old forest for the trees bit! The impossible dream is that we have not been able to interrelate the many teaching styles with the various learning styles. We cannot easily determine the many possible alternate paths the student could take based on his achievement at that point. Therefore, we have not been able to make available the "new" technological learning aids.

THE NEW PENCIL

The teaching/learning process which has been in use for the past 500 years has finally reached the point whereby the results are counter-productive. The instructional tools in use prior to the microprocessor-based learning aids tend to be group oriented with little regard to the individual. Eaton Conant from the University of Oregon has completed a study of the first four years of elementary school and discovered that the amount of time the teacher can give to an individual student is severely limited. Conant found that in a class with 25 to 30 students the average teacher was unable to devote more than 1 to 2 minutes of individualized instruction per student per day. The individualized instruction programs I have worked with all seem to become, sooner or later, self-paced rather than individualized for each student. The success of programs like TICCIT have shown a high degree of success, but at an enormous cost.

We have at our fingertips the tools which will change the delivery system. Notice I said "will" not "could," for these tools are available right now. These are instructional tools such as calculators and learning aids like the Little Professor, Wise Owl, Dataman, the Speak and Spell, and the individual, personal computer.

A SUGGESTED ALTERNATE PROCESS

Several years ago when I first read George B. Leonard's *Education and Ecstasy*, I thought how nice it would be to have that kind of delivery system (although I'm sure I did not use those words since I was in the midst of the delivery system, hence I did not recognize it). In his book Leonard states,

> Every child can delight in learning. A new education is already here, thrusting up in spite of every barrier we have been able to build. Why not help it happen?

We thought then that was so very far into the future—a 1984 kind of future. But 1984 is only five years away and the necessary technology is here now! I would recommend reading Leonard or even reading it again. It is even more relevant now than when it was written in 1968.

But where can we go from here? We don't want to burn it all down, as they were advocating in the sixties, and start all over again (although that is a tempting thought). No, rather we must build on the present structure. The present educational establishment must be won over, for if not, the consequence might indeed be grave. What can we see in schools today? That is, not what is in schools today, but what is currently available, right now, to be placed in schools. In order to provide each student with a truly interactive environment, learning aids must be provided much as those materials (books, paper and pencils) are provided for the present passive one. These microprocessor-based learning aids should be provided, either along with or eventually in place of their present book allotment. In some specialized areas, a simple calculator or a programmable calculator might be provided or even a speech-generating device for language arts should be provided. Eventually, however, a computer is needed for each student, just as an English grammar book is needed for each student. Without considering the instructional aspects, I would guess that the first thought relative to this concept is one of cost. This is perfectly natural, especially when one is familiar with the huge cost of computer-based education of only a few years ago. But with the reduced cost of the present microprocessor-based learning aids, amortized over about five years, the cost becomes a little more than one hundred dollars per year per student. That certainly compares favorably to the cost of the student's textbook allotment per year.

The student's environment needs to have a number of characteristics which are not now provided in the present delivery system. Among these are random access to any portion of the instructional material. Presently much of the student's time is wasted while waiting for a match between his point in the instruction and the serially presented instruction. Allowing this type of interaction permits the teacher to assist the student as needed rather than to be "on stage" all the time. Aligned with this is the concept of interactivity. The use of the individualized computer permits this kind of inter-action which no teacher can presently match. The courseware of the computer is precise, patient, and always available to the student. Another attribute of the "new" learning environment is a giant step toward achieving that impossible dream mentioned earlier: individualized instruction. We've all attested to the impossibility of the record keeping task

involving 30 to 150 students each on possibly as many different programs. With the existing learning aids the record keeping chore is much simplified. We could keep track of the response and modify the student's program accordingly. The student would be branched to his level and a record kept, informing the teacher of both the student's progress and the validity of the instructional material. This permits the teacher to adjust as appropriate. Also unlike current serial media such as books or films, the courseware could be updated as the need arises. One must also re-member that color, motion, and sound to which we have all become accustomed, is very much a part of this environment—and still at the before-mentioned price.

But what do we need to do in order to achieve this kind of learning environment? The technology already is available. First, we must decide to do something about it; or, I suppose we might decide not to decide. Assuming we decide to look seriously at the present educational delivery system, we must build on what already exists. We must not start with bringing in hardware-calculators or microcomputers. No, we must first start with the content of education, the curriculum itself. We must be careful not to think in terms of how does this fit into the curriculum, for the present curriculum itself must be examined. We must start with the needs of society. The jobs re-quiring unskilled or semi-skilled workers are rapidly diminishing; the curriculum must reflect that. A more sophisticated instructional content requires a more sophisticated delivery system.

We must involve the practitioners, the teachers, and we must have the support of the administrators. This is not a simple task, for we are dealing with attitudes. The tendency will be to cling to that which is known and with which one is comfortable. We must tread lightly but deliberately. We must define an instructional process which fits the society that presently exists. We must very judiciously look at our present resources. Rather than to seek additional monies, we might better reallocate existing monies and resources. We have pumped millions of dollars into the system to buy more of the same, i.e., if two aids don't help in the classroom then let's have four; if Miss Jones does well with an overhead projector then let's get one for every teacher; if Johnny is successful using the cassette player then let's have all children use the cassette player. Unless you believe in miracles, more of the same does not promise a solution. We have at least thirty years of data to show the extent of the improvement of our educational system using more money without changing the delivery system. It is here that the Instructional Development Process mentioned earlier can apply:

DESIGN — A process which meets the needs of students relative to our available resources;

DEVELOP — The appropriate content, produce the necessary material and acquire the needed learning aids;

EVALUATE — The content, the materials, and the process itself.

What if we do not change the system? Fortunately, the human species is very adaptable. But what will our society be like while this adaptation takes place? More and more workers will find that they are not trained to survive. Even now we are finding business and industry needing to train their new employees in the very basic skills. In many cases, they are finding it necessary to bring them up to literacy. We have hardly begun to exploit the human potential. We know that our students are capable of achieving much more, but the scores are going down. We have at our fingertips the technology to reverse this trend. Not since the advent of the printing press have we had such an opportunity to influence the quality of life. All around us we see evidence that we have, in McLuhan's words, reached the Neo-tribal or electric age, everywhere, that is, but in the world of education. It might well be that the time has come when we must stop letting schooling interfere with our children's education.

Seymour Papert of M.I.T. sums up our concept of the microprocessor in education with the following.

> When we talk about computers in education people ask how we mean to "computerize" subjects. But this is the wrong image. We do not mean to "computerize" anything. Think of the computer as like a pencil. The pencil is always present and has many uses for scribbling, for writing, for arithmetic, for drawing. But we do not talk about "pencilizing" education. The personal computer will be there to be used in many ways like the pencil. Like the pencil, it should serve education, it should never dictate it. And it will serve it as an instrument for writing, for drawing, for doing arithmetic, for composing music and for many other purposes as well. It will be used for fun, for games as well as for deliberate learning.

RESOURCES

Understanding Media: the Extensions of Man. Marshall McLuhan. McGraw-Hill Book Co., 1964.
Training, Technology, and the Educational Delivery System. Dustin Heuston. WICAT Inc. 1978.
Ibid.
Teaching Students through Their Individual Learning Styles: A Practical Approach. Rita Dunn and Kenneth Dunn. Reston Publishing Co. 1978, Reston, Virginia.
Education and Ecstasy. George B. Leonard. Delacorte Press, New York, N.Y. 1968.

COMPUTERS IN EDUCATION: A NON-ORWELLIAN VIEW

George A. Miller

In one of its television commercials, IBM—that giant of the business machine industry—has an actor express satisfaction that the prices of computers have continued to come down year after year. Unlike most wonders brought to us through the medium of television advertising, this one is worth knowing about. In these times, it is indeed a marvel that anything could become both better and cheaper.

Also marvelous is the industry's ability to predict that reductions in price will continue for another decade. New memory technology is presently moving from research through development to production at a rate that, in constant dollars, promises to halve the price of computer memory elements every eighteen months. The cost of memory, which has always controlled the cost of computer systems, is rapidly becoming a negligible factor. It is as if the price of books became independent of the number of pages they contained.

By the late 1970s, this trend had progressed to the point where small but sophisticated computer systems—called microcomputers in the trade—could be offered for sale for less than a thousand dollars. At that price they became available to small businesses, laboratories, clinics, and schools—even to home hobbyists. Enthusiasts claim that the still lower prices ahead make a mass market inevitable; they envision a new day dawning with all the freshness of a dream. Personal computers will be as common as television sets, but far more useful: introducing them in classrooms will save our schools; locating them in homes will draw families back together; learning to program them will make us a more clever society. There will be computers to educate the young, to help the worker, to entertain the old. Browsing through the literature that has sprung up around this fad should convince anyone that it is already far more than a fad.

According to the heralds of this revolution, we are rapidly approaching a time when, if a man were permitted to write all the programs, he need not care who should write the laws of a nation. Computing is a young person's game. And while it may take a few years for those educated prior to the triumph of the transistor to die off, the computer culture is inevitable. We may as well face it and start educating our children to live with it. Where savage children form their early concepts by playing with mud and industrial children by piling block on block, children of the future will cut their conceptual teeth on a keyboard. The flow of information and the control of process will unfold to them as easily as space and time to their grandparents. Their habits of thought will orient toward goals and solutions, with all the precision that algorithms impose.

That is supposed to be the good news. Never before was rational man so plausible an idealization.

I am less optimistic. I grant that computers are here to stay, that they demand a kind of closed-system thinking that is acquired only after considerable practice, and that they are bound to have a continuing impact on our personal and social lives. I am less convinced, however, that millions of rational people solving problems algorithmically will add up to a rational society. Indeed, I am not even convinced that computers make individuals rational, that a few years of thinking like a computer can change patterns of irrational thought that have persisted throughout recorded history. No amount of rational thinking with computing devices will prevent our descendants from understanding irrational behavior—Othello's jealousy, for example.

On the other hand, I do not side with those who see in computers the major threat to all human and humanistic values. Just as the smiling engineers overestimate what computers can do for us, the scowling humanists overestimate what computers can do to us.

Unless something totally unexpected intervenes, events will take a middle course. Computers will multiply; more and more people will know how to use them; scientific and technological feats will continue to be accomplished that would have been unthinkable without them. But after work, people will go about their feuds and love affairs in the same old ways. Chess will probably be destroyed as an interesting game for humans, but the important games people play will continue to cause as much anguish as they always have. A human being assisted by a computer is still a human being.

Computers are consummate imitators. Given enough information about how any system works, a computer can work the same way. It can imitate the trajectories of the planets, the circulation of the blood, the heating of a nuclear reactor. The imitation is as accurate as the scientific theory on which it is based.

But not everything that happens in the real world is worth imitating. It might be possible, for example, to imitate the windblown motion of every leaf in a forest, but no one would try. The computation would be too tedious even for a machine. Some things are simpler than any imitation of themselves. To put a particular forest breeze into a computer would replace a natural beauty with a mathematical obscenity so complex that no one could ever know whether it had been correctly done. Even the most avid computer fan would render unto computers only that which is the computer's, and unto the forest that which is not.

While you are working with a computer, it has a way of filling your mind, of stretching it until the program's abstract functions and their interrelations leave no place for other thoughts. At such times of concentration, it is easy to forget that there are more things in heaven and earth than you are thinking of. Good scientists must constantly remind themselves not to mistake a theory for the reality that inspired it. For long stretches of time, a scientist may be more engrossed with an imitation than with the real thing, but in the long run the real thing wins every time. It has to. Marvelous as computers are, they cannot replace the world in which theory must be anchored, the world in which our ancestors evolved, the world in which we hope to survive.

So I take enthusiastic pronouncements about the computer revolution with a grain of salt. Science fiction to the contrary, we are not about to bring Nature to her knees. The robust banalities of life and death will go on as before, but the trimmings will change. People will continue to take advantage of each other whenever they can, meanwhile mumbling about brotherly love one day in seven, but some people will have computers to help them.

It is precisely because I do not expect human nature to change very much that I welcome the coming mass market in microcomputers. The more computers there are and the more people who understand and have access to them, the less chance there is that some technocratic elite will use them to exploit everyone else.

My worry is that computers will not become cheap enough fast enough. A thousand dollars is cheap only by comparison to the million dollars that the same amount of mechanical intelligence would have cost ten years ago. It is still a large sum to poor people, who are always the easiest people to exploit.

If such considerations ever lead the American people to stretch the Bill of Rights to include freedom of computation, they might enpower the government to make computers available to everyone. The government might, for example, create another federal bureaucracy, this one in charge of computers for the poor. Each neighborhood might have a building where anyone could go to learn the basic concepts and to develop those special skills appropriate to their own particular use of computers. Each of these neighborhood computer centers would employ a staff to maintain the system and to advise and train new users.

Alternatively, if the impulse to create new bureaucracies could be curbed, this service might be added to some already existing social institution. The school system would be the natural one. Not only are schools already dedicated to teaching; their students are the right age to learn computing, to enjoy computer tricks and treats. If computing must go into the schools, I would keep it largely an extra-curricular activity, somewhere in the fun fringe of academic subjects. A mandate to make computer power available to everyone is not a mandate to rub their noses in it.

But even if our social conscience does not demand it, it seems inevitable that computers will invade the schools one way or another. Given that prospect, the important topic to discuss is the terms of the surrender. But some background may be necessary here.

Sometimes an idea takes command while we are not looking. It is the first idea to occur, and no one challenges it with an alternative idea. I believe that is what happened in educational circles with respect to computers.

If you were to ask most educators to free-associate on the question of computers in education, I am reasonably sure that the best informed would start talking about CAI—Computer Assisted Instruction. The implicitly accepted idea in CAI is that computers should be programmed to imitate teachers. It is not a bad idea. Its advantages are well known by now: questions and answers can be prepared by subject-matter experts; information on success or failure can be given to a student immediately; instruction can be individualized, enabling each child to learn at his or her own pace; teachers' time is freed for those activities that teachers enjoy most.

Unfortunately, there are also disadvantages. Computer imitations of teachers are not very good, because the theory of instruction on which imitations can be based is not very good—most CAI seems to be based on the theory that teachers are drill sergeants. Moreover, mechanical devices have a high mortality rate in most schools.

The educators would probably close their remarks on CAI with the observation that it is better for teaching some things than others. Since the usual format for CAI is symbols-in-symbols-out, it is hardly surprising that the best results are obtained when students are tested in a symbols-in-symbols-out situation; answering questions, for example, or talking about some topic. What the educators would be saying in their closing observation, therefore, is

that teaching students to talk about selected topics does not exhaust the goals of education. When a student is expected to do something more than respond with linguistic answers to preformulated questions—to think, for example—drill alone is not sufficient.

I mention these familiar issues, not to argue on one side or the other, but simply to bring to mind the general direction that most educational thinking has taken with respect to the use of computers in schools. Educators following this line will welcome the new, cheap technology just as eagerly as I do. Small, cheap computers might be given away, as books are. There are already hand-held gadgets that drill a student in arithmetic and spelling, and similar devices for drilling more complex skills only await the cheaper memory elements. Imagine children taking their teachers home every night: it might make us wonder why they have to leave home every morning in the first place.

Teachers do more than drill their students, however. Among many other things, they serve as sources of information. And that side of teaching can also be imitated mechanically: CAI can be based on the theory that teachers are question answerers. Of course, this theory is almost as unfair as the drill-sergeant theory, but at least it introduces a little variety.

As one example, I have been interested in the possible educational value of automated dictionaries. I imagine putting a small dictionary into a computer's memory so that a user can simply type a word at the keyboard and ask for either a definition or a structured list of related words. Commercial word processing systems containing lists of commonly misspelled words are already available. I would simply lengthen the list, add syntactic and semantic information, and put it into the schools. Then I would adapt word games that would be fun enough to motivate children to use the system. I speculate that easy access to an automated dictionary would accelerate vocabulary growth. Vocabulary size is generally considered to be important. It is, for example, one of the most dependable indicators of whatever it is that intelligence tests test.

Whether CAI is used in the accepted manner, where the machine poses the questions and the student gives the answers, or in the reverse manner, where the student poses the questions and the machine gives the answers, it still adds up to question-and-answer education. I find it somewhat disconcerting to realize that much education—particularly higher education—does indeed resemble the conditioning of whatever verbal habits are required to talk on various subjects. But talk, even knowledgeable talk, is merely a symptom of the educated condition, not a substitute for it.

The educational assumption that computers should imitate teachers still has considerable vitality. Indeed, a rival idea does not occur to most people until they begin to think how they would teach children about computers. Following the CAI approach, an expert on computers might write a series of questions and answers to be posed to students by a computer, and these questions would lead a learner step by step into complicated ways of talking about computer systems and their applications. At some point in preparing this CAI program, most people realize that it is like having a solar-powered sunlamp. Talking about computers when you have a computer available is a little silly. Since the computer is sitting there, why not use it to compute?

In this application, the CAI approach is like teaching swimming by textbooks without getting wet. In fact, it is even worse, because the computer is both textbook and water; yet the learner still doesn't get wet. Computers are not very good teachers, but they can be excellent computers.

The suggestion that young children should learn to compute by computing usually triggers the bull-in-the-china-shop question: can children really be turned loose on expensive and highly technical equipment? The answer is yes. In the first place, the equipment is not so expensive anymore. In the second place, if it is too technical for children, we should simplify it. Seymour Papert, a mathematician at the Massachusetts Institute of Technology, has been trying to do just that: powerful programming languages do not have to be forbiddingly complex. If Papert and others like him succeed, young children will be able to learn about computing by computing.

The important educational idea here is not limited to, or even chiefly concerned with, teaching children to operate computing machines. When you compute, there must be something that you are computing. Computations do not occur in a vacuum. If you are trying to program a computer to imitate something, you must learn the theory of that thing (or construct your own theory of it). If you want to make a computer parse sentences, you must know (or invent for yourself) a theory of syntax on the basis of which automated parsing systems can be designed. If you want your computer to imitate an ecological system, you must know (or invent) a biological theory of niches. And so on.

It is apparent, therefore, that many other subjects can be taught as part of teaching children to use computers, a possibility that makes this new idea a rival to the accepted view that educational computers should imitate teachers. How strong a rival it will become remains to be seen. A great deal of work must be done before we will have a clear picture of its potentialities and limitations.

The tendency to greet new ideas with "Yes, but. . ." can be upsetting, but it should not be suppressed. In this case, the "yes, but" is reasonably obvious.

Just as CAI emphasizes how to talk about a subject, so learning by computing emphasizes how to speculate about a subject. But if you want to educate people who can determine which speculations are true out there in the real world (wherever that is), you had better not chain them to a computer keyboard. Somehow they will have to learn how to look at the real world—at real languages, real ecosystems, or whatever.

So where does that leave the computer in education? I think the answer is clear. Computers are coming, but we cannot let them run the whole show. In the long run, the real thing wins every time.

WHAT'S YOUR OPINION?

1. When children program a computer, they embark on an exploration of how they themselves learn.
2. Formal thinking does not develop until a child is at least 12 years old.
3. Children who program computers use very concrete computer models to think about thinking and learn about learning.
4. When you learn to program a computer, you seldom get it right the first time.
5. The computer's main application in the classroom should be to stimulate thinking.
6. Undoubtedly, there will be a massive penetration of computers into the schools.
7. Computers will make little difference in how people learn and think.
8. We will not see an increase in the computer's impact on educational systems without proper planning.
9. Computers may become a wasteland of *Star Wars* games instead of helping young people to develop their intellect to the fullest extent possible.
10. In early education, programming will become even more important than mathematics.
11. The "cutting edge" of the literature on the relationship between computer technology and education is not found in the educational journals.
12. Changes made by computers relate for the most

part to the rearrangement of established programs rather than to the creation of radically new programs demanding substantially new methods and expertise.

13. Students using computers generally tire more quickly than they would in group instruction involving changes of pace, wider perceptual fields, and social experiences.

14. The computer's holding power on students' attention can become a useful educational tool.

15. Instead of inducing mechanical thinking, contact with computers might be the best conceivable antidote to it.

16. Today's school curriculum tends to infantilize the child.

17. Children should learn without a prescribed curriculum; each should design his or her own curriculum.

18. Programs in BASIC require so labyrinthine a structure that only highly motivated and brilliant children learn to use programming techniques for more than trivial ends.

19. The computers in education today are limited by the mixing of old instructional methods with new technologies.

20. We have reached a point in the history of education when radical change is possible, and the impetus for that change is the computer.

21. The use of computers in education is a step in the direction of freeing children so that they can participate in human kinds of activities.

22. Without making extensive use of computers in school instruction, our students will grow up with an outdated method of instruction to live in a world of modern technology that will not only overwhelm, but perhaps control, them.

23. The computer is no more a threat to the teacher than is a slide or film projector.

24. Once computers minimize the time spent on joint involvement in menial tasks, the instructor can share with, listen to, and care about students in a much more individualized and personal way.

25. The microcomputer can radically change the lifestyle of this country.

26. One thing is certain: the process by which students learn is going to change.

27. The widespread integration of computing into schools will shift the focus of education from end product to process.

28. The process of problem solving remains hidden from most students.

29. The present delivery system of education can no longer meet the desired level of productivity.

30. The teaching/learning process that has been in use for the past 500 years has reached a point of counterproductive results.

31. Each student needs a computer just as each student now needs textbooks.

32. We must either decide to do something about computers or decide not to decide.

33. Schooling is interfering with our children's education.

34. Computers allow us to learn about learning while providing a facility for learning.

35. Today's curriculum greatly underestimates the capacity of children to deal with complexity. It arbitrarily postpones the introduction of problem-solving skills to so late a point that most children either lose interest or become so dependent on guidance that they never master these skills.

36. Just as the internal combustion engine revolutionized transportation, so will the computer alter education.

37. Education today is experiencing an intellectual crisis, following a reactive policy and trying to solve new problems with obsolete remedies.

38. The public needs to understand that computer problem solving is itself a basic intellectual skill with academic and vocational payoffs.

39. The future work force is at the mercy of the country's system of education, which is no system at all.

40. The computer is the first technological innovation in education that will enable the educator to respond fully to the individual learner.

41. As its basic educational advantage, the computer provides a vehicle for education that is responsive at all levels to the individual learner.

42. People outside the field of education are unimpressed by its quality of thinking or practice.

43. There has been surprisingly little discussion of the ultimate goals of education in a computerized society.

44. The potential contribution of computers in education is viewed in terms of the processes already present in the traditional classroom instead of in terms of activities that are not now found in schools because they require the use of the computer.

45. In the future, home instruction and study via computer will become increasingly important, and the burden of responsibility will shift to individuals and families.

46. Computers are uniquely able to teach absolutely anything, including teaching about computers.

47. Integrating computer usage into the curriculum is difficult because it means changing all the methods that schools have developed over the years.

48. Many youngsters who do not do well in school are secret computer geniuses because nobody is

telling them what to do when they work on the computer.

49. Personifying a microcomputer may be counter-productive in its effect on a child's understanding. In the long run it blocks the development in elementary school children of a real understanding of computers.
50. It is no longer necessary that every item on a production line look alike or that every student receive the same linear instructional sequence.
51. Children should be taught that machines are like people and that people are like machines.
52. The computer is one of the greatest things to enter the field of education since the invention of movable type.
53. Computers can be useful in sex education because adults dislike discussing such matters openly.
54. While using a computer, the learner is in a passive state, dependent on the programmer.
55. The eye-hand coordination required for computer games could lead us to forget about gross motor development.
56. The in-class computer offers greater opportunity for student-centered learning.
57. Many popular computer games are making little warmongers of our children.

EXERCISES

1. List ten situations in which a computer is better suited than humans to perform certain tasks.
2. Compare computers to humans under the following headings: Input, Processing, Output.
3. What qualities do humans possess that computers lack?
4. What attributes make computers better than people for certain jobs?
5. Researchers are making progress in discovering the nature of the human thought process, the "source" of the mind, and the connection between mind, soul, and brain. What are your theories on this subject?
6. Is it theoretically possible to develop machinery capable of pseudohuman "thinking" without first fully understanding the human thought process?
7. Are computers effective in the classroom? Can you find published results of recent studies?
8. Does your educational system plan to evaluate the use of computers in the classroom?
9. Discuss how classroom volunteers might be used in a computer awareness course.
10. Read Seymour Papert's *Mindstorms.* Can your teaching techniques benefit from his methods?
11. Find out if your present classroom microcomputer can be interfaced with a "turtle." (Contact TERRAPIN, Inc., 678 Massachusetts Avenue, Cambridge, MA 02139.)
12. How might religious groups use CAI [Computer Assisted Instruction] to spread their beliefs?
13. Is a child's attraction or addiction to a computer basically a bad thing? When might it be good and when bad? Discuss.
14. What type of child works best with computers? Discuss.

COMPUTER LITERACY

The term *computer literacy* has become a buzz word that has taken on a range of meanings. To some teachers, a "literacy program" means a concentrated course in BASIC programming; other teachers cover topics in "computer awareness," offering little or no programming experience at all. It is generally felt, however, that computers are the coming thing and that everyone should have some knowledge of what they do, how they do it, and what their implications are for us all. The articles in this section help to define computer literacy, provide topics for course outlines, and clarify the issues and problems involved in producing computer literacy among teachers, students, and the public generally. The detrimental effects of inadequate or nonexistent training programs are also discussed.

Clearly, the need to develop literacy courses at all levels is urgent. The information explosion, the shift in emphasis to science and knowledge-based industries, and the pervasiveness of computers in everyday life demand that educational systems be restructured to develop a computer-literate society. In this section, Molnar, Luehrmann, Eisele, Billings, and Ershov suggest that the ability to use computers has become as basic and necessary a part of formal education as reading, writing, and arithmetic. Suggested topics for computer literacy programs are presented by the Schools Committee Working Program (SCWP), Klassen, and Eisele. Bork and Franklin discuss the role of the personal computer in education and include a comparison with time-sharing.

The Next Great Crisis in American Education: Computer Literacy

Andrew R. Molnar

In the early 1960s, educators found that a large proportion of the persons who taught scientific subjects were inadequately prepared in subjects they taught and that there were gross inadequacies in the instructional materials available to teachers (United States Office of Education, 1969). The launching of the Soviet earth satellite Sputnik brought a renewed interest in science and became the catalyst for a major curriculum reform movement. Unfortunately, the educational reform did not ameliorate or solve the major social problems of our times and the reform movement waned.

Current events have conspired to create a new educational crisis. The fundamental assumptions and social consensus about education which evolved after Sputnik are now under question. Like it or not, we as a nation are now engaged in the social process of renegotiating the form and substance that American education will take for the foreseeable future.

We still face many of the same problems of the past, but in a new context. A synthesis of three major studies of the needs and practices in our nation's schools supported by the Office of Program Integration of the National Science Foundation (NSF) concludes that, in large part, today's problems derive from declining enrollments, increasing costs, the relatively ineffective teacher support structure, and a back-to-basics movement (Office of Program Integration, 1978).

From *Volume 5: Proceedings from Second International Learning Technology Congress and Exposition,* February 14–16, 1978. Society for Applied Learning Technology. Reprinted by permission.

Declining enrollments. A recent study, *The Condition of Education,* reports that the elementary school population is expected to decline in size for the next five years; the secondary school population has now started to decrease; and the college age population is expected to increase slightly until 1980 and then decrease (Golladay, 1977).

Increasing costs. In spite of the decreasing enrollments, per-student expenditures, total expenditures, and the percentage of Gross National Product (GNP) spent for education are expected to increase. The percentage of GNP spent on education (7.9 percent) now surpasses both the percentage for health (7.6 percent) and defense (5.5 percent), and the percentage spent on education has exceeded that spent on defense since 1973 (Golladay, 1977).

Ineffective teacher support. Since declining enrollment means less external funds, it follows that fewer new teachers are being hired and the average age of the faculty is increasing. In addition, 13 percent of science, 12 percent of social studies and 8 percent of mathematics teachers felt themselves inadequately trained to teach one or more courses assigned to them. The lack of funds also has led to fewer replacements of dated textbooks and equipment. Further, it is reported that over half of all science and social studies and two-thirds of all mathematics classes use a single textbook and many teachers use no supplementary aids other than the chalk board (National Science Board, 1975).

In general, teachers tend to be less prepared and find it more and more difficult to keep abreast of the current developments in science and technology. They tend to be supported with one, often dated, textbook and little or no supplementary materials. This has led to a condition similar to that of the pre–Sputnik era.

Back-to-basics movement. After a decade of curriculum revision, a strong public reaction has occurred which seems to stem from a dissatisfaction with the innovations of the 1960s and a concern over declining national test scores. Half of the adults with children in school believe that schools should devote more attention to teaching basic skills (Golladay, 1977). This has resulted in the feeling that reading and computational arithmetic are the building blocks of education. While many still feel that science is important, they also feel that reading, arithmetic, vocational skills and remedial courses are more important. As a consequence, about 50 percent of students take no science after grade ten (Office of Program Integration, 1978). In general, there is a trend toward the relaxation of science requirements in our nation's schools.

The trend away from science is occurring at all levels of education, from the inner city schools to the most prestigious universities. The science curriculum has been attacked as too diverse, too complex, and too difficult. There is a trend toward a more basic curriculum and more basic skills. The current movement has been characterized as a withdrawal from complexity and the acceptance of "minimalcy." Is this reactive policy adequate to cope with the changes occurring in our society? Are there other policies more suited to our times and conditions? What is the nature of the changes which are occurring in our society?

OUR CHANGING SOCIETY

Our economy is in a period of significant and fundamental change. The lack of low-cost energy sources and the diminishing supply of raw materials have led to a shift from the production of industrial goods and services to a greater emphasis on science and knowledge-based industries. An extensive study of the U.S. economy concludes that for the year 1967, 46 percent of GNP was produced by information industries and that nearly half the labor force held information-related jobs and earned 53 percent of the labor income (Porat, 1977). Dr. Daniel Bell (1973) points out that the growth rate of professional and technical employment is twice that of the average. This group has increased from 3.9 million in 1940 to 13.2 million in 1975, thus making professional and technical persons the second largest of eight occupational divisions, exceeded only by semi-skilled workers. Information has become a national commodity and a national resource and has altered the very nature of work. We as a nation have moved from being predominately an industrial society to being an information society.

The "information explosion" is probably felt most in the area of science. It is estimated that 100,000 scientific and technological periodicals are published each year throughout the world. In the United States, 80,000 technical reports are produced per year and this number is increasing at a rate of 14 percent per year. There are 2,000,000 scientific writings of all kinds produced per year or 6,000 to 7,000 articles per day (Anderla, 1973). This enormous growth in information has increased the diversity and complexity of science. Dr. Herbert Simon says that these developments have changed the meaning attached to the verb "to know"; in the past "to know" meant "to have stored in one's memory," but today knowing now shifts from having actual possession of information to the process of having access to it (Simon, 1971).

The United States over the past two decades has been the major user and prime exporter of high technology. Today, statistical indicators show that the United States is fast being overtaken in innovation of new technology by more dynamic foreign economies (National Science Board, 1975). Our technological lead in computing, which some feel offers the best solution for increased national productivity, is also waning. The U.S. Department of Commerce reports that British, French, West German and Japanese computer firms with strong government support will offer severe competition in the near future (*U.S. Industrial Outlook,* 1976).

A number of foreign governments are now working cooperatively with commercial firms and educational institutions in their countries to mount a challenge to our leadership. They are investing large sums of money into research and development of computer-based industries. More significantly, they have placed a high priority on the development of computer-based skills in their educational systems. The key to the success of this technological challenge lies in adopting new educational methods which make the computer an integral part of the educational process from kindergarten to the university and which permit people to experience computer uses and practices on a day-to-day basis (Molnar, 1977).

In summary, it is evident that problems of the economy, science, education and the computer are all interdependent and highly related. Science-driven innovations spur the economy and create new jobs. Computers increase productivity but require a more skilled and professional labor pool with a broader education and a greater familiarity with the tools of science. And international competition for the lead in knowledge-based industries is likely to increase in the near future.

THE POWER OF THE COMPUTER

The impact of computers on science has been revolutionary. Computers permit scientists to organize and access huge quantities of information. While operating at speeds of up to a picosecond (a trillionth of a second), computers shorten the time necessary for lengthy calculations and enable scientists to solve problems that were once considered beyond their capacity.

The computer provides science with a powerful tool for coping with the complexity of knowledge and the ever-expanding information base. As a tool, the computer is no less important to education. However, the computer, which has become indispensible to the operation of science, business, and government, does not play a major role in American education.

Integrating the computer into education. Computers and even hand calculators have made obsolete many subjects and have relegated the calculation of

square root, logarithms and fractions in education to the level of importance of dipping candles and tanning hides. Just as automated information has ended jobs in industry, it has also ended subjects in education. One might ask, what happened to the slide rule? The world's largest producer of slide rules has discontinued their production. Within seven years after it was created and three years after it became widely available, the hand calculator has driven the slide rule out of education and has created a new threshold for problem-solving in science and mathematics courses. This development has occurred, in most cases, without planning and in spite of educators.

Several commissions have studied the problem of integrating computers into education. The President's Science Advisory Committee concluded that if educational computing is to find a useful place in colleges, substantial revision of course material in the various disciplines is necessary. This recommendation was reiterated by the Commission on Instructional Technology, the Carnegie Commission on Higher Education, and the Conference Board of the Mathematical Sciences (Molnar, 1977).

The computer as an object of science. A meeting of school experts was convened by the National Science Foundation to consider the impact of the hand calculator on elementary school mathematics. A mathematician and author of many popular textbooks observed that the first six years of mathematics in our schools is devoted to learning the four basic functions of addition, subtraction, multiplication and division. He asked, "If we introduce into the first grade calculators which automatically perform these functions, what will the children do for six years?" Indeed, what will children do?

Technology and knowledge are inextricably linked. If we look at the current curriculum we will find whole areas of knowledge built around technology such as the inclined plane and the pendulum. Dr. Seymour Papert of M.I.T. finds that young, elementary school children, given the availability of a computer, are capable of solving complex problems in physics, geometry and physiology. They are capable of writing computer-based poetry and music (Molnar, 1976).

The computer Dr. Papert uses drives a device called a "Turtle," which has audio and light-sensitive receptors (ears and eyes). He uses this device to help teach "Turtle Geometry"—a mathematics embedded in the world of an electromechanical turtle. He teaches physiology with a computer-driven "worm"; music composition with computer-driven music box; and English with a computer-generated poetry.

The significance of Dr. Papert's work is that it demonstrates that today's curriculum greatly underestimates the capacity of children to deal with complexity and arbitrarily postpones the introduction of problem-solving skills to a point so late in the curriculum that most children lose interest or become so dependent on guidance that they never master these skills. Computing provides a new way of thinking and as such should be introduced as early as possible. The power of the computer eliminates many manual skills that are prerequisite to mastery and provides a powerful general problem-solving tool that permits students to cope with problems of complexity.

THE SOCIAL COSTS OF ILLITERACY

Many schools and colleges have initiated programs to integrate the computer into the classroom. Dartmouth College has been a leader in integrating the computer into the academic curriculum. Dr. John Kemeny, president of Dartmouth College and researcher on the atomic bomb, says "It took twenty of us twenty hours a day, six days a week for an entire year to accomplish what one Dartmouth student can do in one afternoon" (*Time*, 1977, p. 61).

At Dartmouth, the computer is considered as important to the student as the library, and consequently students are permitted to use the computer, free-of-charge, any time of the day, for any reason. I am told that while other universities have difficulty in attracting students, Dartmouth accepts one of eight applicants. A recent survey of applicants to Dartmouth found that the most frequently cited reason for wishing to attend was Dartmouth's reputation for instructional computing.

Dr. Donald Michael (1968) writes in *The Unprepared Society* that there is a growing separation between those working creatively with computers and the rest of the population. He says that "ignorance of computers will render people as functionally illiterate as ignorance of reading, writing, and arithmetic." It is clear that if we are to have equity in our educational system, all students must have access to computing and must become literate.

Some argue that computer literacy is the responsibility of the individual and can be learned after one leaves school. However, there is a psychological cost involved in reclassifying and relearning concepts once learned. This especially is true when the new concepts make previous models obsolete. Imagine the engineer who graduates with honors but has not been exposed to computers and must compete for a job in industry now permeated with computers. Imagine the drill-press operator who graduates from a vocational school only to discover that machinists in modern factories don't use machines but instead program

computers to run machines. A student who graduates without being exposed to computers has had an incomplete education. To retrain after graduation creates an unnecessary human waste and incurs a high unacceptable social and psychological cost.

WHO IS RESPONSIBLE FOR COMPUTER LITERACY PROGRAMS?

Some argue that the private sector that will benefit most from the sale of computers should support the development of computer literacy. Dr. Arthur Luehrmann of the Lawrence Hall of Science says that publishers do not teach reading because people may go out and buy their competitors' product. Therefore, computer vendors or publishers cannot be reasonably expected to provide such services (Luehrmann, 1977). Consequently, the burden of computer literacy must fall to the educators.

But why is computer literacy also a national problem and not just a local problem? Several studies have concluded that the lack of good computer-based educational materials is the major obstacle to the widespread use of computers and that this need is only partially being satisfied by local efforts—but at costs which are prohibitive and unnecessary when viewed from a national perspective (Molnar, 1977).

The Federal Government is the largest single user of computers in the United States. It has 10,000 computers and spends approximately $10 billion dollars a year on equipment and personnel. Computers have become indispensable to the operation of government. However, Federal agencies which use the computers to make significant gains in productivity and to improve the general well-being of the public also must be concerned with public understanding and acceptance of these systems. An uninformed and uneducated citizenry may limit or reject technological advances.

We tend to underestimate the degree to which the technological literacy pervades our society until we try to introduce technology into other cultures. Attempts to introduce computers into some less-developed nations have not succeeded because of the lack of a significant number of computer literates. Energy-rich nations have developed national programs to exploit their resources; we must develop our human resources. In an information society, a computer-literate populace is as important as energy and raw materials are to an industrial society.

It has been recognized that considerably more than half of the increase in American productivity has been due to scientific and engineering advances. Many economists feel that the major capital stock of an advanced nation is not its physical equipment, but rather the body of knowledge amassed from science and the capacity to train its people to use knowledge effectively (Gilpin, 1975).

In a democratic society, it is not only a right but also an obligation for all citizens to participate in the action of their government. Some feel that due to the high cost of equipment and training, only big government and big business will benefit from the use of computers. Others feel that the advent of small personal computers will solve this problem. They argue that information networks and services will make it possible for the public to benefit from the information without having to learn a computer language. In either case, citizens without any idea of what computers can do will be no better off (Bemer, 1975). Computer literacy is a prerequisite to effective participation in a information society and as much a social obligation as is reading literacy.

EDUCATION IN A COMPLEX SOCIETY

Our society is growing more and more complex. The information explosion has created a discontinuity in the nature of our educational needs. Science curricula designed to meet these needs have been criticized as being too difficult and too complex for most students. Many feel that we should reduce the amount of science taught and instead teach more basic skills. However, the computer is ideal for dealing with complexity, and difficulty is not inherent in the subject matter but rather in our ability to cope with it. The computer provides us with a problem-solving tool capable of overcoming these difficulties.

Will computers reduce the high cost of education? It is unlikely, in the short run, that computers will reduce the costs of instruction. On the other hand, will proficiency in simple computational arithmetic prepare students for an information society? Some say we did not invent automobiles by breeding better and better horses. Just as the internal combustion engine revolutionized transportation, so will the computer alter education. After all, how cost-effective is it to efficiently teach skills that are obsolete, for jobs that no longer exist, in a society that demands knowledge about computers? Instead, we must ask what is *basic* in a society predominately information oriented.

We should take a long view of the question of cost. It is estimated that 15 percent of the major ideas in regard to computing have originated at universities. In addition, some feel that the federally supported university research in the field of semi-conductors was the basis for the electronics revolution and led to our international domination of the computer and aerospace industries (Molnar, 1977). It has been said that the single biggest impediment to the further growth of the multi-billion-dollar microelectronic industry is the fact that the vast majority of Americans are uneducated in the use of the computer (Luehrmann, 1977). In short, the academic community has created innovations whose contributions to our GNP are at least as large as the national cost of education. Further, a computer-literate populace will facilitate the creation of new markets.

A study of innovation found that much of the knowledge used in developing innovations was based upon the knowledge received during the innovator's formal education. The study concluded that in spite of the fact that results of research are published in journals which are widely available, scientific knowledge does not become a relatively freely available good until it becomes part of the educational curriculum (Gibbons & Johnson, 1974). How do we introduce innovations into education? Education is textbook-bound and today's books make little or no reference to computer-based advances. A national effort is needed to introduce computing into the educational curricula and into our nation's textbooks.

Some countries with centralized educational systems have already begun systematic efforts to achieve computer literacy. In the United States, where the responsibility for education is shared at the local, state and federal levels, only collective action can bring about the needed change. Education today is in an intellectual crisis; we are following a reactive policy and are trying to solve new problems with old remedies. Other nations are beginning the task of adapting to a changing world. If we do not begin soon, the next great crisis in American education will be the computer-literacy crisis.

There is a story of the commuter which ran to catch the train and on arriving late commented, "If I had run faster, I would have made it." A bystander said, "No, if you had started sooner you would have made it."

There is a national need to foster computer literacy and if we are to meet this need, we must ensure that high school graduates have an understanding of the uses and applications of the computer in society and its effect upon their everyday lives. We must permit students to use the computer as it would typically be used in business, science, and government. We must increase the quality of education through the introduction of computer-related curricula in a wide variety of academic subjects at all levels of education. A nation concerned with its social needs and economic growth cannot be indifferent to the problems of literacy. If we are to reap the benefits of science-driven industries, we must develop a computer-literate society.

REFERENCES

Anderla, G. *Information in 1985: A forecasting of information needs and resources.* Paris, France: Organization for Economic Co-operation and Development, 1973 (ERIC Document Reproduction Services No. ED 088 462).

Bell, D. *The coming of the post-industrial society.* New York: Basic Books, 1973.

Bemer, R.W. The frictional interface between computers and society. *Computers and People,* January 1975, *24,* 14–19.

Gibbons, M., & Johnson, R. The roles of science in technological innovation. *Research Policy,* 1974, *3,* 220–242.

Gilpin, R. *Technology, economic growth and international competitiveness* (A report for the Subcommittee on Economic Growth of the Joint Commitee, Congress of the United States, 94th Congress, 1st Session). Washington, D.C.: U.S. Government Printing Office, 1975.

Golladay, M.A. *The condition of education* (U.S. National Center of Educational Statistics). Washington, D.C.: U.S. Government Printing Office, 1977.

Luehrmann, A.W. *Research, development and planning for computers and the learning society.* Presented to the Hearing of the U.S. House of Representatives, Science and Technology Subcommittee on Domestic and International Scientific Planning, Analysis and Cooperation. October 12, 1977.

Michael, D.N. *The unprepared society.* New York: Basic Books, 1968.

Molnar, A.R. The new intellectual technology. *The Journal: Technological Horizons in Education,* 1976, *3* (3).

Molnar, A.R. National policy toward technological innovation and academic computing. *The Journal: Technological Horizons in Education,* 1977, *4* (6), 39–43.

National Science Board. *Science indicators,* 1974. Washington, D.C.: National Science Foundation, 1975.

Office of Program Integration (OPI). *The status of pre-college science, mathematics and social studies education.* Washington, D.C.: National Science Foundation, January 13, 1978.

Porat, M.U. *The information economy.* (Department of Commerce, Office of Telecommunications and the National Science Foundation, Division of Advanced Productivity Research and Technology). Washington, D.C.: U.S. Government Printing Office, 1977.

Simon, H.A. Designing organizations for an information-rich world. In M. Greenberger (Ed.), *Computers, communications and the public interest.* Baltimore: John Hopkins Press, 1971.

Time, 1977, *110* (26), 61.

U.S. Industrial Outlook, 1976. Washington, D.C.: U.S. Department of Commerce, 1976.

U.S. Office of Education, Bureau of Research. *Educational research and development in the United States.* Washington, D.C., December 1969.

COMPUTER ILLITERACY—A NATIONAL CRISIS AND A SOLUTION FOR IT

Arthur Luehrmann

THE PROBLEM

Computing plays such a crucial role in everyday life and in the technological future of this nation that the general public's ignorance of the subject constitutes a national crisis.

The ability to use computers is as basic and necessary to a person's formal education as reading, writing, and arithmetic. As jobs become increasingly oriented toward the use of information, society demands and rewards individuals who know how to use information systems. The American computer industry, which leads the world today, depends for its future upon a mass market of computer-literate workers and consumers.

Yet, despite computing's critical importance today, the overwhelming majority of this country's general public is woefully ill-prepared to live and work in the Age of Information, as some have called it. How many high-school graduates have taken a hands-on course in computer use? How many teachers are prepared to teach such a course? How many company presidents can operate their own computer departments? Yet, they could probably do a respectable job with most other departments. How many legislators can interact with a computer-based information-retrieval system? How many office workers are ready for office automation—or even know what they want from office automation? How many consumers are ready for general-purpose home computers that they can program themselves?

The answer to all these questions is the same: very few such people exist today.

Why is this true? Vocational incentives are powerful enough. People with programming skills command jobs with far higher salaries than are average for people with similar education; and word-processing specialists earn more than clerk-typists. Corporate profitability incentives are equally strong, because the success of businesses depends as much on the creative use of information as upon the efficient use of material and energy resources. Personal incentives are also great. The children and adults I see learning to use computers display an unusual intensity of concentration and an evident satisfaction with their results.

Clearly, it takes more than incentive to cause things to happen. There must also be a mechanism—an educational mechanism, in this case—if our society is to emerge from our preliterate state of computer ignorance. *The present educational mechanism is grossly inadequate to the task—a situation that must change and change quickly.*

Two kinds of computer education are needed. First, all future students should acquire basic skills in computer use, including hands-on operation,

From "Computer Illiteracy—A National Crisis and a Solution For It," by Arthur Luehrmann. In BYTE, June, 1980. © BYTE Publications, Inc.

programming, and problem solving, during their early secondary-school years. They should also make further use of these skills in other courses in mathematics, science, language, etc., and in vocationally oriented courses in word processing, accounting, and the like.

The need for a second kind of computer education is dictated by the fact that most of us have finished our formal education. School-based programs will take care of future needs, but today's adults have pressing incentives to develop their own computer skills. How can that be done?

OBSTACLES TO COMPUTER EDUCATION

While computer *awareness* can be arrived at by means of books, lectures, films, and television shows, computer *literacy* can be reached only by practice. Therefore, if schools are to provide students with basic computer literacy, they must give each student many "laboratory hours" at the keyboard of an interactive computer system. While surveys show that most secondary schools have some sort of computer, nevertheless, the average student probably spends less than an hour at a computer keyboard during all of his or her precollege years. *With a very few exceptions, therefore, it is fair to say that computer literacy is not now a part of the curriculum.*

To provide computer literacy, four specific needs have to be met:

- adequate and appropriate equipment in every secondary school
- an available, usable curriculum with materials for students and teachers
- one or more teachers in each school trained in teaching computer use
- community, political, and financial support for such school-based programs

Each of these needs can be satisfied rather easily; that should be grounds for optimism. Nevertheless, each need is currently faced with a significant obstacle.

The inexpensive microcomputer, more than any other event, has made school-based computer education a possibility. The development of small time-sharing systems about ten years ago brought hardware costs per student terminal down to about $10,000—a major breakthrough, but still far too costly for most schools. Worse yet, time-sharing systems lack robustness against hardware failure: 97% uptime is achievable and sounds good, but it means that there is no computer one day per month, and no computer class. The new personal computers have brought the cost down to from $1000 to $2000 and have increased robustness dramatically: 97% uptime for personal computers means that out of a collection of ten machines, nine are working all the time and all ten are working most of the time. Class goes on.

On the other hand, the use and administration of a collection of separate personal computers is often extremely difficult. Since personal computers are not linked to a shared-file system, it falls to the teacher to make duplicate cassettes or floppy disks for each machine, to shelve the copies, to retrieve them, to check them out, to check them in, and to periodically revise all copies when a program change is made. Furthermore, loading a program from a cassette is both time-consuming and unreliable. We have found in our Lawrence Hall of Science computer classes that it takes 5 to 10 minutes to succeed in loading ten program tapes into ten computers.

Adding floppy-disk drives cuts the loading time down, but only at great monetary cost. Furthermore, it does nothing to alleviate any of the problems of maintaining a library of hundreds of floppy disks.

Although there have been a few steps in the right direction, some good enough right now for school use, the industry has not yet solved the relatively simple problem of combining a set of microcomputers with a large, centralized, tree-structured file system of the sort found on any decent time-sharing system. That is what schools need, and probably many businesses, also.

The lack of curriculum is another major obstacle to computer education. We simply cannot expect 25 to 50 thousand school teachers to invent curricula and prepare materials for students to use. The fact that anyone is teaching computing today is powerful testimony to their commitment and to the interest computing seems to generate among teachers.

The traditional secondary-school book publishers have nothing to offer schools; instead, they resort to peddling books designed for the college market or the hobbyist market—usually programming manuals full of syntax rules and definitions but with little relevant problem-solving semantics. Specific new materials are needed for the schools.

Another obstacle is the lack of trained teachers and educational opportunities to learn to teach computing. I know of only a few schools of education that offer content courses appropriate for a future computer teacher, and they are usually pre-service courses for new teachers. In this job market, what is needed is in-service training for existing teachers who are in the process of becoming computer teachers.

The lack of such a program in schools of education is difficult to explain, especially in these times. It represents just about the only economically viable possibility for an in-service program. The teachers I know would willingly pay for a good program, even if they are at the top of the ladder in their current field.

The last significant obstacle to school-based computer education is the lack of public clamor for such a program. Evidently, if the school is to teach computing, members of the community must foot the bill. Parents who see computer education as little more than game playing are bound to treat it as a frill and give it a lower priority than what they perceive as "the basics." They need to understand that computer problem solving is itself a basic intellectual skill with academic and vocational payoffs.

My recent experience in consulting with schools in several districts in California has given me grounds for optimism about the state of community awareness and concern. I find, for example, many parents whose work involves computer use and who speak convincingly about the need for school-based programs. Other parents are simply impressed that their children are visibly excited by the computer class at school. Although concerned about rising costs and the general quality of education, they seem to recognize that computer education needs to be evaluated on its merits.

WHO WILL TAKE THE NECESSARY STEPS?

There is a role for everyone: the computer industry, textbook publishers, universities, teachers, parents, and government agencies.

The computer industry has to recognize that there is a billion-dollar market for computer equipment in secondary schools (26,000 schools, times fifteen computers per school, times $2500 per computer). After that soaks in, they have to design and produce an appropriate computer *system* for school use, along the lines suggested earlier: microcomputers connected in a network to a hard disk and printer, plus a tree-structured file system with account security and cross-account access.

The textbook publishers need to support—perhaps in combination with computer manufacturers—one or two substantial curriculum-development projects aimed at producing materials that concern not just the syntax rules of a programming language, but which also focus on general problem-solving applications. I used to think that this was too big a job for the private sector, but the potential $50 million annual sales volume changed my mind (26,000 schools, times 300 students per year, times $6 per student manual). A proper job of writing, evaluating, rewriting, field trials, and more rewriting would cost a few million dollars, perhaps, but that can be easily recovered in short order.

University schools of education need to gear up to handle both pre-service and in-service training needs of future schoolteachers of computer classes.

Teachers with an active or latent interest in computing need to inform themselves of career opportunities in this emerging field, find out what other teachers are doing, and put pressure on the schools of education to satisfy their training needs.

Parents need to know why Johnny and Janey should learn to compute as well as read and write. Then they need to develop community support for programs in their junior high schools and high schools.

Finally, government agencies have to keep a close watch on the way computer education develops and evolves in the schools, and possibly to intervene at critical points. In particular, if the private sector is unwilling to risk investment in curriculum, or if certain communities cannot afford to pay for equipment, the federal government should help to do so, for compelling reasons. Possession of basic computer skills is a distinct vocational and intellectual advantage to the possessor. Declining prices of personal computers put them within easy reach of people who now have the advantages of above-average income and the education to recognize the benefits of knowing about computers. The disadvantaged will be left behind. It is an entirely appropriate use of federal funds to provide broad social access to new and powerful skills.

WHAT ABOUT THE ADULTS?

It is probably true that most of the people who need to know about computers and their uses during the next five to ten years are already in the work force. They are, quite frankly, at the mercy of the "US system of continuing education"—which is no system at all. Among their options are going back to school, evening classes at a community college or university, extension courses, technical training institutes, topical professional seminars, and self-study.

My standing advice to persons faced with such alternatives is to first enroll in a course that will teach them to write computer programs, and to run and debug them by means of hands-on use of an interactive computer system. Such a course should offer both formal instruction and at least ten hours of computer use by the individual. (Beware of lecture and reading courses alone, as well as those using punch-card equipment.)

Such a course should cost less than a hundred dollars and will determine pretty clearly what the next step should be. If the experience has been a good one, then the person may want to take more advanced courses, or to look for specific career-oriented programs in the computer field, or to buy a personal computer and study on his or her own.

SUMMARY

As a nation we depend more and more on computer technology, on computer applications, and on the success of our computer industry. However, we are also a nation of computer illiterates. The means exist to set in motion education programs that will change the situation.

All we have to do is decide to do it.

Syllabuses for the Future

Schools Committee Working Group

One of the major concerns of the Schools Committee during recent years has been that most syllabuses in so-called "Computer Studies" have not kept pace with current trends. They do not produce a contemporary awareness of the computing world nor do they reflect the pace of technological change. The first Working Party which tried to offer guidance on syllabus design produced, in 1969 and revised in 1970, a document called "Computer Education for All." The success of this document has, to a certain extent, frustrated several valiant attempts at revision.

The present Working Party has approached the matter by identifying, within existing syllabuses, topics which are considered to be of lasting value and by adding areas which might be relevant for the next decade. We have tried to produce an answer to the question posed to the British Computer Society in 1985 [sic] by a secondary school head-teacher: "What should my colleagues be teaching all children about computers?"

In listing the selected topics, members have added a paragraph of explanation, not only of the meaning of the topic itself but also an indication of how a teacher might present the topic to pupils. We would recommend that the topics be included *somewhere* within the normal secondary school curriculum for *every* student either as part of a computing course or as topics studied within other subjects, e.g. general studies, humanities or mathematics.

The Working Party recognised that the current educational debate, epitomised by the recent Green Paper and the published curriculum guidelines from Her Majesty's Inspectorate was making the establishment of computer studies courses even more difficult

From "Syllabuses for the Future," by the Schools Committee Working Group. In *AEDS Monitor,* November, 1979, by the Association of Educational Data Systems. Reprinted by permission.

within an overcrowded curriculum. The move towards a narrower range of subject options has meant that time and resources are not always available for a subject which has, in some cases, enjoyed the status of only a fringe activity.

It is the hope of this Working Party, however, that if a school undertakes an overall review of the curriculum during the next few years, the following list of topics should be considered for inclusion as a *priority,* reflecting as they do the environment and society in which our students will inevitably develop. We leave it to the ingenuity of teachers to find ways to incorporate our suggestions, in whatever order is thought appropriate, within the core of their curriculum.

1. The automatic control of processes. Processes, in the widest sense of the word, have been automated since early times. With the advent of the computer and, in particular, the micro-computer, developments in the automatic control of processes are infiltrating much of our modern living at an ever increasing pace. This is exemplified by an acceptance, as commonplace, of the fact that many of our large industries no longer have need for the higher manning levels which were so common in the past. It is necessary for our pupils to gain a basic understanding of the underlying principles of automation through a study of present developments and possible future trends. A visit to a local engineering works could indicate the extent to which mechanical handling techniques have been introduced.

2. The concept of input-process-output. Pupils should be aware of input-process-output sequence in other than a computer context (e.g., a laundry or dry-cleaning shop). This should help them to appreciate the need, especially in an extremely high speed system, for a standard form of input. They should also be aware of the various means of converting input from a form convenient for people into a form designed for machine. The emphasis should be on the principle rather than on the means of conversion. It should be recognised that, during the processing stage, a computer system undertakes a number of tasks according to a predetermined sequence, thus transforming the input data into a form ready for output. Pupils should also be aware of the ways in which the output from a machine is designed to serve the direct needs of people, for example the computer generation of letters and bills which arrive in the home or the control of traffic by means of coloured lights.

3. Coding systems. In carrying out data processing tasks, a computer repeatedly transforms the input data using precise codes and rules. These transformations may not always be apparent to the operator of a computer system. The input, transmission and manipulation of data involve a wide range of coding techniques from which suitable examples can be selected. Teachers could choose from codes used for punched cards, printing devices, braille output, graph plotters and number representation. Having used some of these codes or seen them in action, students may be interested in inventing their own codes and in using them to complete simple communication tasks.

4. Preparation of input—Interpretation of output. Pupils should be aware of the degree of precision needed when specifying input for a computer. They should have first hand experience of data collection and checking and should be alive to the possibility of data containing errors despite such checking. The preparation of forms for data collection, so that subsequent transfer of data is made easier, can be experienced at first hand. Pupils should appreciate that computer output is not infallible and is simply information which can be used as the basis on which to make decisions, and, as such, may require a degree of interpretation. Most computer programs contain routines for checking data but it is impossible for the computer to produce valid results from incorrect or incomplete data.

5. Using computer program packages. A computer package is a program or set of programs designed to output results which depend upon data supplied by the user. The user needs to be familiar with any manual of instructions and must have a knowledge of the operational procedure for the particular computer system.

The use of such a package does not require any knowledge of the computer programs themselves. It is possible that the data will need to be structured in a certain way, conforming to a particular set of rules; indeed, this may provide some of the educational value of the exercise. A package should be viewed, and treated, as a tool by means of which an extremely powerful information-processing system can be easily controlled by an unsophisticated user.

6. Information storage and retrieval. Pupils should be aware that the computer has made possible the storage of vast amounts of information. They should know that such information can be made available for use, either in a general way or on a restricted basis, but that convenient access is possible only if the information is structured in some way. Libraries offer examples of both manual and computer-based systems for retrieval of information. Businesses use computer data-bases to help them make up-to-date management decisions and to guide their transactions, for example, in international airline booking systems.

Pupils will wish to make use of computer-based storage and retrieval systems alongside other techniques of study. The increase in the amount of information held in the world's libraries has been likened to an explosion. However, new techniques have enabled students to have ready access to recent and relevant research.

7. Hardware in context. It is not necessary to emphasise a study of hardware for its own sake, because technology changes and what is available today may well be out of date in five years time. However, as pupils are made aware of particular applications of the computer by means of case studies, it will be natural to consider the role played by particular pieces of hardware, to appreciate the facilities offered by them and to consider the relative merits (and disadvantages) of alternative devices. Pupils should view hardware as tools which are intended to be convenient for the job being undertaken.

8. Special-purpose and general-purpose computers. A general purpose computer is one which, supported by a team of programmers, analysts and operators, provides a range of computing facilities for a number of users. These systems can be found in large organizations such as local authorities, manufacturing companies and commercial groups and may combine central processing with links to terminals. Some computing activities can be performed by processors which are specifically designed for a single task, for example, the body scanning X-ray system for medical diagnosis or the hand-held calculator used by salesmen. The advent of the microprocessor has made the computer more universally available for such special purpose roles, especially where size is at a premium.

9. The effect of the cashless society. Pupils need to be made aware of the ways in which cash transactions in banks and shops are being replaced by the electronic transfer of funds from one bank account to another using computer systems operated by special cards carried by the customer.

In a supermarket, individual items are identified by a computer readable commodity code. As well as enabling the details and total of a customer's purchases to be calculated, these codes can give the store an automatic record of the stock position and an indication of buying behaviour. The sociological implications of these developments should also be studied.

10. Computers and people. The creation of files of information about people raises questions of accuracy, access and morality which are not easily answered by regulating the behaviour of those in positions of power and control. There are several sensitive areas of public life in which such files may be used or abused, for example, police work and the law, the use of computers to establish the credit worthiness of people, the holding of pupil records in a school. In such areas great care must be taken to make the system foolproof, secure and flexible.

One danger is that decisions on the feasibility and design of such systems will be left to the analyst who may or may not have a social conscience. One safeguard must be to inform our future citizens of the ways in which these systems can be used for their benefit or against our interests.

11. Communications systems. Throughout the last hundred years, communications have been successively revolutionized by the introduction of the telephone, radio, television, satellites and computers. Data may now be transmitted at high speed to almost any part of the world, enabling the use of links between computer systems in different continents.

Networks provide for the sharing of computing resources, by routing requests for processing to the most appropriate location, without the user necessarily being aware that this is taking place. A data base, for example on weather conditions, can be accessed from any point in a given region. The problem of maintaining the data base is then left to a single forecasting station.

12. Computer manipulation of text, number, picture and spoken word. Pupils should appreciate that there are various means of communiating information and that such information can be transmitted, edited, summarised and re-arranged using a computer. The various viewdata and teletext systems are common examples of such manipulation. Direct communication with the computer has been greatly simplified by the development of devices which recognize spoken words and the patterns of text and handwriting. Word processing is already making an impact on office practice. A study of the automation of office procedures could start with a consideration of the information processing activities in the schools' own administration. In design work the computer can support the creative process by allowing exploration of possible models before final decisions are taken. It should be recognized that the computer can also be involved in the implementations of the design by producing the working drawings or by controlling the machine tools.

13. Artificial intelligence. How closely can computers parallel human intelligence? The computer has already taken over relatively complex, though routine, human tasks. Industrial robots are carrying out manual skills and have used pattern recognition and object manipulation to control assembly lines. Some mental tasks, such as language translation, have also been undertaken by the computer. Although progress has proved difficult and is the result of continued, intensive research, the development of

intelligent programs will be of increasing importance in the future. A practical exercise for pupils would be to learn a new but simple board game and then to be asked to investigate what has been learned and how that learning has taken place.

14. Computers and employment. One effect of the use of computers to automate industrial processes is that some jobs are lost but that others are created. During a working lifetime people will be called upon to perform several jobs and will require continuous learning and retraining. It may also mean that at any one time many people will not be 'at work' in the traditional sense. This requires a radical rethinking of society's attitudes to the unemployed.

As technology advances, the decision to implement a computerised system may be based more on social than on technical considerations and will require the participation of the people involved. So that such participation can be effective, the concept of a "lifetime of learning" means more than just retraining for a new job.

15. Computers in the economy. A business and commercial organization can be likened to an information processing system. Over the years, these have made increasing use of computer facilities to improve their efficiency. Also, the mere existence of a computer had led some organisations in new directions, for example in banking services. We have reached a stage where the removal of computing systems would cause the economic collapse of many of our institutions.

It is important to acquaint our pupils with the ways in which automatic data processing systems are modelled on human organizations, but to help them recognize the essential human factors which remain. Examples could be drawn from assembly line manufacturing in the engineering industry and computer-managed learning systems.

COMPUTER LITERACY

Dan Klassen

In review, it seems rather inevitable that what had been a quiet and, perhaps, peripheral aspect of education has rapidly moved to center stage. Improving computer literacy had been the activity of a small band of educators, overwhelmingly trained in the disciplines of mathematics and computer science. But now computer literacy is being embraced by educators from diverse disciplinary backgrounds.

From "Computer Literacy," by Dan Klassen. In *Topics,* Association of Computing Machinery (SIGCSE, SIGCUE). January, 1981. Reprinted by permission.

At the abstract level, computer literacy presents few problems. It is an honorable goal with few negative connotations. It is seen as providing a basis for improving national productivity and the well-being of all citizens. It is one of the cornerstones of a society built on technology. It is, according to some, necessary for survival. Like motherhood and apple pie, it is difficult, perhaps even un-American, to oppose computer literacy.

What is computer literacy? What do computer literates know? How can we separate the computer literates from the computer illiterates? How can schools promote and ensure the development of computer literate students? These are difficult questions. Simple answers do not exist. Agreement among experts is difficult to find. However, if computer literacy is to become a reality, we need to begin to struggle with these questions and seek to formulate answers which can be used to guide future efforts in this rapidly developing field.

The ES3 Task Group on Computer Literacy, in an attempt to begin to provide answers to these pressing questions, has focused its efforts on the development of a definition of computer literacy. It is hoped that this definition can be used to help structure and guide educational programs and activities designed to improve computer literacy.

DEFINING COMPUTER LITERACY

The work of the task force was organized around the computer literacy objectives developed by the Minnesota Educational Computing Consortium's Computer Literacy Project. These objectives were chosen because they attempted to cover the entire range of topics which might be included within the domain of computer literacy and because they had already been reviewed by experts in computer science, education and industry. The objective provided a convenient starting point and functioned as a vehicle for gathering reactions and suggestions from interested task group members.

The original list of objectives, along with specific and general comments of task group members, follows. It should be noted that Minnesota is probably the leading state in its work on computer literacy at the precollege level. There has been substantial National Science Foundation funding on this topic in Minnesota in the past, and a new project was recently funded.

In addition, an annotated bibliography has been developed, of possible interest to educators wanting to learn more about the concept of computer literacy. You can order a copy of the "Computer Literacy Concept" bibliography at no cost from MECC, 2520 Broadway, St. Paul, MN 55113.

COMPUTER LITERACY OBJECTIVES—COGNITIVE

Hardware[a] (H)

*H.1.1 Identify the five major components of a computer: input equipment, memory unit, control unit, arithmetic unit, output equipment.

*H.1.2 Identify the basic operation of a computer system. Input of data or information, processing of data or information, output of data or information.

*H.1.3 Distinguish between hardware and software.

*H.1.4 Identify how a person can access a computer; e.g.,
1. via a keyboard terminal
   a. at site of computer
   b. at any distance via telephone lines
2. via punched or marked cards
3. via other magnetic media (tape, diskette)

*H.1.5 Recognize the rapid growth of computer hardware since the 1940s.

*H.2.1 Determine that the basic components function as an interconnected system under the control of a stored program developed by a person.

*H.2.2 Compare computer processing and storage capabilities to the human brain, listing some general similarities and differences.

Programming and algorithms (P)

NOTE: The student should be able to accomplish objectives 1.2–2.8 when the algorithm is expressed as a set of English language instructions and in the form of a computer program.

P.1.1 Recognize the definition of "algorithm".

*P.1.2 Follow and give the correct output for a simple algorithm.

*P.1.3 Given a simple algorithm, explain what it accomplishes (i.e., interpret and generalize).

*P.2.1 Modify a simple algorithm to accomplish a new but related task.

P.2.2 Detect logic errors in an algorithm.

P.2.3 Correct errors in an improperly functioning algorithm.

---

*Denotes core objectives

[a]Note that the coding is H—Hardware, P—Programming and algorithms, S—Software and data processing, A—Applications, and I—Impact. Also, for each statement the first digit after the letter refers to a cognitive level: 1 indicating a low level, generally a skill or knowledge of facts and 2 standing for a higher level of understanding, requiring some analysis and/or synthesis. The final digit is merely a count of items within each level. While no priority is intended with the final digit, there has been an attempt to place the ideas in some sort of logical sequence.

P.2.4 Develop an algorithm for solving a specific problem.

P.2.5 Develop an algorithm which can be used to solve a set of similar problems.

Software and data processing (S)

S.1.1 Identify the fact that we communicate with computers through a binary code.

S.1.2 Identify the need for data to be organized if it is to be useful.

S.1.3 Identify the fact that information is data which has been given meaning.

S.1.4 Identify the fact that data is a coded mechanism for communication.

S.1.5 Identify the fact that communication is the transmission of information via coded messages.

*S.1.6 Identify the fact that data processing involves the transformation of data by means of a set of predefined rules.

*S.1.7 Recognize that a computer needs instructions to operate.

*S.1.8 Recognize that a computer gets instructions from a program written in a programming language.

*S.1.9 Recognize that a computer is capable of storing a program and data.

*S.1.10 Recognize that computers process data by searching, sorting, deleting, updating, summarizing, moving, etc.

*S.2.1 Select an appropriate attribute for ordering of data for a particular task.

S.2.2 Design an elementary data structure for a given application (that is, provide order for the data).

S.2.3 Design an elementary coding system for a given application.

Applications (A)

*A.1.1 Recognize specific uses of computers in some of the following fields:
a. medicine
b. law enforcement
c. education
d. engineering
e. business
f. transportation
g. military defense systems
h. weather prediction
i. recreation
j. government
k. the library
l. creative arts

A.1.2 Identify the fact that there are many programming languages suitable for a particular application for business or science.

*A.1.3 Recognize that the following activites are among the major types of applications of the computer:
a. information storage and retrieval
b. simulation and modeling
c. process control—decision-making
d. computation
e. data processing

*A.1.4 Recognize that computers are generally good at information processing tasks that benefit from:
a. speed
b. accuracy
c. repetitiveness

*A.1.5 Recognize that some limiting considerations for using computers are:
a. cost
b. software availability
c. storage capacity

*A.1.6 Recognize the basic features of a computerized information system.

*A.2.1 Determine how computers can assist the consumer.

*A.2.2 Determine how computers can assist in a decision-making process.

A.2.3 Assess the feasibility of potential applications.

A.2.4 Develop a new application.

Impact (I)

*I.1.1 Distinguish among the following careers:
a. keypuncher/keyoperator
b. computer operator
c. computer programmer
d. systems analyst
e. computer scientist

*I.1.2 Recognize that computers are used to commit a wide variety of serious crimes, but especially stealing money and stealing information.

*I.1.3 Recognize that identification codes (numbers) and passwords are a primary means for restricting use of computer systems, of computer programs, and of data files.

I.1.4 Recognize that procedures for detecting computer-based crimes are not well developed.

*I.1.5 Identify some advantages or disadvantages of a data base containing personal information on a large number of people (e.g., the list might include value for research and potential for privacy invasion).

I.1.6 Recognize several regulatory procedures; e.g., privilege to review one's own file and restrictions on use of universal personal identifiers, which help to insure the integrity of personal data files.

*I.1.7 Recognize that most "privacy problems" are characteristic of large information files whether or not they are computerized.

*I.1.8 Recognize that computerization both increases and decreases employment.

*I.1.9 Recognize that computerization both personalizes and impersonalizes procedures in fields such as education.

*I.1.10 Recognize that computerization can lead to both greater independence and dependence upon one's tools.

*I.1.11 Recognize that while computers do not have the mental capacity that humans do, through techniques such as artificial intelligence, computers have been able to modify their own instruction set and do many of the information processing tasks that humans do.

*I.1.12 Recognize that alleged "computer mistakes" are usually mistakes made by people.

*I.2.1 Plan a strategy for tracing and correcting a computer-related error such as a billing error.

I.2.2 Explain how computers make public surveillance more feasible.

*I.2.3 Recognize that even though a person does not go near a computer, he or she is affected indirectly because the society is different in many sectors as a consequence of computerization.

I.2.4 Explain how computers can be used to impact the distribution and use of economic and political power.

COMPUTER LITERACY OBJECTIVES–AFFECTIVE

Attitude, values, and motivation (V)

*V.1 Does not feel fear, anxiety, or intimidation from computer experiences.

*V.2 Feels confident about his/her ability to use and control computers.

*V.3 Values efficient information processing, provided that it does not neglect accuracy, the protection of individual rights, and social needs.

*V.4 Values computerization of routine tasks so long as it frees people to engage in other activities and is not done as an end in itself.

*V.5 Values increased communication and availability of information made possible through computer use, provided that it does not violate personal rights to privacy and accuracy of personal data.

V.6 Values economic benefits of computerization for a society.

V.7 Enjoys and desires work or play with computers, especially computer-assisted learning.

V.8 Describes past experiences with computers with positive-effect words like fun, exciting, challenging, etc.

V.9 Given an opportunity, spends some free time using a computer.

The Role of Personal Computer Systems in Education

Alfred Bork and Stephen D. Franklin

While we can view the educational applications of personal computer systems in hardware terms (for example, single user, stand-alone computer systems based, most often, on the newly developed microprocessor technology), for our purposes it is more productive to focus on the mode of use in learning situations implicit in the notion of a personal computer.

The early part of this paper will focus more generally on how computers of any type can be utilized for educational purposes. Much of this discussion will apply to time-sharing systems even through the importance of such systems in educational environments is likely to decrease dramatically. Part of the discussion will apply to the old-fashioned batch environments.

We have chosen consciously to use the word "education" in preference to "instruction" because we wish to indicate an outlook which balances consideration of both the instructional authority and the learner. As the term "student" may not be appropriate for a person who happens to be using a computer to learn something, we shall refer to people using computers simply as "users."

In the next few sections, a descriptive classification of educational uses of computers is given. As with

From "The Role of Personal Computer Systems in Education," by Alfred Bork and Stephen D. Franklin. In *AEDS Journal*, Fall, 1979. Reprinted by permission.

most taxonomies of human activities, this description reflects fundamentally arbitrary distinctions, man-made rather than imposed by external circumstances. Although the categories may be expressed as though they reflected logical dichotomies, they are often not entirely distinct.

One obvious example is whether the user programs the computer or simply uses programs written by others. Certain educational modes demand that the user become a programmer of the computer, specifying in some programming language the algorithm to be used to accomplish particular tasks. Often this user employs a standard programming language, writing programs in that language for some special purpose related to education. At other times, the user programs in a highly specialized language developed for particular situations, in which case our "obvious" distinction becomes extremely fuzzy. The fact that almost all programming involves using programs (compilers, interpreters, operating systems) written by others blurs the distinction further. Yet, from the user's point of view, a distinction can be made between programming and not programming.

THE COMPUTER AS AN OBJECT OF STUDY

Computer Science has grown as an intellectual discipline as computers have assumed an increasingly important role in our society. We will not attempt to enumerate all the areas that computer science has come to encompass. Instead we shall mention three that seem to be of particularly broad import and applicability.

1. *Computer Programming and Problem Solving.* An excellent case can be made for the use of computer programming as a vehicle for the systematic algorithmic expression of the solution of certain types of problems. The development and refinement of such solutions is a form of training for analytic thinking which is applicable to broad classes of problems. Even if one doesn't subscribe to this second statement, one can still appreciate the value of computer programming as training for dealing with abstractions and abstract reasoning. Thus we are encouraged by the increasing availability of courses and curricular material on computer programming.

2. *Social Impact of Computing.* The computer is the dominant tool of our time and, as such, is having a profound influence on our society. Knowledge of the technical aspects of computer science does not guarantee understanding of the consequences of this technology. But such understanding should be based, in part, on acquaintance with the capabilities and limitations of computers.

3. *Computer Literacy.* This heading combines elements of the two previous ones. It is concerned with people who will not be computer professionals. In a society where computers are playing an increasingly important role, it is essential that people be acquainted with computers and their capabilities. Computer literacy goes beyond programming, but most computer literacy courses involve some programming efforts on the part of the participants. Computer literacy courses are presently offered primarily at the college level; opinions on how to run such courses vary greatly. It seems likely, even inevitable, that they will migrate into high school and even junior high school curricula.

THE COMPUTER AS AN INTELLECTUAL TOOL

In this category the most obvious educational use of computing again involves the user as programmer. However, the user considered in this section is programming not to become acquainted with the computer and its capabilities or as a paradigm for algorithmic thought but because it aids in understanding a subject matter which is itself the focus of interest. A typical activity might be the use of the computer within a physics course to improve the user's skill in solving physics problems and even to add new dimensions to problem solving. Using the computer, we can tackle more realistic and meaningful problems, ones more like those encountered in actual experience than the typical "laundered" textbook problems.

The most dramatic uses of the computer as an intellectual tool are in situations where it makes possible entirely new approaches to the curriculum. For example, using the computer to provide a numerical approach to differential equations, one can reorganize completely the first quarter course in college physics; the approach to Newton's laws of motion leads quickly and directly to a student's understanding differential equations and their use in predictive models of physical systems.

USING PROGRAMS PREPARED BY OTHERS

The uses of the computer as an intellectual tool that we have discussed thus far presuppose some programming on the part of the user. However, present computer users and those of the future likely are to be involved primarily with programs written by others. That is, the most common type of computer use in the future (as in the present) is not in writing one's own programs, but in using programs prepared by others. (As we noted above, even people writing their own program are almost always doing so using programs written by others.)

As personal computers become more and more available in educational institutions, in the home market, as part of people's jobs and in public environments such as libraries, we can confidently expect that the sales of such hardware will depend on very large amounts of materials being prepared for the user, requiring minimal training to use. Many of these materials will be educational in nature and even more will have some educational component, if only to help the user learn how to use the materials fully.

A wide variety of materials are possible, and schemes for descriptively classifying them vary widely. Some schemes are based primarily on computer considerations, while others are based on educational considerations. We favor the second approach as in the following enumeration of educational uses of the computer which do not require the user to program.

Drill and practice

While we can debate the importance of practice in learning, almost all conventional educational procedures rely on it to some extent. Thus a student learning calculus, perhaps to use in the physics course mentioned above, needs practice in taking the derivatives of all the common functions. Similarly, few students in elementary school master basic arithmetic without practice. However, when we speak of practice, it should be clear that we mean more than the opportunity to work examples correctly; implicit in our use of the term is that the learner receive feedback which tells when an example has been worked correctly and when a mistake has occurred.

Providing the student with feedback on the correctness of an answer, problem after problem after problem, can be an exceedingly tedious task for a human. The computer can do this task and more, generating a large number of problems of a given type within specifications provided by those responsible for the design of the educational drill and practice program, keeping records, determining when the student has reached a satisfactory performance level, and referring the student to non-computer sources of assistance (such as books, video segments and people).

A student's tolerance (and need) for routine, repetitive practice may exceed an instructor's (or parent's) available time or patience. Many people find that the desire to do something well is, in itself, very compelling (competency motivation). Just the tireless patience of a computer makes drill and practice on such a medium valuable.

Moreover, interactive computer-based problems can take on added dimensions. Successive problems can be chosen and presented based on the responses to previous ones. The computer can present problems with missing information or with redundant or contradictory information. Before solving the problem, the learner must request additional information or ask what of the (contradictory) information is to be discarded.

Drill and practice with remediation

An important elaboration of drill and practice material is the provision of remediation tailored to the difficulties the individual learner may be having. Remediation sections can be simple, showing how to work a missed problem, or large, complex, interactive learning sequences of the tutorial type we shall discuss next. Because the remediation sequence is intertwined with the drill and practice, it can use the data of the problem and the circumstances of the learner's mistake. Incidentally, our choice of the term "remediation" lies in the meaning of the root term "remedy," something that corrects or removes an evil of any kind, and in spite of the condescending connotations that the adjective "remedial" has acquired.

Tutorial programs

The concept of the tutorial program, a dialog between learner and the educational designers of the computer program, is in some ways close to the oldest and most personal form of transmitting knowledge, the conversation between an individual and an experienced teacher.

Information, techniques, and attitudes are developed within an environment in which the learner is invited and encouraged to play an active role rather than the passive role of the audience in a lecture or with video material. The term "dialog" is appropriate since well done materials resemble the type of dialog one finds in Plato. The educator is not telling but is leading the learner by means of carefully planned questions, each successive question depending on the learner's previous response. It is not inappropriate to note here that the word "educate" derives from the Latin "to lead out."

An important subcategory in science and mathematics courses is the notion of an interactive proof. Such proofs, in noninteractive form, occupy much lecture time, with the instructor deriving new results from those already obtained. In interactive computer environments, the users can be asked to create the proof insofar as they are able, being offered various types of assistance along the way.

Before leaving this category, note should be taken of a use of computers that bears a superficial resemblance to tutorial programs—the computer as page turner. Certain programs present large chunks of text, ask intermittent questions ("TYPE 1 FOR YES, 0 FOR NO"), but do not vary the material presented significantly on the basis of the user's response. While the educational value of such programs is open to discussion, it is clear that the term "dialog" is not appropriate (although some case can be made for the term "monolog").

Testing

The importance of evaluation of student progress is almost universally acknowledged, as is the difficulty and unpleasantness of the task. Part of what computers should be used for is to do what humans do not enjoy doing, so test generation, administration, grading, recording, reporting and summarizing are tasks appropriate for the computer. As with drill and practice, testing materials can be based on problem generators and other devices for randomizing the materials. Each quiz or test can be unique, allowing a student to take different versions of the same quiz several times and different students to discuss the quizzes with each other.

While some would insist that the computer is too expensive and important a resource to be "wasted" on such things as interactive testing, we cannot agree. Firstly, testing is an important part of education. Secondly, current economic and technological trends make it clear that the cost of human time is a more important consideration in economic projections than the cost of machine resources. Finally, in this area as in others, the economic reality already often demands that one use the computer because other approaches are unrealistic, inadequate or both.

Testing with learning

One of the most recent developments in testing, related to the remediation ideas already discussed, is that specific immediate aid can be offered to students having difficulties on an interactive quiz or test, often aid precisely tailored to their difficulties and at a time when they are eager to learn the right way to do it. The interactive test can be an intimate blend of testing and learning, unlike most traditional modes of testing that offer no immediate opportunity to improve. Interactive testing with learning provides students that opportunity at a time when they are most open to taking advantage of it. In our own experiences with students, this mode of educational computer usage produces the most favorable student reaction.

Controllable worlds

The computer can be used to generate rich, creative, manipulable environments for the learner, environments difficult to manipulate and experiment with in the real world, even environments which are impossible. This type of computer use is a simulation; we use the computer to model some portion of a real or imaginary world. We prefer the term "controllable worlds" because it stresses the effect rather than the mechanism.

One form of controllable world has the computer duplicating or enhancing a typical laboratory environment. The user is provided with a range of experimental capabilities, perhaps with many of the same factors that would occur if the experiment were carried out in the laboratory. (One factor which is missing is the possibility of injury if the experiment is not done correctly.) The user can gather data rapidly in a variety of situations and may be permitted to perform experiments that cannot be done in an ordinary laboratory (e.g., remove gravity). In addition to providing experimental capabilities, this environment allows the student to be guided, at first gently and then perhaps more firmly, into generalizing on the basis of data and testing the hypotheses so formed. Thus we can help every student arrive at the conclusions that were the aim of the materials.

The laboratory environment can be extended greatly. Whole realms of experiences can be provided which are difficult or impossible to realize in the world as it exists. Inasmuch as experience is the basis for intuition, these controllable worlds can give the user a feel for phenomena and the consequences of theories that was previously available only to the deeply talented or after much study. Thus, the role of the controllable world is extended from that of the ordinary laboratory to that of a tool for building insight and intuition, the basis and perhaps inspiration for later formal study. In such a world, the learner can be in complete control, changing variables and studying, with the guidance of the program or auxiliary materials, the types of situations that lead to more secure later knowledge. While building intuition is the avowed goal of many courses, rarely can conventional modes of education address it directly.

WHY USE THE COMPUTER?

We have discussed some of the educational uses of the computer, but why the computer is such an effective learning aid and why it will become much more widely used in the future may not be clear.

Much of what has happened in formal education during historic times is understandable as a reaction to the increasing numbers of people who needed increasing amounts of education. As long as only a few people needed to learn a very limited scope of material, apprenticeship methods, informal and later formal, were satisfactory. But as the number of learners and what they needed to learn increased, learning strategies had to be modified. Most of our current educational methodology at all levels is shaped by the pressure of large numbers. Thus, the lecture, the textbook and later electronic reading and broadcasting media are all mechanisms to disseminate knowledge to large numbers of people. All are essentially one-way media, with communication flowing from the instructional authority to the student; they provide little if any capability for the authority to respond to individual learners.

Something has been lost in this process. Teachers and students in formal educational institutions yearn for the situation where they can work together closely. Indeed, great amounts of resources are devoted to making this possible precisely in those situations where the quality of education is perceived to be most critical. Thus, graduate education, at least at the later stages, depends primarily on one-to-one contact. Educational psychologists, even with the very diverse views of the learning process, almost all agree that the optimum setting for education is when one teacher works with one student or a small number of people.

Perhaps the most well-known attempt to develop an effective small group learning system is the Socratic dialog. Socrates worked with a small group of people, usually no more than three or four at one time. What modern jargon would call the learning activity was an active conversation in which everyone participated. In no sense did Socrates lecture; Plato often depicts other participants as talking more than Socrates. A major component of most lectures is the conveying of information; Socrates did little of this. Instead he continually queried his students, asking questions that depended on the answers given to earlier questions, always framing new questions for his listeners to react to. There were no time pressures. Presumably, if Socrates had engaged in a number of similar dialogs at different times with different people, both the directions these dialogs took and their duration would have varied considerably.

The computer is the first technological innovation in education that enables us to start moving back, even with a large number of learners, to a situation like that of Socrates where the educator can respond fully to each individual learner.

We do not claim that a computer dialog, even when prepared by a group of excellent teachers, can emulate fully the Socratic situation. But it is the only educational tool with which we can approach that situation with a large number of learners. Each learner can proceed at a different pace and can engage in an individual learning process with educational materials responsive to his or her particular needs. We cannot clone Socrates, but we can use computers to give today's large number of learners more of the type of learning experiences that his students had.

Not all existing computer materials reach these goals; rather, much of it is a poor reflection of what is possible and a better reflection of the shortcomings of our past practices. But we are slowly learning how to create more active, more personalized, more interactive, more effective materials.

Since we wish to focus on the educational advantages, we shall not discuss the economic arguments in favor of educational computing. Such arguments must include some assessment of the value of education to our society. The most basic educational advantage that we see in the use of computers is that, unlike almost any other medium, the computer provides a vehicle for education which is responsive at all levels to the individual learner.

Because of its unique advantages as a responsive, active learning mechanism, we can use the computer to create more effective educational systems than our present ones. But this future is far from certain. The computer can be used in the most banal ways or in ways that are antithetical to the best goals of creative education. Modern educators with a commitment to meeting the needs of the individual learner must play an active role in shaping the future use of computers in education. This effort must not be confined to one level of education but must take place on all levels.

THE FUTURE—TYPES OF HARDWARE

The vast majority of educational use of computers in recent years has employed time-sharing systems, a central machine providing services simultaneously to many users. Most universities still continue to purchase such systems as the principal vehicle for educational applications. There is a strong indication, however, that the personal computer, a small stand-alone computer used by a single person at a time (or, at most, by a small group of people), will be the focus of future educational activities.

In this discussion, a distinction is made between developmental systems, as used for the creation of educational materials, and delivery systems on which the learner uses these materials. In the past, the same computer system was often used for both purposes. This situation was more a reflection of the hardware available (and the then-current understanding of the process of writing programs on one machine to be run on another) than it was of an underlying similarity between what is required for developmental work and for delivery. When we say that personal computers will be the focus of educational activities we are referring to the delivery of educational materials.

The personal computers likely to be the major delivery systems for direct use by learners are not the lowest level of those currently available. These systems, although interesting, have many serious deficiences for educational use. The basic software on most such systems is much more appropriate for the creation of small, simple and limited programs than for designing, writing and maintaining the complex and extensive educational applications we have discussed above. These systems often have poorly designed keyboards (e.g., one popular system has the "stop the world, I want to get off" key immediately above the "return" key). Many support only upper-case letters; many allow very few characters per line and few lines per display; many display characters whose graphics quality is exceeded by the scrawl of a first grader. The graphics capabilities are typically crude. (A popular inadequate approach to graphics is to provide a handful of special characters, line segments at different angles.) Their mass storage devices do not provide easy, quick or reliable storage and transportation for large programs. They most often have fixed character sets, on whose quality we have already commented, and do not allow all the types of characters needed for educational purposes. Few have color capabilities. Thus, in addition to their technical shortcomings, the lower level of systems currently available do not come close to the minimum level of visual appeal that one would accept in a book or piece of video material.

But the personal computer situation is changing rapidly. The newer systems are providing more extensive and reliable capabilities. New software systems are being implemented that reflect the understanding of software that has been gained over the past decade. As the market grows and becomes more competitive, we can expect better hardware and software to become available. The rising curve of technology helps in that we are learning to build computer systems, particularly microcomputer-based systems, at a very rapid rate. This technological advance is reflected in decreasing costs (for fixed capabilities) and increasing capabilities. As mass production of integrated systems becomes the norm, there will be further cost savings. The home computer market will be an important factor. Some estimates predict many millions of computers in individual homes within the next few years.

The existence of the home market and parents' interest in providing educational opportunities for their children are major reasons supporting our assertion that personal computers will be the focus of educational activities in the future. Without going into great detail, we can mention a few others. Thanks to declining hardware costs, any institution or individual that can only now afford to start using computers is more likely to be able to afford a small personal computer than larger, more expensive systems. Many institutions will buy one, to see how it works out, whereas the institution might not have even made the experiment had it entailed a more substantial initial investment. The small cost of a complete unit also makes buying a system feasible purely to get access to the learning materials that the system supports.

To apply a somewhat different set of reasoning in considering why personal computer systems, rather than time-sharing systems, are likely to be the focus of educational activities in the future, we turn to a direct comparison.

PERSONAL COMPUTERS VERSUS TIME-SHARING SYSTEMS

The personal computer, on occasion connected for a brief period to another system, will be the major educational delivery system of the foreseeable future. Several important considerations make this almost a certainty.

A major issue concerns which type of computer leads to a clear marketing path for large-scale distribution of computer-based educational materials. Many different time-sharing systems exist, different in hardware and in operating systems. These differences affect large complex programs much more fundamentally than they affect small simple ones. Effective computer-based educational materials are not small simple programs; they are complex because learning, even learning simple matters, is a complex process.

For a program to be widely marketed in a time-sharing environment, where the hardware is so expensive that it cannot be purchased for a particular use (unless that use is extremely extensive), the vendor must supply the program for a variety of systems. The initial expense and the difficulties of maintaining dozens of versions of a program make this approach unlikely. If we had highly standard languages and highly standard interfaces with operating systems, the problem would not exist. But there seems almost no chance of such standardization adequate to meet the needs of large, complex programs.

Most transportability efforts which have assumed standard languages have accommodated only simple programs. In the educational area, the CONDUIT program is the most extensive effort in this direction. But the programs CONDUIT distributes, although carefully refereed, do not represent the best computer-based learning materials because those materials are not simple to transport. Any organization, commercial or nonprofit, which restricted itself to only a few machines would cut off sizeable portions of the market.

Another approach to using time-sharing as a delivery environment has been to employ a communications network so that users at remote sites can access the central machine, most often over telephone lines. Thus far, the economic viability of this approach is very far from established. Unless the distance between the local site and the central machine can be bridged by a local phone call, communications costs typically exceed the cost of computer services. Another major difficulty with this approach comes with graphic capabilities, capabilities that are essential to full effective educational use of the computer. The rate at which graphics can be displayed in a time-sharing system is slow (full animation is impossible). While many time-sharing systems have difficulty accommodating even moderate numbers of users at 1200 baud (a minimally acceptable data transmission speed for graphics), experience has taught us that even fewer remote communications links can transmit data reliably at this rate. Thus complex pictures are often out of the question. We can hope that communications costs will drop or that capabilities will improve. While the latter seems likely, the prospects for the former are far from bright. Communications costs may not rise and communications capabilities will undoubtedly improve, but the economic-technical prospects in communications cannot compare with those in computers.

If we look at the issue of transportability on personal computers, we see a much different situation than we have on time-sharing systems. With personal computer systems, a program need not work on every machine. The user can buy or lease the hardware along with the course material.

This new marketing concept in computers can be difficult for those with traditional backgrounds to understand. Yet, we can already see successful examples. One such is Computer Curriculum Corporation, which leases to school districts complete systems, hardware and software, covering basic arithmetic and language skills for elementary children. Currently, this company's system is a time-sharing one, and thus the system is leased to serve the entire district rather than an individual school. If an integrated educational package used a personal computer, a school interested in buying a particular set of educational materials initially might buy just one unit to try the materials out. Thus, prospective users have a simple entry-level way of trying out the materials over an extended period of time. This entry-level tactic is important as a marketing strategy.

Another approach to transporting software on personal computers is to transport the entire operating system, something that is not possible with time-sharing systems. An excellent example of this idea is the work done at University of California San Diego (UCSD), under the direction of Professor Kenneth L. Bowles, in creating a portable operating system using Pascal. The UCSD Pascal system, in-cluding its sophisticated screen-oriented editor, runs on several different types of personal computers. The basic idea of this approach is that most sophisticated, complex programs depend on features and conventions that are often particular to the operating system in which they run. Rather than confining oneself to programs that do not use these features and thus severely limiting what one can do, it makes more sense to transport the entire environment which the program needs to function.

Another important consideration is the extreme complexity and the concomitant reliability problems of time-sharing operating systems as opposed to stand-alone operating systems. General purpose time-sharing systems are among the most complex programs in widescale use. When a time-sharing system crashes, every user on the system is affected for the entire period the system is down; on the other hand, a personal computer with problems affects only one user. There is, however, another side to this point. When one finds a "bug" on a time-sharing system, one can correct it for everyone. Maintaining and updating software on stand-alone personal computer systems is a much less easy procedural problem. Some of the complexity of time-sharing systems arises because of the need to support several users simultaneously and because the overhead on such systems, requiring a considerable fraction of the computer, cuts down on what is effectively available to the users. On the other hand, some of the complexity results from the fact that the time-sharing system is providing a range of software and capabilities that personal computers do not. Another reason for this complexity is that time-sharing systems have complex resource allocation algorithms which provide the flexibility to meet peak demands from individual users.

System stability over time is another important issue. New versions of operating systems appear, sometimes fixing known bugs and supporting new capabilities. While it is often said that user programs will be unaffected by the change, it is our experience that large complex programs have problems with new operating systems. On a good personal computer system, we can continue to run programs under several versions of the operating system, gradually phasing in the changes on a program-by-program or, at least, disk-by-disk basis. Thus, we currently are running programs using two different versions of the UCSD Pascal operating system.

We already have mentioned the difficulties a time-sharing system may have supporting graphics, particularly when the system is being accessed from a remote site. No such problems exist with stand-alone systems; information can flow to the screen as fast as it is generated. One immediate consequence is that simple animation is possible even with some of the minimal personal computers. Such capabilities are just not possible in time-sharing systems except in very limited ways.

Time-sharing systems, however, currently provide important communications facilities that personal computers do not. On a time-sharing system, users can exchange messages, maintain central records, and access central libraries of programs and data; and, as mentioned above, all users can maintain and update programs more easily. However, capabilities such as these can be supported on personal computers by having them communicate occasionally and briefly with a central system.

These communications capabilities exemplify, to some extent, an area where time-sharing systems currently have an advantage over personal computers, not for any inherent technical reason but merely because they have been around longer. Better examples might be the richness of software tools (including various text editors and library facilities), different methods of file organization and access, and a broad variety of languages. We can expect such capabilities to be available on small single-user systems in the future. In fact, it is even reasonable to demand them.

A totally different area where one might compare time-sharing systems and personal computers concerns the internal institutional problems involved in a school's acquiring one or the other. A cooperative interdepartmental effort is usually necessary for a school to acquire a time-sharing system, even a small one, of sufficient sophistication to provide some of the advantages we have discussed. These departments must get together on what they want, often accepting undesired compromises or an imposed solution. A similar process even may go on within a department. These political considerations can be reduced to some extent with personal computers. On the other hand, if each individual faculty member is allowed to choose a different personal computer, the institution may very well find that maintenance of these diverse systems and future cooperative action is impossible. There have been a number of cases where one person's equipment was worthless to anyone else. Some central considerations are still necessary. That is, personal computers may allow one to avoid some political problems (e.g., the need to find groups of allies to move forward), but they are not a panacea.

SOME FINAL REMARKS AND A LOOK AHEAD

We have focused on the delivery of computer-based educational materials, outlined the variety and possibilities of such materials and argued that the personal computer is the vehicle which provides for learner access to them. We have not discussed the development process or type of computer system which is a reasonable vehicle for development. The major reason for our silence on this subject is that the arguments for using personal computers as development systems are considerably less compelling.

It is something of an accident in past history of computer-based educational materials that development and delivery systems were the same. Many people still assume, often implicitly, that this dual-purpose use of the same system will continue. Any careful analysis of the situation suggests that developmental work requires considerably different and more extensive capabilities than are needed in a delivery machine.

Another important issue is the software needed for developmental purposes, both the basic software environment required for work on any complex program and the specialized software needed in creating computer-based educational materials. This subject is much too extensive to discuss here, but we present our opinion (prejudices) as revealed in our current work. That work is taking place using the UCSD Pascal system which seems an effective system for complex programming, including that being considered. Our project is developing special software tools modeled, in part, on our previous (time-sharing) production system. For additional detailed information on these issues, please consult the authors.[1]

As we anticipate future developments and trends in education, a great many problems are apparent—financial, social and educational. The educational advantages of the computer, its increasing capabilities and the decreasing cost of computer technology are some of the few bright spots to be seen. There can be little doubt that the computer will be a major component of education in all areas. The time scale involved probably will be something on the order of a quarter of a century but could possibly be significantly less. However, the mere existence of computer technology is not a guarantee that it will be used in creative and constructive ways. The computer is the first technological innovation which allows education of large numbers of people in a manner which is truly responsive to the individual learner. But only the involvement and commitment of educators of vision can ensure that it is used in that manner.

[1] Address: Professor Alfred Bork, Department of Physics, University of California, Irvine, CA 92717.

A Case for Universal Computer Literacy

James E. Eisele

The major premise argued here is that knowledge and understanding of computers and computing, skills for using computers, and positive attitudes toward their productive roles in society are desirable and necessary goals of formal education. The reason for taking such a position is that computers have assumed a pervasive role in everyday life in such important functions as communications, transportation, education, governance, consumerism, entertainment, and employment. In addition to its direct impact on these lifelong functions the computer has, itself, increased the importance of computing as a major human function.

Given the pervasiveness of computers in everyday life there is another concern which argues favorably for universal computer literacy. This concern is one which deals with ethical use of computers both as a producer and consumer of computer services. As producers of computer services all individuals must carefully attend to all the implications of their services and the effects they have on both other individuals and society, in general. As consumers of computer services individuals need to take precautions to attribute to computers only those powers that are rightly theirs and not to rationalize human error by inaccurately ascribing them to a mere machine.

These concerns have led to the conviction that all people have a right to, and would benefit greatly from, opportunities to learn about computers, at least during time spent in formal educational institutions. Though specific teaching and learning objectives would vary among individuals, the concerns mentioned above seem to argue for the inclusion of learning opportunities in the curriculum for:

1 Developing skills to use computer applications which bear on persistent life situations such as communications, transportation, education, governance, consumerism, entertainment, and employment;
2 Developing computing proficiency as a skill for everyday use at home and on-the-job;
3 Developing ethical practices in providing computer services to others;
4 Developing ethical practices of consumption of computer services;

From "A Case for Computer Literacy," by James E. Eisele. In the *Journal of Research and Development in Education*, Volume 14, Number 1, 1980. Reprinted by permission.

5 Developing positive attitudes toward the pervasive role of computers in contemporary society.

USING COMPUTERS IN PERSISTENT LIFE SITUATIONS

The time is rapidly approaching when the ability to make intelligent use of computers will be prerequisite to everyday life situations such as riding subway cars, using telephones, driving automobiles, watching television, obtaining news, and learning new skills and/or making career choices. Certainly not all of these activities now require computer use, but enough of them do now require some use (by end users) of computers that the very near future seems quite clearly to support this claim. Examples of day-to-day activities which may currently involve use of computers by the end user include gasoline filling stations, libraries, toys and games, and instant (24 hour) bank services. These systems are easy to use and require little technical skill. However, there are services currently available for accessing news stories with computer terminals which may one day replace the daily newspaper and which will require some elementary skills of computer use.

DEVELOPING COMPUTING PROFICIENCY

Home use and on-the-job use of computers for management and planning, information processing, computing, and even communication is not uncommon today. Home budgeting, menu planning, and learning activities via computers are found in countless homes today. Increased utilization of computers in business, industry, and government has sent many career employees back to school to learn enough about computing to keep them up-to-date in their jobs. There is little doubt that the use of computers in the home and on the job will continue its rapid increase, and those who can effectively use computers will benefit greatly from the ability.

ETHICAL PRODUCTION OF COMPUTER SERVICES

Computer operations will continue to be a mystery to many naive users of their services. Outright fraud in the form of overcharges to users is one potential threat of unethical practice. Perhaps equally dangerous—though, no doubt, with less harm intended—is the inappropriate demand that users compromise their needs or wishes for the convenience of the developer or provider of computer services. Providers of computer services must acquire the sense of ethics which fosters the concept that services, by definition, should be what users want and not what the provider of the services feels that users *should* want.

This inappropriate view of the nature of service is all too prevalent in computer operations (as well as many other industries) today. In fact, many people readily accept the decision of the storekeeper to stock only the brand or style that he, personally, prefers. When the computer services operator decides which applications will be available (aside from decisions based on *real* constraints), the general welfare of the users is not well served. Like any truly successful service, the consumer of computer services must be assured that his best interests are kept in mind at all times. As the influence of computers over our lives becomes increasingly greater, this concern takes on awesome dimensions.

ETHICAL CONSUMPTION OF COMPUTER SERVICES

There are, indeed, two sides to most coins. Consumers (users) of computer services must accept the responsibility of employing computer services in the best interest of all mankind. This responsibility of ethical consumption is multi-faceted. Users of computer services must accept responsibility to pay their fair share for these services. They must try to remain within the constraints set by the provider of services and not become a hoarder of excessive amounts of computer capability. Users should make every effort to become highly proficient so that they can make the most efficient and cost-efficient use of these services. And, hopefully, users—be they willing or unwilling ones—will someday cease blaming computers for human weakness which will never be overcome as long as computers are seen as the culprits, excusing us of responsibility for our own behavior.

ROLE OF COMPUTERS IN SOCIETY

This last category is not unrelated to the others, but it is still significant in its own right. Just as the introduction of other technologies—the printing press, the mass production of automobiles, and airplanes, for example—left an indelible mark on civilization, so have computers had a profound effect on life and lifestyles. Disregarding for the moment the question of quality of effects, individuals used to learn to cope with changes brought about by technology in order to remain healthy and contented. Coping with change, however wrought, can be both painful and sad. Nevertheless, inevitable changes in society which remain unaccepted by the individual can cause frustration, unhappiness, and disillusionment.

Unfortunately, a fine line exists between accepting the inevitable and opposing that which is believed to be wrong. This may be the eternal curse of humankind! Any technology can be used to attain evil ends and these results, too, affect life and lifestyles. Obviously, injurious effects of computers and society must be opposed rather than accepted as a way of life and this must be understood, as well.

FOSTERING UNIVERSAL COMPUTER LITERACY

Universal computer literacy is not yet a goal of educational institutions in America. But, then, neither is driver education, despite the wholesale slaughter which occurs daily on our highways. Perhaps, though, schools and society will take computer skills more seriously and will seek ways of making computer literacy an important goal to be attained. If so, there are some reasonable steps which can be taken to make the goal attainable. Some of these steps are worth noting.

Identifying goals and objectives

First, computer skills, knowledge, and attitudes necessary to function effectively need to be determined. This can be accomplished by analyzing current requirements in various categories (such as the five presented here) for now and for the foreseeable future. Given the help of experts, teachers, business and industry personnel, and other interested parties, this should not be a difficult task. However, leadership for this effort must be acquired to get the activity underway. The source of that leadership is now questionable and should be of considerable concern.

An example of this step is available from the effort to define appropriate goals and objectives for the United States Schools in Europe's Darmstadt Career Center, as reported by Kauffman (1976).

The overall goal for Computer Education is computer literacy. This consists of being able to:

  I. Understand the functions and use of the components of a computer system.
 II. Utilize a systematic problem-solving technique in developing solutions to a problem.
III. Analyze the role of computer technology in society. Understand its past, present and possible future impact upon human life.

Goals and program objectives

 I. **Understand the functions and use of the components of a computer system.**
 1. Define the following terms: A) Computer, B) Flow Chart, C) TTY, D) Input-output.
 2. Describe in general terms how a computer system works.
 3. Describe how to use and read a calculator, digital

clock and thermostat.

4. Able to use hand-held calculator to solve a math problem.
5. Operate a telephone, radio, etc.
6. Operate the TTY to call-up and execute a library program.
7. Show respect for equipment by not misusing item.
8. Define the five main components of the digital computer.
9. Define the following terms: A) CPU, B) TTY/CRT, C) Card Reader, D) Line printer, E) Disc, F) Magnetic Tape, and G) Paper Tape.
10. Describe in writing the interaction of the various components of a computer during the execution of a program (hardware and software).
11. Operate the TTY and CRT.
12. Load and list a program using paper tape.
13. Demonstrate respect for equipment by properly caring for the school computer center.
14. Able to read a "run book."
15. Describe the steps involved in "bringing up the system" and relocating memory.
16. Discuss the interactions of the total computer system—information and machine cycles.
17. Bring-up system and allocate storage.
18. Run a data processing job on the school computer system from a "run book."
19. Operate the computer from the console or control panels.
20. Operate special features of a computer system such as DS. EDIT, OS COPY and File Management.
21. Operate the card reader, magnetic tape, disc and line printer.
22. Describe the function in a computer system of each of the following: Bits, Bytes, Words, Binary, Octal, Hexadecimal representations and Binary, Octal and Hexadecimal arithmetic.
23. Perform arithmetic operations involving decimal, hexadecimal, octal and binary numbering systems.
24. Describe the function of each of the following components of the CPU and arithmetic logic unit, control unit and registers, buses.
25. Operate the special features of the operating system such as OS EDIT, OS COPY and File Management.

II. Utilize a systematic problem-solving technique in developing solutions to a problem.

1. Describe steps in problem-solving approach.
2. Able to list the sequence of events involved in solving a problem.
3. Describe in written or oral form, the process involved in a "Flow Chart" solution.
4. Critique a given solution and suggest alternatives.
5. Draw a Flow Chart.
6. Appreciate the usefulness of a problem solving approach by using flow charts to analyze personal problems.
7. Write a computer program in BASIC to solve a problem.
   7.1 Algorithm
      1. Be able to define
      2. Describe sequence of operations
      3. Write
   7.2 Develop the logical sequence (flow chart) to solve a problem.
   7.3 Based on sequence write a program.
   7.4 Correct errors.
   7.5 Write documentations describing the program.
8. Compare the problem-solving approach utilized in computer area with other problem-solving modes such as the problem-solving techniques used in science.
9. Load and execute a program on the TTY and CRT from paper tape and disc.
10. Operate TTY and CRT.
11. Appreciate the usefulness of using the problem-solving approach by developing programs on his/her own to solve problems.
12. Set up a computer to run a specific program.
13. Program in at least two computer languages.
14. Define and describe the function for each of the following: subroutine, updating, and sorting.
15. Describe a computer program in sufficient detail as to communicate the basic components of the program to a computer programmer.

III. Analyze the role of Computer Technology in society; past, present and impact on our future.

1. List and describe ways in which the computer is being used in government communications, military and business.
2. Describe how recent computer technological advances have affected her/his family and school.
3. Describe the possible negative effects of a technological invention for society and the environment.
4. Analyze a specific innovation and be able to point out possible uses and misuses.
5. Appreciate the proper utilization of technology as it assists people without hurting society and the environment.
6. Describe the historical development of the digital and microcomputers.
7. List and describe the ways in which computers are being used in government, business, military and communications.
8. Based on previous knowledge, speculate about the future uses of computer technology in society.
9. Discuss the potential misuse of computer technology in the area of individual freedom and identify areas of value conflict.

10. Identify and describe various occupations related to computers.
11. Analyze various viewpoints concerning the utilization of computer technology and note major differences and similarities.
12. Explain a tentative personal decision about the value of computer technology to himself/herself and to society.
13. Describe the potential uses of computer technology in society.
14. Describe in detail the utilization of computer technology in two areas of personal interest—i.e., Business and Communications.
15. Explore at least two occupational choices related to computer technology.

Planning appropriate curricula

With the goals and objectives clearly in mind, the next step is to decide on appropriate curricula. Decisions must be made as to the grade levels at which computing is to be taught, the subject areas to be used (or the decision to make computer science a separate subject), and the kinds of activities and materials which will be used, in general. This step should result in a broad plan, spanning several grades preferably including at least the first two years of college, for teaching and learning about computers.

At this point in the planning, attention should be given to providing adequate resources for implementation. The broad plan should be adequate for identified resources such as instructional materials, computer software, computer hardware, and telecommunications capability. These resources should be acquired as early as possible in this stage of planning.

Preparing and organizing staff

The teaching staff will, themselves, require certain computing competencies and should be given the opportunity to develop or refine these skills. Inservice training often can be provided by someone on the staff who has demonstrated interest and ability. A useful source of training aids can sometimes be obtained from the manufacturer or distributor of the computer hardware purchased.

Other staff members may need training. These should be support personnel assigned to supervise the program who can watch over equipment and maintain system library materials. Unless the people assigned this role are experienced teachers, they should be oriented to the unique needs and characteristics of the educational environment.

Organizing the computing facility

The physical facility in which students are to be taught and allowed to practice their comparing skills should be carefully designed for maximum efficiency.

Hiring a consultant who has experience with this task may save money in the long run. Decisions about the amount of electric power needed, location of terminals or microcomputers, arrangement of printers, monitors, and mass storage devices, etc., must all be made prior to actual use.

SUMMARY

There seems to be sufficient reason for including computer literacy in the curriculum. Support of this view is found in the pervasive nature of the role of computers in our lives and the current lack of programs aimed at universal computer literacy. Computers already are involved in many everyday experiences, have increased the importance of computers for problem solving at home and have raised serious concern with ethical considerations regarding production and consumption of computer services. Clearly, a justification exists for universal computer literacy.

Once the commitment to foster universal computer literacy through formal education is made, certain activities can be helpful, if not necessary. Setting goals and objectives, planning curricula, preparing and organizing the staff, and organizing the computing facility are among the most important tasks which must be performed.

REFERENCES

Kauffman, Draper, T. Jr. *Teaching the future*. A guide to Future-Oriented Education. Palm Springs, California. ETC Publication, 1976.

MICROCOMPUTERS IN EDUCATION: NOW AND IN THE FUTURE

Karen Billings

Although computers are indispensable to science, business and government, they have not realized their full potential in American education. In an information society, a computer-literate populace is important, and we may go through a crisis trying to develop it.

Just as the 70s became the decade of computer technology, the 80s must become the decade of computer education. For the past 15 years I've

From "Microcomputers in Education: Now and in the Future," by Karen Billings. In *Kilobaud Microcomputing*, June, 1980. © 1980 by Wayne Green, Inc. Reprinted by permission.

witnessed the tremendous growth of computer technology. However, until recently, I've seen relatively little interest among school personnel to provide student access to it. The marketing of personal computers, microprocessor-based games and word-processing machines has generated a recent surge of interest. Computers have become so prolific that the educators can't ignore them any longer.

Not only has the degree of interest changed but so has the kind of interest. For example, language-arts teachers are finding a new classroom tool. For some time they have used the computer in tutorial or drill and practice modes. Now the word-processing features and text-editors have made the computer a writing tool.

THE TEACHER'S VIEWPOINT

What is exciting for one teacher is threatening to another. Although we can provide some teachers with the hardware, software and training, microcomputers may still not become a part of every classroom.

I understand why teachers 10 years ago weren't too excited about using mark-sense cards and transporting them to and from an IBM 360 at a nearby campus. Later, even with the more appropriate user languages and an extensive library of instructional programs, computers captured the interest of few teachers. Part of the problem was the justification of the cost and the inconvenience of time-sharing equipment. Furthermore, it was difficult to convince other colleagues that this was an instrument to be controlled, not feared.

Some teachers are philosophically opposed to computer use because of its 1984 image. Others refuse to get involved, sure that it's another fad that will die away like so many other curriculum innovations. Still others just don't want to bother, content to let the younger members of their staff take the responsibility.

Teachers do not think they will be replaced by a computer, but expect their role with students will change as they each learn to communicate with these machines. Could the microcomputer destroy traditional schooling altogether? Some people envision the gradual disappearance of books and the absence of schools as we know them. Teaching will be done at home on the computer with lots of drill and practice exercises.

While this scope of teaching may sound futuristic and threatening, I am convinced that software to change the classroom environment and provide a unique kind of motivation for students will eventually become available.

THE STUDENTS

Teaching with a microcomputer has given me a chance to experience a potentially important resource in American education. I see the students excited by its interactivity, open-endedness and versatility in presenting text, sound and graphics. They are really being exposed to a "mind multiplier."

The students are much less afraid of the computers than are their teachers. They have more access and more time to get involved. Programming gives the student a chance to control the computer rather than being controlled. It emphasizes the process as well as the product. I can recall few other instances in school where a student describes an action, then executes it on command. Programming has enabled some of my students to share "intellectual products" with each other.

INTO THE CLASSROOM

Some educators want to see microcomputers fit into the existing school curriculum, while others want to see them change it. To be usable tools, they must be employed in a manner consistent with the philosophy of the teacher and the curriculum of the school. Most teachers will consider themselves liaisons between computer and student. They will not become hardware experts or programmers, but they will know enough to teach students how to use the equipment. Drill programs, tutorials, games and simulations can be written to fit into almost any curriculum. But teachers must determine the ratios of those different uses, the amount of "hands on" experience and the possibility of programming. To make these decisions, teachers will have to consider their individuals skills and interests, the atmosphere in the classroom and the philosophy of the school.

To use computers successfully, teachers must know what they want the machine to do in their classroom. They need information on the development of microcomputer use in schools and on available educational software to make their own decisions about equipment and software.

A recent report by *Conduit* (see box) revealed a variety of computer uses at the college level, including complex problem solving, simulations, model building and manipulation of large data bases. Drill and tutorial uses accounted for less than ten percent of computer use in instruction, although the percentage increases when interactive services are offered.

I suspect that the percentages are almost reversed for the elementary and secondary levels. Drill and practice, together with games, account for most of the computer time.

Two obvious reasons are the age or sophistication of the users and the nature of the equipment. Teachers are under pressure to emphasize skill building and to raise test scores. Drill and practice programs can create better-skilled students, and the public would love to see the trend of declining test scores reversed. The educators must use what is on the market or produce it themselves. Games are most available commercially, and drill and practice programs are considered the easiest to write.

HARDWARE, SOFTWARE AND PERSONNEL PROBLEMS

The use of microcomputer technology is hindered currently by a relative nonexistence of appropriate instructional software. It's also hindered by lack of information about what people are doing in education. A clarification of its role at the elementary and secondary levels is needed.

People outside education think the problem lies with the staff, not with the hardware and software. They're not exactly impressed by the quality of thinking or practice in the areas of education. If we educators want money for instructional computing when everyone in the schools is being asked to cut back, we will have to convince the public of its benefits. We will have to be able to show them what the computer can do better, and not just replicate in the learning process. It's going to be a tough challenge to make the computer an appealing tool so that taxpayers will buy it, and a lasting tool so the students will really gain from it.

Since I remain so optimistic about the potential of the microcomputer, I have to be realistic when it comes to solving some of the problems of using microcomputers in education. These solutions are not immediate, easy or inexpensive, but they are possible.

People are doing what they can. Teachers and parents are buying their own microcomputers; they are buying or producing their own software. They are taking courses, subscribing to computer journals and attending conferences to learn. Administrators are helping by budgeting for microcomputers and by searching for ways to train teachers in microcomputer use.

Some school districts are supporting teams of teachers and students to produce the needed software. Typically, a teacher who is knowledgeable about programming, available software and computer equipment organizes a team of programmers (usually high school programming students) and teachers with specific needs. The teachers discuss their objectives and the programmers write accordingly. The teachers critique and the programmers revise during the process, each time coming closer to the type of

Some creative computer educators in the country have helped schools and computers to adapt to each other. Ludwig Braun, at the State University of New York, Stony Brook, is a leader in developing pre-college curricula. Tom Dwyer and Margot Critchfield, of the University of Pennsylvania at Pittsburgh, produce appropriate materials for computer users. Karl Zinn, of the University of Michigan, Ann Arbor, has instituted some valuable projects. Alfred Bork, University of California, Irvine, and Arthur Luehrmann, University of California, Berkeley, contribute to science education. David Moursund, University of Oregon, Eugene, and Robert Taylor, Teachers College, Columbia University, focus on teacher training at preservice and in-service levels. Joyce Hakansson, consultant to the Childrens Television Workshop in New York City, is coordinating the development of hardware and software for very young children. Patrick Suppes, of Stanford University, is responsible for many of the drill and practice materials on the market. Sylvia Charp, Philadelphia Public Schools, provides critical insight to the process of implementation. Bob Albrecht, People's Computer Company, and Seymour Papert, Massachusetts Institute of Technology, are strong advocates of children controlling the computers. The Elementary and Secondary Subcommittee of the Association for Computing Machinery, headed by Moursund, is busy this year gathering information nationwide about instructional applications. The Minnesota Education Computing Consortium (MECC), Lauderdale MN, serves as a model for leadership as a state organization. *Conduit* (University of Iowa, Iowa City) is an important resource for disseminating reliable software at the undergraduate level. *The Computing Teacher*, published by the growing International Council for Computers in Education (available through University of Oregon, Eugene, OR), is the first journal that all educators should subscribe to. All of these people and many others too numerous to mention, openly share their ideas, and are also responsible for some major group efforts in instructional computing.

programs that teachers can use directly in their classrooms.

The software currently on the market is largely the result of hundreds of different people, all writing independently of each other, for different microcomputers. The level of their programming skill varies as do their standards for their programs. Given the technical problems with using cassette tapes, we risk buying a program that's of questionable quality or one that won't load on our machine.

Some major, organized efforts to produce educational materials for use with microcomputers exist. Publishers who do this are taking risks when they enter this unpredictable market. (Can you imagine trying to do cost projections, or finding the right person to head the effort?)

QUESTIONS FOR EDUCATORS

Should a school buy one complete system (with printer, disk and memory expansion) that provides more capabilities and applications or several microcomputers that provide more hands-on experiences for students?

Selection of this hardware poses philosophical questions for educators. Should we select one all-purpose machine that does limited drill and practice and that has limited programming potential? Should we, instead, select a dedicated computer that has excellent drill and practice programs, and a different machine on which students can learn to program? Should the computer be in control of the student or should the student be in full control of the computer? Is there a machine that serves both student and teacher needs in the classroom? What computer can carry out both administrative and instructional functions and is it better than buying two separate pieces of hardware?

TENTATIVE SOLUTIONS

Only when we can tell equipment manufacturers what we want the computer to do and when we can afford to pay for it, will we have the appropriate hardware. If and when we can show software houses and publishers that we will support their educational programs, we'll get the desired instructional software. As long as small businesses are purchasing more microcomputers than schools, the hardware manufacturers and software developers will direct their efforts in that direction.

It is exciting to look at the potential of the microcomputer in the classroom. It is frustrating to list all the things that must be done, but also rewarding to see the progress. The problems involved with putting microcomputers to their full use in the classrooms have complex and costly solutions, but I am confident that education will solve these problems as soon as it's humanly and technologically possible.

Programming, the Second Literacy

A.P. Ershov[1]

The title of this talk is, as I fully realize, a metaphor which may sound rather risky. On the one side of the cupula is the name of an exotic, though already very popular, profession which requires specific abilities

[1]Computing Center, USSR Academy of Sciences, Siberian Branch, Novosibirsk 630090, USSR

and an extensive training, while on the other side is the general virtue, the most fundamental property of modern man.

In spite of that, I shall try to show that such a metaphor is both instructive and effective. I have no desire to exhaust the audience with lengthy reasoning or to trick it and therefore shall outright present the scheme of exposition of the main thesis.

First, it will be easier to juxtapose programming and literacy if we remember that literacy is an historical category which has its source, its beginning, and its development. (The USSR is a country of practically complete literacy. Ten years ago literate people in this country constituted 99.7% of the population over the age of nine. One hundred years ago the literate part of Russia's population was slightly over 20%. Even now there are about 800 million illiterate people in the world.)

Second, it must be noted that both literacy and programming are based on technological inventions, those of the printing press and of the computer, respectively.

Third, both literacy and programming express the organic ability of man, that is, the ability prepared by the organization of his nervous system and displayed in all social functions of people; in communication, work, the contemplation of nature and the struggle against it.

Fourth, and, presumably, the most important, is the fact that literacy and programming art not only run parallel and are connected by bridges of analogy, but they also supplement each other, forming a new harmony of human mind.

This last thesis is worth an immediate, if brief, commentary.

One is accustomed to understand literacy as an ability of man to grasp and express knowledge in text form. From our childhood we hear a terse yet profound formula of Maxim Gorky: "Love the book, the source of knowledge." Still, however, the problem remains of how to pass from knowledge on to action. "Suit the action to the word, the word to the action," one of Shakespeare's characters said. This is precisely where programming comes in.

In pre-book times, the integrity of word and action was natural and permanent. The accumulation of experience and knowledge was based on direct and constant contacts between an old teacher and his younger pupil. Of course this method of education was far from being the best because it narrowed the basis for forming general notions and restricted the possibilities of constructing a theory of the subject

From "Programming, The Second Literacy," by A.P. Ershov. In R. Lewis and E.D. Tagg (Eds.), *Computers in Education* (Proceedings of the 3rd IFIP World Conference, Lausanne, Switzerland, July, 1981). Reprinted by permission.

taught and studied? but, on the other hand, no problem of passage from word to action ever arose, as the moment of truth was sensed not in the instant of mental inspiration, but after a goal had been achieved. To put it in modern terms, the education was object-oriented.

The appearance of books blew up the integrity of word and action; it separated the process of knowledge accumulation from its application and created new varieties of craving for knowledge and new sensations of truth understanding.

Every language developed special words and expressions to define knowledge-thirsty people with whom books came first. In all such expressions, from "bookish mind" to "egg-head," there was a shade of contempt, unjustified on the whole, but at times well-deserved.

For, as Montaigne observed back in the 16th century, "a scholarship of a purely bookish nature is a pitiful scholarship." Indeed, it turned out that the accumulation of knowledge through books requires new executive mechanisms of man. That implies that the problem of programming arose long before the first computer was manufactured. Computers stimulated the problem of programming just as book printing had stimulated the problem of literacy. The latter problem had made Jan Amos Komensky and his "Great Didactics" and "Mother's School," which laid the foundation of modern school, whereas the former problem is a challenge to ourselves. I ardently hope that we shall produce from our ranks a great teacher who will be able to equip the generation entering the 21st century with a vision of the future school.

Literacy and ability to act are not separately self-sufficient. If only one of the two factors was to develop, the problem would still remain. It is very difficult to say what brings people more suffering: ignorance or inactivity. Goethe warned that "nothing is as dangerous as active ignorance," but we know from experience that ignorance prospers when educated and cultured people lack an active attitude toward life. We know that literacy is not only the ability to read, but also the way to bring up an intellectual man.

To my mind, we now have to require of education much more than before. That is perhaps the reason why I conclude this introduction by an additional thesis that the second literacy is not only the ability to write computer instructions, but also the way to bring up a man who is resolute and prudent at the same time.

THE WORLD OF BOOKS

Let us return to the starting point of the exposition of our metaphor, that is, to book printing, or, to be more exact, to the book itself. I shall permit myself to give a short quotation from an encyclopedia, because the laconicism of an encyclopedic text makes it all the more expressive:

> BOOK, a printed work (in older times, a manuscript as well) in the form of stitched or bound printed sheets. . . In the Middle Ages books were copied by monks in monasteries and were, mostly, of clerical character. As towns developed, town scribes that replaced the monks copied both clerical and secular books. Book printing, which was invented in the middle of the 15th century, brought about a revolution in book production and publishing. The casting of type, the invention of an engine-press, stereotypes, the wide use of type-setting and rotary press made the book a powerful means of dissemination of knowledge and cultural progress. (Minor Encyclopedic Dictionary, Moscow, Sovetskaya Entsiklopediya Publishing House, 1936).

I honestly hope that some day a distant descendant of ours will summarize our difficult cause of computer construction and programming in as lapidary and epic lines.

I happen to have read several works on the history of books and progress of literacy. They present a most interesting chapter in the history of our civilization. In spite of the fact that book printing and computer technology formations are separated by a time interval of five centuries, their comparison will reveal many similar properties of both an engineering and social nature, the more so if one takes into account the difference in speed and throughput of communication channels. In book printing modes we shall find changes of generations based on progress in the means of production and technology. As in the computer business, we shall learn the history of large manufacturing companies that have all the typical trends of mass production: such as fearless absorption of engineering novelties and then fusion with technology standards, market and sales organization, dramatic confrontations combined with the inevitability of "big" and "small" business coexistence, the appearance of secondary industries of raw materials and parts.

The engineering history is accompanied by social history; authors and publishers appear, as well as booksellers and readers. A new notion is formed, that of the intellectual production, giving rise to a new form of property. Information becomes a commodity. An especially interesting chapter in the social history of book printing is the formation of a mass user, the readers. Strangely enough, this aspect is insufficiently covered by modern research.

Interdependence of book printing progress and universal literacy necessary for this progress, their combined impact that brought about the concept of universal education, the mass character of all such activity—that's just the problem which awaits its researcher, that's just the combination of historical processes that we are bound to experience while computers are introduced in all spheres of human activity.

Let me cite but a few facts illustrative of the tempo, scope and interaction in the development of book printing and literacy.

The first editions of Iohannes Gutenberg, the inventor of the printing press, date back to 1445 (Oelius Donatus' Latin Grammar "On the Eight Parts of Speech" and the famous 42-line Bible). Towards the end of the 15th century, but long before it ran out, there were over a thousand functioning printing houses in the world whose total yield came close to 10 million copies, exceeding overnight the existing fund of handwritten books; yet there are no visible signs of the saturation of the book market. The data for 1962 testify to the fact that on the average every inhabitant of the Earth bought two books. The average family in the USSR buys annually some 30 books, yet there is a constant book shortage. A simple extrapolation of these figures gives an estimate of 40 billion books annually as the potential book consumption of the world nowadays.

There seem to be profound similarities between books and computers. They possess a number of common features that set them off against all the other consumer goods. Other consumer goods are specialized and designed for a certain function. The ratio of the volume of production of such an article to the number of consumers is expressed by a small constant. Books and computers are different. Both books and computers embody an information model of the world in all its multivariousness and changeability. It is unreasonable to expect that man's curiosity and thirst for information will ever be expressed by a small constant.

Allow me to refer to the Soviet experience once again in order to demonstrate the interdependence of literacy and book printing over the last century (data from the editions of the Soviet Encyclopedia):

Year	% of Literacy	The annual volume book publishing (in billions)
1897	28.4	
1913		0.12
1926	56.6	
1933		0.49
1939	87.4	0.46
1946		0.46
1959	98.5	1.24
1970	99.7	1.36
1976		1.78

If the analogies we have drawn are true, then this table will give us an idea of the dimensions and scope of work to be carried out to prepare the encounter of the world of computers with the world of man.

THE WORLD OF COMPUTERS

Mass media, popular science literature and advertising have already imprinted on our mentality, notwithstanding the short age of computers, the habitual image of a typical computer—the screen of a display with a keyboard, tape drives, the intricate lace of paper tape, endless listings, the blinking lights of the control panel, angular cases stuffed with electronic machinery. Technically speaking, all this is subsumed under a single term: the main frame. If, however, we try to visualize the place of computers in the world of man on the basis of such an image, our ideas will be not only superficial but erroneous too. The computer of the future is not so much a gigantic electronic brain, packed into a spacious and carefully guarded glass building of an international bank or into a no less carefully guarded underground refuge of a command and control post. It is rather a tiny slice of a silicon crystal set into a miniature frame which is entangled in the finest web of wires. Such a detail will be an integral part of practically every industrially produced article.

You naturally understand that it is microprocessors I have in mind. Although they first appeared slightly over a decade ago, they are produced nowadays by dozens of millions annually. Their most spectacular application is in the production of various pocket calculators. But this is only the above-water part of the iceberg. I am deeply convinced that the appearance and development of micro-processors is the most revolutionary technical innovation of the 20th century. It has a number of important aspects and implications, and I shall single out only those which are most relevant for the line of analysis pursued in the present paper.

- A micro-processor with the speed of 100,000 operations per second, the internal memory of 5000 digits (words) and the volume of external memory equal to the number of characters in a book of medium length can be made the size of a matchbox, requires a day's work for its fabrication, and may be produced in practically limitless quantities.
- Such a micro-processor, when it makes part of an article of industry, be it a consumer article or a means of population, imparts to the latter entirely new properties and exerts a strong influence on the character of the man-article interaction.
- The integration of a micro-processor in the design of an article exerts an equally strong influence on the methods of design and requires that the above-mentioned properties of an article should be taken into account, understood and implemented.

Considerations of time preclude my going any deeper into these things, although they might have been made the most fascinating part of my paper. Technical literature abounds in the analysis of new problems deluging specialists in the organization of production, planners of working sites, engineering psychologists, designers—in short, all specialists in the field of engineering and technology. Thousands of professions are undergoing a fundamental change. Millions of people—operators, adjustors, typists, bank employees, stewards, librarians, fitters, secretaries, assemblers—acquire entirely reorganized working sites where computers become their partners and inter-locutors. Even if this partner is friendly and reliable, a fundamental psychological and intellectual re-construction should take place for a man to preserve his integrity and dignity in the new environment. Even nowadays there are millions of people involved in this process (in West Europe alone the number of terminals and data communication ports is close to a million). In two generations communicating with a computer will become the concern of practically every person involved in social production.

However, there emerges one serious obstacle on the way of this exponential development whipped up by a number of various factors. At present the ability of man to impart his knowledge to the computer is hopelessly lagging behind his ability to manufacture this computer. Whereas the cost of manufacturing a micro-processor is expressed in man-hours, the cost of producing software for it rockets up to man-months. The logistic curve of Barry Boem, showing the dynamics of the ratio of the hardware and software costs in designing an information processing system has become, owing to incessant repetition, so habitual that it causes no worry. Of course programming specialists are working to the best of their ability to make the programmer's labors more productive. Yet elementary calculations show that even if we accept the hypothesis of a ten-fold productivity in twenty years' time it will be necessary to engage all the adult population of the world in programming in order to supply all the manufactured micro-processors with programs.

Unfortunately the majority of the worried organizers of industry nowadays will wave these calculations away as yet another paradox of a type to which we have become accustomed in our complicated world. Up till now there are many self-confident managers who still believe in the old maxim that demand gives rise to supply and that one can always find a good specialist if one is ready to pay well. A parallel with literacy will help us solve this paradox as well. Says Arthur Clark, who has already been in the 21st century by the sheer power of his foresight: "In the future every man incompetent in the sciences will turn out, honestly speaking, to be lacking in education. And if he prides in this custom nowadays,

he will find himself in exactly the same position as the illiterate medieval barons declaring proudly that they have secretaries to do the counting and writing."

The medieval barons and their offspring do not exist any longer, every man has learned to count and to write, and secretaries have acquired new masters and new obligations.

The same is bound to happen with programming: managers who have no idea of computers and pro-gramming will go off the stage, professional pro-grammers will become systems analysts and systems programmers, and ordinary programming will be mastered by everyone. This is precisely what I call the second literacy.

We thus proceed from the world of computers to the world of programs.

THE WORLD OF PROGRAMS

Monsieur Jourdain, a character of Moliére, was amazed to learn that he, while totally unaware of the fact, had been speaking prose throughout his life. The advent of computers, having given life to computer science, or informatics, proved an eye opener for mankind, which, like the fascinated Monsieur Jourdain, has discovered that it lives in a world of programs, and that the productivity of the information model concept adds a new dimension to what St. John meant when saying: "In the be-ginning was the Word."

Yes, we do live in a world of programming and keep programming most of the time, whether we realize it or not.

It is perhaps open to argument which is the single most momentous scientific breakthrough of the 20th century. But if we take the top five or even three discoveries, the general consensus will be that one of these is the fact that the development of an organism proceeds as implementation of a genetic program encoded in its genes. While further discussion of this is hardly appropriate here, I'd like to observe, in passing, that the computer science terminology, far from being a metaphor, catches the very essence of the intracellular growth and development processes, for which molecular structures and chemical pro-cesses provide some kind of circuitry and instructions repertoire.

The human organism is virtually saturated with programs. Each and every physiological process may be viewed as a vast, involved and carefully checked out program library, where an analysis of program structures (or call graphs—as a computer scientist would dub them) can lead to far-reaching conclusions and predictions concerning the organism's behavior.

Actually, the entire domain of production rela-tions, especially in the production process itself, functions according to certain programs. A stable production process is always internally formalized, its effect being conditional on the smooth running of human-operated programs. Moreover, even in a stochastic process, like hunting or driving, it is only the sequence of events which is random and unpredictable, while reactions to them are nearly always carried out by automatically operated programs.

Take learning, i.e., acquisition of knowledge, or rather, of a capacity to do things—it is also programming. Prof. Seymour Papert, who was among the first psychologists and educationalists to have adopted a programming-oriented approach, convincingly argued in a series of his publications, of a decade ago, that a child learns to do something only after he has fully comprehended how this is to be done. As long as such comprehension has not been achieved, there is no point in repetitive training. Significantly enough, this applies not only to sequences of logically motivated reactions to previously identified stimuli, but also to real-time programs, including all kinds of motor actions (i.e., sports, music, games, etc.).

Everyday life, especially that of a city dweller, is a program-oriented activity. Anyone who follows a regimen might proudly refer to himself as a programmer, once he backtracks his crammed early morning routines running from the alarm clock sound to the working day start. Just ponder a little over the home tidying-up procedure, and you are sure to realize that creating a similar program would be a major challenge to top professional computer scientists engaged in developing applied program packs.

We tend to grumble over the social ailments of our times, such as escapism and passivity, and call for a more active and responsible attitude to life. But what is it like? Plainly speaking, it is an ability to formulate a program of action and to follow it.

Thus, the world of programs is by no means confined to the stuff fed into computer memories. It is above all the enormous stock of operational knowledge accumulated by mankind, which is being merely actualized now in computers, robots and automatic devices. A still greater amount of programs is stored in the gene pool of all the living creatures: its actualization is a basic task of biology with its new branches, notably of genetic engineering. Developmental psychology and the theory of behavior are also molding new concepts essentially similar to those of computer science.

Now, given all this, we come to confront the problem of fundamentalized programming, i.e., attempting to identify in it certain "natural entities" that might help bridge the gap between the machine world and the living one, between the programs of nature and those compiled by man. If it is our wish to place these natural entities within the conscious command of man, we have no choice but to include them as operational cognitive values into the structure and content of public education.

Let us consider the premises for, and possible obstacles to, implementing this plan.

GENERAL PREMISES

So, we wish to teach children the laws of programming. One doesn't need to actually know these to realize that they would constitute a quite peculiar body of know-how. It is still to be found out to what extent this knowledge can be made accessible to children, yet the general impression is that their intellectual and operational potentials are far from being exhausted. Just think how much younger the technical sports, in particular swimming and gymnastics, have become over the recent years. I am not sure about the West, but in my country cars are still expensive, and more often than not one is, so to say, past his prime by the time he raises enough money to buy a car. A lot of people ask acrimoniously, just how many lives lost in traffic accidents could have been saved if everyone had learned to drive at the age of 14 or 15.

However, it is absolutely impossible to load down children with the condensed experience of the entire mankind. There are other risks inherent in such attempts. There is a children's song familiar to everyone in the USSR, in which the singer Alla Pugachyova humorously portrays the dismal life of a little school boy who wonders why he has to cope with college level problems in his first grade and have no time for fun at all.

Everyone knows the romantic story by Rudyard Kipling about Maugli, the boy raised by wolves who eventually found his way back to the people. Similar cases sometimes occur in the tropical countries, yet with a much less happy outcome, and psychologists observe what they call a "Maugli effect, or syndrome" in young children unable to regain their faculties ruined by an alien environment or psychic overstrain. This imprinting is a natural phase in a child's development; moreover, every one of us can be said to be a Maugli of his early years with regard to what happened and what was learned at that time.

Over the past decades developmental psychology has accumulated enough evidence pointing to the crucial importance of the early age in the learning period. Returning to my previous line of discussion, I'd like to remark that the problem of how to teach a child an ability to coordinate his actions and foresee their results is very far from the methodological issues involved, for instance, in the professional training of computer scientists. On the one hand, the setting has to be made natural to a child, while, on the other hand, it has to be rich enough to enable him to create, as the psychologists put it, a "theory" of the comprehended phenomenon.

It is my conviction that laws of programming and information processing do actually exist. They manifest themselves, on the one hand, in the form of operational rules reflecting the immediate experience of mankind. We all happen to know that Latin phrase *Divide et impera,* taking it mostly for a concentrated expression of political cynicism. It was not until modern mathematics and computer science embodied it in the branch-and-bound method that it was recognized as a powerful and productive heuristic tool of solving problems. Thus, on the other hand, the programming laws link up with mathematical education to compose a united, though not yet constructed, basis to foster operational and combinatorial thinking, abstract reasoning and an ability to act.

There is a simple programming problem which always impressed me as a sound example of a transition from knowledge to action. I shall write out the consequent stages of transition from a notation that expresses knowledge to a program that expresses the operations required to raise a number x to the nth degree (where n is an integer): *See figure below:*[2]

$$x^0 = 1 \qquad x^0 = 1 \qquad x^0 = 1 \qquad \text{if } n = 0$$
$$x^{n+m} = x^n x^m \quad x^{n+1} = x^n x \quad x^{2n} = (x^n)^2 \quad \text{if } n \text{ is even } (x^{n/2})^2$$
$$x^{m.n} = (x^m)^n \quad x^{2n} = (x^n)^2 \quad x^{2n+1} = x^{2n}x \quad \text{if } n \text{ is odd } x.x^{n-1}$$

degree $(x,n) =$ if $n = 0$ then 1 else if even n then degree $(x.n/2)^2$

else $x =$ degree $(x, n\text{-}1)$ fi fi.

I challenge everybody to suggest an interpretation of the facts and knowledge involved here at each stage in the transition from the obvious knowledge to a rather ingenious program. I would say only, that if we were able to compile every program in this way, while making coherent informal comments in the process, that would be exactly the fundamentalized programming we are looking forward to.

THE COMPUTER AT SCHOOL

The question of whether or not computers should be allowed into schools is becoming somewhat scholastic these days, following the emergence of

microprocessors. Computers have *already* found their way to schools and will pour there in ever growing numbers. What is required now is a concerted intellectual and organizational effort to direct this process into a controlled and educationally viable channel.

There exists, of course, an actively professed view that using a programmed computer is little different from having a problem's solution in advance, and that electronic aids encourage nothing but mental laziness. Probably one of the best cartoons the *New Yorker* magazine carried in recent years pictured poor Johnny watching in dismay a heap of pocket calculators in front of him, while the equally exasperated Mammy keeps repeating the same question: "Now, look here, if you have five pocket calculators and then take away two of them, how many will remain?"

Such warnings against the risks inherent in "push button" education had been heard before as well, yet the solid experience substantiated by our work with children of various ages proves the contrary: it boosts the activity, inquisitiveness, and hence, the abilities of a child. However, the major factor here is the actual operational setting which must be *stimulating.*

Ways and means of using computers to activate education are infinitely diverse: the only limits that exist here are set by our lack of fantasy or insufficient knowledge of child psychology.

Half of the kids at my local school have memorized the historical dates after a teenage programmer designed a data base of historical dates and set it on a computer, while another one quizzed the school teacher on it and caught her on several errors.

I am not sure which firm it was that started producing a toy computer for checking English spelling. A speech synthesizer pronounces a word, the child types it on a keyboard, the computer checks it and responds. One cannot expect a good speech synthesizer to be built into a pocket-size toy, yet the designers managed to benefit from its faults making it sound like Pinocchio. You can easily imagine the enthusiasm of a child who hears the thin voice of Pinocchio telling him "Try again, try again, and don't fail this time!"

Just one more observation of some interest. The school leavers taking entrance examinations at a university were invited to consult a computer information system. Queues kept forming in front of the terminal. Two university lecturers were sent in to help those waiting in the queue. Yet, the young people seemed unwilling to approach them and preferred standing in line to the computer. Their comment was: "We don't care about showing poor knowledge to a computer, but one feels embarrassed to do so in front of a teacher." In fact, the computer proves to be a more convenient source and controller

---

[2]Author Erskov refers here to a programming language which, unless known, may not provide the "simple programming problem" he identifies above.

of knowledge for children in many respects. Firstly, it is an all-knowing partner, while, secondly, it is no more than an instrument, a thing. A computer creates a play setting which is all the more precious in training, for opposite to real-life situations one can quit a game without damage to one's self-respect. Examples of this kind can be multiplied.

There are, however, more serious arguments in support of bringing computers into schools. I have already mentioned the work of Prof. Seymour Papert from the Artificial Intelligence Laboratory of the Massachusetts Institute of Technology. His recent paper "Redefining childhood: the computer presence as an experiment in developmental psychology" generated common interest when he presented it at the IFIP-80 Congress, held in Japan and Australia. Prof. Papert predicts a total invasion of the child's world by the computer, which is to become an intellectual tool manipulated by the child as spontaneously as a pen or pencil, but with an infinitely greater variety of purpose. Interpreting the observations made by Prof. J. Piaget, which indicate that a child makes most of his intellectual findings individually, provided his environment is rich enough, Prof. Papert points out that once the environment is computerized, this unprecedented change in operational setting will call for new concepts in developmental psychology. Prof. Papert mentions, by way of example, alphabetic language acquisition being noticeably speeded up, and an earlier development of combinatorial abilities, which will make these fundamental skills available to children virtually before adolescence. Among other positive effects triggered by this shift is that it may help overcome the infantilism and feeling of dependence which is so widespread in modern urban societies.

In fact, this positive conclusion made by Prof. Papert could be taken to constitute the climax of my analysis. No great imagination is needed to visualize the enormous shifts in practical education, once this educational goal is achieved.

CONCLUSION

I opened this paper with a metaphor. Now I can reveal what it implied. We are facing the prospects of an effectively unlimited development and spread of electronic computers in society. A computer is becoming an intellectual tool and partner in virtually every sphere of human life and activity. The need to actualize an informational world model in computer science terms and the ever-growing complexity of the environment make it imperative, and also possible, to greatly enhance the intellectual power of mankind. A significant role in this onward movement of the human intellect belongs to the laws of information processing, ways of knowledge-action transition, ability to write programs and reason on them, as well as foresee what they will lead to. A careful conceptual analysis will yield a sum total of knowledge concerning these items, which, combined with mathematical and linguistic conceptions, will provide a foundation of future general education. A computer will be more than a technical tool in the learning process. It will bring about a renovated intellectual background, a new operational setting to be organically and naturally exploited by the child in his development at home and at school. The opportunities offered by the computer and the new educational tasks will make a profound effect on the very foundations of developmental psychology, as well as on the existing didactic principles and educational approaches. Realization of these opportunities will shorten a child's way to intellectual maturity, increase his activity, improve his preparedness to occupational performance, including an ability to take part in the second industrial revolution precipitated by computers and new automation technologies.

In other words, programming is a second literacy. This is still a metaphor, yet the one which, in my view, brings to a focus the goals and the content of the present conference.

WHAT'S YOUR OPINION?

1. Students who have not been exposed to computing are at a significant disadvantage compared with those who have had such exposure.
2. Choosing to ignore the prevention of computer illiteracy will create greater disparity and frustration between those who understand technology and those who do not.
3. Many students are now bringing the literacy of the computer age into the classroom.
4. The computer has become indispensible to the operation of science, business, and government but does not play a major role in American education.
5. Computers and hand calculators have relegated the calculation of square root, logarithms, and fractions to the level of dipping candles and tanning hides.
6. The ability to understand and use computers is

a measure of a person's level of computer literacy.

7. Historically, teachers have rejected technological innovation, and the computer is not likely to be an exception to this trend.
8. If we are to have equity in our educational system, all students must have equal access to computing.
9. A student who graduates without being exposed to computers has had an incomplete education.
10. In an information society, a computer-literate populace is as important as energy and raw materials are to an industrial society.
11. Computer literacy is a prerequisite to effective participation in an information society and is as much a social obligation as is reading literacy.
12. Computer knowledge does not become a relatively freely available commodity until it is part of the educational curriculum.
13. To become computer literate, a student must spend many laboratory hours at the keyboard of an interactive computer system.
14. Computer literacy is being embraced by educators from diverse disciplinary backgrounds.
15. At the abstract level, computer literacy presents few problems; it is an honorable goal with few negative connotations.
16. It is difficult, perhaps even un-American, to oppose computer literacy.
17. It will be a challenge to make the computer so appealing a tool that taxpayers will buy it and so lasting a tool that students will genuinely gain from its use.
18. The introduction of calculators should precede the introduction of computers into the classroom.
19. It would be a good thing if every student had a computer.
20. Just as the 1970s became the decade of computer technology, the 1980s must become the decade of computer literacy.
21. Standardization of curriculum is aided by computers.
22. It is relatively simple to distinguish computer literates from computer illiterates.
23. All high school graduates should have taken at least one course in computer awareness.
24. All elementary school graduates should have taken at least one course in computer awareness.

EXERCISES

1. If we introduce into the first grade calculators that automatically perform mathematical functions, what will the children do for the next six years?
2. Should computer literacy be considered a core element in the back-to-basics movement?
3. How can we separate computer literates from the computer illiterates?
4. Investigate the meaning of the term *word processing*. Should an introductory word processing course be a requirement in the core curriculum for all elementary, junior high, and high school students?
5. List reasons justifying the teaching of computer literacy in elementary schools.
6. List the courses a student should take in high school to be adequately prepared to enroll in a university computer science course.
7. Draw up a course outline for teaching computer literacy to the grade level of students you currently teach. Could you personally teach such a course if your principal requested it?
8. Compare the types of video games found in arcades to microcomputer games.
9. Survey your local business community to determine how many guest speakers on computer-related topics are available. Make a list for future reference, and share your resource with colleagues.
10. Investigate how "The Source" data base works. Determine services offered, costs involved, and equipment required.
11. List ten instances in which you would teach *about* computers as opposed to teaching *with* computers. Explain your choices.
12. What is meant by *programming style*? Should it be a major topic in any programming course?
13. What is the purpose of a logic flowchart for program documentation?

THREE

Teacher Education

For years, experts have warned that courses must be devised to prepare teachers adequately, at all levels of education, for the coming technological revolution. Now the so-called information society has arrived, but most teachers still lack the knowledge and skills needed to cope with new methods of instruction, particularly those involving computers. The articles in Chapter 3 provide a substantial introduction to what is being done to help alleviate the need for contemporary teacher training in computer use.

Hedges and Rawitsch offer suggestions for teachers of educator-training sessions and workshops. Taylor, Poirot, and Powell define (a) the basic universal computing competencies required for any schoolteaching, (b) the additional computing competencies needed by teachers of computing, and (c) the additional computing-related, subject-specific competencies needed by teachers of subjects other than computing. Dennis, Milner, and Dickerson and Pritchard likewise state the need for teacher training and describe instructional models for training pre-service and in-service teachers to use computers.

Suggestions for utilizing advanced technology to increase nationwide productivity and the effects of microcomputers and technology generally on education are discussed by Molnar. Moursund and Jay express causes and solutions for teachers' anxieties about computers and computing, and Myers outlines five concerns for literacy and training programs: money, trained teachers, high-quality courseware, use and misuse of computing knowledge, and dependence on computing. Listed in addition are organizations involved in educational computing and suggested reading materials.

Teacher Education

Jim Poirot, Robert Taylor, and Jim Powell

INTRODUCTION

This paper deals with a subset of the issues and areas related to designing overall, computer-literate teacher training. To appreciate its focus and accept some of its omissions, one should be aware of the following constraints that the task group placed on itself. First, it was unanimously agreed that definitions should be in terms of competencies to be achieved rather than in terms of programs or courses to transmit those competencies. Second, because the computing competencies needed by the teacher who must teach computing as a subject are more extensive than those needed by other teachers, the competencies needed only by the computing teacher should be treated as a separate module. Third, though integrally related to each other, the competencies needed by the teacher are quite different from those needed by the teacher's teachers, the staff of institutions actually doing the teacher training. It was agreed, therefore, that specifying the competencies needed by the teacher's teacher would be a separate module of work. It was also agreed that it should only be undertaken after competencies needed by the teacher had been specified.

The task group saw the competencies needed by teachers at the school level as all belonging to one of three sets. The first set encompasses those basic universal computing competencies required for any schoolteaching, regardless of level or subject. The second encompasses those additional computing

From "Teacher Education," by Jim Poirot, Robert Taylor and Jim Powell. In *Topics,* Association of Computing Machinery (SIGSCE, SIGCUE), January, 1981. Reprinted by permission.

competencies needed only by the teacher who must teach computing as a subject in its own right. The third encompasses additional computing-related, subject-specific competencies needed by teachers who teach subjects other than computing.

This paper outlines the competencies in all three sets. It incorporates critical suggestions received as a result of wide circulation of two earlier papers on the topic [1,2]. We also trust it will stimulate useful discussion and criticism. We hope it provides some guidance to those wondering what teachers should know about computing.

COMPUTING COMPETENCIES NEEDED BY TEACHERS

Three sets of computing competencies follow. The first (1.0) includes those which *all* teachers must have, regardless of their level or discipline, even if that discipline is the teaching of computing itself. The second set (2.0) includes those needed only by the teacher of computing as a subject. It should be noted this second set presupposes the first. The third set (3.0) includes additional competencies for teachers who use computing to support or enhance instruction in subjects other than computing.

1.0: Universal Computing Competencies Needed by All Teachers

These are the computing competencies which all school teachers should have to teach effectively in a society permeated by computers.

They relate to either or both of two goals: (1) to *understand* computing and (2) to *use* computing. They can be stated partially in terms of competencies listed in ACM's "Curriculum '78" [3] and partially in terms of different competencies, derived from other sources. A number of such other sources are listed in the references at the end of this paper. They reflect the abundance of diverse work that has taken place in the past decade, relating computing to education.

1.1: Competencies

In terms of these universal competencies, *every* teacher should:

C1.1 be able to read and write simple programs that work correctly and to understand how program and subprograms fit together into systems;

C1.2 have experience using educational application software and documentation;

C1.3 have a working knowledge of computer terminology, particularly as it relates to hardware;

C1.4 know by example, particularly in using computers in education, some types of problems that *are* and some general types of problems that *are not* currently amenable to computer solution;

C1.5 be able to identify and use alternate sources of current information on computing as it relates to education;

C1.6 be able to discuss at the level of an intelligent layperson some of the history of computing, particularly as it relates to education; and

C1.7 be able to discuss moral or human-impact issues of computing as they relate to societal use of computers generally, and educational use particularly.

The above competencies should be transmitted within the general preparation programs for *all* teachers by having those programs include the topics listed below (T1.1 through T1.5). For those being trained to teach computer science, those topics will represent only a small subset of what must be learned about computing and its uses (see Section 2.0). For all other teachers, however, apart from the subject-specific competencies covered in Section 3.0, these topics cover much of what must be learned about computing by the teacher who is to be minimally literate.

1.2 Topics of Study

T1.1 *Programming Topics:* Includes development of simple algorithms and their implementation in a programming language, programming style, debugging and verification, task-specific programming for educational applications.

T1.2 *Computer Terminology:* Includes software (e.g., operating systems, time-sharing systems, etc.), hardware (e.g., CRT, tape, disk, microcomputers, etc.), and miscellaneous items (e.g., documentation, testing, vendors, etc.).

T1.3 *Classic Applications of Computing in Education:* Includes representative experience with problem solving and test manipulation, simulation, drill and practice and complex tutorial systems including complete student progress recordkeeping, and educational administrative systems.

T1.4 *Human/Machine Relationships:* Includes artificial intelligence, robotics, computer assistance in decision making (e.g., medical, legal, business, etc.), simulations, and computers in fiction.

T1.5 *Information on Computers in Education:* Includes periodicals, important books, online inquiry sources such as ERIC, professional societies such as ACM, AEDS, NCTM, time-sharing networks, networks of computer users, and hardware vendor groups.

In T1.1 procedures or algorithms are at the heart of computing so teachers should learn what they are by implementing simple examples such as: a procedure to average a class's grades; a game to guess what number the computer is thinking of; or a procedure to display a large box on the screen and then make it shrink to disappearance.

Teachers need to be able to implement such procedures in only one language, but should be able to read at the same, or a greater, level of difficulty in a second so that the *idea* of a language, its strength and limitations, springs from personally experiencing functional differences between two languages. Within the limitations of simple programs teachers should be taught to write well structured code, easily readable by others, and to document their code in acceptable fashion.

T1.2 should be integrated throughout the course of study. In order to successfully use computing, the vocabulary of the field must be understood. What is the difference between a tape, a floppy disk, and a disk? Why use one over the other? These are general ideas, but some minimal understanding of them is necessary to actually use computers.

T1.3 should certainly familiarize the teacher with several of the existing well developed CAI systems cited in Section 3.0 below. Teachers will not develop new ideas about what could be done in their areas unless they see the best of what has been done; neither will they get a full understanding of what cannot be reasonably well done by computer without such exposure. For example, acquaintance with the physics system designed by Bork [4], with CCC drill and practice systems based on Suppes's work [5], or with PLATO work[6] should serve to acquaint the teacher with the CAI issues.

Since many teachers end up in administration and since administrative uses of computers affect the teacher, some introduction to one or more representative administrative systems should be included. A student record system would probably be a reasonable choice for illustrative study—it deals with information familiar to the teacher without using financial details some might find difficult to understand.

Teachers should also be familiar with super calculator modes of computer use as classic

application. As home computers become more common, perhaps little formal work in this area will be necessary. Clearly word processing must be covered; every teacher does so much word processing manually that none should be left ignorant of how much word processing help the computer can give.

With respect to T1.4, the long range and the immediate implications of computing as a form of artificial intelligence should be taught. The excitement of learning to think about thinking and of contemplating the powers and limits of human intelligence are so significantly linked with computing experience that this aspect must be studied—the opportunity is too great to pass up. Artificial intelligence may best convey both the power and limitation of computing in education. Acquaintance with any of several perspectives on this experience is essential and can be taught using such projects as the LOGO work [7] or the SOLO work [8]. A growing body of fiction about computing can also contribute effectively to the teacher's insight into the emerging world [9, 10].

With respect to T1.5, teachers must know where to look to keep abreast in this rapidly changing field. Course work and instruction should therefore routinely call attention to and require the trainee's use of a range of sources of information about computing and education.

The ideas presented above represent a minimal set of competencies which should be obtained by every teacher. The topics presented provide a framework to achieve this minimal level of competency. In addition to these competencies, every teacher should also acquire the competencies listed in either Section 2.0 or Section 3.0.

2.0: Competencies Needed for the Teacher of Computing

While every classroom teacher should have the general set of computing competencies suggested above, the teacher of computing needs more. The likelihood that he or she will, in addition to teaching, be forced to function as a general resource to faculty, administration, and students only increases the need for more extensive competency in computing.

Since much of the knowledge required for such a teacher is similar to that required of anyone desiring to be a computer professional, many of the computer competencies defined in the recent ACM Curriculum Committee report "Curriculum '78" [3] apply to the teacher as well. This sector therefore relies extensively upon that report.

2.1: Competencies

The core material recommended for teachers of computer science represents essential elementary material, as well as material especially designed for educators. Computer science teachers should:

C2.1 be able to write and document readable, well structured individual programs and linked systems of two or more programs;

C2.2 be able to determine whether they have written a reasonably efficient and well organized program;

C2.3 understand basic computer architectures;

C2.4 understand the range of computing topics that are suitable to be taught as well as the justification for teaching these topics;

C2.5 know what educational tools can be uniquely employed in computer science education.

The first three competencies are of the sort commonly needed by all computing professionals and are listed in Curriculum '78 as among those to be covered by the undergraduate computer science degree program. Competencies C2.4 and C2.5 are not commonly needed by all computing professionals. They are essential only in the preparation of computer science teachers.

For individuals who are to serve as a computer resource person for their school or school system, two additional competencies have been identified.

C2.6 develop the ability to assist in the selection, acquisition, and use of computers, interactive terminals and computer services which are suitable to the enhancement of instruction; and

C2.7 be able to assist teachers in evaluation, selection, and/or development of appropriate instructional materials which utilize computing facilities.

2.2: Topics of Study

These competencies should be transmitted through a series of courses and other vehicles developed through joint efforts of teacher education programs and the computer science program. We present below a list of topics that should be included in the program.

T2.1 *Programming Topics:* Includes advanced algorithms, programming language, blocks and procedures, programming style, docu-mentation debugging and verification, elementary algorithm analysis, applications.

T2.2 *Software Organization:* Includes computer structure and machine language, data representation, symbolic coding and assembly systems, addressing techniques, macros, program segmentation and linkage, linkers and loaders, systems and utility programs.

T2.3 *Hardware Organization:* Includes computer systems organization, logic design, data representation and transfer, digital arithmetic, digital storage and accessing control, I/O, reliability.

T2.4 *Data Structures and File Processing:* Includes data structures, sorting and searching, trees, file terminology, sequential access, random access, file I/O.

T2.5 *Computers in Society:* Computers and their effects on governments, careers, thought, law, personal behavior; privacy and its protection; information security and its preservation.

T2.6 *Teaching Computer Science:* Includes: (1) knowledge of learning theories as they apply to learning about computers, (2) knowledge of *several* appropriate curricular scope and sequences for a variety of program goals (e.g., literacy, careers, college preparation, personal problem solving).

Curriculum '78, along with a vast amount of research in computer education, supports the inclusion of topics T2.1 through T2.5. Knowledge of programming topics, software organization, etc., are essential for the computer professional of today.

The teaching of computing is a unique computer profession. Knowing how to program, however, does not, in itself, qualify a teacher for teaching computer science. Materials on why and how to teach computer topics included in T2.6 are invaluable to the teacher of computing and should be included within a program of study training such teachers.

Competencies C2.6 and C2.7 of the previous section are required for those individuals serving as computer resource personnel for a school system. These competencies should be transmitted through the computer science program and the teacher preparation programs. The following topics will assist in developing the required competencies.

T2.7 *Advanced Topics in Computer Science:* Includes advanced topics in computer organization, operating systems, architecture; data base systems; computer communications.

T2.8 *Computers in Education:* Includes detailed knowledge of learning/teaching research as it implies effective design of institutional computing styles and systems, administrative uses of computing in our educational setting.

Including study of Computers in Education will increase the teacher's ability to assume a role of leadership in providing direction to school systems in integrating computing into their curriculum. This additional computer background should allow the computing teacher to act as a resource person to assist in fostering development and implementation of computing throughout the school, even when the other teachers know nothing of computing.

3.0: Subject-specific Computing Competencies Needed by Teachers

In addition to the set of universal competencies needed by all school teachers, there are additional level- and subject-specific competencies which teachers should have. Any given teacher will require at least one of these, but no one of them will be universally appropriate for all teachers. The definitions of those competencies spring entirely from the vast and highly diverse body of experience with using computing in education over the last decade. Sources representing some of this work are listed in the bibliography. The competencies can be stated generally, irrespective of the teacher's eventual level of subject; the topics, though, will vary considerably, depending on both.

3.1: Competencies

In terms of these subject-specific competencies, the teacher should:

C3.1 be able to use and evaluate the general capabilities of the computer as a tool for pursuing various discipline- or level-specific educational tasks;

C3.2 be able to use and evaluate alternative hardware and software systems designed to function as tutors or teacher aids;

C3.3 be familiar with alternative hardware and software systems designed to perform school administration; and

C3.4 be familiar with information and quantitative techniques of study in the (teacher's) subject.

These competencies should be developed by the teacher preparation program, tailored to suit the trainee's intended teaching level and subject. We will not present an exhaustive list of topics corresponding to these subject-specific and level-specific competencies. Instead, we will present model topics for a few selected subjects and levels.

3.1.1: Topics of Study for Teachers of Early Childhood (Primary Grades 1–4)—TEC

TEC3.1 *Computerless Preparation for Computing:* Experience with a wide range of computerless but computing-related activities that children can participate in to enhance their readiness to understand and work with computers.

TEC3.2 *Games and Simulations:* Experience with a wide range of games and simulations that stimulate children to explore and better understand fundamental concepts and strategies of basic learning.

TEC3.3 *Tutorial Systems:* Experience with simple and complex tutorial systems focusing upon mathematics, spelling, reading, and other elementary topics, including bilingual variations of such systems.

TEC3.4 *Exploratory Programming Systems:* Experience with well developed exploratory systems where child-appropriate I/O subsystems such as robots are programmatically manipulated by the child in a discovery or problem-solving approach.

Less work has taken place in the area covered by TEC3.1 than one might expect. Despite the likely widespread availability of micro-processors in the immediate future, computerless computing activities can still be very useful. By contrast with heavily machine-dependent activities, they provide a more contemplative, less involved opportunity to examine some of the fundamental ideas connected with computing. They thus allow those using them to deepen their understanding *even if they have access to computers.* Typical examples may be found in some of Papert's work [11] and in Taylor [12].

Vast quantities of games and simulations are available for TEC3.2, but careful choices should be made in selecting them. Many are not well written, either from a programming point of view or from a child-user point of view, and none should be selected unless it is both. Some of the best work in this area at this age level came out of the People's Computer Company, under the initial stimulus of Albrecht [13].

With respect to TEC3.3, though much has been developed, not all of it is good. The experience of the teacher should certainly include at least one good system and some discussion of what lies behind it. The work of the CCC group under Suppes is certainly a worthy example in this category [14].

Finally, new exploratory systems relevant for TEC3.4 are appearing, but the pioneering work is still for illustration. In particular, the XEROX work which produced SMALLTALK [15] and the LOGO work, particularly as Seymour Papert has advertised and sustained it [16], is outstanding.

Microprocessors can be the primary machine type used, but not to the point the trainee is left ignorant of the advantages of larger shared systems.

3.1.2: Topics of Study for Teachers of Foreign Language—TFL

TFL3.1 *Games and Simulations:* Experience with a wide range of games and simulations designed to provide cultural background and informal language learning, using the culture as context and the language as the medium of communication in the game or simulation.

TFL3.2 *Tutorial Systems:* Experience with tutorial systems designed to enhance the learning of a foreign language through a carefully arranged body of interactive experiences driven by competency-based, computer-administered testing.

TFL3.3 *Foreign Language Text Editing:* Experience with a powerful text editor used to create and manipulate texts in a foreign language.

Under TFL3.1, simulations based on relevant activities and situations in the language-culture can provide insight into the langauge difficult to obtain in other ways. These, and many popular computer games, should also be used to provide a more informal language practice for learners. This practice can take two forms: (1) *translating,* and (2) *informally using* the language. Teachers should become familiar with the practice of translating all user text of appropriate games and simulations into the target language, thus preparing to have their students do such translation. Teachers should also have wide experience with playing games whose text is entirely in the target foreign language and which expect all player responses to be rendered in that language. Such playing in a foreign language can be a valuable informal enhancement. Experience with a wide range of such games and simulations may also suggest new, more appropriate ones which the teacher can create or have others, including students, create. Some attempt to create such new material (or new variations of old material) should be part of every foreign language teacher's training. Naturally, where audio is available, it should be appropriately used.

There are many examples of language drill and practice suitable for use under TFL3.2. Work such as that done by Suppes [17] at Stanford should certainly be familiar to language teachers, though alternatives certainly exist [18]. Work in this area should rely as heavily upon audio and graphics as possible, thus cutting down on the automatic tendency to always translate from the native language and to develop competence only in reading and writing the foreign language.

TFL3.3 should ensure that teachers become comfortable with using a suitable computer text editor to manipulate text in the target foreign language. With appropriate accent mark capabilities, such editors can encourage language learners to practice much more prose writing and thus enhance their overall command of the language.

3.3.3:   Topics of Study for Teachers of Physical Science—TPS

TPS3.1   *Exploratory Programming Systems:* Experience with well defined exploratory systems through structured, discipline-appropriate languages; systems must include graphic capabilities, systems must be programmably controllable by the student, and be oriented to discovery through problem-solving activities relevant to the physical sciences.

TPS3.2   *Tutorial Systems:* Experience with tutorial systems designed to enhance learning of the physical sciences through a carefully arranged body of interactive experiences driven by competency-based, computer-administered testing.

TPS3.3   *Games and Simulations:* Experience with stand-alone games and simulations designed to enhance understanding of specific physical phenomena or significant past experiments.

TPS3.4   *Classroom/Laboratory Management:* Experience with automated management of people learning, time and resources including automated inventorying, laboratory information/ reference systems; in general, uses of the computer to provide the science teacher with more time to work with individuals.

The possibilities under all three topics for physical science teachers have been extensively explored already by Bork [19] and others [20]. Their careful work and well documented analysis should be extended and incorporated in the training of physical science teachers. Such training should include experience with relevant examples which illustrate the three topics; it should also require each trainee to construct selected, similar small modules of computer-supported instruction as a normal part of teacher training.

SUMMARY

This paper has addressed the computing competencies needed by the precollege teachers. These competencies are listed in three groupings. These groupings are based on the involvement of the teacher in computer-related activities. The first set of competencies represents the basic computing skills needed by all teachers. These are essential if teachers are to assist society at large to become computer literate. The second set relates to teachers who want to specialize in teaching of computing and/or the utilization of computing background. The third set provides the proper background to allow the teacher to utilize computing in presenting subject-related material. Because of the variation of subject matter, implementation examples have been given for teachers of grades 1–4 (early childhood), for teachers of foreign languages, and for teachers of physical science. These examples are not meant to be all-inclusive, but to indicate the level of necessary background knowledge.

Before graduating from a teacher-training program, all teachers should be required to acquire the first set of competencies and *either* the second or third set. This requirement will prepare each teacher for the utilization of computing in the classroom. No attempt has been made to package the competencies into specific courses. It is felt that each environment will possibly require a different technique for the introduction of the material.

Another group of individuals that needs to be considered are the current in-service teachers. The above-described competencies are as important for them as for our future teachers. In-service courses must be developed to provide the indicated background for in-service teachers.

CONTRIBUTORS

Vivian Coun, University of Missouri-Tolla, Rolla, Mo.
Richard Dennis, University of Illinois, Urbana, Ill.
Dan Isaacson, University of Oregon, Eugene, Oreg.
David Moursund, University of Oregon, Eugene, Oreg.
John W. Hamblen, University of Missouri-Rolla, Rolla, Mo.
Jerome R. Kaczorowski, Bremen High School, Midlothian, Ill.
James Lockard, Buena Vista College, Storm Lake, Iowa.
Dick Ricketts, Multnomah County Education Service District, Portland, Oreg.
Stan Troitman, Wheelock College, Boston, Mass.

REFERENCES

1. Poirot, J., Powell, J., Hamblen, J. and Taylor, R. Computing competencies for school teachers—A preliminary projection for the teacher of computing. *National Educa-*

tional Computing Conference Proceedings, Iowa City, Iowa, 1979.

2. Taylor, R.P., Hamblen, J., Poirot, J. and Powell, J., Jr. Computing competencies for teachers—A preliminary projection for all but the teacher of computing. *National Educational Computing Conference Proceedings*, Iowa City, Iowa, 1979.

3. Curriculum Committee on Computer Science (C3S). *Curriculum '78:* Recommendations for the undergraduate program in computer science. (Preliminary Draft, dated Autumn 1978).

4. Bork, A. Learning to teach via teaching the computer to teach. *Journal of Computer-based Instruction, 2*, November 1975.

5. Suppes, P. Computer-assisted instruction at Stanford. *Man and Computer*, Karger, 1970.

6. Smith, S. and Sherwood, B. Educational uses of the PLATO computer system. *SCIENCE, 192*, April 1976.

7. Papert, S. Teaching children thinking, Logo Memo 2, MIT AI LAB, Cambridge, Mass., October 1971.

8. Dwyer, T. The art of education: Blueprint for a renaissance. *Creative Computing*, September/October 1976.

9. Mowshowitz, A. (editor). *Inside Information: Computers in Fiction*, Reading, Mass.: Addison-Wesley, 1978.

10. Taylor, R.P. (editor). *Tales of the Marvelous Machine: Thirty-Five Stories of Computing*. Morristown, N.J.: Creative Computing Press, 1980.

11. Papert, S. Teaching children to be mathematicians vs. teaching about mathematics. Logo Memo 4, MIT AI LAB, Cambridge, Mass., July 1971.

12. Taylor, R.P. Computerless computing for young children or what to do till the computer comes. *Proceedings of the 2nd World Conference on Computers in Education*. Amsterdam: North Holland, 1975.

13. PCC (collective authorship). *What to do after You Hit Return*. Menlo Park, Calif.: People's Computer Co., 1975.

14. Suppes, P. and Macken, E. Evaluation studies of CCC elementary school curriculums 1971–1975. Palo Alto, Calif.: Computer Curriculum Corp., 1976.

15. Kay, A. A personal computer for children of all ages. *Proceedings of ACM National Conference*. Boston, August 1972.

16. Papert, S. Personal computing and the impact on education. Edited transcription of a talk delivered at the Gerald P. Weeg Memorial Conference, as printed in the proceedings. *Computing in College and University: 1978 and Beyond*. University of Iowa, 1978.

17. Suppes, P., Smith, R. and Beard, M. University-level computer-assisted instruction at Stanford: 1975. *Instructional Science* 6 (1977). Amsterdam: Elsevier Scientific Publishing Co.

18. Tanable, Y. et al. CAI in language education. *Proceedings of 2nd World Conference on Computers in Education*. North Holland/Elsevier, 1976.

19. Bork. A. Preparing student-computer dialogs—Advice to teachers. PCDP. Irvine, Calif.: University of California, July 1976.

20. Dwyer, T.A. Some principles for the human use of computers in education. *International Journal of Man-Machine Studies 3*. July 1971.

OTHER REFERENCES

21. Atchison, W.F. Computer science preparation for secondary school teachers. *SIGCSE Bulletin, 5, 1*, 45–47 (1973).

22. Computers and the Learning Society report of hearings before USHR, October 1977. U.S. Government Printing Office, 1978.

23. Conference Board of the Mathematical Sciences Committee on Computer Education. *Recommendations Regarding Computers in High School Education*. Washington, D.C.: CBMS.

24. *Conference on Basic Mathematical Skills and Learning*. Euclid, Ohio: U.S. Department of Health, Education and Welfare, 1975.

25. Dennis, J.R. Undergraduate program to increase instructional computing in schools. *Proceedings of Ninth Conference on Computing in the Undergraduate Curriculum*. East Lansing, Mich.: 1977.

26. Dennis, J.R., Dillhung, C. and Muiznieks, J. Computer activities in secondary schools in Illinois. *Illinois Series on Educational Applications of Computers*, No. 24. University of Illinois, 1977.

27. Esterson, D.M. Problems of implementation: Courses for pre- and in-service education. *Information and Mathematics in Secondary Schools*. North Holland Publishing Co., 1978.

28. IFIP Technical Committee for Education, Working Group on Secondary School Education. Computer education for teachers in secondary schools: Aims and objectives in teacher training. *AFIPS*. Montvale, N.J.: 1972.

29. Leuhrmann, A. Reading, writing, arithmetic, and computing. *Improving Instructional Productivity in Higher Education*. Educational Technology Publications, 1975.

30. Molnar, S. Computer literacy: The next great crisis in American education. *Oregon Computing Teacher, 6, 1*, September 1978.

31. Moursund, D. Report of the ACM teacher certification subcommittee. *SIGCSE Bulletin, 9, 4*, December 1977, 8–18.

32. Poirot, J.L. A course description for teacher education in computer science. *SIGCSE Bulletin, 8*, February 1976, 39–48.

33. Poirot, J.L. and Groves, D.N. *Beginning Computer Science*. Manchaca, Tex.: Sterling Swift Publishing, 1978.

34. Poirot, J.L. and Groves, D.N. *Computer Science for the Teacher*. Manchaca, Tex.: Sterling Swift Publishing, 1976.

35. Conference Board of Mathematical Sciences. *Recommendations Regarding Computers in High School Education*. Washington, D.C.: April 1972.

36. Taylor, R.P. Graduate remedial training in computing for educators. *SIGCSE Training Symposium Proceedings*. Dayton: February 1979.

37. Taylor, R.P. (editor). *The Computer in The School: Tutor, Tool, Tutee*. New York: Teacher's College Press, 1980.

38. National Science Foundation, Science Education Directorate. *Technology in Science Education: The Next Ten Years*. Washinton, D.C.: July, 1979.

39. *Topics in Instructional Computing*. (A special publication of SIGCUE), 1975.

Training Preservice Teachers to Teach with Computers

J. Richard Dennis

The purpose of this paper is to present a position regarding training in instructional applications of computers (IAC). But from a more general point of

From "Training Preservice Teachers to Teach with Computers," by J. Richard Dennis. In *AEDS Journal*, Volume 11, Number 2, Winter, 1978. Reprinted by permission.

view, the discussion here can be viewed as an instance of a much larger problem: that of professional skill specialties derived at the preservice training level. Historically, preservice teacher education programs have been decidedly consistent on at least two characteristics:

1. The academic concentrations (majors and minors) offered the preservice teacher largely have been focussed on imparting knowledge that the preservice person eventually would teach to someone else.
2. Training and derived expertise at the preservice level with matters related to the act of instruction itself, and the styles for doing same, overwhelmingly has been biased toward the classical lecture delivery mode.

For a long time, teacher educators have argued that preservice teachers should accrue minor concentrations in alternate subject fields. State teacher certification boards recognize such concentrations and employing school administrators frequently make employee selections on the basis of the potential for alternate assignment of a prospective employee. We do not disagree with this practice as *one* alternative, but are arguing that, as the only alternative, this practice eliminates opportunities for structured, supervised development of prospective personnel in a variety of equally important professional techniques and skills. At the inservice training level, it is very difficult (if not impossible in most cases) to deliver training requiring sustained, intensive concentration of both the trainer and the trainee. Only at the preservice level are such programs most easily managed if one is attempting to address a relatively diverse selection of teachers.

So, we are arguing for more diversity in the variety of minor concentrations available at the preservice level. We would claim that, given such choices, professional skill specialty is just as attractive and potentially valuable to the schools as those with second subject areas.

A PROFESSIONAL MINOR IN INSTRUCTIONAL COMPUTING

The specific professional skill specialty we wish to present here is that of applying computers to the instructional task. That this is a viable area for training is witnessed by several recent studies. Bukoski and Korotkin, in a study conducted by the American Institutes for Research, found that approximately 28 percent of the secondary schools in the nation were active in instructional use of computers. This finding is supported on more regional levels as well. For example, Dennis, Dillhunt, and Muiznieks found 35 percent of the secondary schools in Illinois active in instructional computing. Both studies found growth rates for such activity (in terms of numbers of new schools reporting activity) averaging around 4 percent per year over the past 5–10 years.

There are two important characteristics of instructional use of computers reported by both of these studies that support the proposal being discussed here. First, in schools reporting instructional computing activity, the majority of the activity centered around teaching computer programming. Second, again a majority of the active schools reported very low portions of their total teaching core involved in such matters. This suggests that perhaps instructional computing resources are underutilized in many schools, and that the portion of the student body receiving benefits from such technology is rather small. Even though costs for computing resources appear to be declining, such costs for a typical secondary school are add-on costs. No teachers are (or should be) replaced by introduction of computers into the instructional process. But when budgets become tight, as is the case in many schools of late, those add-on costs most easily justified and most likely to survive scrutiny are those clearly benefiting the larger portions of the school community.

From still another point of view, using computers in the instructional process, as those teachers actually doing so will attest, is an activity that requires concentrated energy in order to become proficient. Only a few very eager teachers have been able to muster such concentrations of energy and/or time on the job (inservice). An alternate route to impacting on schools is through functional expertise derived by a diverse segment of the potential teaching corps at the preservice career stage.

Following is a description of a program at the University of Illinois, Urbana, which addresses the growing role for teaching personnel with credentials in a conventional subject area as well as functional competence in using computers in the teaching of *that* subject.

The general characteristics of this program are as follows:

1. An opportunity to acquire the technical background in computer programming adequate for job demands of instructional computing.
2. An intensive throughout-the-school view of instructional computing, coupled with a discipline-specific instructional computing methods experience.
3. Hardware and software background adequate for conditions likely to be found in schools today, but also adequate for dealing with the changes likely to be experienced over a period of 5–10 years.

4. A concentration on the relevant findings from research areas such as learning, teaching, curriculum development, and evaluation. Too often, research on the teaching/learning processes is discounted as having virtually no value to practitioners. The position of this program is that some research in education is pertinent to effect design/delivery of computer-based instruction.
5. An opportunity to demonstrate proficiency in instructional computing through a task-centered practicum. This would be comparable to a microteaching experience so often recommended as a precursor to practice-teaching in a discipline, but would concentrate on the tasks of teaching with computers.
6. A controlled practice teaching experience in a setting where computers are available for use in the instruction of the candidates' teaching major.

From a more detailed point of view, the basic program consists of five parts extending for at least four semesters. Following are detailed descriptions of the parts.

I. Background in Computer Science
   Normally, this consists of a beginning and an advanced undergraduate programming course. Generally, the goal of this part of the program is to develop reasonable skill as a computer programmer. In addition, there is a three-hour elective in computer science selected from among advanced systems programming, hardware, numerical analysis, logic design, or an applications course relevant both to educational computing and to the teaching major.

II. Instructional Computing—The Total School View
   A. The literature and existing resources of instructional computing.
   B. Survey and analysis of the variety of educational uses of computers and general characteristics of each computer-managed instruction, drill and practice, tutorial, simulations, instructional games, problem solving, evaluation and test-item banking, record keeping and processing.
   C. Studies of various hardware characteristics, capabilities, and the effects on school application. Consideration of specific instructional activities as they would be implemented by alternate hardware systems, and the accompanying changes in teacher behavior and responsibilities. The systems considered include programmable calculators, micro-processors, and large-scale network systems. Included is a thorough consideration of both batch and interactive instructional applications.
   D. Reviews of relevant research on learning, teaching, curriculum, and evaluation.
   E. Social and legal implications of computers in schools and society, privacy, computer security, computers in the home.
   F. Models of system management and operation in schools; implications for personnel access and management.
   G. Strategies and issues in hardware/software procurement and maintenance.
   H. Authoring languages for IAC—(e.g., TUTOR, BASIC, IDF, PILOT, COURSEWRITER, PLANIT, CAISP, TEACH-SCHOLAR). Characteristics and techniques of authoring in such languages.

III. Instructional Computing—The Content-Specific View.
   (An array of one-semester courses sectioned to be specific to the teaching major of the student.)
   A. Critical survey and analysis of instructional computing within the content area of the teaching major.
   B. Integrating instructional systems with classroom instruction; role analysis and designation within classroom management models peculiar to the discipline.
   C. Design and evaluation of courseware in the teaching major.
   D. Automating evaluation and record keeping in the discipline.
   E. Projects and materials design.

IV. Task-Centered Practicum in Instructional Computing
   An opportunity for repetition of fundamental practice skills. Teacher competencies are defined in the following categories:
   A. Preparation and use of controlled, interactive, computer-based instruction.
   B. Preparation and use of computer-managed instruction.
   C. Design, implementation, and utilization of simulations.
   D. Facilitating computer problem solving.
   E. Prescribing student evaluation and record keeping.
   F. Resource allocation and management.

V. Practice Teaching
   Students practice-teach in schools having instructional computers available. Of course, participants all practice-teach in their subject major.

The competencies which this program strives to establish have been derived from the experiences of a large number of instructional computer users identified for this purpose. An intensive survey was conducted, following the Delphi procedure, to achieve a unanimity on the desirable knowledges and skills in the area of instructional computing. Table 1 presents those abilities rated as somewhat

---

TABLE 1 Important knowledge or skills for instructional computing

1. Familiarity with computerized teaching materials (i.e., instructional programs) in a variety of fields.
2. Ability to integrate computerized teaching materials into a course.
3. General knowledge of the functioning of CMI (computer-managed-instruction) systems.
4. Understanding of effective design of drill and practice materials.
5. Ability to apply computerized drill and practice in a variety of teaching situations.
6. Familiarity with computer simulations and models.
7. Experience in preliminary design and construction of a simulation.
8. Knowledge of the uses of simulations as teaching tools.
9. Ability to evaluate the effectiveness of a course that uses computerized teaching materials.
10. Ability to determine the computer needs of a school.
11. Ability to draft specifications (request for proposals) which set down the needs and desires of the school and invite proposals/bids from potential suppliers.
12. Ability to be highly critical of suppliers' proposals and their machines.
13. Ability to assemble data about proposed equipment to facilitate decision-making (costs, performance data, hardware characteristics, software support, etc.).
14. Familiarity with instructional games.
15. Knowledge of how to use instructional games appropriately and effectively in teaching.
16. Physical familiarity with computer equipment, i.e., everday operation and use of a range of different machines.
17. Knowledge of trouble-shooting procedures and means of access to professional help, i.e., knowing how to determine if a piece of equipment is ailing, and if it is, knowing whom to call to fix it.
18. Knowledge of sources for computer materials.
19. Knowledge of how to improve less than adequate instructional computer programs.
20. Ability to evaluate the effectiveness of instructional computer programs.
21. Ability to instruct others in the social role and impact of computers in society.
22. Knowledge of alternative uses of computers in schools, e.g., as class-record-keepers, term-paper-editors, etc.
23. Awareness of the value of involving students in the development of computerized instructional materials.
24. Knowledge of processes of involving students in instructional materials development.

---

or very important to proficient instructional computing by a majority of these users.

SUMMARY

This paper describes an instructional model for training preservice teachers to teach with computers. The preservice career level is seen as the appropriate time for such training because intense, long-duration experiences are required to develop functional competence with the instructional medium. Opportunities are rare for undergraduates to develop expertise with alternative instructional styles or media. But such expertise is much more difficult to develop inservice because of increased demands on the energies and attention of the personnel.

Stages of Development in Introducing Computing to Teachers

J. Richard Dennis

Although studies both nationally and regionally have shown steady growth of instructional use of computers since the 1960s (Bukoski and Korotkin, 1976; Dennis, Dillhunt, and Muiznieks, 1977), their studies also show that such activity involves a very small portion of the teachers in any school. Also, there is ample evidence of the spreading influence of computing to the spectrum of subjects found in a typical secondary school. One of the major reasons cited for such narrow impact of instructional computing is the lack of teachers prepared for using computers.

The thoughts presented here are concerned with teaching *with* computers, although the comments also apply to those who would teach *about* computers.

The training models discussed have been developed and implemented in teacher education programs of the Department of Secondary Education, University of Illinois, Urbana. At this writing the models are being considered for implementation in three other teacher education institutions.

There are two conventional avenues of learning for teachers: preservice and inservice. Training at each of these career levels has distinct characteristics. With preservice, an individual can enter into relatively intensive and lengthy learning experiences. Learning skills are at their sharpest and, due to minimal other distractions in the learner's life, attentions usually are focused intently. But preservice teachers have little experience on which to act or to judge their learning. Consequently, training must be structured to reflect

From "Stages of Development in Introducing Computing to Teachers," by J. Richard Dennis. In *Proceedings of NECC,* June, 1979, by the National Educational Computing Conference. Reprinted by permission.

the view of the practitioner. At the same time, preservice personnel are being prepared for the future. Particularly when training is in an area involving rapidly advancing technique or technology, prospective teachers require a foundation from which to act.

The inservice career differs considerably. Practicing teachers seldom enjoy long periods in which to intensively pursue a new topic. Personal learning skills are not as sharp, and attentions are fragmented. During the course of a school day a secondary teacher must attempt to deal productively and personally with 125–150 different people. During this time they must shift gears cognitively several times on only a few moments notice between class periods. Where the previous 50 minutes may have been spent in diagnostic and remedial teaching of basic arithmetic skills, the teacher may have to shift next to a lesson in precalculus for very talented students.

Clearly, inservice teachers have their attention on practice, and only where time will permit on the improvement of same. But the latter is a luxury. New plans for altering or improving instruction must be capsulated in such a way that concepts may be grasped and skills acquired from relatively short and infrequent investments of time. The only exceptions to this are summer or sabbatical training. Career teachers, however, frequently have other demands on their summers and the tightening of school budgets recently experienced (and expected) has made a sabbatical leave a rarity in public schooling.

A MODEL FOR INSERVICE TRAINING IN AIC

For the practicing teacher, training for classroom use of computers requires special consideration of the job context and the constraints on personal time and energy already discussed. With such constraints in mind we shall describe three stages of inservice training designed to bring a practicing teacher to a level of competence in teaching with computers. These stages are: (1) Awareness Stage (2) Implementing Stage (3) Maintenance of Growth Stage. Each of these stages has unique information needs and specific ability goals to be achieved.

At the *Awareness* stage, two types of teachers are encountered. First, there are teachers who teach in schools already having instructional computing resources, but who are not personally involved. The second type teacher encountered is the one from a school not yet having instructional computers. Both of these teachers are very much interested in the questions: What could *I* do with an instructional computer? For the teacher from an unequipped school, there is an almost equally important question to address at the awareness stage: How would my school get an instructional computer if desired?

For each of these types specific ideas are needed on how a computer might support or facilitate instruction in their subject. But one must keep in mind that seldom do these teachers have much background with computers or even the working vocabulary. So, relevant information must be framed in the context of day-to-day instruction with very little technical reference to the computer. Generally, such an information program is the subject of a session lasting a few hours. An essential attribute of such a program is the opportunity to view and to experience firsthand a variety of instructional computing activities. Such examples should be chosen from materials that have had actual classroom use, and wherever possible should include some description or other information on how the computer activity is integrated with (and benefits) regular instruction. Also at this stage, teachers receive their first introduction to the characteristics of the various instructional computer styles that influence their quality, effectiveness, or motivating power.

For the teacher not currently in a computer-equipped situation, an awareness program also should include a discussion of methods others have used successfully to bring computers into a school. For this teacher it is almost mandatory that a responsible administrator be a co-participant in the awareness activities. Both the teacher and the administrator should be convinced of the need to define as explicitly as possible the uses they will make of a computer *before* attempting to purchase major amounts of equipment. In the absence of such careful procedure, the risks are great of acquiring equipment in some way incompatible with or inadequate for uses likely to emerge later.

Inservice teachers at the *Implementing* stage of instructional computing require two kinds of training, both of which imply rather intensive commitments for a period of time. One of these is a detailed look at instructional computing methods and their characteristics. Integrated with this training should be a growing expertise with instructional programming. The inservice teacher is much more action oriented than the preservice counterpart. In most cases, this precludes a succession of experiences from programming instruction to intensive looks at computerized instruction. For the inservice person, we recommend the integration and simultaneous growth of these abilities so that classroom implementation (and experiences) may begin very early in the training period.

For gaining a background in computing, one productive technique is to progress from *reproducing* instructional programs created elsewhere to *creating* original instances oneself. In this way the teacher can learn rudiments of a programming language (commands, formats, etc.) while quickly achieving an activity usable in the classroom. This postpones until later the more difficult tasks of developing program algorithms. In the meantime, valuable classroom experiences with computers can be derived in the instructional environment. These piloting experiences help to rapidly build perceptions of those applications of a computer likely to be of maximum personal use.

The teacher has a particularly difficult problem in providing appropriate resources during this implementing stage. This is most easily solved in cases where the teacher training can be exported to the audience's school *and* computing equipment is already there for use. Where either of these conditions is not present, the teacher must take steps to ensure that efforts expended on pilot implementations can be transferred easily to the eventual equipment and software configuration installed at the schooling site.

Another often overlooked demand is that resources be readily available to the trainee. All facilities must be made as easy to access and use as possible. Example programs must be ready and must work. Documentation must be available and must be accurate. In part, such demands serve as a model to the trainees. More important, however, is the need to eliminate or avoid as many levels of frustration for the trainees as possible. We already have said that for the practicing teacher, time is at a premium. Any nonproductive use of this resource has significant deterring effects on the audience.

A successful curriculum map for inservice training at the implementation stage is shown in Figure 1. Note that the plan reflects the central theme of a subject characteristic of the orientation of an experienced teacher. Integrated with this focus are the detailed studies of the various instructional computing styles as they are deemed appropriate to the particular teacher and subject. Note also that this plan includes provision for informational resources to those implementing teachers also involved in initial computer resource procurement. These teachers will require a wide variety of information about hardware, software, and applications. They usually will need extensive consultation and assistance in relating desired computing tasks to equipment needs.

Many attempts to install new programs or activities into secondary school practice have failed during the implementing stage. During the 1950s and 1960s many attempts at installing new curricula or new instructional models in the United States were made. Many people were trained to use the various new curricula. They went away from training apparently highly motivated to proceed. But a short time later it was not uncommon to find a lapse to more

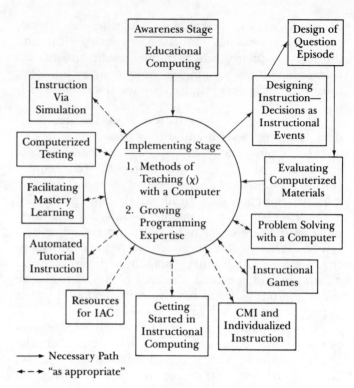

FIGURE 1. Curriculum map for IAC training (inservice)

conventional curricula or instructional models. Sustaining the efforts was another matter indeed.

The same phenomenon is observable in some instances of instructional computing installation. Resources are made available, teachers receive initial training, perhaps to the extent of having an initial set of computer activities prepared, but some time later the teachers have not progressed into expanding their repertoire. And not infrequently, initial efforts have ceased altogether.

Sustaining implementation efforts in education is not a new problem. Some would argue that this is neither the responsibility nor the concern of the trainer. This author cannot accept such a view. Instead, the implementing stage must be structured to include a sustained new information flow, readily available consultation on problems surrounding implementation, and a great deal of hand-holding. Periodic debriefings on past experiences are in order. Consultations of an advisory or confirming nature are needed to reinforce correct application of past training.

Practicing teachers probably should not attempt major implementations in isolation. Several teachers attempting similar implementations can provide each other with a level of support and consultation difficult to achieve from outside the school. Added to this are needed periodic third-party debriefing, confirmation, and future efforts sessions to sustain momentum, to confirm perceptions, and to reconcile observed weaknesses in recent efforts.

To date, only a few teachers at the pre-college level have progressed to what we are calling the *Maintenance of Growth* stage of instructional computing expertise. It is at this stage that the teacher ceases somewhat incidental computer instruction activities or experiments and, instead, establishes a major role for the computer in the classroom environment. That role may range widely depending upon the teaching strengths or interests of the teacher, the nature of the subject, the teacher's view of the objectives of the subject, etc. One teacher oriented toward individualized instruction may set about the creation and implementation of an elaborate instructional management facility. Another teacher, wishing to emphasize a minimal level of performance in processes or procedures of the subject, may design and implement several simulations. A department, wishing to improve and expedite its testing program, may set about to create a computerized test-item banking/test construction system. A group of foreign language teachers, wishing to inject another dimension of culture education into their program, may elect to construct simulations of trips to foreign lands—each decision in such a simulation providing information about economic, religious, social, or political characteristics of the country and the implications of same for the foreign traveler. The possibilities for intensive or group projects at this stage are boundless.

The role of the trainer changes radically at this stage. Where before, the trainer had an initiating responsibility, now the educator need only assume an on-call posture. The computer-using teacher has come of age. The on-call consultations will serve largely to prevent reinvention of wheels. These wheels normally take the form of computer software systems available elsewhere and tailored to achieving certain instructional tasks. The trainer is in a better position to survey available materials. The teacher still may solicit evaluative opinions, but the motivation for such solicitations clearly is more courtesy or flattery than uncertainty.

From this point on, the computer-using teacher is self-perpetuating. The trainer has achieved a goal.

Implementing the inservice model

Institutions normally involved in teacher education regularly have engaged in dissemination of knowledge about new programs or instructional models. For such institutions to engage in continuing education programs such as that described above requires major changes in staffing patterns and acceptable faculty activities. Such changes are not impossible. But because of classical rank and pay evaluation procedures, the role, for example, of a facilitating consultant and evaluator is a difficult one to reconcile to higher education administrations.

One way to bootleg such input to small numbers of schools is to organize preservice teacher education and educational research efforts in the same schools where instructional computer implementation is taking place. The research component of such a trilogy provides a justification for major levels of contact and effort by the trainer. Of course the scale of such efforts is limited.

That such services are valuable to schools or teachers attempting major implementations partly is attested to by the growth and popularity of teacher centers over the past several years. One of the major functions such centers provide is an opportunity for interaction among teachers either looking for ideas or looking for consultation on personal implementation efforts. Without sustaining input during the awareness and implementation stages of teacher change, new ideas for schooling rapidly fade and die in their infancy.

BIBLIOGRAPHY

Bukoski, William and Korotkin, Arthur. "Computing Activities in Secondary Education," Educational Technology, Vol. XVI, No. 1, January, 1976, (pp. 9–21).

Dennis, J. Richard, Dillhunt, Clifford and Muiznieks, Viktor J., "Computer Activities in Illinois Schools," The Illinois Series on Educational Application of Computers, Department of Secondary Education, University of Illinois, Urbana, Illinois, Number 24, June, 1977.

REFERENCES

Austing, R.H., Barnes, B.H., Bonnette, D.T., Engel, C.L., and Stokes, G., Editors. Curriculum '78: Recommendations for the Undergraduate Program in Computer Science—A Report of the ACM Curriculum Committee on Computer Science. CACM, 22, 3, 1979.

Baker, J. Computers in the Curriculum. Phi Delta Kappa Fastback No. 82. Bloomington, Indiana: Phi Delta Kappa, 1976.

Dennis, J.R., et al. Computer Activities in Illinois Secondary Schools. Urbana, Illinois: Department of Secondary Education, University of Illinois, June, 1977.

Frederick, T. Computer Science Education For Students Training To Be Teachers. In S.D. Milner (ed.), Topics in Instructional Computing (Volume I): Teacher Education. New York: ACM, 1975.

Hargan, C. and Hunter, B. Instructional Computing: Ten Case Studies. Alexandria, Virginia: Human Resources Research Organization, 1978.

International Federation for Information Processing Technical Committee on Education (TC-3). Computer Education for Teachers in Secondary Schools: Aims and Objectives in Teacher Training. IFIP, 1972.

Milner, S. (ed.) Topics in Instructional Computing (Volume I); Teacher Education. New York: Association for Computing Machinery, 1975.

Minnesota Educational Computing Consortium. Computer Literacy Study—an Update. St. Paul, MN: MECC, June 2, 1978.

Minsky, M. Form and Content in Computer Science. *JACM*, 17, 2, 1970.

Rothman, S. and Mosmann, C. *Computers and Society*. (2nd. ed.). Chicago: SRA, 1976.

Sanders, D. *Computers in Society*. (2nd. ed.). New York: McGraw-Hill, 1977.

Understanding How to Use Machines to Work Smarter in an Information Society

Andrew R. Molnar

TECHNOLOGICAL INNOVATION AND PRODUCTIVITY

A Government Accounting Office study concludes that all industrial nations are now using advanced computer technology to improve their manufacturing productivity. While the United States uses more advanced technology than any other country in the world, it is concentrated in a few high technology industries. Elmer Staats, the Comptroller General of the United States, concludes that the greatest hope for increasing the rate of productivity growth lies in advances in technological innovations. He says that a national policy of full employment requires technological innovation on a scale that has not been achieved for over a decade.[1]

It will not be easy to improve the rate of productivity. Many factors are working against increases. First, the growth of our work force is slowing down and this will lead to labor shortages in the 1980's. Second, fewer workers will be supporting an increased number of retired people. In 1950 our country had a ratio of 7.5 workers to one retiree. Today, the ratio is 5.4 to 1 and by the year 2000, it will be 3.1 to 1. Already in the auto industry the ratio is 3 to 1 and is expected to be 2 to 1 by 1990.[2] Finally, the increased use of technology will require a highly skilled work force. Therefore, we are likely to see a shortage of skilled workers and high unemployment among the unskilled and those whose jobs will be made obsolete by innovation.

From "Understanding How to Use Machines to Work Smarter in an Information Society," by Andrew R. Molnar. In *T.H.E. Journal*, Volume 7, Number 1, January, 1980. Reprinted by permission.

MICROELECTRONICS—COMMUNICATIONS AND PRODUCTIVITY

There are many positive factors working to increase productivity.

Agriculture. Small computers are used to assist cattle breeders in working out optimum feed schedules so that cattle will arrive at market at maximum weight. Farmers also use microcomputers for pest management. *Computer models* are used to evaluate the rate of spread of insect populations and to prescribe when and how much insecticides to use to minimize ecological damage and costs.[3]

Industry. New, *computer-aided management* tools permit planners to compare manufacturing costs for dozens of products in numerous countries over a several year period and to simulate the consequences of various corporate actions. One computer model is based upon 20,000 individual forecasts of cost variables such as wages, materials, productivity, transportation, and exchange rates, all of which are updated periodically.

The use of *computer-aided design* has been found, on the average, to produce a gain in productivity by a factor of six. One study concludes that any organization with over 25 draftsmen can justify the use of computer-aided design and drafting.[4] Engineers use computer graphics to simulate the structural characteristics of a car and simulate the assembly of components and road tests before it is built. The Cadillac Seville was designed in record time in this manner.[5]

Business. Microelectronics is changing the business office. It is estimated that while the average factory worker is capitalized with $25,000 per worker, the average clerk or secretary works with only $500 to $1,000 of equipment and is not very productive.[6] While costs of the office have doubled over the last decade, productivity has remained about the same. Today, microprocessors are now being used for typing, editing, accounting, filing and billing. It is predicted that microelectronics will cause an organization revolution in the office of the future much like the assembly line did for the factory worker.[7]

Information systems. *Prestel* is a British computer-based information system that uses an ordinary television set as a display and has revolutionary potential as an *electronic publishing system*. The central computer is dialed through your telephone and the information is displayed on your television screen. You can call up any of 25,000 pages of information on such topics as financial data and consumer reports and after viewing have it automatically charged to your phone bill. Information is provided by 100 information providers such as the stock exchange, Reuters, and others. This online information library offers interesting opportunities for optimizing decisions and for providing the general public with access to information that has not been widely available.[8]

Print media. It has been estimated that the average reader of a newspaper does not read 90% of what is contained in it. It is also estimated newspapers print only about a tenth of the information available to them. One newspaper found that computerized subscription lists make it feasible to collect and store on-line reader interest files and to tailor and print supplements economically for as few as 1,000 readers. Anthony Smith, a British television producer, says that tailoring information to individual needs involves a revolution in social attitudes as much as technology in that consumers and not editors decide what information will be seen.[9]

Computerized printing allows for timely and tailored publications. Encyclopedias can be immediately updated and printed without waiting for new editions. If you wish a textbook for your classroom, you can order a book from a publisher and specify any chapter you may wish to have included from a long list of available works. If you want a personalized book for your child, you can send the publisher the child's name and receive an adventure story in which the child is the main character. Personalized printing offers interesting possibilities for instruction and motivation.

MICROCOMPUTERS AND EDUCATION

In a recent report, *Technology in Science Education: the Next Ten Years*, J.C.R. Licklider of MIT says the world is rapidly moving into the "information age" and information technology is flourishing everywhere but in the field of education. He concludes that education is not only missing an opportunity, it is failing to discharge a responsibility.[10]

In the past, computer use has been limited by expensive time-shared equipment systems. The economics of this situation has now shifted in favor of microcomputer systems. One publishing company advertises a math series for grades 1–6 for 10 cents per student hour.[11] Dallas Independent School District plans to deliver bilingual instruction for 50 cents per student hour.[12]

Dr. Karl Zinn of the University of Michigan says that it is not safe to extrapolate from the experiences with equipment which led users to consider computer efficiency as more important than learning convenience. He says most research on CAI systems has been obsoleted by a revolution in microelectronics and new research will have to be done in a context which is different in qualitative and quantitative ways.[13] Innovative uses of microcomputers are beginning to occur in all sectors of education.

Minnesota Educational Computing Consortium (MECC)

In 1979–80, MECC will transition from an exclusive time-sharing system linking 200 institutions to a combination of time-sharing and microcomputers. MECC has purchased 700 Apple II microcomputers; 555 for elementary and secondary schools and 145 for higher education. Kenneth Brumbaugh, manager of user services, says the Apple II has several advantages over time share. First, you don't have to rely on telephone lines and this reduces long-distance charges. He says it gives you a full-time servant, rather than a part-time assistant with many masters. Second, a microcomputer can do things a large system can't. It permits you to teach music and music composition. You can generate a music scale on the CRT and then hear the notes you write. It has voice input and output and color graphics and animation. Third, programs already in the central system can be easily down-loaded into the microcomputer.[14]

MECC will use the system to teach computer programming and computer applications. They anticipate the greatest growth will be in the use of applications especially in elementary schools and special education. Micros will be used to teach about computers and will be used in colleges to interface laboratory devices and experiments. Programs are available in science, business law, math, music, and reading, as well as for scheduling, cataloging, records, and testing.[15]

The State University of New York at Stony Brook

SUNY at Stony Brook has established a National Coordinating Center for Curriculum Development (NC3D) which has as its purpose to increase the number of minority high school students in engineering. They have placed Commadore PETs in three minority high schools to teach programming, and to motivate students through computer conferences. Students are permitted to sign out a microcomputer overnight and microcomputers are available in a youth center on weekends. The teachers have developed programs in math, science, and language art. They also use the Huntington II simulations in science and social science.[16]

University of Wisconsin—AUTOCOM

Dr. Gregg Vanderheiden of the University of Wisconsin has developed a device called Autocom for severely handicapped individuals. It is a portable personal aid which utilizes a microprocessor that fits in the person's lap and allows a cerebral palsied user with little motor control to generate and print messages. The device facilitates and accelerates communication and written work. It can also be used as an input/output device for computers and opens up CAI for the handicapped.[17]

Massachusetts Institute of Technology—LOGO

Dr. Seymour Papert of MIT has been working with children in the elementary grades using microcomputers to teach computing skills and the acquisition of knowledge in mathematics and science. He concludes that (1) a student in the lower quarter of an average third grade ought to be able to do something he feels to be interesting with the language within ten minutes of introduction and should be able to move from there and be able to conceive, write and debug his own programs; (2) teachers without previous knowledge of programming should be able to learn after a half year of in-service training to write programs which will change the interface between the user and the system.[18]

Papert says the literacy problem cannot be solved by teaching only a programming language. Each lesson should be concerned with some subject domain. For example, one unit in the LOGO project is about the behavior of mealworms. The students devise and conduct experiments centered around such questions as "Can worms see?" and "How do they find food?" This is not a programmed simulation. The students design their own models and decide which features to include and practice formulating their own hypotheses and observations in the mathematical language of computation. They learn computing, problem-solving and subject matter.[19]

This year the LOGO Project will be implemented in the Lamplighter school in Dallas, Texas. Third grade students will have free, unlimited access to microcomputers both during school hours and at home.

Intelligent videodisc

The National Science Foundation (NSF) is supporting proof-of-concept projects to determine the feasibility of combining a low-cost videodisc and a microcomputer into a single system that has the power and logic of the computer and the visual and audio features of television.[20] Videodisc is capable of presenting a half-hour television program or providing random access to 54,000 frames (enough space to store the Encyclopedia Britannica) or 8.6×10^{10} bits of digital information.

A videodisc player is now available for $695 and the discs sell for between $5.95 and $15.95. While microcomputers vary widely in price, it seems likely that in five years an intelligent videodisc system might cost about $1,200. Dr. Victor Bunderson of WICAT in Ogden, Utah is developing a prototype course in biology which involves tutorials, simulations, practice items and a reference retrieval index. Dr. Robert Kadesch and Dr. Richard Brandt of the University of Utah are developing courses in electronics and physics.

Curriculum development

Of course, today, the most serious problem is the need for high-quality courseware. A distributor of microcomputer courseware warns that 95% of all the programs carried probably should never have been offered for sale and that buyers should be careful and selective.[21] In the interim, some materials exist and others are becoming developed. CONDUIT, a non-profit, university consortium concerned with the dissemination of computer-based education programs is now disseminating microcomputer materials.[22] The Northwest Regional Educational Laboratory is establishing a national clearinghouse for K-12 microcomputer-based, instructional material.[23] In addition, the National Science Foundation and the National Institute of Education are initiating a new program to begin in 1980 for development and research in mathematics education with microcomputers and information technology. Other NSF programs are supporting research and development on the use of microcomputers in schools, universities, museums, laboratories and homes.

COMPUTER LITERACY

A number of foreign governments are investing large sums in research and development for computer-based industries. More significantly they have placed a high priority on the development of computer-based skills in their educational systems.[24]

In October of this year, French President Valeri-Giscard d'Estaing set aside a special week for computers in society and in speeches stressed the importance of the computer industry to the country's economy. The government wanted this activity to act as a catalyst to spark a debate among French citizens on the place of information technology within society.[25] The French also plan to install

10,000 microcomputers in high schools throughout the country over the next ten years as part of a national plan to make a computer literate society.[26]

In a response to an initiative by their Prime Minister, the British Science Research Council has established a major program of academic research to help the United Kingdom maximize the benefits from microprocessors and electronic technology. The plan calls for the support of a program of five year projects to expand existing commitments in computer-assisted instruction with a goal for creating 1,000 to 2,000 work stations using microcomputers. Fifty researchships per year will be offered to attract doctorate and masters students to the field. A national centre will be established for research on increased uses of microprocessors in measurement and instrumentation as well as research to anticipate the next generation of silicon chip design and automation.[27]

American educators are increasingly recognizing the importance of computing to education. A recent survey of business schools shows that an increasing number are requiring students to have a familiarity with computers and data processing and many are making computer courses an integral part of the curriculum.[28] Harvard University now includes a requirement that all students have at least an elementary acquaintance with the use of computers and freshmen are required to demonstrate their ability to handle computer-related skills.[29]

Professional associations are helping to define computer needs in education. In the area of computer science, the Association for Computing Machinery (ACM) has up-dated their "Curriculum '68" recommendations for undergraduate computer science programs and has recommended core curriculum and courses for undergraduate, community college and secondary school programs.[30,31] The Institute of Electrical and Electronic Engineers (IEEE) has also developed model curriculum for computer science and engineering.[32] In addition, the ACM is completing a study of computers in society and computer literacy and will soon publish a recommended curriculum for computer literacy. The ACM maintains an on-line, annotated bibliography of several thousand books and articles in this area. ACM committees have also published recommendations for computing competencies for school teachers who are and are not teachers of computer science.[33]

State-wide educational agencies have also taken an interest in computer literacy. The Minnesota Educational Computing Consortium has developed and validated the *Minnesota Computer Literacy and Awareness Assessment Test* of computer knowledge. The test is designed to measure knowledge attitudes and skills of computer literacy.[34] In April of 1979 the test was administered to a state-wide sample in Minnesota.

Researchers are also attempting to clarify the important dimensions of computer literacy. The Human Resources Research Organization (HumRRO) has analyzed twenty-four college and university programs designed to increase the level of computer literacy among students and faculty. They define computer literacy as what a person needs to know and do with computers in order to function competently in our society. They found that programs stress (1) skill in writing algorithms and computer programs, (2) knowledge of computer applications in one's field, and (3) understanding of computers and their impact on society. They also found that exemplary programs usually had strong administrative support from academic leaders, provided students with ready access to suitable facilities and integrated computer-based learning into regular courses.[35]

As part of a long-range planning committee for NSF, Dr. Arthur Luehrmann of the Lawrence Hall of Science has recommended that a basic curriculum in computer use be developed. The course, he says, should aim not merely at teaching the syntax of a common computer language, but should mainly show students how to perform meaningful tasks, thereby improving their analytic and problem-solving skills. Students should learn to structure problems in a logical form, to express ideas as algorithms, to simulate real systems as computer models, to process text, to construct graphs, and to search data bases among other skills.[36]

Recently Congress has expressed an interest in this problem. Committees of the U.S. House of Representatives have held hearings on "Computers in the Learning Society" and a bill to establish a "National Commission to Study the Scientific and Technological Implications of Information Technology in Education."

In testimony before Congress, Dr. F. James Rutherford, Assistant Director for Science Education, noted that the National Science Foundation has a special mandate to foster computer technology for research and education. Dr. Rutherford has identified four areas that NSF will concentrate its resources to accomplish these goals. 1) Fundamental research and development, 2) curriculum revision and development, 3) faculty training, and 4) microcomputers.

Dr. Richard Atkinson, the Director of the National Science Foundation, has added his support to these activities. Dr. Atkinson has said that the NSF has long had a special interest in advancing the use of computers in science and education and he feels that the time is right to develop a new research strategy that will satisfy both the requirements for broad national goals and the goals of the country's school systems.[37]

THE POTENTIAL IMPACT OF TECHNOLOGY ON EDUCATION

What do these developments and innovations portend for education?

The work place. Personal computers will allow more education to take place in the home and will permit home study for students, the handicapped who cannot travel to school, and the professionals who wish to continue their education. Conversely, inflation and taxes are likely to decrease the importance of salary as the prime incentive in business and on-the-job fringe benefits like computer-based continuing education will become an attractive feature of a desirable job. In addition, telecommunications will permit many to use word processors and intelligent terminals at home thereby allowing work at locations other than the place of employment.

The form of communications. Exponential increases in information and the high costs associated with print technology are likely to end an era of the comprehensive library. We will see a rapid expansion of on-line, specialized information systems. Rapid access to vast quantities of data and information will create qualitative changes in scholarly research and instruction and open up new democratic forces in our information society. Microcomputers will be used as text-to-speech devices, voice-operated typewriters and word processors for personal filing systems. Electronic mail and teleconferencing will increase the speed and quantity of national communications.

Curriculum and the student. Computer-augmented problem solving and computer-aided memory will reduce the difficulty and complexity of problems in all disciplines and are likely to be a catalyst for major curriculum revision efforts. Intelligent devices will tutor and advise students and provide small but powerful computation facilities. There will be a greater emphasis on problem-solving, algorithms, graphics, dynamics and data processing at all levels of education. Transition to computer-based curricula is likely to cause an enormous stress in our educational system. Students who have not been exposed to computing will have had an incomplete education and will be at a significant disadvantage when compared with those who have. We can no longer advise the less able to take vocational or clerical courses, for they too will require technological skills to operate computer-driven tools and word processors. Students without experience with computers will be ill prepared for the world of work.

PRODUCTIVITY AND EDUCATION

Will all of these innovations improve productivity? Dr. Allen Rosenstein of UCLA notes that history has demonstrated that possession of scientific knowledge is not easily converted into economic strength or improved quality of life. He says that knowledge gained from basic research is an international commodity while expertise of the Nation's professions is the commodity that increases productivity.[38] Of course, professional expertise depends on education.

Some assume that market factors will solve the productivity problem. If business wants profits, they will use more innovative technologies. Unfortunately, many businesses are not using high technology such as computer-aided design and computer-aided manufacturing because they lack the capital necessary to make the transition and cannot find the skilled personnel necessary to operate the technology. Universities face a similar problem and lack incentives to teach such courses. Universities also face another special problem. The demand for people with computer experience is so great that the best students are leaving for jobs after their Bachelor's degrees and are not pursuing advanced degrees. The most talented faculty are also leaving. This has depleted the number and quality of those teaching at universities. Dr. John Hamblen concludes after a study of manpower needs that the cause of many problems associated with computer usage is the overutilization of under-educated people. A sufficient number of properly educated people is not available nor will be in the foreseeable future.[39] A recent committee of academic and business leaders in computing has expressed grave concern about this problem and have recommended a rejuvenation of university computer science programs.[40]

If we are to increase national productivity through the use of computers, we must find some way to train a sufficient number of computer specialists, and those scientists and professionals who will use computers to create a critical mass in the work force. But this is only part of the problem; if we are to have a computer literate society we must also train university and school teachers to use computers in their classrooms.

Access to information and communications may turn out to be one of the most significant social forces in the information society. Information has always been an important social, political and economic force. Information can be transformed into power. Low-cost, computer-communications have the potential to expand that power base. However, if individuals are not computer literate and do not understand how these systems work, they will be unable to meaningfully participate in actions that affect their lives.

In summary, it is becoming increasingly clear that if we are to meet both national needs for increased productivity and local needs for educational change, greater cooperation by all sectors will be required as well as an organized redirection of our nation's efforts and resources. In an information society, human capital is the wealth of a nation and education is the process for refining that resource. If we do not soon revitalize our educational institutions to meet this challenge they are liable to become what Peter Drucker has already dubbed "the railroads of the knowledge industry."

FOOTNOTES

[1] *Technological Innovation and the U.S. Economy,* National Academy of Sciences, Washington, D.C., November 14, 1978.

[2] "Danger: Pension Perils Ahead, Approaching the Other Side of the Baby Boom," *TIME Magazine,* September 24, 1979, p. 68.

[3] "Agriculture Pests Up Against New Enemy: DP." *Computerworld,* June 26, 1978, p. 14.

[4] Sperry-Univac Worldwide News Education, Research, and Training, Volume 79.040 CIDC Order No. U6324, 1979 Blue Bell, Pa.

[5] Decker, Robert W., "Computer-Aided Design and Manufacturing at G.M." *Datamation,* Vol. 24, No. 5, May, 1978, pp. 159–165.

[6] Anderson, Robert H. "Programmable Automation: The Future of Computers in Manufacturing," *Datamation,* Vol. 18, No. 12, December, 1972, pp. 46–52.

[7] Stewart, Jon, "Computer Shock: The Inhuman Office of the Future," *Saturday Review,* July 23, 1979.

[8] "Science in Europe/British May Use Telephones, TV's to Tap Data Base," *Science,* July 7, 1978, pp. 33–34.

[9] Smith, Anthony. "All the News that Fits in the Data Bank." *Saturday Review,* July 23, 1979.

[10] *Technology in Science Education: The Next Ten Years,* Deringer, D. and Molnar, A. (Eds.), National Science Foundation, Washington, D.C., July 1979.

[11] Mathematics Series, Milliken Publishing Company, St. Louis, Missouri, 63132.

[12] Dooley, Ann, "For Bilingual Instruction School Shifting Teaching Aid to Micros," *Computerworld,* November 6, 1978, p. 63.

[13] Zinn, Karl, "The Impact of Microcomputers on College Teaching," *Pipeline,* Vol. 4, No. 2, Spring, 1979.

[14] "MECC Recommends APPLE II for MN Schools," *The Journal,* Vol. 6, No. 5, September, 1979, p. 28.

[15] *1979-80 Microcomputer Report of the Minnesota Computing Consortium,* July, 1979, (2520 Broadway Drive, St. Paul, Minn. 55113)

[16] Braun, Ludwig, "An Odyssey into Educational Computing," IFIP, Computers in Education, 1979.

[17] Watson, Paul, "The Utilization of the Computer with Hearing Impaired and the Handicapped," Symposium on Research and Utilization of Educational Media for Teaching the Deaf, University of Nebraska, April 19, 1979.

[18] Papert, Seymour, Abelson, H., di Sessa, A., Watt, D., Weir, S. Final Report of the Brookline LOGO Project, and Assessment and Documentation of a Children's Computer Laboratory, 1979.

[19] Abelson, Hal and Paul Goldenberg, "Teacher's Guide for Computational Models of Animal Behavior," MIT AI Laboratory, AI Memo 432, April, 1977.

[20] Molnar, Andrew, "Intelligent Videodisc and the Learning Society," *Journal of Computer-Based Instruction,* Vol. 6, No. 1, August, 1979, pp. 11–16.

[21] Robert Elliots Purser's Reference List of TRS 80, PET and APPLE II, P.O. Box #466, El Dorado, Calif. 95623.

[22] CONDUIT, P.O. Box #388, Iowa City, Iowa 52244.

[23] Northwest Regional Educational Laboratory, 710 S.W. Second Avenue, Portland, Ore. 97204.

[24] Molnar, Andrew, "National Policy Toward Technological Innovation and Academic Computing." *T.H.E. Journal,* Vol. 4, No. 6, Sept./Oct., 1977.

[25] Blumenthal, Marcia, "In Week of Special Events, French Public Shown How DP Influences Everyday Life," *Computerworld,* October 1, 1979, p. 4.

[26] *Electronics,* July 19, 1979.

[27] *Nature,* April 19, 1979.

[28] Karten, Howard, "Computer No Longer Simple Support Device: 'B' Schools Found Encouraging DP Studies," *Computerworld,* August 13, 1979, p. 18.

[29] Woodruff, Jay, "New Harvard Curriculum Includes DP Requirement," *Computerworld,* May 28, 1979, p. 15.

[30] Austing, Richard (Ed.), *Special Issue on Computer Science Curricula,* ACM/SIGCSE Bulletin: A Quarterly Publication of the Special Interest Group on Computer Science Education, Vol. 9, No. 2, June, 1977.

[31] Austing, Richard (Ed.), "Curriculum '78: Recommendations for Undergraduate Program in Computer Science. A Report of the ACM Curriculum Committee on Computer Science," *Communications of the ACM,* Vol. 22, No. 3, March, 1979.

[32] *A Curriculum in Computer Science and Engineering,* IEEE Computer Society, 5855 Naples Plaza, Long Beach, Calif., 90803, 1977. Also *A Library List of Undergraduate Computer Science, Computer Engineering and Information Science,* 1978.

[33] Taylor, Robert, et al., "Computing Competencies for School Teachers: A Preliminary Projection for All But the Teachers of Computing," and Poirot, James, et al., "Computing Competencies for School Teachers: A Preliminary Project for Teachers of Computing." Proceedings of the National Educational Computing Conference, University of Iowa, 1979.

[34] Klassen, Daniel, Minnesota Educational Consortium, 2520 Broadway Drive, St. Paul, Minn., 55113 (1979).

[35] Hunter, Beverly, "What Makes a Computer-Literate College?" Conference on Computers in the Undergraduate Curricula, University of Denver, 1978.

[36] *Technology in Science Education: The Next Ten Years,* National Science Foundation, Washington, D.C., 1979.

[37] Statement by F. James Rutherford, Subcommittee on Science, Research and Technology of the House Science and Technology Committee, October 9, 1979. Also see "Computer and the Learning Society," Committee on Science and Technology, U.S. House of Representatives, June, 1978.

[38] Rosenstein, Allen. "Education for Professions and the Future Quality of National Life," *T.H.E. Journal,* Vol. 5, No. 5, Sept./Oct., 1978.

[39] Hamblen, John, "Computer Literacy and Social Impact of Computers: Education and Manpower," ACM Meeting, Williamsburg, Virginia, July, 1978.

[40] Feldman, Jerome, et al., "Rejuvenating Experimental Computer Science: A Report to the National Science Foundation and Others," University of Rochester, January, 1979.

Computerphobia: What to Do About It

Timothy B. Jay

Many instructors, whether they admit it or not, are afraid of computers. I validate my observation from discussions, either formal or informal, on the topic of computers and computer-assisted learning with administrators, teachers, students, and instructional technologists, who admit these fears. Computerphobia is but one branch of a larger technophobia in our society that has been engendered by our recent period of rapid technological growth and development. People either keep up or give up.

Computerphobia is unfortunate and uncomfortable. It must be overcome. Instructors need the sense of control, confidence, and authority that comes

From "Computerphobia: What to Do About It," by Timothy B. Jay. In *Educational Technology,* January, 1981. © 1981 by Educational Technology Publications, Inc. Reprinted by permission.

with understanding technology. Instructors need to use this technology as an effective and productive tool in educational settings. Most important of all, learners need to experience the more creative, diverse, and motivated learning that is promoted by this technology when in the hands of knowledgeable instructors.

Before looking for the remedy for computer-phobia, we have something to gain by examining the phenomenon in more detail. Understanding the etiology of computerphobia is part of the cure. Let us look at the symptoms and the causes of this electronic nightmare.

THE SYMPTOMS OF COMPUTERPHOBIA

Computerphobia appears generally in the form of a negative attitude toward technology. The negative attitude takes the form of (a) resistance to talking or even thinking about computer technology; (b) fear or anxiety, which may even create physiological consequences; and (c) hostile or aggressive thoughts and acts, indicative of some underlying frustrations. We may see these resistances, fears, anxieties, and hostilities in some of the following:

- a fear of physically touching a computer;
- a feeling that one could break or damage the computer or somehow ruin what is inside;
- a failure to engage in reading or conversation about the computer, a type of denial that the computer really exists;
- feeling threatened, especially by students, and others who *do* know something about computers;
- an expression of attitudes that are negative about computers and technology, for example: (a) feeling that you can be replaced by a machine, (b) feeling dehumanized, or (c) feeling aggressive toward computers (let's bend, fold, and mutilate these cards!). Such feelings are indicative of an underlying feeling of insecurity and lack of control; and
- a type of role reversal, whereby the person assumes the role of slave to technology rather than the master of a fine tool.

There may be other characteristics, but these are the ones manifest in many of those afraid of computers.

CAUSES OF COMPUTERPHOBIA

The causes of computerphobia are diverse and may vary from individual to individual. I assume that there are both individual and institutional sources of these problems; therefore, I trace the causes back to simple beginnings, such as:

Figure 1
A model for a computer seminar

A two to three day session, depending on the experience of the participants and the amount of introductory material to be presented.

Participants should come from a variety of positions: administrators, teachers, students, and technologists. They should also have various levels of expertise, although most will be beginners.

An introduction to the literature and philosophy of instructional technology.

Reinforce the idea that they are "in control" of technology.

Reinforce the idea that they do not need to be programmers or experts in electronics to use the technology.

Provide hands-on experience with both hardware and software.

Use both time-sharing and microcomputing systems, if possible. With either system, many computer neophytes have been extremely gratified by just touching the computer keyboard for the first time.

Reinforce the idea that *they* are the experts in knowing how to instruct learners.

- a failure on the part of the phobic to "keep up" with technological advances that affect his or her life. This reflects a simple failure to keep up with readings in popular and professional literature about technological advances;
- the institution or organization for which a person works may have failed to take his or her job into consideration when planning to use this new technology. A recurrent theme in educators' stories is that administrators buy equipment without (a) planning for its use, (b) assessing teachers' attitudes, (c) evaluating job changes, or (d) finding out how the computer technology will affect a particular individual. A resulting feeling is having an "unknown force" about to "attack";
- a failure of institutions to provide incentives to educators to keep up with technology. These incentives take the form of time off, training, paying for courses at local colleges, and/or incentives to develop one's own courseware to further personalize the use of the computer.

The phobia develops because people and institutions have not assessed how the computer might affect a particular person.

REMEDIES FOR COMPUTERPHOBIA

The cure for computerphobia must come from sources within the phobic and from the support of the system in which he or she works. Basically, the cure must result in a change in the attitude and behavior of the phobic. Some of the following are suggested:

- individuals, on their own, can begin a course of personal education, doing readings about computer technology in terms of current hardware and software developments; and
- institutions must begin promoting computer literacy both with learners and instructors. Teachers need time off, monetary incentives, and encouragement to attend seminars and courses in computer technology and educational reform. A model for a computer seminar is presented in Figure 1.

THE FUTURE OF COMPUTERPHOBIA

Unfortunately, my projections for the future predict an increase in the incidence of computerphobia, for the following reasons:

- lack of funds for teachers to attend seminars;
- lack of funds for incentives;
- increased *student* awareness of computer technology, while teachers remain uneducated;
- increased impact of the computer on educational systems without proper planning; and
- more pervasive use of computers in society in general, due to declining costs of the hardware.

I am concerned about those who won't come out of the closet. I am concerned about the instructor afraid to pick up this journal in the first place! The task is ours: find a computerphobic; give the phobic this article and a flashlight (for closet reading). The future will look brighter for all.

How Can Educators Become Computer Literates?

Darlene Myers

SUGGESTIONS AND CONCERNS

The development and growth of our children into happy, productive, contributing citizens is the most precious inheritance [sic] we can leave to our universe. *The Year of the Child* and *The Year of the Family* have encouraged many of us to become actively concerned about the role the family and educational systems play in preparing our children for the future.

From "How Can Educators Become Literates?" by Darlene Myers. In *The Computing Teacher*, November, 1980. Reprinted by permission.

Unfortunately, many families have placed the responsibility of rearing, guiding and educating their children in the hands of the schools, rather than accepting their full share of the responsibility. How effective could a mother or father be with 20 to 40 children around them constantly? I think any individual would have to agree that it would be a formidable task to take care of more than just the basic needs. Yet, we are shocked and disappointed to find our educational systems inadequate and unsatisfactory. In an editorial by Dr. Ludwig Braun[1] in *Byte* magazine, he lists eight reasons for dissatisfaction with the educational system in America:

1. Significant increase in the number of dropouts (New York has a 40% dropout rate before high school graduation).
2. Increase in the number of students performing below their grade level.
3. Declining SAT (Scholastic Aptitude Test) scores.
4. Decrease in the average daily attendance.
5. High levels of youth unemployment.
6. Continuing decline of educating students in the sciences.
7. Increased concern about increased costs incurred by the requirement to "mainstream" handicapped students.
8. Unacceptable levels of failure in state-mandated competency tests.

Dr. Braun goes on to say, however, that, "In each of the indicators cited above, there is evidence that the computer can provide assistance to the teacher in addressing these needs."

The almighty computer solves another human dilemma? Hardly. There are numerous concerns. Here I have listed five of them:

  I. Money
 II. Trained teachers
III. High quality courseware
IV. Use and misuse of computing knowledge
 V. Dependence on computing

I. Money

The first concern of any program is usually money. Yet the consistent drop in hardware costs for mini and microcomputers makes this equipment no more expensive than the microfilm-microfiche reader-printers housed in many of our libraries today. While no one can deny the importance of money to any program, there are other considerations. C.N. Opie of the Hertfordshire County Council Advisory Unit for Computer-based Education in England stated recently, "While money is important, machinery is useless without careful planning, standardization and support at ground level."[2]

Dr. Braun, Director of the Laboratory for Personal Computers in Education at the State University of New York at Stony Brook has urged that computers enter our educational system "in an orderly, intelligent manner. . .in contrast to our experience with television. . .(which was) dominated by commercial interests." Dr. Braun warns that if the "educational community does not move forcefully and soon to ensure proper support for teachers and students in making intelligent use of personal computers, computers will become the *wasteland* of "Star Wars' games, instead of helping our young people to develop their intellects to the fullest extent possible."[3]

II. Trained teachers

This statement brings us to the second concern: trained teachers and librarians. What can the teacher, librarian, information specialist or even lay person do to become "trained," or at least informed about educational computing?

The problem is significant enough that Congressperson Downey (D.-N.Y.) is trying to get $4 million allocated from the U.S. Budget to encourage computer literacy in the nation's classrooms,[3] and Arthur Luehrmann, Director of Computer Research at the Lawrence Hall of Science, University of California, Berkeley, believes that computer illiteracy is a national crisis. He says, "Computing plays such a crucial role in everyday life and in the technological future of this nation that the general public's ignorance of the subject constitutes a national crisis. The ability to use computers is as basic and necessary to a person's formal education as reading, writing and arithmetic."[4] Dr. Luehrmann also states that adults wishing to become "literate" are at the mercy of the U.S. system of continuing eduation, "which is no system at all."

This section is designed especially for the educator who needs or wants to know more about computing. What is available to aid those wishing to take on this challenge? Here are some suggestions:

1. Find out the position of your school or school district on computing. Are there any proposals for computer-related learning projects, or computing equipment acquisitions being made?

2. Find out what is being done in your local area in the way of personal computing. Are there any local computer clubs? Local computer shows sponsored by universities, colleges, the DPMA (Data Processing Management Association) or the ACM (Association for Computing Machinery)? Do any of the local university or college computer centers offer non-credit courses to introduce computers, programming or special packages, such as SPSS (Statistical Package for the Social Sciences) which may be of use to you?

3. Visit local computer stores for a demonstration and comparison of microcomputers. Find out: if you can add your name to their mailing list; if they have a computer center; if they have any publications that might be beneficial. (Note: Radio Shack now provides, on a national basis, free BASIC computer programming language instruction for educators. In the Seattle area one can receive three college credits through one of the local universities for attending the nine sessions of four hours each. It is obvious that Radio Shack uses these sessions as a sales technique. But the sales pressure is very, very low. They trust that the proficiency developed on the TRS-80 computer during the class is sufficient to persuade those present to acquire the same equipment for their classroom or personal use. For non-teachers, the cost of the class is approximately $90 for 36 hours, or $30 for each of the 3 levels. In some areas, state contracts are being negotiated which would allow educational institutions up to a 20% discount on the purchase of TRS-80s. Other manufacturers, such as APPLE, may be able to provide sizeable discounts for bulk purchases.)

4. Become aware of the literature—books, journals, reference works[5] and technical reports. At the end of this section you will find two lists: "Computing Books for the Beginner" and "Texts for the Educator." All are fundamental introductions designed to ease the pain of your first inquiry into computing.

5. Become aware of the organizations involved with educational computing on both the international and national levels. (A list of some of these is supplied later in this article.)

6. Become aware of individuals whose names frequently appear in the literature, or who are nationally known as innovators in educational computing. Some of these might be:

BOB ALBRECHT (Menlo Park, California) One of the founders of People's Computer Company and the Community Computer Center; author and educational consultant on computer subjects.

KAREN BILLINGS (New York, New York) Microcomputer Resource Center, Columbia Teachers College, 525 West 121st, N.Y., N.Y. 10027. (212) 678-3740.

DR. LUDWIG BRAUN and JO ANN COMITO (Stony Brook, New York) Laboratory for Personal Computers in Education, State University of New York, Stony Brook, N.Y. 11794. (516) 246-8418. In addition to having a laboratory of various personal computers and software, they teach computing to teachers in the continuing education program and help them develop programs for use in their own classrooms.

JUDY EDWARDS (Portland, Oregon) Ms. Edwards is the Director of the Computer Technology Program at the Northwest Regional Educational Laboratory. The lab has recently been funded by the National Institute for Education for a special project called MicroSIFT—this stands for MICRO Software and Information For Teachers. It is a project to assist elementary and secondary school educators in curriculum development as well as self-development. The project is so new that only a few letters have been sent out, one of which informs teachers of workshops and seminars being offered. They are collecting micros for the Project (hopefully one of each kind) so they can quickly access software received and provide reviews. Reviews of software are to begin Fall, 1980. The project also plans to supply a list of newsletters as well as cost comparisons for various microcomputers.

AL BORK (Irvine, California) Educational Technology Center, University of California, Irvine, CA 92717. (714) 833-6945. Professor Bork is making super contributions to CAI (Computer Aided Instruction).

7. Attend conferences and symposia held especially for educators, either in the field of education or computer science. One of these is the *National Educational Computing Conference* (formerly Conference on Computers in the Undergraduate Curricula). Annual meetings are held in various places throughout the United States. Contact the organizations involved with educational computing so you will begin receiving notices about future workshops and tutorials.

8. Subscribe to journals on educational computing. Two of the more prominent titles are *Computing Teacher*[6] and the *Journal of Educational Computing*.[7] In these publications you will find articles, book reviews and meeting announcements on educational computing.

9. Form your own "invisible college" of colleagues, friends and acquaintances that can supplement your knowledge and keep you informed of current happenings.

10. Find a "computer buddy" whose opinion you trust, and who will help you with unfamiliar computing terms and techniques.

11. Make sure "your library" (be it at school, the public library or even your personal library) contains current literature and information on computing for you and your students.

12. Make sure that you have an awareness of the pros and cons of computing. Keep your own literature files up-to-date. Be ready and willing to support your requests for training and equipment with backups from the literature and personal inquiries.

Once you have done all these things, you will be on your way to becoming an innovator for computing in your educational setting.

III. High quality courseware

Although the development of high quality educational courseware is a problem, doors are beginning to open with special software projects like Micro-SIFT,[8] which supplies microcomputer information and software for teachers, and CONDUIT,[9] which aids in the search for and selection of computer-based materials considered to be appropriate for use in an undergraduate curriculum. MECC (Minnesota Educational Computing Consortium)[10] is striving to provide good software for the APPLE computers, and Radio Shack has just published a substantial catalog of software for the TRS-80. (Software in this catalog has been developed by TRS-80 owners and users. Radio Shack has compiled this information—a valuable software tool for TRS-80 users.) Another source often cited by micro users is *Robert Purser's Magazine*.[11] This, too, will assist in locating software which may be appropriate for classroom use.

IV. Use and misuse of computing knowledge

Recently, an article appeared about a community college student in Doylestown, Pennsylvania who used a student terminal to alter his grades. The article goes on to say, "By use of the computer, the young man gave himself four A's, a B and a B+ in place of two C's and 4 F's, and for summer semester gave himself 2 A's and 2 B's for classes not taken."[12] He was charged with forgery and tampering with records. This points out that not only do we have a responsibility to educate, but to educate *responsibly* by presenting the issues of computer fraud, invasion of privacy and computer ethics in the classroom, as well as technological know-how.

V. Dependence on computers

And finally, some are concerned about increased dependence on computers. The June 16, 1980 issue of *Information Systems News,* with a circulation of over 100,000, had this caption on the front page: "DP 'Catastrophes' Predicted for Users." When the question was asked, "Is computer reliance so complete that failure would be catastrophic?" Professor Dennis G. Severance, one of the researchers who spent much of his time working on the report said, "Absolutely yes. Most companies could not continue to operate if the electricity to the computers was shut off."

The article concluded by saying that when the report by Severance and others was done that

management will (perhaps) realize for the first time that its Model T computer, which rumbled into the company only a short time ago . . . now travels at dangerously high speeds, holding most of the corporate memory upon which operational decision making and financial reporting are based. Technicians debate the need for seat belts and bemoan the high cost of air bags, while technology continues the acceleration. Perhaps it is time to slow down or at least take control more seriously.

With the heavy burden of educating our nation about computers, it is especially important that our teachers be well informed on all the issues and have access to information that will assist in averting the computer illiteracy crisis.

ORGANIZATIONS INVOLVED IN EDUCATIONAL COMPUTING

Here is a list of some organizations which are actively participating in educational computing.[13] These organizations are endeavoring through workshops, classes, software development and curriculum development to make it easier for the educator to become informed about computing. They are involved in computing issues and problems and are trying to offer solutions to these problems.

Association for Educational Data Systems (AEDS)

1201 16th Street, NW, Suite 506
Washington, D.C. 20036
(202) 833-4100
Objectives: Provide a forum for the exchange of ideas and information about the relationship of modern technology to modern education.
Dissemination Activities: *AEDS Journal, AEDS Bulletin,* annual convention, workshops, seminars, proceedings, AEDS Handbook, Membership Directory.

Association for the Development of Computer-based Instructional Systems (ADCIS)

Computer Center
Western Washington University
Bellingham, Washington 98225
(206) 676-2860
Objectives: Promote the investigation and utilization of computer-based instruction and/or management. Promote and facilitate the interchange of programs and materials. Help reduce redundant efforts among developers. Institute specific requirements and priorities for hardware and software.
Dissemination Activities: *Journal of Computer-Based Instruction, ADCIS News,* ADCIS Annual Meeting, workshops held prior to the Annual Meeting.

Minnesota Educational Computing Consortium (MECC)

2520 Broadway Drive
St. Paul, Minnesota 55113
Objectives: To coordinate computing activities in the State of Minnesota.[14] To distribute information and provide software, training and access to computers for classroom use.
Dissemination Activities: MECC has two newsletters: *Dataline* concentrates on in-house activities, and *Users*[15] provides information on commercial software, animation hints and articles. MECC sponsors workshops, annual meetings, classes and also provides software.[16]

Society of Data Educators

983 Fairmeadow Road
Memphis, Tennessee 38117
(901) 761-0727 Executive Director: Dana H. Verry
Objectives: Promote data education and assist in teaching data processing to educators.
Dissemination Activities: *Journal of Data Education,* bi-annual film directory, meetings.[17]

Special Interest Group: Computer Uses in Education (SIGCUE)

Association for Computing Machinery
1133 Avenue of the Americas
New York, N.Y. 10036
(212) 265-6300
Objectives: To promote the use of computers in education. Provide a forum for the discussion and exchange of ideas, methods, policy and materials related to all aspects of instructional computing. Offer technical sessions which may consist of invited or submitted papers, panel discussions, seminars and tutorials. Provide workshops devoted to instructional methodology, activities of specific schools or regions, collections of instructional materials and various strategies for using the computer.
Dissemination Activities: *SIGCUE Bulletin;* workshops and seminars.

ACM Elementary and secondary school subcommittee

(503) 686-4408 David Moursund, Chairperson
Objectives: Aid in the use of computers at the precollege level by identifying problems and assisting in solving these problems. Subcommittee has published some preliminary reports on their efforts. Task Groups were set up to handle the problems identified and 17 reports from the various Task Groups were published in the Fall of 1980. Two reports have received special

ACM recognition and will be published in the *ACM COMMUNICATIONS:* one article is on "teaching training" and the other is on "computer science courses for the secondary level."

COMPUTING BOOKS FOR THE BEGINNER*

This is a list of books for the beginner. They are very basic in their approach and do not assume any knowledge about computers on the part of the reader. Each book is labeled a Level I or a Level II. Level I books are best suited to the elementary school level because of the size of print, length of book, illustrations and content. Level II books are for junior high students on up. Surprisingly, there are even a few that are appropriate for all levels. I have assumed that "beginners" are just that—beginners. Therefore, no ages are attached to Level II books. They should be appropriate for anyone taking a first look into the world of computing.

Ahl, David H.
The Best of Creative Computing. Morristown, New Jersey: Creative Computing Press, 1976.
CONTENTS: Collection of articles originally published in *Creative Computing* magazine. LEVEL II

Ball, Marion J.
What Is a Computer. New York: Houghton Mifflin, 1972. 92 p. illus. (drawings are cartoon-like and in color)
CONTENTS: 1. What is a Computer. 2. The History of Computers. 3. Parts of a Computer System. 4. How Software Is Made. Summary. Glossary. Index.
"Excellent for children and adults in building a basic understanding of computers and the popular computing buzz words." LEVEL I/II

Ball, Marion J. and Charp, Sylvia
Be a Computer Literate. Morristown, New Jersey: Creative Computing Press, ©1977. 61 p. illus. (drawings are cartoon-like and in color)
CONTENTS: 1. Introduction. 2. What Are Computers. 3. Kinds of Computers. 4. What Goes on inside Computers. 5. Communicating with the Computer. 6. Language of the Computers. 7. How to Write a Simple Program. 8. How Computers Work for Us. Glossary. LEVEL I/II

*Note: You may notice that some of these books are over a decade old. This should not concern you too much because the history and basics of computing have not changed that much in the past ten years or so. The market can only support so many beginning level books. As a result, very few new books appear on the market for this audience in any one year.
Review by Jean Rogers
Department of Computer and Information Science
University of Oregon
Eugene, Oregon 97403

Berger, Melvin
Computers. New York: Coward, McCann & Geoghegan, ©1972. 46 p. illus. (line drawings are realistic.) LEVEL I

Brown, Clement
Questions and Answers on Computers. London: Newnes-Butterworths, ©1969. 94 p. illus. (line drawings are realistic.)
CONTENTS: 1. Introducing Computers. 2. Elements of Computing. 3. Programming. 4. Data Processing. 5. Computers and Science. 6. Computers in Industry. 7. Microelectronics. 8. Trends in Computing. Glossary and Index.
"Uses a Question/Answer approach. Answers are precise and informative. A few terms may seem strange as terminology varies slightly in the United Kingdom. LEVEL II

Cohen, Daniel
The Human Side of Computer. New York: McGraw-Hill. 84 p. illus.

Fields, Craig
About Computers. Cambridge, Mass.: Winthrop, ©1973. 133 p., illus. (a few realistic line drawings).
CONTENTS: Introduction. 1. What Are Computers and What Can They Do? 2. How Do Computers Differ from Other Machines? 3. How Do Parts of Computers Communicate with Each Other? 4. How Do Computers Communicate with People? 5. What Instructions Do Computers Follow? 6. How Can We Use Computers Easily? 7. How Can People Share Computers? 8. Of What Use Are Different Kinds of Computers? Epilogue; Appendices; Binary and Octal Arithmetic; References; Glossary; Index.

Fleck, Glen, ed.
A Computer Perspective. Cambridge, Mass.: Harvard University Press, © 1973.
"*A Computer Perspective* is an illustrated essay on the origins and first lines of development of the computer.... The book is based on an exhibition conceived and assembled for IBM Corporation...." LEVEL II

George, Frank
Machine Takeover: The Growing Threat of Human Freedom in a Computer-Controlled Society. Oxford, New York: Pergamon Press, ©1977. 193 p. (no illustrations).
CONTENTS: 1. Information and Data Processing. 2. Information Science: How the Story Starts. 3. The Science of Cybernetics. 4. The Consequences of Modern Science. Further Reading. Name Index. Subject Index.

Goldstine, Herman H.
The Computer from Pascal to von Newman. Princeton, New Jersey: Princeton University Press, ©1972.
CONTENTS: 1. The Historical Background up to World War II. 2. Wartime Developments: ENIAC and EDVAC. 3. Post-World War II: the von Newman Machine and the Institute for Advanced Study. APPENDIX: World-Wide Developments. Index.   LEVEL II

Halacy, D.S., Jr.
What Makes a Computer Work? Boston: Little, Brown & Co., ©1973. 64 p. illus. (line drawings are realistic).   LEVEL I

Jones, Weyman B.
Computer: The Mind Stretcher. New York: Dial, ©1969. 120 p. illus. (line drawings are realistic)
CONTENTS: Problem solving, Computer arithmetic, Telling the computer what to do. LEVEL I

Lewis, Bruce
Meet the Computer. New York: Dodd, Mead, ©1977. 47 p. illus. (line drawings are cartoon-like).   LEVEL I

Meadow, Charles T.
The Story of Computers. New York: Harvey House, ©1970. 124 p. illus. (line drawings are realistic).
CONTENTS: 1. Machines That Do Arithmetic. 2. Computers Use Binary Numbers. 3. How Computers Work. 4. You Can Tell Computers What to Do. 5. Going to the Moon—A Problem The Computer Solves. 6. Telling the Weather with a Computer. 7. Computers Can Teach Us. Recommended Additional Readings, Glossary, Index.

Piper, Roger
The Story of Computers. New York: Harcourt, ©1964. 186 p. illus. (photographs).
CONTENTS: 1. Almost Certainly They Have You in Mind. 2. Computers, Are They Human? 3. A Million Thoughts a Minute. 4. How the Computer Gets the Story. 5. Learning Electronic Language. 6. The Computer's Memory. 7. Inside the Computer's Brain. 8. More about the Computer's Brain. 9. The Minds behind the Computer. 10. Computers That Can Imitate. 11. The Smaller, the Better. 12. Careers among the Computers.   LEVEL I

Porter, Kent
Computers Made Really Simple. New York: Thomas Y. Crowell, ©1976. 182 p. illus. (photographs).

CONTENTS: 1. The Computer in Today's World. 2. What Is a Computer? 3. Computer Talk. 4. Thought Processes. 5. More about Language. 6. The Brains of the Computer. 7. Memory. 8. Eyes and Ears. 9. Hands and Mouth. 10. Directing an Idiot. 11. Anatomy at Work. 12. Who's The Boss? Appendices: Binary Arithmetic, Computer Careers, Glossary.   LEVEL II

Rice, Jean
My Friend the Computer. Minneapolis: T.S. Denison & Co., ©1976. 85 p. illus. (line drawings are cartoon-like, photographs).
CONTENTS: 1. What Is a Computer? 2. How Are Computers Used? 3. History of the Computer. 4. How Does a Computer Work? 5. Devices Used to Get Information Into and Out of a Computer. 6. How to Plan a Computer Map (Flow Chart). 7. How to Tell a Computer What to Do (Programming). APPENDIX: How to Use a Computer Terminal, How to Make Paper Tape, Glossary.   LEVEL I

Rusch, Richard B.
Computers: Their History and How They Work. New York: Simon & Schuster, ©1969. 126 p. illus. (Photographs).
CONTENTS: 1. Thinking Things Through. 2. Counting Machines. 3. It's Really Quite Simple. 4. Input, Output and Throughput. 5. You're the Boss. 6. Today is History. 7. Careers Tomorrow. Glossary and Index.   LEVEL II

Spencer, Donald D.
Computers in Action: How Computers Work. Rochelle Park, N.J.: Hayden Book Co., 1974. 150 p. illus. (line drawings are realistic, cartoons, photographs).
CONTENTS: 1. The Computer Age. 2. Computer Evolution. 3. How Computers Work. 4. Getting Information In and Out of the Computer. 5. Computer Storage. 6. Designing the Computer Program. 7. The Language of the Computer. 8. Introduction to Computer Programming.   LEVEL II

Spencer, Donald D.
Computers in Society: The Wheres, Whys, and Hows of Computer Use. Rochelle Park. N.J.: Hayden Book Co., ©1974. 196 p. illus. (photographs, cartoons).
CONTENTS: 1. The Story of Computers. 2. The Computer in Society. 3. Computers in Medicine. 4. Computers and the Fine Arts. 5. Computers and the Law. 6. Computers in Engineering. 7. Computers in Education. 8. Computers in Business. 9. Computers for Control. 10. Computers in Transportation. 11. Miscellaneous Jobs

for Computers. 12. Computers and the Future. A prose Glossary. LEVEL II

Spencer, Donald D.
The Story of Computers. (Rev. ed.) Ormond Beach, Fla.: Camelot Pub. Co., ©1977. 64 p. illus. (line drawings are cartoon-like).
CONTENTS: 1. What Are Computers? 2. Who Invented Computers? 3. What Kinds of Computers Are There? 4. How Does a Computer Work? 5. How Do I Tell a Computer What to Do? 6. What Are Some Useful Computer Terms? LEVEL I

Spencer, Donald D.
Posters on Famous Computer People. Ormond Beach, Fla.: Camelot Pub. Co., ©1978. 20 p. illus. (line drawings are realistic).
CONTENTS: Line drawings of 20 famous computer people with a brief paragraph on their contributions to computing. LEVEL I/II

Srivastava, Jane Jonas
Computers. New York: Thomas Y. Crowell, © 1972. 33 p. illus. (line drawings are realistic).
 LEVEL I

Superman in the Computers that Saved the Metropolis! ★starring★ the TRS-80 Computer Whiz Kids. New York: DC Comics, Inc. for Radio Shack, ©1980. 28 p. illus. (cartoons, color).
CONTENTS: Uses a Superman escapade to introduce the fundamentals of computing. Multiple copies are available from your local Radio Shack store. LEVEL I

Van Tassel, Dennie L.
The Compleat Computer. Chicago, Palo Alto: Science Research Associates, Inc. 216 p. illus. (line drawings are realistic, some color, cartoons, photographs).
CONTENTS: 1. In the Beginning. 2. How Computers Do It. 3. The Software. 4. The Present and Potential. 5. Applications. 6. Governmental Uses. 7. The Impact. 8. Controls, or Maybe Lack of Controls. 9. Your Future. LEVEL II

TEXTS FOR THE EDUCATOR

Here is a list of books that have been written especially for educators who are concerned with introducing computers into their classroom instruction. If you are aware of other timely texts that have not been included in this list, I would appreciate your notifying me. Darlene Myers, P.O. Box U-5373, Seattle, Washington 98105.

Edwards, Judith B. et al.
Computer Applications in Instruction: A Teacher's Guide to Selection and Use. Hanover, N.H.: TimeShare, ©1978. 202 p. illus.

CONTENTS: 1. The Essentials of Hardware and Software. 2. Instructional Uses of the Computers. 3. Selecting Computer-based Instructional Units. 4. Readings in Computer in the Curriculum (i.e., Art Education, Business Education, Instruction for the Deaf and Hard of Hearing, Elementary School, Language Arts, Mathematics, Music, Physical Education, Secondary Science, Natural Science, Social Sciences, Social Studies, Vocational Agriculture).

International Federation for Information Processing. Technical Committee for Education TC-3. Working Group on Secondary School Education WG 3.1.
Computer Education for Teachers in Secondary Schools: an outline guide. (Rev. ed.), ©1971.

This guide is intended for those people who are concerned with the planning of computer courses for the training of teachers. It gives suggestions for the content of such courses and indicates methods by which the concepts of computer science can be explained to students. Included is the study of the computer itself and some indications of the influence of the computer within subject areas and its effect on society. . . .

For more information contact: William F. Atchison, Computer Science Dept., University of Maryland, College Park, Md. 20742. (301) 454-4245.

National Computing Centre, Ltd.
Computer Appreciation for the Majority. J.D. Tinsley, Supervising Editor. Manchester, Eng.: NCC., ©1973. lv. (various pagings) loose-leaf.

. . .The NCC prepared this document for teachers wishing to run a general computer appreciation course. . . .It is in the form of a comprehensive set of teacher's notes and may be used either in a computer course or as a module within another course, such as in humanities, environmental studies or, perhaps, mathematics. . . .The material was tested in classes where the ability of students ranged from the bottom stream of a Manchester Comprehensive school to a group in a Sheffield School, 75% of whom are expected to take a CSE examination in mathematics. . . .The programming language used. . .is BASIC. This language has been chosen because of its simplicity, suitability for both numeric and non-numeric work, and because it is widely available.

Nuffield Foundation
Computers and Young Children. Edinburgh, London, New York: W & R Chambers, 1972. 63 p. illus. (some color).
CONTENTS: Why Computers; Flow Charts; A Classroom Human Computer; Presenting the Program to the Computer; Working with a Computer; Conclusion.
INTRODUCTION: There is no attempt in this book to give the age for which each particular part of the work is appropriate. Chapter 2 begins with work that is suitable for children at the lower end of the primary school; the

end of the book deals with work that is appropriate for pupils at the top end of the primary school and the first years of the secondary school. It must be left to individual teachers to decide just when the time is right to introduce the different stages of the work.

Poirot, James L. and Groves, David N.
Computer Science for the Teacher. Manchaca, Texas: Sterling Swift Publishing Co., ©1976. 262 p. illus. (photographs).
CONTENTS: 1. Computer Development. 2. Arithmetic from the Computer's Point of View. 3. Logic and Boolean Algebra. 4. Flowcharting. 5. Programming, Language and Applications. 6. Instructional Assistance. 7. Administrative Assistance. 8. Games Computers Play. Appendices. Bibliography and Index.

"Although prior computer training would be helpful toward depth of understanding, such training is not assumed. The content is especially designed to be meaningful to a teacher or future teacher, otherwise unfamiliar with the computer, but with a need to teach a course in computer science or to implement the computer in the classroom. Information on the how to and whys of teaching along with the 'what' to teach is included."

REFERENCES

1. Braun, Dr. Ludwig. "*Computers in Learning Environments;* An Imperative for the 1980s" Byte v. 5 no. 7 (July 1980) p. 7–10, 108–144.
2. "Pupils and dp in HCC." *Computing,* v. 8, no. 26 (Thursday, June 26, 1980) p. 17.
3. Kirchner, Jake. "House Bill Urges Computer Literacy Financing." *Computerworld,* v. 14, no. 6 (June 30, 1980) p. 18.
4. Luehrmann, Arthur. "Computer Illiteracy: A National Crisis and a Solution for It." *Byte,* v. 5, no. 7 (July 1980) p. 98–102.
5. Teachers interested in computer-based learning should be familiar with the three-volume work edited by Anastasia C. Wang: *Index to Computer Based Learning.* For more information, contact: Instructional Media Laboratory, University of Wisconsin, Milwaukee, P.O. Box 413, Milwaukee, Wisc. 53201.
6. *Computing Teacher,* Computer Center, Eastern Oregon State College, La Grande, Ore. 97850.
7. *Journal of Educational Computing,* MAEDS, 1925 W. County Rd., B2, St. Paul, Minn. 55113.
8. MicroSIFT Computer Technology Program. Northwest Regional Educational Laboratory, 710 S.W. Second St., Portland, Ore. 98204.
9. CONDUIT, P.O. Box 388, Iowa City, Iowa 52244.
10. MECC, 2520 Broadway Dr., St. Paul, Minn. 55113.
11. *Robert Purser's Magazine,* P.O. Box 466, El Dorado, Calif. 95623.
12. "Signs of the times" *Privacy Journal,* v. 6, no. 8 (June 1980) p. 1.
13. The National Council of Teachers of Mathematics is doing a great deal to help math teachers. They are not included in this list because of their emphasis on a single discipline.
14. Note: MECC has two computer systems which provide access to computing: a Control Data Corporation Cyber

70/73 networking system with 2500 terminals and the APPLE microcomputers. In less than two years, MECC has distributed 1500 APPLEs. These two systems provide access to computing for 92% of the students from kindergarten through college. This represents 75% of the schools in the state for 1979–1980.
15. *Users* may be subscribed to by persons interested in MECC activities.
16. There are two levels of software exchange for each computer system.

CDC Cyber 70/73		*Apple*
Share	Level I	Seeds
Library	Level II	Apple

Level I software has been developed and submitted by teachers throughout the State of Minnesota. MECC looks over all the software that has been submitted in Level I. Those programs of special significance receive a MECC "stamp of approval" and are moved into Level II. For more information, contact MECC.
17. Because membership is quite small, meetings are usually held in conjunction with one of the other societies such as AEDS.

An Analysis of Computer Education Needs for K–12 Teachers

Stuart D. Milner

PROBLEMS AND ISSUES

It is generally acknowledged that one of the most critical problems facing effective and widespread use of computers in learning is teacher education; that is, teachers at all levels need to be educated about the use of computers in the classroom and about their impact on society in general (Milner, 1; IFIP, 2).

Unfortunately, there are numerous unresolved issues that inhibit the education of teachers at both the preservice and inservice levels. Among them are: 1) lack of certification and experience requirements for teaching computer-related courses; 2) a lack of educators' knowledge of computer applications in education; 3) lack of training programs and courses; 4) low priority given to instructional computing; 5) lack of incentives for teachers; and 6) the need for greater administrative commitment and recognition. What is required is a multi-level approach for dealing with the entire set of problems. Each will be addressed in turn.

The need to certify teachers of computer science is pervasive. Currently, only four states in the United States certify teachers of computer science. To

From "An Analysis of Computer Education Needs for K–12 Teachers," by Stuart D. Milner. In *Proceedings of NECC,* June, 1979 by National Educating Computing Conference. Reprinted by permission.

illustrate the real nature of this need, consider the following situation in a large school system which requires a mathematics teacher to take 24 hours of mathematics content; yet, to teach computer science, the state requires no coursework in that area. The problem is not limited to computer science courses. Teachers are not required to take computer education courses in order to teach subjects that involve computing in an adjunctive manner (e.g., computer applications in social sciences). Consequently, legitimate criticisms of computer misuse and of ill-prepared or unqualified teachers of computing exist.

Computer systems and instructional materials are proliferating at an amazing rate. Yet, it is surprising how many teachers and administrators are unaware of what the systems can do and what instructional materials exist. It follows that too many of them do not know how to effectively use computer-related materials.

Generally, in relation to other disciplines, university-based programs, courses, and workshops in computer education for teachers are lacking. Where courses do exist, they are often optional and not well-integrated in degree programs. (A few programs in computers and education do exist, for example, at Teachers College, the University of Massachusetts and the University of Illinois.) In all fairness, though, the demand for such training is not being felt by universities.

Many educators do not seem to see the relevance of computing in the curriculum, and, therefore, it is given a low priority. High school teachers, in particular, sometimes complain that there is no room for computing in existing curricula. But, computer-related materials are being incorporated into text-books and other curriculum materials signalling a philosophical advocacy for computing by curriculum developers. If Minsky (3) is correct in his prophetic statement that "eventually, programming itself will become more important even than mathematics in early education," then we must deal with teacher training to a greater extent than is presently the case.

Because computer science is a new discipline to many teachers, there is a seeming reluctance to pursue the study of it. It involves both new ways of thinking and new approaches to pedagogy.

Paradoxically, teachers seem to recognize the need for training in computing. In a recent survey conducted by the Minnesota Educational Computing Consortium, (4), 85% of 1300 teachers surveyed agreed or strongly agreed that the secondary school student should have a minimal understanding of computers. Only 39% of the entire group agreed or strongly agreed that their training was adequate for using computers in instruction. When divided into users and non-users of computing, 62% of the users felt prepared. In any case, it appears that teachers, in general, perceive the need for preparation in computer use.

Administrative commitment to and recognition of instructional computing is sine qua non for effective and widespread use of computers in education. Administrators must be aware of the kinds of applications that exist and how these can be effectively used in education.

In spite of apparent lack of recognition of and commitment to instructional computing, some administrators do appear to recognize the need for more computer-trained teachers. Dennis (5) surveyed 686 secondary school principals in Illinois and found that 1) 71% expressed a need for computer science teachers; 2) 55% expressed a need for state certification in computer science; and 3) 82% felt some computer science is valuable in the background of any teacher.

Baker (6) conducted a survey of 78 superintendents in 50 states regarding their preferences concerning the roles of computer science and teacher training in secondary schools. Respondents stated their preferences with respect to: 1) a computer science department in secondary schools; 2) every teacher required to take three computer science courses; 3) a computer science department and every teacher trained in basic uses of the computer; and 4) none preferred. When divided into users and non-users of computing, a majority of the users preferred option 3, and the majority of the non-users preferred option 1 or 3.

Generally, administrators seem to have mixed feelings about computer education for teachers. Perhaps a comprehensive national survey would provide data on administrators' attitudes for the purpose of planning and decision making.

In spite of these problems and inhibiting factors, we do have available alternatives that could serve as prototypes for educating teachers. Existing and previous approaches for educating teachers in the instructional uses of computers are summarized in a volume edited by me (1). A few university-based programs exist and range from B.S. degree to summer M.S. degree programs. In addition, non-profit organizations and consortia such as the Minnesota Educational Computing Consortium, the Oregon Council of Computer Education, and Project LOCAL have been very effective in disseminating ideas and materials to schools. Finally, federally funded programs such as NSE's Programs in Pre-College Teacher Development and Information Dissemination in Science Education and Title IV-C programs of the U.S. Office of Education offer still other ways to educate teachers.

A FRAMEWORK FOR TRAINING NEEDS

How much should a teacher know about computer use in education? This is a complex question for which no simple answer exists. We can deal with this question based on what is taught, what certification and experience requirements exist, and what is believed necessary by experts. The matter of certification must be dealt with by school decision makers. The other matters are dealt with through the framework presented in this section.

In order to facilitate planning for and discussion of teacher education in computing, the general framework presented in Figure 1 is given. It deals with the kinds of courses and experiences that are necessary for various types of computer-related teaching. Its conceptualization is based on this author's experiences in providing computer education courses to a variety of teachers over the last nine years, as well as recommendations for courses by the Association for Computing Machinery (7).

Instructional design: An introduction

This course is designed to provide a basis for understanding and applying principles of instructional technology in education. It includes: 1) an overview of instructional technology; 2) aspects of instructional planning, development, implementation, and evaluation (e.g., task analysis, behavioral objectives, presentation strategies); and 3) selected means for individualizing learning (e.g., CAI).

Designing Computer-Based Learning Materials (CBLM)

Depending on background and interests, the student learns how to design, implement, and evaluate instructional materials using computers. The primary performance products are computer-based instructional or management modules. The student demonstrates mastery of selected computer programming techniques germane to project development. The content includes: 1) computer programming for instruction; 2) review of prototype computer-based materials; 3) development of instructional or management modules; 4) implementation; and 5) evaluation.

Programming

In a first course, Computer Programming I, the content recommended by the Association for Computing Machinery (ACM) includes the development of algorithms and the design, coding, debugging, and documentation of programs written in widely used, high-level programming languages. Computer organization is also introduced.

In the second course, Computer Programming II, students are introduced to structured programming concepts, string processing, searching and sorting, data structures, and recursion. Analysis of algorithms is discussed.

These two courses or some equivalent would appear to be relevant to teachers who either major or minor in computer science or who engage in the other types of teaching described in Figure 1.

Hardware and software organization

The ACM has recommended and described other courses in computer science that would follow the two programming courses. These courses involve organizational and design aspects of computer hardware and software. Courses recommended for a major in computer science are: assembly language programming, introduction to file processing, and introduction to computer organization. More advanced courses in operating systems and computer architecture, data structure, and programming languages are also suggested. When planning specifically for teachers, some subset of these may need to be selected especially for those who minor in computer science. Frederick (8) has provided such an example.

FIGURE 1. A framework for training needs
Courses/Experience

Types of Teaching	Instructional Design	Designing CBLM	Programming	Hardware & Software Organization	Computer Uses in Education	Computers & Society
Computer-Assisted Instruction	X	X	X		X	
Computer Science, Data Processing			X	X		X
Computers & Society			X	X		X

Computer uses in education

This course provides a basis for developing, implementing, and evaluating computer uses in education. Following are topics of such a course: 1) computer systems fundamentals; 2) instructional usage modes; 3) considerations in developing an evaluating computer-based instruction; 4) representative projects; 5) issues and problems. In such a course, students get hands-on experience in various applications and demonstrate competence through some form of instructional evaluation or development effort.

Computer and society

A course in computers and society for teachers should deal with systems fundamentals, programming, and applications in a wide variety of areas and their applications. Many excellent textbooks are available for use in such a course, such as Rothman and Mosmann (9) and Sanders (10).

IMPLEMENTING CHANGE

In order to expedite computer education for teachers, school decision makers must 1) identify needs; 2) establish goals; 3) develop certification requirements, and 4) implement teacher education and support options.

The framework discussed in the previous section could facilitate the identification of generic training needs, the establishment of goals, and the development of requirements for teaching computer-related courses by teachers. Although comprehensive national, state, and local action is required, specific actions could be implemented immediately. For example, all preservice teachers could be required to take a course in computer programming even if it is offered in lieu of another content of discipline-related course.

Various types of teacher training and support activities are possible. Some of these were implemented by schools using computers that were identified as exemplary in a recent study by Hargan and Hunter (11). The activities included:

1) Consulting by professional staff or outside experts;
2) Department meetings and demonstrations;
3) Workshops offered for inservice teachers who may not wish to commit themselves to entire courses. . . .(Because microcomputers are being introduced in schools on a steadily increasing basis, workshops may be an expeditious way to train teachers.);
4) Summer curriculum development teams for teachers with previous development experience;
5) Paid release time;
6) Staff development within school systems;
7) Memberships paid in professional organizations;
8) Travel paid to professional meetings;
9) University classes.

Finally, improvement in the existing state of teacher education in computer use requires the resolution of all the problems and issues identified in this paper. A framework for thinking about and planning for teacher education has been presented and suggestions for the implementation of change have been made. Widespread and effective use of computers in education requires such action.

REFERENCES

1. Milner, S. (ed.) *Topics in Instructional Computing (Volume I); Teacher Education.* New York: Association for Computing Machinery, 1975.
2. International Federation for Information Processing Technical Committee on Education (TC-3). *Computer Education for Teachers in Secondary Schools: Aims and Objectives in Teacher Training.* IFIP, 1972.
3. Minsky, M. Form and Content in Computer Science. *JACM,* 17, 2, 1970.
4. Minnesota Educational Computing Consortium. Computer Literacy Study—an Update. St. Paul, MN: MECC, June 2, 1978.
5. Dennis, J.R., et al. Computer Activities in Illinois Secondary Schools. Urbana, Illinois: Department of Secondary Education, University of Illinois, June, 1977.
6. Baker, J. *Computers in the Curriculum.* Phi Delta Kappa Fastback No. 82. Bloomington, Indiana: Phi Delta Kappa, 1976.
7. Austing, R.H., Barnes, B.H., Bonnette, D.T., Engel, G.L., and Stokes, C., Editors. Curriculum '78: Recommendations for the Undergraduate Program in Computer Science —A Report of the ACM Curriculum Committee on Computer Science. *CACM,* 22, 3, 1979.
8. Frederick, T. Computer Science Education For Students Training To Be Teachers. In S.D. Milner (ed.), *Topics in Instructional Computing (Volume I): Teacher Education.* New York: ACM, 1975.
9. Rothman, S. and Mosmann, C. *Computers and Society.* (2nd. ed.). Chicago: SRA, 1976.
10. Sanders, D. *Computers in Society.* (2nd ed.). New York: McGraw-Hill, 1977.
11. Hargan, C. and Hunter, B. *Instructional Computing: Ten Case Studies.* Alexandria, Virginia: Human Resources Organization, 1978.

MICROCOMPUTERS AND EDUCATION: PLANNING FOR THE COMING REVOLUTION IN THE CLASSROOM

Laurel Dickerson and William H. Pritchard, Jr.

The six students entered Mr. Allen's home without knocking. They were smiling and talkative this Monday morning as they assembled in the living room, sitting on the floor, the sofa, and in Mr.

From "Microcomputers and Education: Planning for the Coming Revolution," by Laurel Dickerson and William H. Pritchard. In *Educational Technology,* January, 1981. ©1981 by Educational Technology Publications, Inc. Reprinted by permission.

Allen's favorite chair. The certified parent, Jim Allen (B.A., Marketing), walked into the room carrying a tray of milk and breakfast rolls for the young students, ranging in age from 6 to 14. "We have a real surprise this morning," he said, as he set the tray on the coffee table. "I've arranged for all of you to work with the students in Mrs. Jordan's class through the terminals. I thought you might enjoy reviewing your arithmetic units with another class, rather than using our regular review disks." The children were enthusiastic. As they helped themselves to the tray of rolls, they all spoke at once. "Where's Mrs. Jordan's class?" "Who's in her class?" "How can we work with her kids?"

Jim Allen continued: "Mrs. Jordan's class is in the western part of the state, about 130 miles from here. There are six students there who are studying the same arithmetic units as you are this month. She and I have arranged for all of you to talk with each other by hooking your terminals together using telephone lines. We've worked out a series of questions and problems for each of you. You will begin by asking each other questions, waiting for your partners to answer, and then correcting the answers. If the answers are not correct, you'll be able to work them out together. All communication will be made by typing on your consoles. Instead of talking with each other using your voices, you'll be writing messages back and forth."

Mr. Allen paired each student with a pre-assigned student from Emily Jordan's class, as he continued to answer questions and provide instructions to the six eager learners. By the time the children were ready to work at the terminals, all individual arithmetic questions were distributed, each child knew the name of his or her partner from Mrs. Jordan's class, and the snacks had disappeared.

The children followed Mr. Allen to the den, where six small desks were located, each with an integrated micro-unit containing a console, color monitor, modem, and disk drive. The children sat at their desks, turned on their micro-units, and typed out their introductory messages.

"Hello, John Turner. My name is Maria Delgado. I am your study partner today." The message appeared on the monitor. The response came quickly. "Hi, Maria. This is John. What is my first question?"

Considering the potential of micro-technology, this scenario definitely is *not* whimsical. Small groups of students using that micro-technology is not unreasonable. The rising cost of traditional education and the increased frustration among educators to meet educational demands are real. The growth of the microcomputer industry is so rapid that educators have only begun to scratch the surface of its potential for use.

Microcomputer technology is attracting the attention of increasing numbers of people. A look at the educational community reveals a truly startling amount of activity: new courses are being developed to introduce computer applications to educators; federal grants are supporting studies to determine microcomputer effectiveness; teacher training workshops are being sponsored to teach microcomputer instructional techniques; and teachers and students are discovering increased opportunities to use micro-technology in the classroom. But, so far, this activity is scattered, random among schools, districts, and states, and unincorporated into long-range plans. Only in isolated cases are groups of educators prepared to employ systematic decision-making in the selection and use of microcomputers. Further, this activity notwithstanding, the literature predicts that computer literacy will be the next crisis in education (Lewis *et al.*, 1978; Molnar, 1978–79). Milner (1980) reports that only four states in the nation currently certify teachers in computer sciences (p. 544). The authors are faced weekly with publications presenting information and ideas about micro-technology and its implications for education.[1]

As a result of reviewing this literature, there is no doubt of the potential for computer-based instruction. But, the potential for computer illiteracy poses a challenge to the educational community which must not be ignored. The "cutting edge" of the literature on the relationship between computer technology and education is *not* found in the educational journals. It is found in trade magazines, technical journals, and professional publications apart from the traditional educational arenas. While the educational community reads general information telling the reader "You should use this technology . . . ," other trade, technical, and professional journals are saying "This is *how* to use the technology . . ." Educators must face the possibility that they will be major contributors to computer illiteracy if priorities are not given to the implementation and use of this technology.

In fact, the implications of computer illiteracy are most serious for the recent graduate of a teacher-training institution. Molnar (1978–79) notes that educational institutions are creating "unnecessary human waste" and a "high, unacceptable social and psychological cost" when they graduate students who are not computer-literate (pp. 280, 281). While many teacher-training institutions provide students with opportunities to enroll in technical computer

---

[1] See, for example, the issues of *Newsweek*, June 30, 1980; *Computer*, July, 1980; *BYTE*, July, 1980; *Kilobaud Microcomputing*, June, 1980; all of which featured cover stories on computers in education. *Educational Technology*, of course, devoted a full issue to the topic in October, 1979.

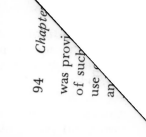
programs, few provide courses supporting computer applications in education. More specifically, even fewer institutions offer courses which apply to the use of computers in the classroom. Institutions train systems programmers, analysts, and technicians, but not educational computer specialists. As a result, the gap between the technical experts and the practitioners in education continues to grow. One major problem lies with the paucity of concentration on the effective ways in which computer technology, specifically microcomputers, can be used to enhance education for the learner. In addition, little focus is given to the effects which microcomputer technology can and will have on the learner.

If the educator is willing to acknowledge the impending computer literacy crisis, then it is important to recognize the relationship which must exist between computer literacy and instruction. The learner must be approached in a systematic fashion when computer technology is introduced and utilized in the classroom. Concurrently, the teacher, or student teacher, must receive the necessary training to effectively use micro-technology. In addition, an awareness is necessary of the impact this technology will have upon the lives of the learners in the future. In an attempt to bridge this gap, several problems are identified. One of the major problems contributing to the literacy crisis rests with the lack of sophisticated training programs for student educators. Perhaps because of the inability of institutional programs to respond rapidly to the need for training in different areas, and certainly because of the rapid growth of the microcomputer industry, student educators in higher education are not computer-literate upon graduation. Unless the teacher can command and direct the technology, the students who follow will not be prepared for the demands of a technological society.

A concomitant problem arises within the public schools and their academic programs: The ability to develop new programs, or radically change methods, is restricted by traditional approaches and administrative constraints. Concentrated efforts to resolve problems in areas of basic skills and budget slashes assume priority over new methods and long-range planning. Choosing not to concentrate on the prevention of computer illiteracy will create greater disparity and frustration between those who understand the technology and those who do not.

A third problem arises from the manner in which educational institutions plan for their financial and programmatic futures. Budgetary programs are created and approved on a yearly basis, thereby precluding the energies necessary to develop long-range future plans for training and instruction. Immediate problems related directly to yearly operating costs,

salaries, and basic skills progr... before attention can be give... development and change. The ... expended over and above ma... instructional and administrativ... not sufficient to include sy... planning and development. Fu... of the budget reduces the ability to take risks, to make major changes, and to program for the future. Changes made, for the most part, relate to the rearrangement of established programs rather than to the creation of radically new programs demanding substantially new methods and expertise.

While the inability of academic programs within higher education results in teachers being computer-illiterate, the problem is magnified, rather than reduced, in the consideration of teacher development programs. Student teachers graduate computer-illiterate and then return to those very institutions that caused their illiteracy for additional training. Even if a focus is placed upon computer-literate graduates, teachers return to classrooms where there exists no planning for the future.

These problems serve to dampen the energies of educators who are aware of the potential of computer technology in the classroom. The lack of systematic support to challenge the problem of computer illiteracy, coupled with growth and visibility of the micro-technology industry, suggests a bleak future. Unfortunately, data collected in a recent survey substantiate this dismal view.

In a survey of Florida's public school administrations, 60% of the reporting districts noted that computers were used in some way for instructional purposes. BUT LESS THAN 40% PROVIDED OR SUPPORTED FORMAL TRAINING FOR TEACHERS in the instructional use of computers. The results of this survey are presented below. The focus was on the instructional use of computers. The authors' contention is that computer literacy will be developed most effectively by using computers in conjunction with instruction—as instructional tools—and that the training of teachers in computer-based instructional use is the key to computer literacy.

THE NEED FOR TRAINING

A questionnaire (see Figure 1) was mailed to the assistant superintendent for curriculum and instruction in all 67 public school districts in the state of Florida. In smaller districts, which did not have such a position, the survey was addressed to the superintendent. The questionnaire asked each administrator whether or not computers were used for instruction; what types of hardware and software were used; whether or not a formal training program

...ded to the districts' teachers and the nature ... a program; and the expectations for future ... computers for instruction within the districts ... private homes. Fifty-five (82.1%) responses were received.

Of the 55 districts which responded, 33 (60%) utilize computers in some way for instructional purposes. Three used maxi-computers; eight used mini-computer systems; 16 used microcomputers; and six utilized a combination of these systems. Twenty-nine school districts employed BASIC, or a variation thereof, for their instructional software language, and four districts identified themselves as users of the PLATO program.

There appears to be a relationship between the size of school district enrollment and responses to selected items on the questionnaire. The larger the enrollment, the more likely were the school systems to use computers for instruction, to support training programs for teachers, and to expect increased instructional use of computers both in their district schools and in private homes.

The relationship between the size of districts and the instructional use of computers presents the most dramatic distinction among all analysis results. *None* of the districts in the smallest enrollment area

(0–2,000) use computers for instruction. *All* of the largest districts (over 25,000) do.

Of the 33 districts which reported using computers for instruction, 20 (60.6%) supported some form of training programs for teachers, and 13 (39.4%) did not. Generally, these training programs reflected one or more formats used by the districts. Seventy-five percent supporting training programs held inservice workshops; 30% utilized existing community college and university courses; and 35% relied on outside consultant training programs.

In the districts which do not now use computers for instruction, ten administrators indicated that they expect their districts to begin doing so within the next five years. Eleven do not expect any use in that time period.

Most respondents (69.1%) expected an increase in the use of computers for instructional purposes within the next five years. Over 70% expect instructional computer use by individuals in their homes to increase markedly.

THE FUTURE

There is evidence that the use of computers for instruction is becoming widespread and will increase in the future. Over 80% of the administrators surveyed

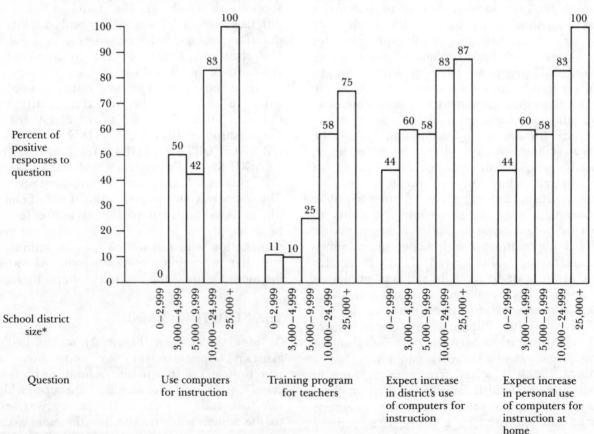

*12 to 15 school districts per size category.

FIGURE 1. Questionnaire responses by school district size

in Florida expect their districts to be using computers in some way for instruction within five years. And, as the cost for such facilities and equipment declines in relationship to the increasing labor costs of teacher salaries, even more districts will be considering the possible use of computer technology. Those already utilizing computers will consider wider implementation activities. The positive, as well as negative, impact of such growth could be great. But to ensure that instructional computing achieves its potential, careful planning must take place *now*.

For computers to be most effectively used for instruction, there are certain "gaps" which currently exist that need to be corrected. First and foremost, there is the gap which exists between the users and non-users of computers for instruction. This also translates into a gap between the rich and the poor, urban and rural, and large and small school districts (as indicated by the survey results). The danger here is that further economic, social, and educational stratification will occur as the "haves" become computer-literate before the "have nots" can even become "haves." As microcomputers continue to become a relatively less expensive luxury, this gap should close naturally, but slowly.

A second gap exists between training for instructional computer use and actual utilization. Evidence of such a problem already existing is shown clearly by a survey conducted in Minnesota of 3,800 secondary level teachers. Fully 35% of the teachers agreed or strongly agreed that all of their students should have some minimal understanding of computers, yet only 39% believed that their training had adequately prepared them to make decisions about using computers in their teaching (Minnesota Educational Computing Consortium, 1978). About one-third of those teachers teach with, or about, computers. Inadequately trained, or in many cases, not trained at all, computer-illiterate teachers cannot turn out computer-literate students. At the present time, the dichotomy between the sophistication of the technology and the sophistication of the training would seem to be increasing: computers are much easier to mass produce than trained teachers. A conscious and deliberate effort of will and planning on the part of teacher-training institutions is required to overcome this gap.

It is this second gap which appears most critical for teacher educators. Although computers are now institutionalized in schools for *management* purposes, there is little understanding of how they can be used for *instruction*. As previously noted, only four states certify teachers of computer science (Milner, 1980). Many students are now bringing the literacy of the computer age *to* the schools rather than receiving

that literacy *from* them. And, to complicate the problem, some school districts have banned the use of hand-held calculators by students as a matter of school board policy.

The lack of preparation and training of teachers is evident and acute. Historically, there is evidence of lessons learned from previous advances of technology in education. The growth of the television industry, and education's general neglect of its potential impact, has changed the complexion of the learner today. Students bring into the classroom an expanded world view and challenge the teachers to provide them with educational material as captivating as the recreational material provided by television. The ability of educational institutions to meet this challenge is discouraging.

Now, education faces the computer age. But, as with television, efforts to accommodate the impact are random and not systematically planned. There is an additional, more serious problem: general television viewing is a passive activity, not requiring active feedback on the part of the viewer. Computer technology demands active participation on the part of the user. Those who interact with this technology are required to respond. The future impact of this difference within the classroom cannot be predicted without careful and deliberate study.

There is clearly a need for computer literacy courses within teacher-training programs. But beyond that, there is also the need for a planned program of study of computers in education within the public school system. Such a program is needed not only to dispel myths about computers, but also to provide a "science" of computers in instruction. Computers can have an exponentially greater impact than television, due to their interactive nature and storage capabilities: therefore, an exponentially greater loss might result if educators, and their students, are not prepared for the future.

REFERENCES

Lewis, A.J., Harrison, D., Kajdan, P., and Soar, R. Future Applications of Electronic Technology to Education. Paper prepared for the Southeastern Regional Consortium Planning Project through a grant from the Florida Department of Education, University of Florida, Gainesville, November 1978.

Milner, S.D. Teaching Teachers About Computers: A Necessity for Education. *Phi Delta Kappan*, April 1980, 544–546.

Minnesota Educational Computing Consortium. Computer Literacy Study—an Update, The Consortium, St. Paul, Minnesota, June 2, 1978.

Molnar, A.R. The Next Great Crisis in American Education: Computer Literacy. *Journal of Educational Technology Systems*, 1978–79, 275–285.

How to Introduce Teachers, Principals and Curriculum Personnel to the Microcomputer

William D. Hedges

If the usage of the microcomputer in our schools is to increase and to be most effective, those of us involved with introducing computers to teachers, curriculum coordinators, principals and other school personnel must concern ourselves with a special problem. This problem is how to teach adults.

We now know that adolescents and adults respond differently in a training context in a number of respects. This article presents tips for working effectively with the adult learner.

TIP ONE: With adults there is a pronounced need to save face. As a rule, we adults are much more worried about "fouling up," committing a gaffe or otherwise appearing foolish in front of our peers than are young children. We tend to be so anxious in this respect that we don't take in data as well as younger students; at least until we have learned to relax with those around us. For example, I have noticed some adult graduate students so tense during a first experience at the console that they don't comprehend the simplest direction on the screen; for example, "Press the RETURN button."

Thus, a first requirement in introducing adults to the computer is to induce a relaxed attitude. They must quickly learn the machine won't bite them and they won't ruin anything if they press the wrong key. One way of establishing this relaxed environment during the first class is to seat each person at the console and begin with a guaranteed success experience. No big lectures at this stage! Put them down with a simple program that just CAN'T GO WRONG. Don't have them sitting there wondering what to do, what button to press, worried they've fouled up and are appearing foolish and too uptight to ask.

To accomplish your goal, use a short program that will take almost any response, short of striking the reset button of course, and will then DO SOMETHING INTELLIGENT with it—no matter how "dumb" the response is. Next, have each student turn the machine off and on several times, load the program, and run it.

I've yet to see an adult who gets up from the console for the first time having succeeded, who isn't ready and anxious to go back for more. On the other hand, let someone arise from a demo that didn't work, that makes him/her look silly, or left the person mystified and you are apt to get: "Well,

From "How to Introduce Teachers, Principals, and Curriculum Personnel to the Microcomputer," by William D. Hedges. In *The Computing Teacher*, January, 1981. Reprinted by permission.

I've had my doubts about the practicality of these things and this merely confirms those doubts." The point is that initial experiences are important in establishing positive or negative attitudes.

The above isn't meant to imply face saving is unimportant for children and adolescents; it *is* meant to stress the cruciality of this factor for adults.

TIP TWO: Avoid overemphasis on speed. It has been thoroughly established from research that we adults can continue to learn throughout life. However, the SPEED of our reaction time tends to slow as we grow older; the POWER or level of complexity of our thinking need not diminish.

The above suggests a reduced emphasis on the snap responses that characterize some teaching. If and when a question is asked, the instructor needs to provide adequate time for a considered response. The value of "wait-time" for chidren and youth has been established by Dr. M.B. Rowe. Such wait time is even more applicable for adults. Average wait time for teachers tends to be slightly over 1.3 seconds; this time interval is too short for many. With adults *and* youngsters, 3.0 seconds is recommended as a minimum interval. This provision for wait-time also tends to improve the quality of responses.

I thought when first reading the research on wait-time that I, of course, allowed adequate time. A check on myself with a stop watch quickly convinced me otherwise; three seconds is a longer period of time than you may think it is.

Of course, there are performance tasks which do require speed (as typing). In these, speed can be gradually developed over time with carefully graduated practice. However, speed at a computer terminal, at least initially, is a guaranteed way to make frequent, unnecessary errors. We humans produce enough errors, syntax and otherwise, without needlessly encouraging even more.

TIP THREE: Peer instruction can be very effective. Adults are accustomed to turning to one another for information—and in a learning mode tend to prefer asking a friend rather than an instructor with whom they are unfamiliar. I find it helpful to organize a class of adults in pairs and, in a few cases, in threes. This means that as one student is working at the terminal the other is watching. I am amazed at how many errors are caught in this way. The error correction is immediate; the partner points out a potential or actual error and it is immediately corrected. This not only saves the instructor, but provides far more rapid and comprehensive feedback for all than any one teacher could ever provide.

Immediate feedback is one of the powerful learning adjuncts of computer-assisted or computer-based education. Hence, why not build it into the learning situation with person-to-person interaction? This pairing also provides for modeling; that is, these educators will be more prone to allow students to work in pairs or small groups rather than in the isolation so typical in many school settings.

TIP FOUR: There is a need for purpose. Adults tend to resent practice for the sake of practice. By having your students work on a simple, clearly defined problem, you establish a purpose; the purpose is to create a product. No child is ever more proud of his "masterpiece" than two adults who have finally gotten the graphic they were striving to produce to work. They will, as excitedly as any child, call others over to see what they've done. At the same time, an effective learning strategy is at work, i.e., the adults learn the commands as they develop the need for them. This suggests another teaching tip.

There is a secondary spin-off from requiring problem definition. We educators have tended to shy away from explicit description of what goes on in the teaching/learning process. This becomes evident as you patiently push students to become very precise about the steps that need to be taken in programming even a simple problem.

TIP FIVE: In programming assignments, insist on blow-by-blow verbal descriptions of what the program is to do. As this is broken down into more and more precise language and finally into the language commands of the program, the students begin to perceive the need for being clear about what they are trying to accomplish; they also begin to see the reasons for requiring such precision. Some will resist precise problem definition and description; they want to get on with the task of programming rather than thinking through a problem in advance.

TIP SIX: Provide periodic sharing. I find it helpful to take a few minutes during each class for each small group to report where they are, what they are doing, problems they may have encountered. This activity places all students in a mode of easy admission of mistakes. Being able to laugh about "bloopers" as they realize everyone else has made just as many makes for a relaxed classroom environment. In addition, some who are having difficulty pick up valuable information from those reporting.

TIP SEVEN: Establish early that each project will be pilot tested by a number of the other students. The idea that field testing of any program is a necessity is a crucial one to implant; it also lets the producers see a needed modification in a program without the instructor being the only person to point it out. A typical author response as a fellow student tries out a program is, "I already see something there I need to change." Also, no instructor can possibly pick up all the needed improvements; he won't make the same responses as beginning students. By knowing they will have their peers "taking" their program, class members are motivated to produce a better product than they otherwise might.

In summary, I have found that adults can and do respond if factors such as those identified above are incorporated by the instructor in his or her teaching. Undoubtedly, some of you will have noted other factors which can improve class operation. I would be interested to know of them.

Teaching Educators About Computing: A Different Ball Game

Don G. Rawitsch

INTRODUCTION

Instructional computing has finally gained the widespread attention that has long been predicted for it. Since about 1978, microcomputers have been available on the market with sufficient capabilities and low enough prices to attract educators. While timeshare computing has been serving as an instructional tool for over a decade, the newest advances in computer hardware are pushing computing in the classroom to new levels of utilization.

This explosion of easy, available, attractive technology has created an insatiable demand from educators who want to learn how to use computers. Teachers especially, interested in the ready-made applications computers can provide, want to know how to operate the computer as well as how to program the computer so that new applications can be developed. This quest for knowledge has produced a demand for qualified instructors in this area, and numerous workshops and classes are now being taught by staff from computer support organizations, college and university faculties, and public and private school teachers with computing backgrounds.

A problem exists, however, in that most people who have the background to teach educators about the computer did not themselves learn from an educational perspective. Instruction in this area has typically been done from a technical or computer science point of view. Many of those who now train teachers sat side by side in classes with computer science students. This kind of instruction produces

From "Teaching Educators About Computing: A Different Ball Game," by Don G. Rawitsch. In *The Computing Teacher*, December, 1981. Reprinted by permission.

good technical people but often does not speak to the needs of educators. It is time to reexamine the instructional approaches used to teach computing to those in the educational profession.

Many aspects of computer technology can be appropriately included in the computing "curriculum" for educators, including:

1) How to operate computers.
2) How to use computer applications.
3) How to integrate applications into the curriculum.
4) How to evaluate applications.
5) How to design new applications.
6) How to program computers.

The first four are the most critical. However, the last two are becoming increasingly popular as educators, having learned to use computers, desire to implement original instructional ideas on the machine. The purpose of this article is not to provide a syllabus for teaching the above topics. Rather, it attempts to identify problems common to teaching any of them. The sample activities referenced are drawn from several of the topics as appropriate.

DEFINING THE PROBLEM

In examining the question of how to teach educators about computers, consider as an example the area of programming the computers used in schools. The traditional approach to programming is to see it as a complete and highly organized body of information which can be broken down into small, distinct pieces. These pieces are, for the most part, the various programming statements or instructions sequentially ordered to make the computer perform a specific task or operation. There are a finite number of these statements, and they can be generally ranked in order of difficulty. The teaching of programming, then, becomes simply the explanation of each statement, starting with those that are easiest to comprehend and progressing to the more difficult ones. When all the statements have been covered, the learner supposedly knows how to program a computer. The fact that computer programming by nature 1) is so organized, 2) is so rule oriented, 3) is so sequential, 4) provides such immediate feedback, and 5) produces results which are so fascinating makes this traditional approach irresistible to many instructors.

However, this traditional approach often works because of the nature of the learners. Students who enjoy computer science and have the aptitude for learning material of this type will probably not have trouble picking up the fundamentals of programming. As a follow-up to the instructor's explanations, such a student will experiment a great deal on his/her own, will discuss the subject with others having the same interest, and will read additional material on programming.

Educators, on the other hand, come from a different environment. They may or may not have a technical or scientific background. Their goals in learning programming are more modest than those who intend to pursue it as a profession. Their interest in learning may stem more from curiosity than from a desire to produce anything specific. Computing is probably not their main field of interest and so they will not be devoting large amounts of time outside of the programming class to improving their newly acquired skills. This type of person needs a different instructional approach.

Listed below are three characteristics of the traditional method of teaching about computing which conflict with the needs of the educator as learner:

1) Computing as foreign turf
   An educator often comes to computing with a large body of knowledge about other fields, but usually none about this one. Instruction in computing often proceeds with the new material without relating it back to what the learner already knows. From the standpoint of self-confidence, the educator may find it uncomfortable to play the role of a novice in terms of computing when s/he is such an expert in other fields.

2) Computing as a discipline, and somebody else's at that
   The areas of computing that are of most use to educators are not difficult to learn; yet, the subject is often cluttered with terminology, details, and incidental concepts that are important to the discipline of computer science but extraneous to the educator. This just reinforces the belief that computing is a mysterious undertaking reserved for computer professionals rather than simply being a method of using a machine to help in the instructional process.

3) Computing as a collection of little pieces
   The approach of explaining computing "piece by piece" often fails to give the learner the "big picture." Each piece of information is totally new to the learner and s/he may not see how it relates to a larger concept. Without an overall road map that shows where all the technical explanation is leading, the new material is apt to maintain an aura of mystery that inhibits the learning process.

Instructors of computing who work with educators need to be aware of these when designing their instructional plan. Each of them represents a problem area, but each problem has a solutuion, which will now be discussed.

SOLUTIONS

1) Computing as foreign turf

Computing need not be strange territory unless the instructor insists on approaching it as an area that has no relationship to any other. If computing can be introduced to the educator as something that relates to a previous experience, it will not appear mysterious or threatening. As a tool for the teacher, computing relates to three areas that teachers encounter in any instructional design: 1) their curriculum, 2) their instructional materials, and 3) their learning activities.

Educators should never be asked to accept computing solely on the merits it may have on its own. Rather, they should first define their *curriculum* goals, and only then decide if the computer has anything to offer them in achieving those goals. Consider the following example from the field of social studies. Listed below are some objectives of social studies teachers, objectives that were important before computers were invented:

STRATEGY—Create new experiences for students.
STRATEGY—Investigate new sources of information.
CONTENT—Present facts to students.
CONTENT—Present concepts to students.
SKILL—Inquiry for asking appropriate questions and evaluating information.
SKILL—Social interaction for learning to work with others.
ATTITUDE—Empathy for living conditions and feelings of others.

This is the place to start with teachers. Then, continue with the concept that there are definite types of instructional computing activities that can assist the social studies teacher in achieving those specific goals, as shown on the following chart. If subject area goals are defined before information on the types of instructional computing activities is given, teachers are more likely to understand that computing relates directly to their subject area.[1]

The first thing a teacher does when confronted with new *instructional materials* is to evaluate them, both for their general quality and for their relevance to the students being taught. Computing applications should be treated no differently. Thus, it makes sense when introducing teachers to computing to cover the evaluation of computing materials immediately after they have learned how to use these materials on a computer. Listed below are questions that might be answered when evaluating computer courseware:[2]

Is computer use appropriate for this activity?
Are the goals of the program clear? What are they?
Does the activity in the program focus on these goals?

DESIRED ELEMENTS IN SOCIAL STUDIES TEACHING

Types of Instructional Computing Activity	STRATEGY Create New Experiences	STRATEGY Explore New Information	CONTENT Facts	CONTENT Concepts	SKILL Inquiry	SKILL Social Interaction	ATTITUDE Empathy for Others
Simulation	X		X	X	X	X	X
Data Base Inquiry		X		X	X		
Information Retrieval		X	X		X		
Drill and Practice		X					

Are the instructions clear? If not, why?
How understandable is the format of the output?
How good is the continuity of the output?
How vulnerable is the program to input mistakes?
How appropriately is reinforcement used?

Discussing the evaluation process, something with which teachers are familiar, before covering how computers work and how they are programmed, helps reinforce the idea that computing relates to other experiences and skills already familiar to the educator.

Computing activities fit into an educator's instructional plan just like any other *learning activity*. Activities can be thought of as fitting into an instructional sequence as follows:[3]

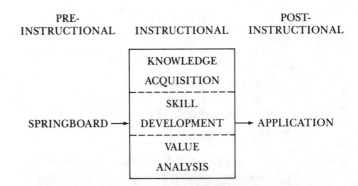

PRE-INSTRUCTIONAL	INSTRUCTIONAL	POST-INSTRUCTIONAL
SPRINGBOARD →	KNOWLEDGE ACQUISITION / SKILL DEVELOPMENT / VALUE ANALYSIS	→ APPLICATION

A computing activity can be used at any place in such a model. A simulation may act as a springboard to a new topic. Tutorials and drills can introduce new knowledge or skills. Data analysis may provide a further application of concepts already learned. Showing that a general instructional model applies to computing activities just as well as to non-computing activities helps to emphasize that computing does not take an educator off already familiar ground.

Just as computing relates to broad areas in every educator's background, past experience can be drawn upon to teach specific computing concepts. The use of analogy is one method of doing this. For example, some educators have difficulty understanding the general idea of how computer programs are written. The following is a useful analogy which also makes for an interesting activity in a training session.

Have a volunteer come to the front of the room and pretend to be working in a mail order business that sells circles and squares to customers. These objects are shipped in both big and small envelopes. If the shipping room supervisor were to tell the employee (our volunteer) how to do the job, s/he might give the following instructions:

Put circles in small envelopes.
Put squares in big envelopes.
Put only one item in each envelope.
Place filled envelopes in a pile to your right.

However, giving instructions in this manner will not work for computers because each instruction contains too many concepts and a computer, being essentially stupid, will not understand. Programming, then, is the art of *organizing* instructions so that a computer *can* carry out a given task. Thus, a computer might be given the instructions in the following format:

1) Take an item.
2) Take an envelope from top of left pile.
3) If envelope is too big, skip to (7); otherwise proceed.
4) If item is a circle, skip to (8); otherwise proceed.
5) Put envelope on bottom of left pile.
6) Skip to (2).
7) If item is a circle, skip to (5); otherwise proceed.
8) Put item in envelope.
9) Put envelope on top of right pile.
10) If more items, skip to (1); otherwise proceed.
11) Stop.

Project this sequence of instructions with an overhead projector and have the volunteer stand in front of a table with a pile of empty envelopes on his/her left, a pile of circles and squares directly in front, and a place for envelopes that have been stuffed to the right. Read through the instructions aloud in the correct sequence and have the volunteer perform the tasks. (A most effective run-through starts with three empty envelopes stacked in top down order small-large-large and three items [shapes] stacked in top down order square-circle-square.)

Of course, following this set of instructions seems unnecessarily time-consuming to humans, but computers make up for this with their amazing processing speed.

Using this analogy, which can be understood without any knowledge of computer technology, might be helpful in making the educator more comfortable with the idea of programming.

Another way to draw on past experiences is simply to call on an educator's common sense. Again turning to programming, a person who has seen computer applications run has a general understanding of what a program can make a computer do. Before discussing a computer language in a training session, participants could be asked to construct a list of what a computer can do, based on their current knowledge. Such a list might end up as follows:

- put stuff on the screen
- accept stuff at the keyboard
- remember things
- do arithmetic
- stop the computer
- make decisions
- skip around
- repeat procedures
- read from a collection of information

Once the list is recorded, the particular statements of the programming language being considered can be matched up to listed items as the statements are introduced. If BASIC was the subject, then the list might ultimately end up as follows:

Purpose	Statement
put stuff on the screen	PRINT
accept stuff at the keyboard	INPUT
remember things	LET
do arithmetic	LET
stop the computer	END
make decisions	IF . . . THEN
skip around	GOTO
repeat procedures	FOR . . . NEXT
read from a collection of information	READ . . . DATA

The critical point is that the educators showed their understanding of programming before they were taught anything about it. What they needed from a computing expert was simply how to "spell" in a computer language.

2) Computing as someone else's discipline

The technical world of computing, being a relatively new field, has brought with it a vast array of new terminology. This terminology should be learned by those being trained in the discipline of computer science. However, educators wishing to learn something about the application of computing to instruction only find these technicalities threatening and inhibiting to learning. Certainly at times it becomes necessary for even the beginner to learn some of computing's technical jargon. But it should be tied to other terms or concepts already understood by the learner.

For example, in explaining the components of a microcomputer system, a list similar to the following is usually used:

1) Keyboard
2) Disk drive
3) Central memory (Random Access Memory)
4) Language card or language chips (Read Only Memory)
5) Central processor
6) Video display screen

While it will become useful for an educator to know these terms eventually, it would be better to discuss components on a more general level first, as in the list below:[4]

1) A place for accepting spontaneous ideas
2) A place from which packaged ideas are retrieved
3) A place to temporarily hold ideas waiting to be processed
4) A place to translate ideas from human language to "procedure" language
5) A place to carry out procedures to get things done.
6) A place to announce ideas after they have been processed

After the generalized descriptions are understood, the technical terms can be matched up to them.

Computer programming is an area replete with new terminology. Instructors of programming training sessions for educators, out of deference to the computer science discipline, sometimes feel obligated to burden the learner with more than is necessary to understand the essential programming process. For example, because professional programmers use flowcharts in the planning of programs, instructors tend to think it is necessary to teach flowcharting to all beginning programmers. Theoretically, the flowchart should bridge the gap between the larger concepts of programming and the actual coding of statements. But the symbolism used in flowcharting is as foreign to the beginner as the code itself. Perhaps the learner actually depends on knowing the programming statement to understand how a flowchart works, which is the reverse of what is intended. Researcher Richard Mayer found that flowcharts did not work well in teaching programming to beginners: "The flowchart aid presented geometric symbols which were apparently familiar to subjects, but the symbols themselves provided only a second layer of code ... rather than an organizing superstructure."[5] Teaching technicalities for their own sake is not helpful in motivating educators to learn about computing.

3) Computing as a collection of little pieces

Computing is a brand new topic to most educators. Thus, almost everything being taught in this area constitutes a new piece of information. In such a learning situation it is helpful to be given some kind of organizing concept into which each piece of information can be placed, and so, given some perspective. Without this, learning about computing for an educator is like attending a meeting without an agenda.

The concept referred to has been called by some researchers an "advance organizer."[6] An advance organizer is simply some easily comprehended "table of contents" which gives the learner "the big picture" prior to receiving the details on each piece of that picture. Two suggested techniques already mentioned can serve as advance organizers in teaching beginners about computing. The list of purposes of a computer program suggested by participants in a training session can serve to organize the programming statements to be taught. The list of microcomputer hardware components in generalized terms can serve to organize a discussion of computer hardware identification.

Computer science students are eager to know everything they can about computers because it is their chosen field. Educators need road maps to the technology because they are not certain just what they would like to explore in this new field. Advance organizers help keep the flood of new information in perspective.

CONCLUSION

In summary, this discussion leads to the identification of three principles to be applied in teaching educators about computing:

1) Ease into the technicalities of computing through the use of concepts familiar to the learner's previous knowledge;
2) Don't distract the learner's grasp of fundamental concepts by introducing extraneous technical information; and
3) Use an organizing model to give the learner the "big picture" before discussing the detailed pieces.

Workshops and classes for educators on general computer knowledge should adhere to these three principles. The first activity should be a demonstration of computer applications in instruction followed by an exercise in evaluating those applications. Educators can identify with understanding and judging applications, regardless of the format. Descriptions of machinery and electronics only serve to get things off on the wrong foot. Educators as learners about comptuing should not be distracted with lectures on "hardware," "software," "core memory," "program execution," "disk operating systems," and the infamous "K" (standing for a memory capacity of about 1000 characters). These labels can be applied later for those who wish to learn the "language" of the computing field. An advance organizer, if only an outline of the session's topics, assures the participants that even when it becomes necessary to get technical, the main point being addressed is the instructional value of computers and that the discussion will soon return to that perspective.

It is becoming a rule of thumb in the computing field that "the software is more important than the hardware." That is to say, the machine is not useful without an effective set of instructions. As computers are introduced into areas like education, where the majority of users do not have backgrounds in the field of computing, we may soon be saying that "training is the most important of all." Yet, the training of educators in the effective use of computers in instruction is a subject that has received slight attention in either educational or computing literature.

We may not yet know the most effective way to train educators to use computers. However, it seems reasonable to assume that this training is different than the way we teach children about computers or the way we teach adult computer professionals about them. Instructors involved in training educators in the use of computers must keep in mind the perspective from which educators come. Such instructors would benefit from a set of instructional principles that apply when teaching about a field entirely new to them.

FOOTNOTES

[1] Minnesota Educational Computing Consortium, "System Library Guide for Social Science," MECC, St. Paul, Minn., 1980, pp. 1–3.

[2] Minnesota Educational Computing Consortium, "Introduction to the APPLE II in Instruction Training Booklet," MECC, St. Paul, Minn., 1980, pp. 10–11.

[3] Glenn, Allen, "Simulations in the Instructional Sequence," *The Social Studies*, Vol. 68, No. 1, Jan./Feb., 1977, pp. 23–26.

[4] MECC, "Introduction to the APPLE II in Instruction Training Booklet," p. 12.

[5] Mayer, Richard, "Different Problem-Solving Competencies Established in Learning Computer Programming With and Without Mean-

ingful Models," *Journal of Educational Psychology*, Vol. 67, 1975, p. 732.

[6] Mayer, Richard, "Some Conditions of Meaningful Learning for Computer Programming: Advance Organizers and Subject Control of Frame Order," *Journal of Educational Psychology*, Vol. 68, 1976, pp. 143–150.

On Being a Change Agent

David Moursund

If our technologically-oriented society continues, then eventually computers will be commonplace. Children will grow up in homes, schools and neighborhoods in which everyone uses computers. Computerized information retrieval, word processing and problem solving will be as widely used as paper and pencil techniques are today.

But that "eventually" may be a long way off. Sure, hardware can be mass produced, and hardware progress continues unabated. Sure, a piece of high-quality software can be widely distributed, making the cost to each end-user quite reasonable.

Unfortunately, knowledgeable end-users cannot be mass produced. The computer is a powerful tool, but it is a complex tool. To use a general range of computer capabilities effectively takes considerable knowledge, training, experience and a measure of courage.

That is where you and other educators come in. You are a computer-knowledgeable educator, capable of helping others to learn about computers. Thus, you are a change agent.

Being a change agent is stressful. This is especially true in the computer field. "How do I know what I am doing is right?" "The computer field is changing so fast—how can I possibly keep up?" "Others seem to know so much more than I." "The field hasn't been researched very well. I fear that I will do more harm than good." "I don't have time to keep up in the field where I got my degree. What chance do I have in the computer field?"

Do you have any of these doubts? I have had all of them, and they continue to reoccur periodically. Be aware that these are common fears! Here are some ways to deal with them.

RELAX! PAUSE FOR A MOMENT. TAKE A COUPLE OF DEEP BREATHS. REALIZE THAT YOU ARE "DOING A NUMBER" ON YOURSELF.

If you are a regular reader of *The Computing Teacher*, then undoubtedly you are in the upper five percent of all educators in terms of your computer

From "On Being a Change Agent," by David Moursund. In *The Computing Teacher*, February, 1982. Reprinted by permission.

knowledge. You know a lot, both relative to other educators and relative to most students. You know enough to help others learn, and you know enough to do some things that will reduce the stress on you.

1. Admit freely and openly:
   a. That you don't know as much as you would like to know about computers, but you are still learning.
   b. That you feel it is very important to help others learn about computers, and that you are committed to doing so.

This type of open and honest attitude is beneficial to you and to your colleagues. It is intellectual honesty—an excellent role model for students.

2. Learn from your everyday environment. You are surrounded by easily accessible opportunities to learn. For example:

   a. Talk to your fellow educators about current and future applications of computers. As you try to express your insights you will receive valuable feedback as well as hearing the insights of others.
   b. If you are a teacher, think carefully about what you teach. Then discuss the problems of computers in education with your students. Learn from them as you help them to begin to understand the role of computers in your teaching area.
   c. Watch science-oriented television programs, especially those on PBS. You will see that computers are an everyday tool in modern science, and you will learn some of these computer applications.
   d. Pay attention to computer and other electronics-oriented ads. Browse in an electronics store. Visit an electronic arcade center.

3. Take a course. (Or, if you can't do that, buy a computer-oriented book and read it.) Check your nearby college or university. Perhaps you can get your school district to arrange an appropriate course. If you can't find what you need, encourage your school district or a nearby school to create an appropriate course.

4. Finally, continue to be a change agent. Eventually you, and thousands like you, will be successful. Then you will be surrounded by computer-knowledgeable people, and you will no longer need to be a change agent in this area.

WHAT'S YOUR OPINION?

1. Teachers must accept a greater emphasis on computing as part of their teaching methodology.
2. Teaching competencies related to computing should be taught in all teacher-preparation programs.
3. Teachers learning about computers should not be taught using classical lecture delivery modes.
4. At the in-service training level, it is very difficult to deliver computer training requiring sustained, intensive concentration of both trainer and trainee.
5. Only a few very eager teachers can muster the concentration of energy and time necessary to integrate computers adequately into their classrooms.
6. Research in education is the most important factor in good design/delivery of computer-based instruction.
7. Ten years from now there will be no problem with in-service teacher training in computers because almost all teachers will already know about computer uses.
8. New plans must be implemented for improving computer instruction for educators so that concepts may be grasped and skills acquired from relatively brief and infrequent investments of time.
9. Teachers should know enough about computers to operate them but need not know about their internal technical operation.
10. When training teachers to use computers, it is important to avoid frustrating the trainees as much as possible.
11. Teachers should not attempt major implementations of computer uses in the classroom by themselves.
12. Education programs that ignore computers are not only missing an opportunity but are failing to discharge a responsibility.
13. Teachers without previous knowledge of programming should be able to write programs after a half-year of in-service training.
14. Foreign governments that are investing large sums of money and placing high priority on the development of computer-based skills for teachers could more profitably invest in other aspects of education.
15. A national center should be established for research in the uses of microprocessors in education.
16. Transition to computer-based curricula is likely to cause enormous stress in our educational system.
17. The most talented faculty members of schools of education are educational technology specialists

who are leaving the schools for more lucrative jobs in the private sector.

18. Many of the problems associated with computer usage are caused by the overutilization of under-educated people to carry out programs.

19. To have a computer-literate society, we must first train teachers to use computers in their classrooms.

20. Teachers using computers must either keep up with the changing technology or give up using computers.

21. All instructors need the control, confidence, and authority that come with understanding the technology they use.

22. It appears that student awareness of computer technology will increase while teachers will remain uneducated.

23. The current lack of funds to serve as incentives for teachers to learn about computing is a threat to education.

24. In general, teachers do perceive the need for preparation in computer use.

25. All preservice teachers should be required to take a course in computer programming, even if it is offered in place of another content- or discipline-related course.

26. Educational institutions do not appear actively to be planning an adequate approach to micro-computer usage.

27. Educators will be major contributors to computer illiteracy if they do not give priorities to the implementation and use of this technology.

28. Educational institutions are training systems programmers, analysts, and technicians, but they are not training educational computer specialists.

29. Students graduating as teachers from higher education are generally not computer-literate.

30. When budget slashes occur, concentrated efforts to resolve problems in areas of basic skills take priority over new methods and long-range planning.

31. The power of the budget reduces the educator's ability to take risks, to make major changes, and to program for the future.

32. Student teachers who graduate computer-illiterate then return for additional training to the very institutions that caused their illiteracy.

33. Even with a focus on computer-literate graduates, teachers enter classrooms where there exists no planning for the future use of computers.

34. The lack of systematic support to challenge the problem of computer illiteracy, coupled with the growth and visibility of the microtechnology industry, augurs a bleak future for education.

35. The training of teachers in computer-based instructional use is the key to universal computer literacy.

36. Computer-illiterate teachers cannot produce computer-literate students.

37. Because of their interactive nature and storage capabilities, computers can have a far greater impact on the classroom than television; therefore, a correspondingly greater loss will result if educators and students are not prepared to use them.

38. There is an insatiable demand by educators to learn how to use computers.

39. Most people who have the background to teach educators about the computer did not themselves learn from an educational perspective but rather from a computer technology perspective.

40. Teachers' interest in learning about computers may arise more from curiosity than from a desire to use them in any particular way.

41. Very few people with imagination, creativity, and a drive to innovate enter the field of teaching. Most of those who do are soon driven out by frustration.

42. In time, teachers will overcome their fear of the computer and view it as a valuable aid.

43. With increased computer usage, the teacher will become less of a lecturer and more of a consultant or facilitator of information.

44. Effecting major changes in the teacher's role through updated training programs should be a high-priority goal for education.

45. A computer curriculum is too diverse, complex, and difficult for anyone but a scientist to learn.

46. We simply cannot expect 25,000–50,000 school-teachers to invent curricula and prepare materials for students to use.

47. Some teachers are opposed to computer use because of its *1984* image.

48. Some teachers refuse to get involved with computers because they believe that it's only another fad.

49. Many teachers don't want to bother with computers and are content to let the younger members on their staff take the responsibility.

50. Brief work sessions or single-term night courses are inadequate to prepare teachers to use computers in the classroom.

51. Substantial experience and training are required for teachers to be able to integrate computers into their classrooms.

52. Generally, the level of computer literacy is low among college-of-education faculty.

53. Using a computer causes too much additional work for an already overburdened teacher.

54. Those who recognize the computer's promise in education must be better salesmen of the concept, and a better sales pitch has to address technology in education in general.

55. The introduction of computers into schools will attract brighter people into the teaching profession.
56. The failure of teachers to implement classroom computer use parallels their refusal to accept and teach the metric system. In both cases teachers believe that the current system is adequate.
57. Education as a profession will become more prestigious with the advent of heavy computer use in the schools.
58. Computers are raising the tension level of teachers because keeping up with computers is exhausting.

EXERCISES

1. What could you do with an instructional computer in your present situation?
2. Explain why some efforts to implement computer education have failed.
3. What causes the failures outlined by Timothy Jay in "Computerphobia"?
4. Write a brief essay explaining why you would like to own a personal computer.
5. Start a scrapbook of computer-related newspaper articles (especially those dealing with education). Document the source and date of each article, and underline the important points.
6. Develop a set of criteria that a school principal could use to determine which teachers should be assigned to teach computer awareness courses.
7. It has been suggested that teachers in the future will need to know how to write computer programs. Is this a realistic and necessary expectation? Compare your response with that of (a) a fellow teacher, (b) a school principal, (c) a computer science teacher, (d) a professor of education, and (e) a parent.
8. In what ways will widespread use of microcomputers change the teacher's job?
9. A foreign university is now offering its entire curriculum at home via computer and communications networks. What are your thoughts about the feasibility of such a school now and in the future?

INTERFACE

Making
It
Happen!

four

Computer Assisted Instruction

Since the early 1960s, computer assisted instruction (CAI) has been touted as the single, ultimate justification for educational computing. Until recently, however, the actual use of CAI in classrooms lagged behind expectations, while applications never quite measured up to the enthusiasm generated in educators since CAI's introduction. Today, the presence of personal computers in schools is causing an impressive rebirth of CAI usage. Though a dearth of well designed, high-quality software persists, the interest shown by software houses, publishers, and others suggests that CAI is about to fulfill its original promise.

In this chapter Chambers and Sprecher provide an excellent summary of CAI's past, present, and anticipated future. Required reading for anyone interested specifically in CAI, this article presents types of CAI, evaluations, costs, languages, appropriate hardware, courseware creation, future developments, and suggestions for implementation. The Chambers and Bork summary of a report for the Association for Computing Machinery (ACM) offers interesting statistics, recommendations, and an assessment of current and projected uses of CAI in U.S. schools. Steely offers suggestions for effective CAI design, while Garson makes a thought-provoking case against the use of multiple-choice tests (a common CAI application). Finally, Forman gives an excellent, in-depth summary of recent CAI literature.

Computer Assisted Instruction: Current Trends and Critical Issues

Jack A. Chambers and Jerry W. Sprecher

1. INTRODUCTION

The focus of this paper is upon the learning situation and upon the use of the computer to provide course content instruction in the form of simulations, games, tutorials, and drill and practice. In the United States this has come to be known as computer assisted instruction (CAI), and in the United Kingdom and elsewhere as computer assisted learning (CAL). Throughout this paper the term CAI should be considered synonymous with CAL.

1.1 Types of CAI

There are several types of CAI, representing distinctions which have been neglected in the CAI literature and in practice. The first relates to CAI which supplements the learning situation, as opposed to that which substitutes for other modes of instruction. The former will be referred to as adjunct CAI [35]. It is illustrated by the short (one-half to one hour) CAI programs available through vendor libraries which are used to support or illustrate concepts. These concepts are then usually discussed in the regular classroom.

In contrast, CAI materials which provide instruction of a substitute or stand-alone variety are usually of longer duration and are generally less well-known

From "Computer Assisted Instruction: Current Trends and Critical Issues," by Jack A. Chambers and Jerry W. Sprecher. In *Communications of the ACM*, June, 1980. © 1980 by the Association for Computing Machinery. Reprinted by permission.

and understood in the educational world. These will be referred to as primary CAI. This approach is represented in the United States by the development of entire credit courses. In the United Kingdom the Open University is experimenting with this type of CAI (as well as with the adjunct type). In many discussions worldwide, primary CAI is being debated as a part of distance learning—a term used in many countries to describe efforts to provide education to large groups over broad distances. Distance learning typically encompasses many types of educational technology, including radio, TV, electronic conferencing and mail, and computers, in conjunction with the more traditional methods such as correspondence courses [32].

A second distinction refers to the simplicity-complexity level of CAI. The author approach, employing an easy-to-learn programming language as well as minimal hardware to support the use of the programs, epitomizes the simplistic approach. However, such simplistic CAI produces limited results; i.e., graphics capabilities, large-scale calculations, and the like are not components of such programs. Conversely, complex CAI, which permits extensive use of graphics, large-scale calculations, authoring aids, etc., requires complex author languages (necessitating extensive time for authors to acquire proficiency in use) and large-scale computing capability to support such use.

1.2 Advantages and disadvantages of CAI

Perhaps the most widely accepted value of CAI is that it involves the individual actively in the learning process. It is impossible for the student to be a totally passive member of the situation, and this very activity and involvement facilitate learning [41]. Another much touted value is the ability of the learner to proceed at his own pace, which has strong implications for both the slow learner and the gifted person.

Reinforcement of learning in such situations is immediate and systematized, which should result in more effective learning, according to established theories of instruction. In addition, the computer in a simulation mode permits students to explore time and space, to mix explosive chemicals together in a simulated laboratory without destroying themselves and the lab, and to investigate complex problems using instruments and methodology which would be excessively costly or not possible at all without the computer.

In addition, the use of computers in this manner frees faculty members or training coordinators to devote more time to the personal, human considerations of their students. Time thus spent with students has been found in a nationwide study of university faculty and students [18] to be *the* most important factor, in students' opinions, in the development of their creative abilities. Thus the use of the computer in these modes should result in an educational environment in which individuals learn more and in which their potential for innovative and creative professional work is more fully developed. Similarly, there should be a greater acceptance of the computer as a helpful tool after the student has used simulations, games, or tutorials.

A final comment regarding the benefits of CAI relates to remedial education. The problems of handling remedial training for students have increased, because the problems of bilingual and disadvantaged students and the inadequate English and mathematics skills of entering university students are being recognized. Computer tutorials, especially in these areas, appear to be both educationally sound and reasonable in cost, if approached in an appropriate manner. Similar cases can be made for the use of CAI to support continuing education and in industrial training programs.

The disadvantages of using CAI in the learning process can be divided into three main categories. In order of importance, these are: (1) the need for teachers and training directors to move from accepted methods that work to a new and relatively untried method in which most individuals have little expertise and which arouses considerable fear and antipathy owing to its heavy technological base; (2) the primitive state of the art, in which a diversity of computing hardware and CAI languages compete with little apparent coordination from professionals in the educational world; in which the majority of available CAI course materials are poorly constructed, largely undocumented, and able to be run on only select computers for which they were written; and in which there are relatively few "experts" to whom CAI users can turn for assistance; and (3) the cost of hardware, CAI course materials (courseware), and individuals to help implement the process—especially since computer vendors initially touted CAI as an ultimate cost saving device. When used as a substitute or replacement method for learning, CAI can be cost saving; however, in actuality CAI is used today mainly as a supplement to enrich learning in the educational scene, and therefore costs should be considered as add-ons.

1.3 Early developments

CAI usage was initiated in the United States in the late '50s and early '60s. Early work was done at Florida State University, Dartmouth, and Stanford.

At Florida State, using an IBM 1500 interactive computer and the newly developed high-level CAI language Coursewriter, several entire university level courses (physics and statistics) were developed and offered for credit. Providing a quite different viewpoint, but occurring in the same general time frame, the Basic language was developed and implemented throughout the campus at Dartmouth. Thus for the first time faculty and students were provided with a simplified programming language which could be learned in a few days and which permitted the development of simplistic CAI programs.

At Stanford in the mid-sixties, Patrick Suppes and Richard Atkinson [65] applied CAI methodology in a different area. Their work represented the first attempt to increase children's skill levels in basic English and mathematics through computerized drill and practice.

1.4 Scope of the paper

With this brief orientation to CAI the authors will first survey current CAI trends and existing centers of activity. This will be followed by a discussion of those studies which have attempted to evaluate the use of CAI in special learning situations. Next, costs will be discussed, and the critical issues in CAI will be highlighted, in order to identify courses of action to alleviate some of these problems. The possible future uses of CAI will then be briefly outlined. The paper will close with conclusions and recommendations.

2. CURRENT TRENDS AND EXISTING CENTERS OF ACTIVITY

The majority of work in CAI appears to be concentrated in four major areas: the United States, the United Kingdom, Canada, and Japan. Although some discussion of CAI throughout the world will follow, the major thrust will be in identifying activities in these four countries.

2.1 The United States

Dartmouth University served as one of the prime sources for adjunct CAI program development for many years. During the early '70s Dartmouth, in conjunction with the Universities of Oregon, North Carolina, Iowa, and Texas, formed a consortium (CONDUIT) to acquire, evaluate, and distribute quality instructional computing materials on a national basis. CONDUIT, supported by the National Science Foundation and the Fund for the Improvement of Post-Secondary Education, is located on the University of Iowa campus, under the direction of James Johnson. It currently offers more than seventy-five computer programs in a variety of fields to support higher education classes [20]. Some CAI programs, mostly in Basic or Fortran, are available both for mini- and larger computers, with a few now available for microcomputers.

A similar effort, but encompassing both pre- and post-secondary education, is ongoing at the Minnesota Educational Computing Consortium at Lauderdale, Minnesota, with Kenneth Brumbough as Director of Instructional Services. One of the major recent accomplishments of this consortium is an extensive comparison of the capabilities and costs of microcomputers and their uses in the educational environment [44]. One result of their study has been the installation of several hundred Apple II microcomputers throughout the state of Minnesota, with an accompanying growth in the development of CAI programs.

Another project emphasizing adjunct CAI programs in Basic that will function on most computers is housed at California State University, Fresno, under the direction of Jack Chambers. This project is concerned with the acquisition, faculty evaluation, restructuring, and sharing of quality CAI materials. Over 135 programs are now available in a diversity of fields for both secondary and higher education. Copies of the library have been requested and distributed to over 125 educational institutions worldwide [1].

Yet another California project is housed at the University of California, Irvine, under the direction of Alfred Bork. This project has been under way for a number of years and has produced a significant amount of courseware of a fairly complex nature supporting instruction in physics at the higher educational level.

At Stanford CAI work continues under the direction of Patrick Suppes. Entire CAI courses are now offered in Russian and mathematics.

The PLATO system, funded by the National Science Foundation and housed at the University of Illinois under the direction of Donald Bitzer, is probably the most well-known CAI project in the world and therefore will not be dealt with in any great depth here. This system uses the Tutor language, a much higher level language than Basic, and requires large-scale computing capability, at least for authoring purposes. Despite this, the system has been extensively used as supplemental to the learning situation. Since the system can produce complex CAI programs having graphics capabilities (including animation), voice output, and the like, it is quite possible that the system will be used even more heavily in the future in the primary CAI mode.

A second major PLATO installation, emphasizing support for music education, is located at the University of Delaware. A third is centered at Florida State University at Tallahassee. At this installation support is provided to select Florida high schools for PLATO-based remedial studies in mathematics.

Other, smaller PLATO installations are scattered throughout the United States.

A final project of interest, emphasizing the use of primary CAI, is represented by the TICCIT (Time-Shared Interactive Computer-Controlled Information Television) project. Funded by the National Science Foundation through a grant to the MITRE Corporation, TICCIT was developed at the University of Texas and Brigham Young University under the direction of Victor Bunderson. Using minicomputers and modified TV receivers, the system was designed to provide basic undergraduate instruction in English and mathematics. It was initially implemented at Phoenix College (Arizona) and the Alexandria Community College (Virginia). The English portion is still in use at Phoenix [45], and both the English and mathematics courses are still in use at Alexandria [59].

2.2 The United Kingdom

Computer assisted learning (CAL), as CAI is known in the United Kingdom, began in the late '60s in scattered but important projects headed by Peter Smith at Queen Mary College, Robert Lewis at Chelsea (both part of the University of London), and James Howe at the Artificial Intelligence Laboratory at the University of Edinburgh. The British government began to be seriously interested in this type of activity at about this time. This interest resulted in funded work at Leeds and, in 1972, in a two-million-pound, five-year CAI project. With Richard Hooper as director, the program began in 1973 as the National Development Program in Computer Assisted Learning (NDPCAL) [31].

The NDPCAL project was primarily concerned with stimulating CAI through development of new courseware and was essentially based on work already underway. Thus Leeds University became the base for projects in chemistry and statistics, Queen Mary College for the engineering sciences project, while the University College and Chelsea College, both of the University of London, combined with the University of Surrey to develop materials in support of undergraduate education in the sciences. This latter project became known as Computers in the Undergraduate Science Curriculum (CUSC).

The NDPCAL project was completed in 1978, and government funding in the United Kingdom is currently at a minor level. However, the project did result in a number of ongoing centers dedicated to the improvement of instruction (with emphasis on CAI) at a number of universities. The authors of this paper visited several of the United Kingdom campuses in late 1979 and found CAI activities to be flourishing, especially at Chelsea College, University College, and Queen Mary College of the University of London; the University of Surrey; and the University of Edinburgh. A significant number of quality CAI programs developed under this project are now in use—between 75 and 100 units from all NDPCAL projects [32]—and exchange programs are now emerging both within the United Kingdom and between United Kingdom and United States institutions. A particularly strong exchange program is housed at Imperial College under the direction of Nicholas Rushby [57]. In addition, enthusiasm runs high and initial work appears most promising at a number of other United Kingdom institutions, especially Anthony Hoare and Frank Pettit's laboratory at Oxford [56].

In addition to the NDPCAL project, the British Open University (OU), which opened in 1969 to criticism, is by most accounts now considered highly successful [47]. The OU is now using the computer in a CAI mode. Although the authors of this paper visited the main campus of the Open University, the extent to which CAI is now in use in the OU is not totally clear. It is apparent, however, that current usage is expected to increase both in the CAI adjunct and primary modes.

Another CAI-related activity currently in the research and experimentation stage in the United Kingdom is Viewdata. This is a computer-based information and communications medium under development by the Post Office. The intent is to provide an interactive nationwide service to the general public and professional community. It will operate via terminals based on TV receivers, the regular dial-up telephone network, and a set of interconnecting computers and databases [26].

2.3 Other activity worldwide

Canada and Japan both have shown strong interests in CAI and have developed centers of activity. Major Canadian centers include the Ontario Institute for Studies in Education, the National Research Council of Canada, Queen's University, Concordia University, and the Universities of Alberta and Calgary [32].

In Japan, experimentation with CAI is in progress at the university and the secondary school level, as well as in industry. Research studies in CAI have been conducted by the Nippon Telegraph and Telephone Corporation, the Japanese Society for the Promotion of Machine Industry, and by scholars at such institutions as Osaka University, Hokkaido University of Education, Aschi University of Education, and others. Research on CAI at the secondary school level is proceeding under the auspices of the National Institute for Educational Research [60].

With the exception of Russia, in which minor CAI activities have been reported [58], the authors are unaware, either through personal experience or the literature, of major CAI activities elsewhere in the world [32]. However, the developing nations, especially India and those of South America and Africa, faced with problems of large numbers of persons spread across thousands of miles, limited funds, and the desire to provide a reasonable education for everyone, are experimenting with distance education. Although their initial attempts are concentrating on radio and TV, they have also begun to look to the British Open University as a model. Thus, as the Open University develops CAI materials and uses them both successfully and financially, the widespread use of CAI for distance learning, particularly of the primary CAI type, can be anticipated [8, 17, 21, 27, 48].

3. EVALUATIONS OF CAI EFFECTIVENESS

The effectiveness of CAI has been defined differently by different investigators. To some effectiveness means the amount of learning that takes place initially. To others it means the degree of retention of learning, or at the very least, whether or not an individual stays in or drops out of a learning experience. Still others are concerned with the learner's change in attitude toward the computer as an instructional medium or simply as a helpful tool in the culture. Finally, owing to the fact that CAI is in its infancy, some are simply concerned with transportability of materials and/or acceptance of the materials for use by others.

In general, well-designed, tightly controlled evaluative studies of the use of CAI are rare. Some have been conducted by this time, however, and trends are becoming discernible. Several of the more prominent studies will therefore be reviewed, followed by a summary of the bulk of the others.

The CAI physics course developed at the Florida State University is in the form of a computer tutorial. Tentative evaluations indicate that instructional time was reduced by 17 percent over the traditional lecture course, and students scored higher on final exams and attained superior conceptual mastery [37].

The medical school of the University of Southern California has used computer-controlled modeling to teach anesthesiology. A lifelike model exhibits a variety of human responses, allowing the student to test his knowledge of anesthesiology. Evaluations using experimental and control groups demonstrated that when the model was used, fewer trials over a shorter period of time were required for students to reach an acceptable level of professional performance [37].

Studies of the CAI Russian course at Stanford, using experimental and control groups, revealed positive results in terms of student performance on examinations, student behavior, and student responses to a questionnaire about the program. Students taking the computer-based course scored "significantly better" on the final exams. In addition, far fewer students dropped out of the computer-based course [37].

Probably the most significant uses of the computer in simulation, game, or tutorial modes are represented by the Chicago City Schools Project (using Suppes and Atkinson's materials), the PLATO project, and the TICCIT project.

The Chicago City Schools Project was begun in 1971 and is continuing today. It affects over 12,000 fourth through eighth grade children in the inner city schools, with 850 terminals providing tutorial lessons in mathematics and reading. Originally designed to improve skills in these areas, the project has had significant results. As an example, the average increase in reading ability in the schools was 5.4 months per pupil for each 10 months of regular classroom instruction. Using the computer tutorial approach, the average rose to 9.0 months improvement for 8 months of instruction [55]. This program is now being formally evaluated by the Educational Testing Service under a grant from the National Institute of Education [64].

Both PLATO and TICCIT have recently been evaluated in a controlled, systematic manner by the Educational Testing Service [2, 46]. Donald Alderman of ETS commented in regard to the outcome of these evaluations as follows:

> The PLATO evaluation covered five fields: accounting, biology, chemistry, English, and mathematics. Computer uses in these fields represented supplemental or replacement instruction for regular classroom work; in no cases were these PLATO programs in lieu of entire courses.
>
> The PLATO materials were used and evaluated at five community colleges: four were a part of the City Colleges of Chicago, the fifth was in Urbana, Illinois.
>
> On the positive side, a large number of students and faculty became involved in the use of these materials, and students' attitudes toward PLATO-type materials did improve. Additionally, a significant positive achievement effect was found for PLATO vs. traditional classroom procedures in the area of mathematics. No further significant achievement effects were found for any other subjects, either in favor of PLATO or in favor of the regular classroom.
>
> The TICCIT evaluation concerned both of the mathematics and English courses in use at Phoenix College and the Alexandria (VA) Community College. These two applications represented entire courses, although *the English TICCIT program included much more personal interaction between students and faculty than did the mathematics course.*
>
> The results of the mathematics evaluation, comparing TICCIT courses to the regular classroom, and adjusting for entrance ability of students, indicated a significant

achievement effect of TICCIT over the regular classroom, although fewer TICCIT students completed the course within the semester than did those in the regular classroom. Additionally, more students had favorable attitudes toward the lecture classes than toward the TICCIT approach, although there did not appear to be any changes in overall attitudes toward additional learning in mathematics.

The results of the English evaluation also indicated a significant achievement effect in favor of the TICCIT approach, and in this situation, the completion rate for TICCIT was the same as for the classroom. Additionally, there were no significant attitude differences in favor of either approach.

ETS' responsibility in this regard was to evaluate the educational aspects of PLATO and TICCIT, and therefore no cost comparisons are available [3].

Does the above mean that such uses of the computer are effective? Certainly those who have become involved with the projects already mentioned would answer that question in the affirmative. Many who have studied the subject from a more objective vantage point also agree.

Overall, a review of the literature revealed the following consistencies:

(1) *The use of CAI either improved learning or showed no differences when compared to the traditional classroom approach* [2, 24, 35, 42, 46, 54, 62, 66].
(2) *The use of CAI reduced learning time when compared to the regular classroom* [15, 24, 35, 42, 60, 62, 66].
(3) *The use of CAI improved student attitudes toward the use of computers in the learning situation* [15, 35, 42, 46, 62, 66].
(4) *The development of CAI courseware following specified guidelines can result in portability and their acceptance and use by other faculty* [1, 20, 36, 41].

There are also some indications that low aptitude students profit more from the use of CAI than either average or high aptitude students [24, 66], and that retention rates may be lower than for traditional means [62].

The studies reviewed thus have shown striking consistencies in results, even though the type of CAI mode used (tutorials, drill and practice, games, simulations) has varied and the learners concerned have ranged from elementary school children through adults in training programs. One factor has remained relatively constant, however. The bulk of the studies have concerned the use of adjunct CAI, in which a classroom teacher is, at the least, available for consultation as needed. In the one major situation of primary CAI in which entire mathematics and English courses were taught through the TICCIT system and evaluated in a controlled manner, comple-

tion rates for the mathematics course dropped considerably below the traditional classroom, and student attitudes toward the CAI mathematics course were not positive. The opposite was true for the English course, as indicated earlier. The apparent cause of these discrepant findings was the more significant involvement of the English faculty with the students in the CAI English course, as compared to the limited involvement of the mathematics faculty with students in the mathematics CAI course. Thus, by implication, primary CAI, and distance learning in general, may achieve results similar to those for adjunct CAI as long as there is sufficient human interaction accompanying the use of the CAI materials. The Open University is currently researching this problem to determine the optimum level of human interaction necessary to produce the most effective results for various learning situations [51].

4. COSTS

Costs account to a significant extent for the lack of use of CAI in learning situations, especially at the elementary/secondary level. As Kearsley [35] has pointed out, although CAI may be perceived as instructionally effective, educators may be reluctant to utilize it if it is perceived as being prohibitively expensive.

The accepted method for assessing CAI costs is to total all expenses for computing hardware, software, telecommunications, courseware, and implementation, and then divide by the total number of student hours used. However, in actual practice, many so-called "hidden" costs are seldom entered into the equation [6]. For example, terminals and line costs are frequently considered user costs and are omitted from the calculation. Similarly, space costs, heat, electricity, etc., are often paid by the educational institution directly and thus are not considered. Also, the life-span of courseware is seldom considered, and implementation costs (staff to develop teaching guides for use of the programs, etc.) are often ignored. Compounding this situation, educators, who have been the major developers of CAI, are seldom good accountants, and thus data as to actual time taken to develop courseware often is reported inconsistently. Cost estimates for CAI, for example, are highly variable. Only recently have patterns been emerging which permit comparison of costs for complex CAI on very large computers with more simplistic programs running on mini- or microcomputers.

Other than hardware costs (which are rapidly diminishing), the cost of developing CAI courseware appears to be the greatest single factor of concern. Various authorities report courseware development time ranging from 50 to 500 hours of preparation to produce one hour of student CAI contact time at a terminal. One hundred hours appears to be the most widely accepted rule of thumb [7, 42, 49, 64]. The key variables appear to be the complexity of the programs produced and the expertise of the individuals involved. Costs per student hour of programs developed to date range from $.50 to $28.50 [41, 52, 61, 64, 67].

In addition to development costs, other factors in the equation must be considered. Materials running on microcomputers have been reported to have the lowest costs. Similarly, the greater numbers of students using the materials, the lower the per-student-hour cost reported. Thus the CUSC programs in the United Kingdom show the highest costs (apparently due to low usage). CAI programs running on microcomputers at the Highline School District in Seattle [61] and those used by large numbers of students in the Philadelphia schools [64] show some of the lowest costs. Thus, in addition to using inexpensive hardware, one major way to lower costs is to share courseware.

Norris [50] has pointed out another appropriate factor quite often overlooked in cost studies of CAI, i.e., that traditional instructional costs have been increasing at the rate of 13 percent per year for the past three years, while CAI costs have been decreasing at 5 percent per year, coupled with a 10 percent improvement in performance. Therefore the cost avoidance aspect of CAI should also be considered.

Finally, as McKenzie [41] has pointed out, if our goals are to improve the learning situation, then costs must be set beside a qualitative assessment of educational change to answer the question: Is it worth the cost?

5. THE CRITICAL ISSUES

The critical issues in CAI today relate to computer hardware, CAI languages, courseware development and sharing, and courseware implementation. Again, the major concern is with the effects of these variables upon improvements in the learning situation in relation to the costs involved.

5.1 Computer hardware

At the current time the availability of microcomputers with their multisensory capabilities and low costs appears to be the technological breakthrough which may well result in significant increases in CAI usage at all educational levels. Eisele [25] feels that an entire new era of educational application is at hand. Critchfield [22] predicts that within the next ten years all educational institutions will have one or more microcomputers, while Matthews [43] points out that in time microcomputers may become more commonplace in schools than some audiovisual devices.

A major advantage of microcomputers is their low cost. A $3,000 investment is currently sufficient for a configuration capable of providing adequate support for CAI. In addition to providing similar capabilities to minicomputers, however, some microcomputers also permit voice input and output, color displays, high resolution graphics, and text editing. Video disk enhancements at reasonable costs appear imminent [38]. Microcomputers are essentially portable and require minimal maintenance. Their disadvantages are in the areas of file handling techniques, processor capabilities, and disk capacity. Thus their strengths lie in their use for instruction in computer languages such as Basic, applicability for production of novel and innovative CAI materials, etc., while a significant weakness is in their handling of standard administrative data processing applications. In this latter regard, although agreeing that microcomputers will likely be prominent shortly on the high school scene, Blaschke [10] has pointed out that a survey of secondary and elementary principals indicated that financial resources for purchases of microcomputers would be more readily available were the microcomputers able to serve the dual purpose of supporting both instruction and administration.

The advent of the microcomputer has resulted in heated debates concerning the relative merits of CAI systems supported by large-scale powerful computing configurations as contrasted to the CAI capabilities of the microcomputers. Bitzer has amply championed the cause of the large-scale CAI systems such as PLATO, while Bork has spoken strongly in favor of the microcomputer approach. Both have recently softened their stances, however—Bitzer by developing the means whereby PLATO materials may be downloaded and run on a microcomputer, although still requiring the large computing capability for authoring [64]. Bork, conversely, seeing the need for students to communicate with one another, now envisions the possibility of a distributed environment, especially for development [12].

Returning once more to the topic of adjunct CAI and primary CAI, it would appear that microcomputers may well provide both the adequate technology and the low cost which, in a distributed network environment, will permit wide-scale use for both types of CAI worldwide. This seems especially likely if microcomputer cost/performance ratios continue to improve as predicted.

Licklider [38], for example, has estimated that by 1988, owing to technological advances, $500 worth of computing equipment could provide a 1-microsecond, 32-bit machine with 32,000 words of fast memory plus console or secondary memory. This type of equipment, with satellite communication in a distributed environment, and with the central machine used for authoring and communications, might well support the type of distance learning envisioned by the Open University.

5.2 CAI languages

CAI languages developed specifically for high-level, complex, interactive use include Coursewriter, developed by IBM; Tutor, developed for PLATO and now marketed by Control Data Corporation; ASET (Author System for Education and Training), developed and marketed by UNIVAC; and CAN, developed and marketed by the Ontario Institute for Studies in Education. All systems provide authoring aids, calculation capabilities, and varying levels of graphics commands. However, they are all machine dependent except CAN, which will function on computers from several major vendors and which is now being prepared for use on a microcomputer [53].

In a different vein, a number of other languages have been used extensively for CAI, owing to some extent to the ease of learning to use them (although they do not have CAI authoring aids). These languages include Basic, APL, Fortran, and Pascal. Each has unique features which appeal to different authors. It is interesting to note that Kearsley [34] in a study of CAI languages found that the emphasis shifted from the use of Coursewriter and Tutor in 1970, to APL, Tutor, and Basic in 1976. Since Basic is the predominant microcomputer language, it is likely to continue to gain in usage for CAI development.

The critical issue indicated in the above, however, is that there is no standard, high-level, complex CAI language which is machine independent, and which combines authoring aids, calculational mode, and graphics capabilities. This is currently one of the major impediments to the widespread use of CAI to support the learning process. Although the possibility of language independence (i.e., the ability to translate automatically from one language to another and thus to achieve portability) has been discussed for some time, such software is not now available.

5.3 Courseware development and sharing

The single most critical issue in CAI today is the development and sharing of quality CAI materials. The majority of CAI courseware currently available is of the adjunct type, developed by individual faculty members for specific purposes. It has largely been written in a machine dependent language and is undocumented. Thus the available courseware is difficult to share and, in many cases, protected by copyright if of significant value. In "The ABC's of CAI" project [1] over 4,000 CAI programs written in Basic were reviewed, and about 3-4 percent were found acceptable by faculty in the fields concerned. To permit sharing of these programs, restricted Basic standards had to be developed and programs restructured at an average cost of 100 hours per program.

In regard to authoring, the authors are in agreement with Alfred Bork that "The notion that computer-based materials can be produced by anybody, completely by themselves, is an archaic concept" [11, p. 20]. This concept has also been reiterated by Dean [23], who believes the team approach, using at least three faculty members, a programmer, and an instructional designer, has the best chance of developing courseware of high caliber which will be acceptable to the greatest number of faculty and students. Howe and du Boulay [33], although not arguing for or against teams, do caution that we not repeat our previous mistakes, and they point out that learning principles should be recognized in the development of future CAI programs.

The team approach and specific learning strategies were used in the preparation of TICCIT materials, while a more singular faculty member approach was used with the PLATO system. As indicated earlier, although student attitudes were generally more favorable toward PLATO, the most significant learning gains over the traditional classroom approach occurred with TICCIT.

Perhaps a more basic question than the individual versus team approach to development, however, centers around the question of faculty motivation to develop and share materials. Both Hawkins [29] and Sprecher and Chambers [63], in broad-based studies, found that direct financial reward was not a primary motivator. Rather, the traditional rewards for the scholarly life appeared to be the goals. Thus, recognition and acceptance by one's peers for courseware development and sharing of such materials, release time, and acceptance of courseware development by peers and by administrators as equivalent to research publications for promotion and tenure, appeared important as means to resolve the incentive question.

5.4 Courseware implementation

Until recently, those concerned with facilitating the use of computers in the curriculum were content to offer seminars on "How to Program," and the like. With the probability of widespread CAI usage at all educational levels, however, a great deal more attention will need to be paid to the question of how best to integrate the CAI materials into the curriculum. Otherwise, as preliminary data indicate, CAI materials will be used as add-ons, with little regard to their effectiveness in the total learning environment.

The CUSC staff at the University of Surrey identified courseware transfer and implementation as major goals of the British NDPCAL project. To achieve these goals, the programs were developed by teams from two or more educational institutions. The programs were all student-tested a number of times, and written student guides were prepared for use with each CAI package.

Although transfer goals were realized, *the ability* to rewrite student guides effectively had to be transferred since faculty tended to reject the original student guides which accompanied the transfer of the programs. The transfer was achieved by including in the documentation copies of all student guides that had been developed and thoroughly tested. In addition, a teacher's guide was also included which outlined the rationale behind the guides, as well as possible uses of the computer program.

Thus, in regard to both adjunct and primary CAI, some type of personal support and written materials from teacher, advisor, etc., appears necessary in order to achieve maximal benefits. Decisions will be required, especially in regard to primary CAI and distance learning, as to the frequency and amount of personal contact and supporting materials which most facilitate learning in these situations.

6. THE FUTURE OF CAI

6.1 Early predictions

In the early '70s several studies were made of the future educational technology in general, and CAI in particular, with 1980 to 2000 as the target prediction dates. The most well-known of these studies was published by the Carnegie Commission [16]. In this study the Commission predicted both widespread acceptance of educational technology by 1980 and the availability of a large quantity of quality courseware. Further, they predicted that by that time, new professions for persons engaged in creating and developing instructional materials on the nation's campuses would have emerged. As indicated throughout this paper, however, widespread acceptance and use of CAI has not yet occurred.

Two other studies also independently predicted significant increase in the use of CAI in higher education. The first used community college representatives and persons from computer-related industries active in CAI (40). The other study was based on faculty response from the nineteen-campus California State University and Colleges [4]. The Luskin study [40] predicted that the major obstacles to the use of CAI would be resolved by 1987, resulting in general acceptance and use of CAI in higher education by that time. Ames in turn [4] found the CSUC faculty predicting a 270 percent increase in CAI usage from 1976 to 1980. Although the accuracy of the Luskin study predictions cannot yet be assessed, personal observations by the authors of the use of CAI within the CSUC system indicates increased usage, but probably not to the extent predicted in the Ames study.

6.2 Predictions, 1980 to 1990

Resulting in part from the failure of current usage to match past predictions, predictions of the future of CAI have become guardedly optimistic. Most writers agree that technological (hardware) barriers are largely resolved or will be in the very near future, and further, that cost reductions due to mass production and consumption for home entertainment and learning will permit cost-effective uses of CAI in both the traditional classroom and in other settings [5, 9, 13, 14, 30, 38, 50]. This cost-effective technology will include large-scale mini- and microcomputers with voice input and output, interactive television, video disk systems, and satellite communication.

There is also general agreement that computers linked with video disks on the one hand, or communication satellites on the other, will play significant roles in nontraditional educational practices resulting in a revolution in courses and learning. Luehrmann [39], for example, sees the use of video disk-based learning materials, purchased or leased outside the usual educational framework and used on the home TV set, as possibly playing a significant role in learning in the future. He sees little change in the United States in the next ten years in regard to the roles played by broadcast or cable TV.

Atkinson [5], Bunderson [14], Hirschbuhl [30], and Norris [50], on the other hand, envision nationally or internationally distributed networks with large, shared databases. The individual could then use video disk materials on stand-alone microcomputers or through the network, access larger databases as needed, communicate with other persons, and the like. Norris spells this out in some detail, envisioning international networks of learning centers with CAI as the main delivery system using video disks, audio input and output, and touch input. He foresees these centers as providing direct learning experiences for individuals or providing sales of developed materials to educational institutions, to industries for training purposes, etc.

Futurists are in most disagreement, however, as to the role CAI will play in traditional educational institutions, especially in situations in which academic credit is granted. As opposed to the views of Luskin [40], Norris [50], Atkinson [5], and others who see CAI as playing major roles in education, both Luerhmann [39] and Charp [19] see matters remaining much the same over the next ten years in the traditional educational setting. Both, however, foresee the increased use of CAI for instruction in the basic skills for areas of reading and mathematics, especially in work not involving academic credit.

Licklider [38] also points out the inherent dangers in the widespread use of technology for education. Chief among these concerns are the possibilities that computers will be used to emphasize facts over concepts and principles, and that they will be used to condition acceptance of political doctrines, dictate personal philosophies, etc. Although most other writers have not dealt with these problems, they are matters of concern if CAI becomes as widespread in its use as predicted.

7. CONCLUSIONS AND RECOMMENDATIONS

A heavily academic background is drawn upon to offer conclusions as to the current stage of the art in CAI. Recommendations are made as to profitable courses of action to follow to help achieve the most educationally cost-effective use of CAI.

7.1 Conclusions

(1) The expectations of the early '60s in regard to widespread use of CAI in education by 1980 have not been met. However, with recent advances in cost-effective CAI uses as exemplified through the micro-computer, rapid increases in future CAI use in the learning situation are foreseen.

(2) The greatest number of advances in adjunct CAI have been made in the United States. This trend is likely to continue with increasing usage throughout the United States—both in the traditional educational systems (higher, secondary, and elementary, in that order), and in geographically distributed learning centers.

(3) The greatest number of advances in primary CAI and distance learning have been made in England via the Open University. This trend is predicted to continue throughout at least the first half of the '80s, with CAI usage via satellite spreading to the developing countries.

(4) The private sector in the United States will resolve technological (hardware) problems connected with CAI early in the '80s. By the mid-80's computers in general, video disks, and satellite communication will be cost-effective for both traditional and home learning.

(5) The problems of compatibility and portability of languages, standard documentation procedures for courseware, etc., will not be resolved by the private sector and therefore must be addressed elsewhere.

(6) The critical issues in the CAI field today which will continue to plague users throughout at least a major part of the '80s relate to the development, evaluation, sharing, and implementation of quality instructional courseware.

7.2 Recommendations

In light of the analyses of the CAI situation worldwide, the authors recommend the following in reference to the use of CAI in the United States.

(1) *A nationwide, standard high-level CAI language should be developed for complex CAI development which incorporates authoring aides, computational capability, graphics capability, multisensory input/output controls, and prescribed documentation standards.*

This approach should build, as much as possible, upon existing frequently used CAI languages, should be as simple to use as possible, and should be capable of running on large, mini-, and microcomputers. Impetus for this development should come from the educational sector, perhaps incorporating a cooperative venture with the private sector. Initial efforts should be funded by the federal government, since such a development would clearly be in the national interest.

CAI authors could then use the language which most meets their needs. Thus, simplistic CAI program development could continue as in the past, with authors using languages such as Basic, APL, etc., while those desiring to develop complex, yet portable, programs could make use of the new standard CAI language.

(2) *Development of quality, creative, transportable CAI materials of the adjunct type should be encouraged.*

Adjunct CAI materials, being mainly of short duration and thus not requiring long-term commitment and extensive funding, can be accomplished by individual faculty or teams of faculty (who have expertise in these activities) supported by assistants to provide programming support. To provide motivation for faculty to engage in these activities, and to provide incentive to identify topics and objectives that are both broad and important to the field, educational institutions are encouraged to look to the established institutional model for rewarding professional accomplishments. Thus, the provision of faculty release time on a competitive basis, recognition by other faculty and administrators that courseware development is an acceptable and laudatory activity, availability of training programs in the area, and acceptance of peer-reviewed and published courseware as equivalents to published research in promotion and tenure decisions, may well help move faculty toward the development of quality creative adjunct CAI materials.

The state and federal governments, in turn, can stimulate such development by funding faculty release time both for courseware development training and for actual time spent developing such materials. In addition, federal funding could be most beneficial for programs designed to change campus attitudes in directions more favorable to courseware development.

Finally, private enterprise could profit through joint arrangements with faculty for the development of CAI materials which could be useful both in the traditional classroom and in nontraditional learning centers, industrial training programs, etc.

(3) *Development of quality, creative, transportable CAI materials of the primary type should be encouraged.*

Since primary CAI materials are usually lengthy, requiring extensive time commitments and heavy funding for development, they could profit from joint ventures by educators, government, and the private sector. The private sector might well take the lead in these ventures; developed materials could be used initially in learning centers, and secondarily in traditional educational settings. As long as educators fill appropriate roles as subject matter and learning theory specialists, and as long as the materials are peer-reviewed and evaluated by faculty and students, the results should be of high quality and should be considered academically respectable.

(4) *Evaluation and sharing of quality courseware should be emphasized.*

Educational consortia, as well as committees within the professional associations of academic disciplines, should be formed to provide peer evaluation, publication, and distribution of CAI materials. In this way, quality courseware will be recognized and distributed, and the necessary professional status will be brought to courseware development so that it will be acceptable as a professional accomplishment in promotion and tenure decisions on the campuses. Again, development in this area should be built upon existing sources; however, additional ones will be needed.

The federal government and the private sector, at this stage, can both profitably play the role of funding agencies for these ventures. Initial efforts, if they are to be acceptable to the academic community (at least in regard to peer evaluation), must come from within its own ranks.

(5) *Appropriate use of CAI materials in the learning situation should be studied and implemented.*

The use of CAI materials to facilitate learning is an entirely different problem from the development, evaluation, and sharing of such materials. Unfortunately, these problems have been intermixed, and this has resulted, at times, in the misuse of CAI materials. To alleviate this condition, educational institutions need to provide release time for their faculties in order that the problem may be researched. On the basis of such studies, courses should be introduced so that students preparing for a teaching career at any level would be provided with a minimal background with which to implement the use of CAI as a learning tool.

Federal and state governments, in turn, should fund such studies as well as release time for the development of courses indicated above.

(6) *Distance learning experiments should be implemented.*

The development of a model for distance learning in the United States might well be a joint venture of the educational sector, private sector, and the federal government. Impetus could come from education, with funding from the private sector and the federal government. The initial model, perhaps organized as a branch campus of a major university or university system with consultation from the Open University, could experiment with primary CAI, satellite communications, microcomputers, level of human interaction required for effective learning, and the like. Although the United States would not be likely to accept one Open University for the entire country, this proposed model could permit in-house development of some of the materials and prototype technological and organizational schema, which could then serve as guidelines for other developments both within the country and internationally.

(7) *Finally, communication of worldwide CAI developments should be enhanced.*

As indicated throughout this paper, although the United States still maintains a leadership role in CAI, important activities are occurring outside the country. At this stage of development, it is particularly important to all concerned that scientific knowledge in this area be communicated worldwide.

Acknowledgments. The authors wish to express appreciation to the persons who gave generously of their time in order to review early drafts of this paper: C. Moore, Monterey, California; L. Bertrando, California Polytechnic State University, San Luis Obispo; D. Reiss, Sonoma State University; L. von Gottfried, California State University, Hayward; and N. Harbertson, California State University, Fresno.

REFERENCES

1. *The ABC's of CAI, Fourth Edition*, California State Univ., Fresno, Calif., 1979.
2. Alderman, D.L. *Evaluation of the TICCIT Computer-Assisted Instruction System in the Community College*, Educational Testing Service, Princeton, N.J., 1978.

3. Alderman, D.L. Personal Communication, Educational Testing Service, Princeton, N.J., Jan. 1977.

4. Ames, R.G., and Carpino, S. *The Demand for Instructional Computing Resources: 1976–1980. California State University and Colleges*, California State Univ., Hayward, Calif., 1977.

5. Atkinson, R.C. Futures: Where will computer-assisted instruction (CAI) be in 1990? *Educational Technology 18*, 4 (1978), 60.

6. Avner, R.A. Cost-effective applications of computer-based education. *Educational Technology 18*, 4 (1978), 24–26.

7. Baker, J.C. Corporate involvement in CAI. *Educational Technology 18*, 4 (1978), 12–16.

8. Basu, C.K., and Ramachandran, K. Educational technology in India. In *International Yearbook of Eduational and Instructional Technology 1978/1979*, A. Howe and A.J. Romiszowski, Eds., Nichols Pub. Co., New York, 1978, pp. 242–250.

9. Bitzer, D. Futures: Where will computer-assisted instruction (CAI) be in 1990? *Educational Technology 18*, 4 (1978), 61.

10. Blaschke, C.L. Microcomputer software development for schools: What, who, how? *Eduational Technology 19* 1979), 26–28.

11. Bork, A. Machines for computer-assisted learning. *Educational Technology 18*, 4 (1978), 17–20.

12. Bork, A., and Franklin, S. Personal computers in learning. *Educational Technology 19* (1979), 7–12.

13. Brown, J.S. Fundamental research in technology in science education. In *Technology in Science Education: The Next 10 Years*, Nat. Sci. Foundation, Washington, D.C., 1979, pp. 11–18.

14. Bunderson, C.V. Futures: Where will computer-assisted instruction (CAI) be in 1990? *Educational Technology 18*, 4 (1978), 62.

15. CAI helping pupils move four grades in three years. *Computerworld 11* (June 13, 1977), 16.

16. Carnegie Commission on Higher Education. *The Fourth Revolution: Instructional Technology in Higher Education*. McGraw-Hill, New York, 1977.

17. Chadwick, C. The multidimensional projects of the OAS in educational technology. In *International Yearbook of Educational and Instructional Technology 1978/1979*, A. Howe and A.J. Romiszowski, Eds., Nichols Pub. Co., New York, 1978, pp. 290–296.

18. Chambers, J.A. College teachers: Their effect on creativity of students. *J. Educational Psychol. 65* (1973), 326–334.

19. Charp, S. Futures: Where will computer-assisted instruction (CAI) be in 1990? *Educational Technology 18*, 4 (1978), 62.

20. CONDUIT. Catalog of CONDUIT reviewed and tested materials. *Pipeline* (Summer 1979), 13–36.

21. Costa, J.M. de M. Prospects for distance education in Brazil. In *International Yearbook of Educational and Instructional Technology 1978/1979*, A. Howe and A.J. Romiszowski, Eds., Nichols Pub. Co., New York, 1978, pp. 297–311.

22. Critchfield, M. Beyond CAI: Computers as personal intellectual tools. *Educational Technology 19* (1979), 18–25.

23. Dean, P.M. Computer-assisted instruction authoring systems. *Educational Technology 18*, 4 (1978), 20–23.

24. Deignan, G.M., and Duncan, R.E. CAI in three medical training courses: It was effective! *Behavior Res. Methods and Instrumentation 10*, 2 (1978), 228–230.

25. Eisele, J.E. Classroom use of microcomputers. *Educational Technology 19* (1979), 13–15.

26. Fedida, S., and Dew, B. Viewdata in education. In *International Yearbook of Educational and Instructional Technology 1978/1979*, A. Howe and A.J. Romiszowski, Eds., Nichols Pub. Co., New York, 1978, pp. 78–86.

27. Garvey, B. Instructional technology in Zambia. In *International Yearbook of Educational and Instructional Technology 1978/1979*, A. Howe and A.J. Romiszowski, Eds., Nichols Pub. Co., New York, 1978, pp. 239–241.

28. Hansen, D.N., and Johnson, B. *CAI Myths That Need to Be Destroyed and CAI Myths That We Ought to Create*. Florida State Univ., Tallahassee, 1971.

29. Hawkins, C.A. Computer based learning: Why and where is it alive and well? *Comptrs. and Education 2*, 3 (1978), 187–196.

30. Hirschbuhl, J.J. Futures: Where will computer-assisted instruction (CAI) be in 1990? *Educational Technology 18*, 4 (1978), 62.

31. Hooper, R. The national development programme in computer-assisted learning. In *International Yearbook of Educational and Instructional Technology 1978/1979*, A. Howe and A.J. Romiszowski, Eds., Nichols Pub. Co., New York, 1978, pp. 173–179.

32. Howe, A., and Romiszowski, A.J., Eds. *International Yearbook of Educational and Instructional Technology 1978/1979*, Nichols Pub. Co., New York, 1978.

33. Howe, J.A.M., and du Boulay, B. Microprocessor-assisted learning: Turning the clock back? *Programmed Learning and Education Technology 16* (1979), 240–246.

34. Kearsley, G.P. Some "facts" about CAI: Trends 1970–1976. *J. of Educational Data Processing 13*, 3 (1976), 1–12.

35. Kearsley, G.P. The cost of CAI: A matter of assumption. *AEDS J. 10*, 3 (1977), 100–110.

36. Laurillard, D.M. The design and development of CAI materials in undergraduate science. *Comptr. Graphics 2* (1977), 241–247.

37. Levien, R.E. *The Emerging Technology: Instructional Uses of the Computer in Higher Education*. McGraw-Hill. New York, 1972.

38. Licklider, J.C.R. Impact of information technology on education in science and technology. In *Technology in Science Education: The Next 10 Years*. Nat. Sci. Foundation, Washington, D.C., 1979, pp. 1–10.

39. Luehrmann. A. Technology in science education. In *Technology in Science Education: The Next 10 Years*, Nat. Sci. Foundation, Washington, D.C., 1979, pp. 11–18.

40. Luskin, B.J., Gripp, T.H., Clark, J.R., and Christianson, D.A. *Everything You Always Wanted to Know About CAI*. Computer Uses in Education, Huntington Beach, Calif., 1972.

41. McKenzie, J., Elton, L., and Lewis, R. *Interactive Computer Graphics in Science Teaching*, Halstead Press, New York, 1978.

42. Magidson, E.M. Issue overview: Trends in computer-assisted instruction. *Educational Technology 18*, 4 (1978), 5–8.

43. Matthews, J.I. Microcomputer vs. minicomputer for educational computing. *Educational Technology 18*, 11 (1978), 19–22.

44. *Microcomputer Report*. Minnesota Educational Computing. Consortium, Instructional Services Division, Lauderdale, Minn., July 1979.

45. Morrison, F. Personal Communication. Phoenix College, Feb. 1980.

46. Murphy, R.T., and Appel, L.R. *Evaluation of the Plato IV Computer-Based Education System in the Community College.* Educational Testing Service, Princeton, N.J., 1977.

47. Neil, M.W. Distance learning in developing countries in relation to the Open University. In *International Yearbook of Educational and Instructional Technology 1978/1979*, A. Howe and A.J. Romiszowski, Eds., Nichols Pub. Co., New York, 1978, pp. 104–115.

48. Neil, M.W. The educational imperative in developing countries. In *International Yearbook of Educational and Instructional Technology 1978/1979*, A. Howe, and A.J. Romiszowski, Eds., Nichols Pub. Co., New York, 1978, pp. 87–90.

49. Neuhauser, J.J. A necessary redirection for certain educational technologies. *Comptrs. and Education 1*, 4 (1977), 187–192.

50. Norris. W.C. Via technology to a new era in education. *Phi Delta Kappan 58*, 2 (1977) 451–453.

51. Northedge, A., and Durbridge, N. The use of tutorials in the Open University. In *International Yearbook of Educational and Instructional Technology 1978/1979*, A. Howe and A.J. Romiszowski, Eds., Nichols Pub. Co., New York, 1978, 34–43.

52. Okey, J.R., and Majer, K. Individual and small group learning with computer-assisted instruction. *Audio Visual Communication Rev. 24*, 1 (1976), 79–86.

53. Olivier, W.P. Personal communication. The Ontario Inst. for Studies in Education, Ontario, Canada, June 1979.

54. Paden, D.W., Dalgaard, B.R., and Barr, M.D. A decade of computer-assisted instruction. *J. Economic Education 9*, 4 (1977), 14–20.

55. Passman, B. Personal Communication. Sperry Univac Corp., Blue Bell, Pa., Jan. 1979.

56. Pettit, F.R. *Computer-Assisted Learning—A Review of the Current Practice in the U.K.* Comptng. Teaching Centre, Oxford Univ., Oxford, England, 1978.

57. Rushby, N.J. *The CEDAR Project.* Comptr. Centre, Imperial College, London, 1978.

58. Rushby, N.J. *Computer-Based Learning in the Soviet Union.* Comptr. Centre, Imperial College, London, 1979.

59. Sassar, M. Personal communication. Alexandria Community College, Alexandria, Va., Feb. 1980.

60. Sakamoto, T. The current state of educational technology in Japan. In *International Yearbook of Educational and Instructional Technology 1978/1979*, A. Howe and A.J. Romiszowski, Eds., Nichols Pub. Co., New York, 1978, pp. 251–271.

61. School shifting teaching aid to micros. *Computerworld 12* (Nov. 6, 1978), 63.

62. Splittgerber, F.L. Computer-based instruction: A revolution in the making? *Educational Technology 19*, 1 (1979), 20–26.

63. Sprecher, J.W., and Chambers, J.A. Computer-assisted instruction: Factors affecting courseware development. *J. Computer-Based Instruction*, 1980 (in review).

64. Sugarman, R. A second chance for computer-aided instruction. *ICEE Spectrum* (Aug. 1978), 29–37.

65. Suppes, P., and Macken, E. The historical path from research and development to operational use of CAI. *Educational Technology 18*, 4 (1978), 9–12.

66. Taylor, S., et al. The effectiveness of CAI. Ann. Convention Assn. for Educational Data Systems, New York, 1974.

67. Time-sharing in education—going, going, but not gone. *Datamation* (Jan. 1977), 138–140.

Computer Assisted Learning in U.S. Secondary/Elementary Schools

Jack A. Chambers and Alfred Bork

SUMMARY

The study reported here was undertaken by the Task Force on Computer Assisted Learning of the ACM's Sub-Committee on Computing in the Secondary/Elementary Schools, with special emphasis on the use of the computer in computer assisted learning. A part of this overall assessment was to determine factors impeding the use of computer assisted learning so that guidelines could be established to facilitate its use.

A sample of 974 school districts was selected to most closely approximate the total population of U.S. public school districts. The district superintendents were contacted through a personal letter and a 34-item questionnaire, in March, 1980. The letter encouraged superintendents to identify a person on their staff to complete the questionnaire and to serve as a future computer assisted learning coordinator. A portion of the questionnaire was devoted to a description of various computer assisted learning publications and programs which the districts could receive free of charge.

A total of 62.3% of the school districts completed and returned the questionnaires. Analyses of the data revealed the following:

1) In 1980, the percentage of school districts using the computer for instructional and/or administrative purposes stood at 90%. It is projected to rise to 94% by 1985.

2) Between 1970 and 1980, the best estimates of instructional usage of the computer showed increases from 13% in 1970 to 74% in 1980. Instructional usage is anticipated to reach 87% of the districts by 1985.

3) Computer assisted learning is currently in use in 54% of the districts, and represents the type of usage reported by the second largest number of districts.

4) Heaviest usage of computer assisted learning is in the nation's secondary schools. The Mathematics departments show the largest usage, followed by the Natural Sciences, Business, and Language Arts.

5) Most computer assisted learning programs in use in the districts are written in BASIC, were

From "Computer Assisted Learning in U.S. Secondary/Elementary Schools," by Jack A. Chambers and Alfred Bork. In *The Computing Teacher*, September, 1980. Reprinted by permission.

acquired from outside the district, are predominately drill and practice, and run on a variety of large, mini- and microcomputers.

6) Secondary/elementary faculty and students give computer assisted learning a high rating.

7) Projections for 1980–85 indicate computer assisted learning will be used by more school districts than any other type of computer application. Usage is anticipated to rise from 54% of the districts to 74%.

8) Type of computer assisted learning usage is predicted to shift from the current emphasis on drill and practice to tutorials by 1985, and ultimately to simulations.

9) Microcomputers are anticipated to play an increasingly significant role in computer assisted learning usage in the school districts.

10) Computer assisted learning usage is projected to continue to be heavy in Mathematics, Natural Sciences, Business, and Language Arts at the secondary level, while also expanding to more significant usage at other relevant high school fields such as Social Sciences. More extensive use is also anticipated at the elementary level.

11) Major impediments to implementation and successful use of computer assisted learning at the secondary/elementary level appear to be financial, lack of knowledge about computer assisted learning and computers, attitudes of faculty, and need for more and better computer assisted learning programs.

12) Major computer assisted learning Task Force activities felt to be helpful by the districts were identified as dissemination of information about computer assisted learning in general and about computer assisted learning funding sources, providing in-service training for faculty, and serving as a clearinghouse for existing computer assisted learning courseware.

RECOMMENDATIONS

In the light of the results of the current study and the authors' experiences, the following recommendations are offered:

1) School districts not now using computer assisted learning should appoint a coordinator to acquire relevant information and to assist in general with the implementation of pilot computer assisted learning projects.

2) School districts now using computer assisted learning should disseminate relevant information throughout the districts concerning the results of the use of computer assisted learning nationwide as well as the specific results of local projects.

Training programs for faculty should be implemented. Liaisons with local higher education institutions and state departments of education should be formed to make use of faculty expertise as consultants and to develop joint funding proposals for submission to federal, state, and/or private agencies.

3) Major government agencies and private foundations should support information dissemination and consulting proposals to assist U.S. secondary/elementary schools to implement and successfully use computer assisted learning. In addition, these agencies should fund proposals to increase the quantity and quality of computer assisted learning programs.

4) The private sector, particularly computer vendors and publishing firms, should form cooperative agreements with secondary/elementary schools and institutions of higher education to help ensure that computer assisted learning programs developed in the future are of higher quality, and are disseminated widely at reasonable costs.

The Case Against Multiple Choice

James W. Garson

It seems to be widely recognized that computers have a great potential for improving education. There is much less agreement about how this potential can best be realized. Although there is a gigantic literature on different strategies for using computers in education, there is surprisingly little discussion of their relative merits in the context of a theory of the ultimate *goals* of education in a computerized society.

This does not mean that the evaluation of courseware (computerized teaching materials) is not attempted. Almost any report on the development and use of courseware discusses the advantages to be found in using the computer, and many support the point with tests that compare the rates of progress of students using different teaching strategies. These tests, however, invariably measure mastery of course material which is taught with traditional methods using multiple choice examinations. Because of the method of measurement used, evaluation tends to focus on how well students perform on rote memorization of standard material. This may help explain why the large majority of present courseware is designed around drill and practice systems that use the multiple choice format. As a result, the potential

From "The Case Against Multiple Choice," by James W. Garson. In *The Computing Teacher,* December 1979. Reprinted by permission.

contribution of computers is viewed in terms of the processes already present in the traditional classroom, instead of in terms of activities that are not now found in schools because they *require* the use of the computer. The very methods and catagories in terms of which we assess courseware may build "buggy-whip" objectives into the uses to which computers are put. A good theory of the goals of courseware requires that we re-examine the criteria of success which are implicit in present research efforts. The purpose of this paper is to lay out some suggestions for new educational objectives, and to use them to criticize present trends in the use of computers in education.

Let us begin with a very basic objective, namely to ensure that our technology serves *human* needs. People should not be forced to support technologies which are not in the public interest. They must be in control of the form of their technology; new technologies should not promote projects and goals which serve only a small group.

Ensuring that the public controls technology for its own good entails a variety of subgoals. An important one of these is that education by machine should not train people in skills better performed by machines. A society which trains both people and machines to fill the same niches is bound to create conflict, and people are likely to lose the competition. A healthy culture develops symbiotic relationships between people and machines, where the special abilities of each define separate, but interdependent roles, leaving to humans the job of controlling the relationship to their own advantage. In a sick culture, people are trapped by technology into playing out roles which harm them with limited means of changing the situation so their dependence on machines becomes a burden.

A typical mechanism for maintenance of that dependence on a unhealthy culture, despite human dissatisfaction, is the creation of new institutions and technologies which take over tasks which people used to perform for themselves, thus eroding their niche further, and increasing their dependence on the very system that makes them miserable. The result is a society where people regard their technology with all the ambivalence felt by a small child towards cruel parents.

I believe we are headed towards a sick relationship with technology in our use of computers in education. Part of the problem is that our traditional educational institutions are not healthy. Mandatory schooling, degree requirements, and the demand that job applicants be overeducated ensure our dependence on an education system which clearly has its faults. Because of our dependence, however, healthy educational goals do not appear as live

options. This is ironic because the new computer technology can provide the very tools we need for mastering technological development.

At present, computers tend to play educational roles that have already existed. Any attempt to re-define the educational niches to take advantage of the liberating opportunities of computers is a serious challenge to the structure of the present system and although these novel applications are widely endorsed, the strains with the present structure argue for their "impracticality" when it comes to their actual *adoption*. We are in danger, then, of being caught in a vicious circle, for as computers take over traditional tasks in education, our dependence on them is strengthened, while our will to reform our institutions around human need is weakened.

One of the tasks that is most in danger of being appropriated is basic to our freedom: the task of planning our own education. The present patterns of computer use reinforce our tendency to place students in passive roles so that the organization of the process of learning is taken on by others. Education is viewed according to the Transfer Metaphor, which takes knowledge to be an object which teachers *insert* into the minds of their students. Success on this model depends on the *means of insertion* (teaching methods) and on the receptivity of the student (motivation). Given such a view, the important issues in applying computers to education are: how knowledge should be transferred, and how to ensure that students will be open to it.

This outlook tends to ignore the importance of the student's *activity* in learning. It is assumed that decisions about the content and form of their experience are to be made by "experts" who know best what students need and how to transfer it to them—as if students were interchangeable receptacles. Current research in instructional psychology has taken a new interest in the processes which are involved in learning. From this point of view, education is seen as the development of a wide variety of *abilities* which are pre-requisites for later learning. Knowledge is not seen as an object which inhabits the mind, but as a reflection of the mastery of a skill. Given that the pace and order of the development of such abilities is found to differ from student to student, there is not likely to be *one* right set of answers to how and what students *should* learn.

Research on reading and memorization underscores the importance of the student's awareness and participation in the control of the learning process. There are children who can recite out loud from a written text, but who cannot read because their own recitation means nothing to them. They clearly have memorized which letter strings go with which words and/or phonemes, but they have not learned to relate this information stored to the *process* of reading. Studies suggest the importance of the student's awareness of what reading is, and of being able to monitor the difference between merely moving one's eyes over the page, and understanding the text. There is evidence that even the task of rote memorization (where the Transfer Metaphor would seem most accurate) requires developed executive abilities which control the process. The lesson we are learning from instructional psychologists is that the development of the ability to take command of one's own education is extremely important to learning.

We have other persuasive reasons for being interested in seeing that students play an active rather than passive role in learning. In spite of complaints about the low "productivity" of our present system of education, we seem unwilling to take advantage of the cheapest way of solving the problem: To teach students to take over the job of learning at the earliest opportunity, thus adding an immense new source of labor without adding any new teaching jobs. When students learn how to provide their own education, the institutions and technologies designed to enforce decisions about what and how to learn are no longer needed. Motivation, or receptivity to learning, is guaranteed by the students' mastery of the learning process and their perceptions of what they must learn to function effectively in society.

The proper goals for computerized education in our view conflict radically with those that are generated by the Transfer Metaphor. For one thing, we would teach the *student,* not the *computer,* the effective strategies needed in learning. We would train students to be able to marshall information for their own purposes and goals rather than defining what *we* expect they should know. We would train students to be able to recognize their own limitations in knowledge and in skills for acquiring new knowledge, and to take effective action in overcoming them. In short, we would do our very best to encourage autonomy in education.

The goal of computer design, then, is not to figure out how to get the computer to play the role of the teacher, but to have it serve as much as possible as a *resource* for the student. The goal of education is to teach students how to master the new resource, and the training is "faded out" as students gain competence. By the way, there is no fundamental reason why this training has to be carried out by the computer.

This attitude about learning has important connections with our need to master technology in general. Students who develop the ability to monitor and control their own education are bound to be more capable at diagnosing the problems with their own technology, and taking effective measures for solving them. As their dependence on the system of education weakens, the opportunity to make meaningful demands of their technology grows.

Another important objective to be considered in constructing courseware is the development of social skills: the ability to communicate effectively with others, to uncover conflicting values and goals, to negotiate compromises, and to develop and execute a plan for the solution of common problems. These skills are needed if human control of technology is to succeed. There is very little one person can do without the support of a group which perceives the problem in roughly the same way, and can focus its energies to resolve it. The present educational system does very little to develop social skills required for social action. Without them, individuals have little opportunity to *recognize,* much less *deal with,* problems which arise when technologies frustrate their own happiness.

Given these objectives the success of courseware is not to be measured according to how well students memorize a body of material. In a world where computers are clearly more accurate "memorizers," we need to find ways to measure the development of information *processing* skills, not how much information the student is able to *store.* The skills that are particularly important are those that allow social action and independent learning. The goals that really matter do not depend so much on the *format,* or even the *content,* of educational materials, but on the degree to which students are encouraged and prepared to take responsibilities for their education, and to work effectively together.

Most courseware now in use is in drill and practice format. The computer asks questions, and the student responds with a multiple choice answer. Tutorial systems print explanatory text between the bouts of question asking and answering, but the student's interaction with the computer is basically the same. It is assumed in programmed instruction that the student is to work alone at a terminal, and that the computer is to determine what questions are to be asked next. This sort of courseware certainly has its uses, but the danger is that it is becoming the predominant method of computer education. It is a danger because opportunities for students to learn social skills and the art of learning may be lost. In the context of an educational system which is already unhealthy, drill and practice is liable to encourage just the kind of dependence which makes enslavement by technology possible.

First of all, consider the effects of this kind of courseware on the values, personality, and intellectual development of the student. It is assumed that it is the computer's job to explain and ask questions, and that it is the student's job to answer them. This recreates the predominant pattern in the standard classroom, while cancelling out other kinds of classroom activity which help develop autonomy. Consider what is missing. Students *do not ask questions.* They are not asked to organize what they are learning in their own way. They are not encouraged to explain things in their own words, to offer opinions, to apply what they have learned to a new situation, or to sway someone with another point of view. It leaves them with few options in determining what and how to learn.

The use of drill and practice also has important effects on the body of material taught. The whole process of question answering and asking pre-supposes that questions have one right answer. Topics which are controversial, where an orthodox answer has not developed, have to be avoided. This encourages the use of pseudoquestions such as "what were the three causes of the Civil War?", which bury controversy by demanding the student to reproduce pat answers from some text. This leaves the student with the impression that all questions have one right answer, and that, for instance, there really *were* exactly three causes of the Civil War. It reduces learning to a trivia game demanding rote memorization of ritual responses. It allows little or no practice in challenging what others take to be the "facts," of assembling data into theories and testing them, or solving novel problems in novel ways. It masks the fact that instructional materials are written by people, who make mistakes and distortions. It demands acceptance of what others have determined to be the case without giving the student any awareness of the process of criticism and development of knowlege. I admit that these are already pervasive features of our present system of education, but that is no excuse of exacerbating them with a computer.

If students are expected to think and reason on their own, they need an apprenticeship in the art of learning. Drill and practice teaches them that only experts know this art, and that to learn they must listen, memorize, and be prepared to answer questions. It devalues their abilities to teach themselves, and to work out solutions to problems they have defined in their own terms.

The truly exciting moments in education come when students have taken an active interest in some topic, and have been able to put something together on their own. Whatever is learned this way is learned painlessly (although not effortlessly) and once learned, not soon forgotten. Drill and practice replaces this kind of self-motivated concentration with a seemingly endless stream of petty tasks. As control over the shape of the learning experience is taken out of the hands of students and teacher and turned over to the programmer, opportunities to practice, and hence to become accomplished at autonomous learning are lost.

A second problem with drill and practice is that it is essentially asocial. Typically, students communicate with the computer at separate stations, in an environment where exchanges between students are discouraged, either by partitions, the noise of the machinery or both. This eliminates the chance for students to work out solutions together, to share information, and to play the role of teacher as well as student. We tend to overlook the potential power of peer tutoring, partly because our present institutions have a vested interest in monopolizing teaching. But a healthy system of education, just like a healthy medical system or a healthy government, should do everything in its power to become useless. One of the best ways to accomplish this in the case of education is to develop teaching and learning skills in as many people as possible, so that learning does not require an elaborate institution staffed by "experts." We cannot expect to be able to wean our students away from formal schooling if they are not allowed to practice nourishing themselves, and each other.

Advocates of drill and practice claim it has three main advantages. First, the question asked can be controlled on the basis of the student's progress, thus "individualizing" the instruction. Second, the use of the computer ensures that students are motivated, by defining a sequence of problems they can manage, and by giving immediate feedback on their responses. Third, students are free to schedule their work at the computer when they like and so can learn to take responsibility for setting their own pace.

I believe that these advantages of programmed instruction are overrated, particularly given the state of the courseware in use today. Let us consider the first claim: that programmed instruction is sensitive to the students' abilities and so can adapt to their individual needs. Since programmers have the responsibility for determining how student progress is to be measured and know how the progress measured determines the kind of material to be seen next they should employ a good theory about how the material should be selected given a person's performance. Patrick Suppes, one of the leaders in the development of programmed instruction, admits that, "those of us who are faced with making these decisions are aware of the inadequacy of our knowledge." Without an accurate theory to go on, programmers must rely on their own intuitions, tempered by what they can manage to program using the resources available.

In admitting this problem, Suppes offers us the hope that by using more programmed instruction, we will be able to generate the data we need to develop theories of learning that will serve as a foundation for being able to make these decisions properly. This motivation for using programmed instruction has it all backwards; it proposes that we take choices about learning away from the student and teacher and give them to the programmer so that research programs can be developed to determine what choice the programmer should make. This is just a proposal to establish a new mechanism that increases human dependence. We are to create instructions which convert capacities which people already have to some measure (to regulate their own learning) into services which must be obtained at a price. When it is pointed out that there is no guarantee that the new institution would provide service better than what people can supply for themselves, the development of a new institution is proposed to improve the performance of the first institution.

Of course it would be a good thing to have accurate theories about learning and there is nothing wrong with using computers to gather data to make the formulation of such theories possible. First, we must have the information we need about effective methods of education before we turn over the decision making to a computer. In fact, the present research suggests that drill and practice may be of limited value, and that people learn better when they have more control over what and how they learn.

The fundamental issue is not so much whether the programmer is properly equipped to make the right choices about what the students' experience should be like, but whether making these choices for students doesn't decrease their ability to learn, and to learn how to learn. We have two options. Either we "train" computers to make good decisions about how to learn, or we can expend the same effort training people to make effective decisions on their own. The second option has the decided advantage that students won't need a computer (or even a teacher) to regulate what they do because they come to their education *with* the skills and motivation to teach themselves.

A second advantage that programmed instruction is supposed to have is: the computer provides discipline and motivation, by forcing students to work in a proper sequence on problems they can be expected to solve. The computer can inform students when their answers are wrong and demand new responses. This ensures they will keep thinking about a problem, and not give up too soon. In fact, in some courseware, students cannot proceed at all unless they get the right answer. Even when there are several thousand possible responses on difficult questions, students on some systems are forced to figure out an answer before they are allowed to go to the next problem. If they cannot solve a problem, they must

seek human help if they are to continue to use the program at all.

Other styles of programming are not so severe and allow the student to ask for a hint (an option that is much less used than it ought to be) or to simply give up and see the right answer. This sort of enforced discipline can be useful on some occasions, but there are dangers in its widespread use. One of the most unfortunate products of our present system of education is people who require external motivation (through grades, the reaction of their parents, etc.) in order to learn. If computers take on the job of providing discipline, students may develop dependence on new forms of external motivation which can only be supplied by computers. It is odd that the primary application of drill and practice is in colleges where the students should be expected to have the maturity to learn on their own. Small children who do not have the experience of mental preparation to work things out for themselves may profit from drill and practice. They may need to be led by the hand through the fundamentals of some topic, in steps that are small and well thought out. By the time the student is in college, however, we would hope that there would be no need for systems that enforce the "proper" behavior.

The advantage the computer has of giving students immediate feedback on their progress cannot be disputed. But this does not argue necessarily *for* the use of drill and practice over other techniques. For example, Marshall describes a method which provides individual instruction with rich feedback, in an environment that encourages students to cooperate in solving their problems. The students are given worksheets to fill out but no limitations are put on where or when they are done, as long as each student completes the work by the end of the day. The teacher roams around the room to help students who are having special problems. Students form groups with their friends, and help each other figure out correct answers. They are free to move around the room at will, to take responsibility for scheduling their work, and to offer and seek help. At the end of the day the teacher reviews common mistakes. This system has the disadvantage that feedback on some incorrect answers may not be immediate, but it has the advantage of involving students in processes which are more valuable: communication, cooperation, teaching, and the control of their learning. Not only that; the feedback available in this situation is more insightful and interesting than any set of canned computer responses could be. Students get feedback only when they need it, (there is no need to provide students with feedback for an answer they know is right) in a context where they must take responsibility for determining for themselves when they are unsure of something. Until computers begin to display the intelligence of children, we may as well choose children over computers as teachers.

The third advantage claimed for drill and practice (one it shares with other forms of courseware) is that students can determine their own schedule for learning. This is certainly the sort of freedom for which I have been arguing. But the design of most drill and practice courseware limits self-pacing. Part of the problem is that when the student has little control over what is being learned, advantages of determining *when* to learn are lost.

In most drill and practice programs, students are trapped into following a sequence which must be continued to a stopping point defined by the programmer. This can be as much as an hour's worth of work away for a slow student. Students who "give up" part of the way through a unit must repeat the whole unit when they return to the computer. This exerts strong pressure on them to complete a unit underway, even if they have good reasons for scheduling part of the unit at some other time. A few programs keep a record of the exact point at which students stopped and will allow them to return to it in later sessions, but even given this added feature, there are problems. Sloppy programming of this option, and computer crashes can still force the student to start in entirely the wrong place. Even when it works, the student is still forced to follow the course material in a sequence defined by the courseware writer.

Some would claim that the solution to this problem is the development of programs that allow the student detailed control over what is to be studied. Certainly programs that allow the student new forms of mobility are worth designing, but it is very difficult to develop systems that can respond intelligently to students' requests. Under most circumstances, students must pay the price of learning a language of commands in order to control what they will do next. Since approaches to command languages vary widely from program to program, the student has to master a computer system along with the topic being presented by the system. We are a long way from the day when standards for control languages can be enforced (we can barely force standards for computer languages), and until we do, we will need to train students to take advantage of the opportunities for control. In the light of this problem there really is no strong argument for the development of drill and practice courseware which allows students significant control over their experience. The reason is that there is an alternative, cheap, and highly effective technology for presenting student controlled drill and practice: the book.

Workbooks were the precursors of drill and practice programs. Though they do not provide the computer's immediate and salient feedback, they do allow students to select what they want to do by moving their eyes and hands. Not only that, they can be used just about anywhere, any time (and they rarely "malfunction"). Drill and practice conspires to lock the student into a fixed sequence of steps which is determined by the programmer. At least with a workbook, the student can participate to some degree in the process of learning. Any convincing argument for replacing workbooks with computers for drill and practice must demonstrate that the advantages of immediate feedback outweigh the disadvantages of lack of student control. If self-scheduling is truly a strong argument for the use of drill and practice on the grounds that it lets students adjust their experience to their abilities and interests, then the same arguments support the view that books are better than computers at presenting this sort of instruction.

There is an advantage that computerized drill and practice has over workbooks which, in all fairness, should be mentioned. Unfortunately, it seems to be poorly appreciated by the developers of drill and practice courseware. Once a workbook is published, it is impossible to change. But when material is entered in a computer, it can be edited easily. This allows the gradual evolution of more effective material without the need for a sequence of costly editions and re-editions. Nevertheless, one of the major criticisms I would make of the courseware I have seen is the lack of careful editing. Not only are there the standard sorts of typographical errors, but the text is often poorly worded, the questions vague or misleading, and the stored answers simply wrong. Judging from what I have seen, most courseware is written hastily, and the writer rarely feels an obligation to improve the program once it is being used by students. This may be due to the fact that courseware developers are funded primarily for the production of an initial product, and not for its maintenance and improvement. Yet, it is by studying the ways in which students respond to the program that the best ideas for improvement come. A good program cannot be written in isolation; it must develop and change during a break-in period that approximates as closely as possible the actual use to which it will be put. Too many programmers assume that they can anticipate all the problems that the student is liable to encounter. The evidence is that this assumption is woefully wrong.

It is bad enough that students have limited means for communicating with, and controlling the computer, but it is worse when the opportunity to obtain feedback from students on possible improvements of the program is ignored. When a poorly written program descends on students in a seemingly immutable form, then engagement in the process of education is in jeopardy. However, if they are expected to play a role in the improvement of the program which defines their experience, they have the chance to develop a feeling of "ownership" toward the process of learning. The invitation to criticize courseware opens up an important educational experience, for it centers conscious attention on the learning process.

Unfortunately, very few programmers have bothered to set up the mechanisms needed to encourage interaction with students on improving their programs. For the most part, evaluation is carried out in the traditional manner, where students play the role of guinea pigs in a psychological experiment designed to measure the variables which the *experimenter* thinks are relevant. Generally what is measured is the student's performance on multiple choice tests, so methods of evaluation which would challenge the whole multiple choice mentality in education are quietly ignored.

The nature of the measuring instrument automatically sets the evaluator at a distance from any effects of courseware other than on the student's memory. In a society where computers are the ultimate memorizers, the emphasis on assessing what the student has memorized is misguided, if only because it tends to train people in tasks better done by a computer. It is at least as important to investigate the less tangible effects of courseware: the effects on students' skills in gathering information on their own, in analyzing it, in applying it to their problems, in motivating themselves to learn, in working well with others in groups; in short, in using educational resources to control the shape of their lives.

Educational psychologists are not especially well trained to measure these factors. Their whole orientation is to take numerical measures of "subjects" under artificial conditions. The researcher studies the results of education, not the process, and so is blind to the effects courseware is liable to have on the personality, emotions, and social behavior of students.

It is time to develop new forms of evaluation that help us assess what is truly relevant. The teachers or programmers who believe that they have nothing to learn from students about the design of courseware are either foolish or arrogant. We must face up to our responsibilities to put our concern for the growth of our students over our interest in verifying some pat theory about why our program will work best. Program developers and evaluators need to spend more time simply watching how students interact with their products right at the terminal. The terminal should be a forum for the programmer's education as well as the student's. There is an immense amount

to learn about computerized education by patient and sensitive observation in the real setting. Effective evaluation demands the skills of a good parent or interviewer, who can elicit student reactions with concern and respect.

Instructional Design and CAI

Don Steely

CAI presents an entirely new medium in the application of instructional design. Until recently, the science of instructional design has been applied primarily to printed materials—texts, teacher guides and student workbooks. And although there is some variation between authors and publishers on how these practices are used in printed materials, there is a fairly standardized approach to how an instructional program is put together, what it includes and what it assumes.

How well will the existing print oriented instructional design techniques work with CAI? If CAI programs are to be instructionally sound and successful, there will have to be significant changes in the existing practices.

Nearly all printed instructional materials are designed around one given fact—each teacher teaches differently. Therefore, instructional programs are guides rather than absolutes. In terms of instructional design, this translates into giving general procedures that all teachers can use, giving alternative methods of teaching and supplying different supplemental activities. Few efforts are made to carefully control instructional details—such as day to day consistency of wording in explaining new concepts, required review schedules, exact correspondence between how a skill is taught and subsequently applied and tested. It is assumed that the teacher will alter the printed materials to suit his/her particular students and his/her way of teaching.

In reality, most teachers do modify the programs they use. A recent study showed that teachers added about 150% more than what the printed teacher guides called for. They asked more questions, gave more explanations, provided more practice and review. Succinctly, there is a very large difference between the printed program that comes from the publisher and what gets taught in the classroom.

Obviously this latitude will not be able to exist in CAI programs. There will be no omniscient, flexible teacher discretion. What is in the CAI pro-

From "Instructional Design and CAI," by Don Steely. In *The Computing Teacher*, September 1980. Reprinted by permission.

gram is exactly what gets taught. The details that are left to the teacher's control must be accounted for. An examination of how these details are dealt with in printed materials and how teachers must modify the resulting programs can imply much about how CAI programs must be designed.

The following analysis will examine a half dozen design concerns in which the details are left to the teacher. The analysis and general comments tend to apply uniformly to the teaching of any subject. However, the specific data we are discussing are based upon a study of teaching certain basic reading skills. In particular, the study dealt with teaching the skill of finding the *main idea* in a passage.

Assumption 1: Students tend to forget what they have been taught unless it is periodically reviewed and practiced.

If you follow main idea instruction from its introduction to its last appearance (about 3 years), you will find that any usage or mention of the skill occurs about once every two months. Can you imagine being taught something new (say an integral calculus concept) one day and not being required to use that knowledge again for two months?

Obviously, if a particular teacher thinks the skill is important, s/he must either reteach the skill each time it reappears or provide intervening practice and review. Most teachers do the latter.

If a skill is considered important enough to teach through a CAI presentation, review and practice for that skill must be scheduled into the program. The practice can be independent or CAI, but it must be there, ideally every 3 days, minimally once a week. Without it, each new appearance of the skill will have to be treated as initial teaching, thus requiring more intensive work and testing.

Assumption 2: When teaching a particular skill, the questions that the teacher asks should be about that skill and not about some other unrelated skill.

If you examine the lessons that teach the main idea you will find that roughly 50% of the suggested teacher guide questions have nothing to do with main idea. The result is that the students do not know what is or is not relevant to main idea and they are distracted from understanding the concept of main idea. Their situation is probably similar to us trying to read a professional article and simultaneously carry on a conversation with our spouse.

If the teacher is serious about having the students understand the skill or concept, s/he must provide additional, relevant questions and examples to ensure that students get the important information.

CAI programs will not have the room for extraneous, irrelevant material. This will require examining what is taught longitudinally—following the development of one skill at a time across all the lessons that

it will appear in to make sure the questions and information are pertinent; logically developed in small steps, and that all unessential material is eliminated.

Assumption 3: If the student has just been taught how to answer certain questions or apply certain skills, the student should be tested on those same applicants and same types of questions.

In independent main idea exercises, about 50% of the question forms and applications have not been taught. Although generalization of a skill does require application to a variety of examples, those examples must be of the same general type. These were not. The analogy runs something like this—you learned to drive a car and they make you take your first driving test in a truck!

Again the responsibility falls to the teacher. If s/he decides to seriously teach the skill, s/he must provide additional tests on those forms that have been taught. S/he must decide when the students sufficiently understand the new skill.

The implication for CAI is careful control of example questions and forms. By isolating the longitudinal development of the skill, it is possible to provide the increasingly less structured, more general form required for generalization without introducing nontaught types of examples.

Assumption 4: When the teacher presents a new skill to the student, that presentation should be unambiguous—there should be only one interpretation of what is being taught.

In the usual print program, there are often several possible interpretations that the student could come away with from any particular lesson. For example, in my right hand I have a blue box of matches. I hold it up and call it "glerm." "Glerm" could mean: 1) a matchbox, 2) something blue, 3) something in my right hand, 4) an object, etc. All are possible interpretations—only one is correct.

The teacher is responsible for straightening out the students by asking more questions, giving additional examples and providing additional explanations.

CAI programs will have to be much more careful about how concepts and skills are taught. A devil's advocate approach must be used on each presentation in an attempt to try to misunderstand what is being taught. There must be one, and only one, interpretation of what is taught.

Assumption 5: When students are tested on a skill they have just learned, the questions should make them apply what they learned and not be giveaways.

However, about 50% of the independent workbook questions have spurious prompts—clues, pictures, bolded words or absurd possibilities in multiple choice questions—that make it possible for the student to answer the question without applying any knowledge of what is being tested. The questions are not all of the order "Who is buried in Grant's tomb?" but many approach that form.

The teacher is expected to determine when the students sufficiently understand the concept and can go on to additional or new work. If the teacher feels the students need more work, s/he must provide the additional questions.

CAI programs must provide fair, informative tests void of spurious prompts that give the mistaken impression that students know something they may not. Yes/No questions and multiple choice questions, although easiest to use with CAI, are susceptible to guessing. The more difficult question form, generating the entire answer, will certainly provide the kind of feedback that is required.

Assumption 6: When the teacher asks the student a question, the student should be reasonably able to answer it.

When we examine main idea lessons, we find about 50% of the questions suggested in the teachers guide are either ambiguous or the questions have not been taught or reviewed within two months.

The teacher can handle this problem by rewording the question to a clearer form or by providing that intervening practice.

CAI programs must ensure that the questions are not ambiguous, especially if the student must generate the entire answer rather than using a simpler response form. A combination of the devil's advocate approach for ambiguity and adequate review can accomplish the goal.

In each of the six cases above (a few of possibly dozens), the lack of detailed instructional design procedures that worked satisfactorily in print programs presents problems for CAI programs. Instructional design practices for CAI must be infinitely more precise and concerned with detail than the practices currently used with print materials. Without this concern for detail, CAI will also require that a teacher be present to do the same work that the print programs require.

Search of the Literature

Denyse Forman

A search of the literature reveals that most educators would agree with Splittgerber[45] that the instructional utilization of microcomputers can generally be divided into two broad categories; namely, computer

From "Search of the Literature," by Denyse Forman. In *The Computing Teacher*, January 1982. Reprinted by permission.

managed instruction (CMI) and computer assisted instruction (CAI):

> The latter, CAI, is defined as a teaching process directly involving the computer in the presentation of instructional materials in an interactive mode to provide and control the individualized learning environment for each individualized student. These interactive modes are usually subdivided into drill-and-practice, tutorial, simulation and gaming, and problem-solving. . .
>
> In contrast, CMI is defined as an instructional management system utilizing the computer to direct the *entire* instructional process, including perhaps CAI as well as traditional forms of instruction which do not require the computer such as lectures and group activities. CMI has some or all of the following characteristics: organizing curricula and student data, monitoring student progress, diagnosing and prescribing, evaluating learning outcomes, and providing planning information for teachers (Splittgerber, p. 20).

The definition of CAI has been further refined by Chambers and Sprecher[11] to distinguish between adjunct and primary, simplistic and complex CAI. According to these researchers, adjunct CAI refers to a program or series of programs which supplements the learning situation whereas primary CAI describes programs which provide instruction of a substitute or stand alone variety. Simplistic CAI can be developed by using easy-to-learn programming languages but complex CAI requires authoring which permits such features as the extensive use of graphics and large scale calculations.

However, for the purposes of this discussion, the terms CAI and CAL will be used interchangeably to include the broad range of possible applications of computers in education. The remainder of this section of the report will review the current literature regarding the use of computers in education.

THE EFFECT OF CAI ON ACHIEVEMENT

Arguing against the need to prove over and over again that CAI "works," Eisele[18] points out that there is "little likelihood that sufficient evidence will ever exist that will assure educators—with any noticeable degree of confidence—that any *delivery system* will perform adequately if the criterion is stated in replicable learner performance" (Eisele, p. 1).

Similarly, Gleason[21] observes that few serious researchers are now interested in comparative studies, i.e., studies which attempt to compare the results of computer assisted instruction with the results of other strategies because of the extreme difficulty of controlling the number of significant variables in any learning situation (Gleason, p. 16).

Aiken and Braun[1] argue that although the trend has been to use statistical techniques to measure the effectiveness of CAI materials, they feel that attitudinal studies would appear to be a more promising approach. They point out that "statistical results have been meaningful only as measures of *performance;* other methods will have to be considered if we are to have meaningful measures of *learning*" (Aiken and Braun, p. 14).

However, although researchers caution against placing too much emphasis on statistical results, decision makers are demanding proof that CAI is effective, often without fully understanding what they mean by "effective."

As Chambers and Sprecher[11] point out,

> To some effectiveness means the amount of learning that takes place initially. To others it means the degree of retention of learning, or at the very least, whether or not an individual stays in or drops out of a learning experience. Still others are concerned with the learner's change in attitude toward the computer as an instructional medium or simply as a helpful tool in the culture. Finally, owing to the fact that CAI is in its infancy, some are simply concerned with transportability of materials and/or acceptance of the materials for use by others (Chambers and Sprecher, p. 335).

To further complicate the issue, the number of methodologically sound evaluations of the effectiveness of computer assisted instruction are rare and conclusive results are difficult to find.

However, there are a number of well designed and tightly controlled studies from which some generalized conclusions can be drawn regarding the effectiveness of CAI in the learning process:

1. The use of CAI either improved learning or showed no difference when compared to traditional classroom approaches.[9,16,17,20,23,29,34,41,50]
2. The effect on achievement occurred regardless of the type of CAI used, the type of computer system, the age range of the students, or the type of instrument used to make the measurements (Hallworth and Brebner, p. 175).
3. When CAI and traditional instruction are compared, equal or better achievement using CAI is obtained in less time.[16,17,20,29,34,42]
4. Students have a positive attitude towards CAI, frequently accompanied by increased motivation, attention span, and attendance in courses (Hallworth and Brebner, p. 178).

In addition to the above consistencies, a number of other interesting and significant factors relating to the effectiveness of CAI are reported in the literature:

1. Tutorial and drill modes seem to be more effective for low-ability students than for middle or high-ability students;[8,16,17,20,26,42]
2. Many reluctant learners become active and interested learners when involved in computer supported programs;[20,26]
3. The bulk of the studies showing CAI to be effective have concerned the use of adjunct CAI in which the classroom teacher was readily available;[11]
4. Poor attitudes on the part of instructors and administrators have resulted in overt sabotage to the computer learning process;[14]
5. Foreign languages and science are two areas in which CAI programs consistently have been shown to be effective;[17]
6. CAI is helpful to students reviewing materials with which they had prior familiarity;[17] and
7. Retention rates may be lower than for traditional means.[45]

Although a number of fundamental questions regarding the effectiveness of CAI have been answered, an increasing number of researchers are arguing that there are many more complex questions that still need to be explored and that more subjective, less quantitative approaches are going to have to be used.[1,11,13,14,18,21,31,42]

The types of questions that educators and administrators are currently asking of the research are concisely summarized by Gleason:[21]

1. What are the most effective CAI strategies? What type of feedback is most effective? How often? At what point in the program? What types of learner interaction are most productive? Which instructional paradigms are most effective in the various content areas?
2. What are the interactions of individual learning styles in CAI? How much cognitive complexity can the learner manage? What concept-learning strategies are most appropriate for which types of learners?
3. What are the effects of individual learner characteristics such as memory span, perceptual skills, sensory preferences, intelligence, motor skills, etc.?
4. Which hardware configurations are most effective and efficient in various types of program? Audio? Touch-sensitive screens? Videodisc? Light pens? Etc.
5. What affective characteristics of the learner are important? Motivation? Persistence? Delayed gratification? Locus of control? Etc.
6. What are the most effective strategies for program development?
7. What are the most effective strategies for integrating CAI with other instructional activities? (Gleason, p. 16)

The answers to these questions will provide further information regarding the development of courseware and the integration of instructional technology into the classroom. In the meantime, educators can continue to plan and implement computer programs on the basis of studies that have been completed. As Paden[41] points out,

> If the profession is serious about improving instruction, these experiments provide tips galore: use the computer to improve study habits, to highlight important concepts, to process data, to "individualize" instruction, to give examinations, to provide prompt feedback to students, to keep records, and to add pizzazz to content instruction. Some of this will improve performance. Some of it will improve student attitudes. Other aspects will reduce the drudgery of teaching for the instructor (Paden, p. 18).

But he also cautions, as does a search of the literature on the effectiveness of CAI, that expectations of greatly improved performance from CAI presented as an addition to conventional instruction seem unrealistic.

Dence[17] expresses a similar opinion in regard to the most effective current and future use of CAI in the instructional setting. She points out that current studies in ATI (Aptitude-Treatment Interactions) are attempting to identify ways to measure individual student characteristics to determine which approaches will benefit students with specific characteristics. Educators have begun to identify the student characteristics such as response pace, initial levels of achievement, and prior familiarity with subject matter as characteristics that respond well to CAI, and Dence suggests that further research in areas such as locus of control, split-brain research, cognitive style, anxiety level, and personality types will assist educators in designing courseware and in making recommendations for the effective use of CAI in educational settings. She adds that "where significant differences are found between CAI and traditional instruction, it is imperative to identify and quantify why those differences occurred" (Dence, p. 54).

She concludes:

> The result of direct research will have a great impact on the use of CAI by extending the interpretation and applicability of prior findings. CAI can then be used in those situations where the indication is that it will enhance learning for individual students or groups of students. More traditional methods of instruction can be retained for those situations where they are the most effective (Dence, p. 54).

THE COST EFFECTIVENESS OF CAI

Kearsley[29] has pointed out that although CAI may be perceived as instructionally effective, educators may be reluctant to use it if they perceive it as being prohibitively expensive. Economically, the debate over the uses of CMI and CAI focus on 1) the relative advantages that the computer has over traditional, perhaps less expensive instructional methods; 2)

whether, in fact, less expensive means are available to effect the same instructional gains as the computer; and 3) whether technological advances have reduced the costs to a point where school districts can implement computer based instruction (Splittgerber, p. 21).

Cost estimates for CAI are highly variable and are difficult to establish with any degree of accuracy, particularly as CAI can be delivered on a variety of timeshare or microcomputer hardware systems. There have been a number of studies which have assessed the cost effectiveness of timeshare systems,[6,7,8,11,23,29] but studies providing information regarding inexpensive microcomputers and commercially available courseware are difficult to find.

However, regardless of whether CAI is being delivered via timeshare or microcomputer technology, the hardware purchase and maintenance costs, the courseware purchase and courseware development costs, and the cost of the provision of training and support services to educators must be taken into consideration in any estimate of the cost effectiveness of CAI over traditional instructional methods.

More specifically, estimates of cost effectiveness need to consider hardware purchase and maintenance costs as amortized over the number of years of use the system is intended to provide and as distributed over the number of students who will be using the system.

Similarly, courseware acquisition and development costs are dependent on a number of factors which influence any estimate of the overall cost effectiveness of CAI. For example, software development and acquisition costs are reduced in proportion to the number of students using the courseware, particularly if the courseware is being provided for handicapped or remote students who have traditionally been more expensive to educate than regular students. Costs are also reduced if the courseware is simple in design and if it has a long lifespan uninterrupted by updates or revisions. Whenever possible, it is generally more cost effective to purchase commercially available courseware than to develop it.

In addition, any decision regarding the cost effectiveness of CAI must take into consideration whether the courseware and the costs are being incurred to replace or to add to regular instruction.

These variables have made it difficult to assess the cost effectiveness of CAI, particularly with the newer microcomputer technology.

It has been estimated that a very adequate stand alone system costing $5,000 to $6,000 and used for 1500 hours throughout a school year will cost 50 cents an hour. Courseware development cost estimates range from 50 cents to $750 per student hour.[11,23] Courseware acquisition costs are highly variable, ranging from $3.00 for a single program to $600 for a series of programs that can be used by an entire elementary school, but 50 cents an hour would be a generous estimate. Therefore, whether courseware is acquired or developed, the cost of CAI using a microcomputer hardware system can be estimated at $1.00 a student hour. Hallworth and Brebner[23] estimate that timesharing computer cost is between 66 cents to $1.00 per student hour. They point out that when 16 bit microprocessor systems become available, with multi-user software using hard disks, these should support up to at least 16 users on a school CAI system and it may be reasonably expected that for this number of users, and possibly for a smaller number this system will reduce the cost per student hour to 20 cents or less. With the overall cost of education per student hour for the Calgary Board of Education being $2.22 with $5.56 for special education students,[23] CAI, whether on timeshare or a microcomputer system, compares very favourably.

Norris[39] has pointed out that traditional instructional costs have been increasing at the rate of 13% a year for the past three years while CAI costs have been decreasing at 5% per year, coupled with a 10% improvement in performance. Hirschbuhl[26] also points out that "in a period of run-away inflation on a nearly global basis, the per character cost of computer technology has been reduced a thousand fold, the reliability increased twenty fold, and the accessibility increased by a like magnitude" (Hirschbuhl, p. 62). He estimates that by 1990, computer industry hardware will become 32 times as cost effective as present day hardware. It can be safely assumed that as hardware capabilities increase and costs decrease, CAI will become more and more cost effective.

In addition, the hidden benefits must be considered. Braun[8] reports that in a computer program in the District of Columbia in which 700 students were involved, there was an increase in student attendance at a tax cost saving to the public of $30,710. Extrapolating this to the entire student population, Braun argues that the productivity gain would be on the order of $1 million per year. Similarly, based on a study on attrition in a community college system in Ontario, Braun estimates that by using CAI mathematics the province's dollar gain or cost-productivity gain index per year would be $9,600,000. He concludes that "the value of these two studies is that they demonstrate that the use of the computer to aid instruction *can* result in a substantial gain in the use of the tax dollar for education" (Braun, p. 10).

It has also been pointed out that hardware originally purchased for CAI has been doing double duty in administration, guidance, record keeping and library functions; that truancy and vandalism were reduced in schools where CAI was being used with disadvantaged students; that by using the computer, educational institutions can offer more flexible scheduling and wider course alternatives; that curricula can be more attuned to the pace of change; that instructor costs are saved in providing distance and continuing education; and that new knowledge can be brought into education much sooner.[8,11,23,29,39]

The hidden costs include maintenance costs for hardware, the inevitable higher costs for courseware development which are anticipated to account for over 90% of total costs by 1990,[23] and the cost of a support mechanism to introduce and integrate CAI into the instructional setting in a manner which guarantees the benefits which have been shown to be possible.

If the cost estimates of CAL are adjusted to include the hidden costs of software, courseware, inservice, maintenance and support, they may well be higher than traditional per-student-hour costs. They must, however, be weighted for their cost effectiveness. Deltak, Inc. compared their industrial training programs and found that a five-day instructor-led course of 10 students was more costly than a computer enhanced, learner-paced multi-media approach at a ratio of $1,120/$680.[42] That is, traditional training is 65% more expensive than CAL.

Kearsley, in his article "The Cost of CAI: A Matter of Assumption," concluded:

> The fact that CAI results in a higher per student hour cost is based upon a fairly dubious assumption that the instructional effectiveness of CAI is the same as traditional instruction. This is most certainly an invalid premise. Almost all comparative studies of CAI have shown that it reduces the time required for a subject by 25–50 percent while still resulting in the same end performance. CAI permits a very detailed monitoring and evaluation of student performance and instructional effectiveness which is essentially impossible in traditional instruction. CAI also permits certain kinds of instruction which could not be done by any traditional means (e.g., medical simulations of dying patients). Students are overwhelmingly positive about CAI, and they express strong preferences for this mode of instruction across all subjects. Thus, an hour's worth of CAI may be instructionally equivalent to two hours or more of traditional instruction. If we accept this, then cost estimates which show CAI as costing the same as or slightly more than traditional instruction in fact give CAI the edge.[29]

When used as a substitute or replacement for traditional methods, particularly when considering the education of special students, CAI can be cost saving. However, at the present time, CAI is used today mainly as a supplement to regular instruction either in enrichment or remediation and as such, its costs must be considered as add-ons to traditional instruction. Considering the benefits, educators must ask whether the added expense is worth it.

FURTHER CONSIDERATIONS

In addition to the effect that CAI reportedly has on achievement and education costs, a search of the literature reveals that researchers have identified a number of other factors that can be identified as advantages to CAI.

These advantages include the computer's ability to individualize the instructional process;[34] to simulate experiences not possible at all without a computer;[13,29,34] to keep students informed of their progress through immediate feedback and achievement summaries;[34] to provide immediate and systematized reinforcement; to provide instruction that has been systematically prepared, sequenced, tested and revised;[34] and to allow students to review previous instruction, request special help, or to continue on to enrichment activities.[34]

In addition, researchers argue that because the computer involves the individual actively in the instructional process, learning is facilitated;[11] and that CAI frees the teacher to devote more time to the personal, human considerations of their students, a factor which has been identified by Chambers as being the most significant in the development of creative abilities, according to students.[12]

The rationale for introducing computers into the schools on the basis of cost effectiveness and instructional benefits is a potent argument, particularly in light of the public's perception in Canada and the U.S. that the educational system is both costly and unsatisfactory.

Braun[8] identifies a number of factors which indicate the public's dissatisfaction with the education system in the U.S. These factors include the significant increase in the number of dropouts; an increase in the numbers of students who are performing below their grade levels; unacceptably high levels of youth unemployment; a continuing decline in the education of U.S. students in the sciences; and the spiralling costs of programs for the education of the handicapped, the gifted, and the learning disabled.

He offers the arguments of Dr. Dustin Heuston of WICAT as further rationale for the immediate and widespread introduction of the computer into the present educational system. In "Technology and the Educational Delivery System," Heuston points out that

1. The current U.S. educational system is insensitive to additional investment and cannot be improved

without the dramatic change producible with new technologies.
2. The current educational delivery system provides about 15 seconds of personal attention per hour whereas with computers that proportion could reach almost 100%.
3. After expensive and extensive efforts at improvement, the present educational system has reached its maximum effectiveness.

Thus Braun and Heuston argue that the only effective means of increasing the productivity of the present educational system is through the introduction of technology into the instructional process, and as Braun points out, computers will move into homes and schools, whether or not anyone does anything to ensure their effective use.

Splittgerber[45] summarizes:

> Supporters forecast an imminent breakthrough in the use of computers, due primarily to decreasing costs and increased availability of minicomputers; curricula and software improvements; the trend toward accountability; the requirement for improved school productivity; and the expansion and personalization of instruction (Splittgerber, p. 25).

THE COMPUTER LITERACY ARGUMENT

Perhaps the most powerful argument for the immediate and widespread introduction of computers into the school system is Luehrmann's argument[32] that "the ability to use computers is as basic and necessary to a person's formal education as reading, writing, and arithmetic" (Luehrmann, p. 98). He contends that computing plays such a crucial role in everyday life and in his nation's technological future that "the general public's ignorance of the subject constitutes a national crisis" (Luehrmann, p. 98).

The requirements for living and working in what has been called The Age of Information have been clearly described by Andrew Molnar[36] who argues that "if we are to continue to benefit from the expanding frontiers of knowledge, we must devise new ways to expand human capacity and reasoning . . . and we must create new intellectual tools to extend human capacity to reason."

In his presentation, "Education for Citizenship in a Computer-Based Society," Daniel Watt[51] points out that although in the past only a small percentage of the population ever had direct contact with computers, in the future, as the nation's economy becomes more dependent on information processing and high technology, "we can expect the overwhelming majority of our working population to have significant interactions with computers as part of their daily work" (Watt, p. 2). He insists that "only public schools can help insure that all citizens have equal access to the opportunity for computer literacy education, and only the public schools in our society have the responsibility for the education of citizens who can make effective decisions about the impact of technology on society" (Watt, p. 6).

The important point being made is that computers will soon be everywhere and students who have not been exposed to them will be at a decided disadvantage when competing with those who have; and society generally will be at a disadvantage when confronting issues that have to do with the impact of computers on the individual and on society. In short, our students must become computer literate.

The definition of computer literacy has been evolving as educators and researchers have become more knowledgeable about what it means to be literate and as computers extend further and further into society.

Initially, when computer literacy was identified in 1977 as one of the Ten Basic Skills by the American Council of Supervisors of Mathematics, computer literacy was generally described as what students should know about the uses of computers and what computers can and cannot do.[40]

The Human Resources Research Organization (HumRRO) defined computer literacy as what a person needs to know and to do with computers in order to function competently in our society.[38] The University of Oregon advised that computer literacy referred to the non-technical and low-technical aspects of the social, vocational, and educational implications of computers.[38]

However, it is generally believed that these definitions no longer suggest adequate goals and objectives for a computer literacy program. As David Moursund points out, computer literacy initially tended to mean a level of understanding at which the student could talk about but could not actually work with a computer.[38] However, this level of understanding is now considered to be computer awareness rather than literacy.

Luehrmann[32] argues that computer literacy must mean the ability to *do* computing and not merely to "recognize," "identify," or "be aware" of alleged facts about computing that have been supplied by a book or a teacher. Further, he states that "it is intellectually improper to inculcate beliefs and values about a subject that do not arise out of direct experience with the content of that subject" (Luehrmann, p. 6).

Based on an interpretation of the common meaning of literacy and following a traditional understanding of what it means to be literate, Daniel Watt[50] defines computer literacy as "that collection of skills, knowledge, values and relationships that allows a person to

function comfortably as a productive citizen of a computer oriented society" (Watt, p. 26).

He further divides the concept of computer literacy into four distinct interrelated areas which, summarized, include:

1. The ability to control and program a computer to achieve a variety of personal, academic and professional goals;
2. The ability to use a variety of preprogrammed computer applications in personal, academic and professional contexts;
3. The ability to understand the growing economic, social and psychological impact of computers on individuals, on groups within our society, and on society as a whole; and
4. The ability to make use of ideas from the world of computer programming and computer applications as part of an individual's collection of strategies for information retrieval, communication and problem solving (Watt, p. 27).

Watt concludes that "the failure of schools to make a major commitment in this area now can have disastrous consequences for both the education of the public and the future of public education" (Watt, p. 27).

IMPEDIMENTS TO IMPLEMENTATION

If the evidence for the widespread and immediate introduction of computers into the school system is so overwhelming, why is there such a gap between the actual and potential use of computers in education? A search of the literature reveals that there are a number of factors which researchers have identified as being impediments to the exploration of the full potential of the computer in education:

1. Insufficient funding from the appropriate sources to support the original purchase of hardware, software, courseware, and to establish the necessary support services for the successful integration of the technology into the educational system. [13,29,33,37,45]
2. The primitive state of the art in which there is a confusing diversity of languages and hardware systems. [11,29]
3. CAI materials that are poorly constructed, largely undocumented, and able to run only on the equipment for which they were written. [11,29]
4. Lack of knowledge among educators as to how to effectively use CAI materials and the computer in the learning situation, particularly at the moment when limited financial resources restrict the number of systems available per classroom. [11,29,37]
5. The attitude among teachers, familiar with and comfortable using tried and tested methods,

that the computer is not a tool but an intelligent machine destined to replace them as teachers.[11,14,29,45,48]

In order of importance, Chambers and Bork[13] found the impediments to the implementation of computer assisted instruction to be 1) funding; 2) lack of knowledge about computer assisted instruction and computers in general; 3) attitudes of faculty; and 4) the need for more and better computer assisted instruction modules (Chambers & Bork, p. 28).

In addition to the above impediments to the implementation of computer assisted instruction, critics cite the lack of information about the effectiveness of CAI, the tremendous financial commitment to a technological innovation that is new, untried and uncomfortably similar to educational television, depersonalization of the educational process, and lack of support from teachers and teachers' organizations as reasons why it is advisable to adopt a wait-and-see attitude.

POTENTIAL, ACTUAL, AND PROJECTED USES OF THE COMPUTER IN EDUCATION

A search of the literature reveals that there are various applications which have been identified as being reasonable and effective uses of the computer in education. As described and envisioned by such researchers as Bork, Franklin, Haugo, and Watts, these applications include the following:

1. *Administrative applications* which include such activities as keeping track of accounting, payroll, inventory and employee records and of attendance, grades and student records. The computer has also been used in administration in class timetabling and in simulating models to forecast the implications of decisions and changes in the educational environment.[6,24,49,52]
2. *Curriculum planning applications* such as the resource information file which was developed and is being used in Alaska to provide teachers with information on available educational resources.[49]
3. *Professional development applications* which not only provide teachers with new skills and an understanding of the uses of computers in education, but could also provide highly informative and imaginative professional development courses in other areas of education.[52]
4. *Library applications* which involve the computer in maintaining records of holdings, managing intra- and inter-library loans, and enabling users to search files for relevant titles and information.[52]
5. *Research applications* which enable a school or district to analyze data collected on a regular basis or for special purposes.[52]

6. *Guidance and special services applications* which include computer administration and scoring of selected standardized tests; provision of guidance and career information using a computer; and the administration of tests and the analysis of data to assist special education personnel with the diagnosis and remediation of learning problems.[52]
7. *Testing applications* which include computer assistance in the construction, administration, scoring, and evaluation and analysis of test results.[6,52]
8. *Instructional aid applications* which are described by Watts[52] as the use of the computer in the same manner that any audio-visual device or piece of laboratory equipment may be used to demonstrate or illustrate concepts or to allow students to manipulate parameters without having to duplicate a real world situation.
9. *Instructional management applications* which assist the teacher in providing individualized or small group instruction by using the computer to manage the student's learning experiences and to monitor and assess progress.[1,6,24,45,52]
10. *Computer assisted instruction applications* which involve the computer in taking over a central part of the instruction of the student[1,6,24,45,52] and which can include a number of different modes of interaction with the student:
    a. Drill-and-practice programs take advantage of the computer's tireless patience and ability to provide immediate feedback and reinforcement to prescribe, provide and monitor potentially very complex drill-and-practice activities which can be tailored to a student's individual needs.
    b. Tutorial programs, depending on the capabilities and the storage capacity of the computer system, are dialogues between the learner and the designer of the educational program. The computer acts as a "tutor" to teach the student concepts and skills. The worst of such programs are simply page turners which present passages of text and then ask the student to answer a question on what they have just read. The best type of tutorial, called "dialog," leads the active learner through a series of carefully planned questions to some new understanding or knowledge of the topic at hand.
    c. Simulations or controllable worlds are programs in which the computer can be used to simulate or generate environments for the learner so that he can change variables and explore situations in a manner that might have been too expensive, too restricted by time limitations, too dangerous or too impossible to allow the student to explore in the real world.

11. *Computer awareness and literacy applications* which involve the computer in preparing students to understand and to be able to use computers in our future computer oriented society.
12. *Computer science applications* which include teaching students about computer architecture, operations, programming and applications.[52]

Chambers and Bork[13] selected a sample of 974 school districts, which closely approximated the total population of U.S. public school districts to assess the current and projected use of the computer in U.S. public secondary/elementary schools, with special emphasis on the use of the computer in computer assisted instruction (Figure 1).

It was found that approximately 90% of all school districts responding are now using the computer in support of the instructional process. Most computers are leased or owned by districts and large computers are more in evidence than are micros and minis which the study found to be equal in popularity. It was also found that the most popular applications in order of usage are the teaching of computer languages, computer assisted learning, data processing applications, using the computer as an instructional aid, and using it for guidance and counselling applications (Chambers & Bork, p. 11).

In computer assisted instruction applications, the predominant use is in drill and practice, although it was noted that simulations are also receiving a good deal of use. At the secondary level, predominant use is occurring in Mathematics, Natural Science, Business and Language Arts (Chambers & Bork, p. 15).

Chambers and Bork's study showed a dramatic change from the past. From an estimated 13% in 1970, instructional computer usage had leaped to 74% in 1980 with the type of instructional usage changing from predominantly problem-solving and the acquisition of EDP skills, to a much heavier emphasis on computer assisted instruction. They also found that while the quantity of instructional computer usage in the schools had increased significantly, the richness and diversity of usage had not increased proportionately. They attribute this to the industry's concentration on providing hardware to the schools while not being able to provide adequate and satisfactory courseware to support the use of the hardware, and to the lack of adequately trained staff to enable effective use of the computer in CAI.

For the period 1980–1985, 94% of the districts surveyed anticipated using the computer with 87% of this percentage indicating that they would be using the computer to provide support for instruction. Types of instructional usage were projected to continue as in the past with 74% of the districts indicating that they would be providing computer assisted instruction. It was also anticipated that tutorials would assume greater usage with drill and practice receiving less. Chambers & Bork suggest that this shift in emphasis will perhaps move towards simulation by 1990. In support of Chambers and Bork's findings is Hirschbuhl's table which projects increased levels of acceptance and utilization areas for CAI by 1990 (Figure 2).

Watts[52] points out that there are schools in which a dozen applications of the computer in education are already to be found and he concludes, "the challenge is there for all schools to successfully introduce computers and to develop their potential in education" (Watts, p. 22).

FUTURE TRENDS AND RECOMMENDATIONS

A search of the literature indicates that most educators and researchers are cautiously optimistic about the future of computers in education.

As discussed earlier, the major impediments to the widespread introduction of computers into the education system are:

1. Insufficient funding to purchase hardware and courseware;
2. Insufficient and inadequate courseware that has been designed to run only on one system;
3. The confusing diversity of hardware systems and languages;
4. Lack of knowledge among educators as to how to effectively use the computer in an educational setting; and
5. The concern of teachers that the computer is either too difficult for them to learn to use or that it is destined to replace them in their job.

Although Chambers and Bork report that "it is predicted that by 1985 the current major problems

FIGURE 1. Trends (U.S. experience)

	% of School Districts Sampled
1. Districts Using Computers	1980 – 90% 1985 – 94%
2. Instructional Usage	1970 – 13% 1980 – 74% 1985 – 87%
3. CAL	1980 – 54% 1985 – 74%
4. Application Priority	1. Math 2. Science 3. Language Arts 4. Business
5. Emphasis Shift	Drill and Practice ⟶ Tutorial ⟶ Simulation

Source: ACM Report on CAL, Chambers/Bork 1980

FIGURE 2. Levels of acceptance and utilization areas for CAI

	HOME PRESCHOOL	SECONDARY SCHOOLS	HIGHER EDUCATION	INDUSTRY	COMMUNITY INST.
1977 ACCEPTANCE	Zero	Widely dispersed emerging	Widespread	High level limited implementation	On the horizon
1977 UTILIZATION	None	Basic skills (heavy)	Skill and survey type instruction (moderate)	Testing and training drills (light) Basic skills and conditioning programs (light)	Vocabulary and procedural info in health areas
1990 ACCEPTANCE	Widespread	Widespread	Universal	Heavy	Broad by social and health institutions
1990 UTILIZATION	Heavy use in concept development	Universal for skill development and high level concept development	Extensive for entry level courses and high level professional development and continuing education	Heavy in specific training skills and management development	Heavy use by health industry for upgrading diagnostic skill. Heavy use for rehabilitation and deterrent programs in criminal justice.

Source: Hirschbuhl, *Educational Technology* 18, 4 (1978), p. 62.

in the use of computer assisted learning will have been reduced to the level that the hardware problem has now reached in 1980" (Chambers & Bork), at the moment, the above impediments must still be considered major concerns.

It is generally agreed that hardware barriers have been or shortly will be resolved and cost reductions will help eliminate funding problems and permit the cost effective use of CAI.[2,4,10,11,26,29,31,39] In support of this prediction, Gleason[21] reports that a recent study by the National Science Foundation estimated that there are already 200,000 microcomputers in American elementary and secondary schools and projects one million units by 1985.

It is also generally agreed that the technology for instructional use in educational settings will likely include mini- and microcomputers capable of standing alone or networked and incorporating a touch-sensitive input device, image projection, colour printing device, voice input and output, interactive television, videodisc systems and satellite communication. According to the research, videodisc technology will play an increasingly significant role in creative and effective innovations in education.

A number of researchers—Atkinson, Bunderson, Hirschbuhl—predict distributed networks with large shared databases which would enable individuals to use stand-alone microcomputers or access larger databases or communicate with other users.

Hirschbuhl[26] argues that, "the power of interactive visual, sound, computer simulation, control, and change of variables along with the mind extending

ability of computer prediction offer teaching capabilities never before realized" (Hirschbuhl, pp. 52–53). He envisions brain waves used as input to Computer Assisted Dialogue CBE systems, laser libraries for the visually handicapped, talking computers to provide books for the blind, listening computers that understand unconstrained natural speech; in short, applications that will have far-reaching implications for education.

Although it is generally accepted that hardware is going to be the most easily solvable problem in implementing CAI in the future, it is still considered to be absolutely essential that 1) educators constantly monitor new hardware products and their potential usefulness to CAI, and that 2) wherever there is a central organization planning the activities of a group of computer using educators, there should be uniformity of hardware and cost reducing bulk purchasing arrangements with manufacturers.

Although Atkinson[2] believes that "by 1990, the cost of computer-assisted instruction will be so cheap and its applications so broad that it will be viewed as an educational necessity" (Atkinson, p. 60), Bitzer[4] points out that "the next steps in producing useful educational computer technology are far more complex and include some of the most difficult applications of a computer" (Bitzer, p. 61).

He agrees that limited applications that can take advantage of increased low-cost technical capabilities are already available but argues that hundreds of different stand-alone systems are not going to provide an "educational system consisting of high quality material organized in an overall educationally efficient manner" (Bitzer, p. 61). He believes that the most difficult questions must still be answered and that we cannot afford to underestimate how much those answers are going to cost.

The first of these problems is the continuing diversity of hardware systems with their differences in languages and their limitations in only running the courseware that has been written for that system. Although some researchers believe that this will continue to be a problem, Attala[3] argues that hardware advances in the development of microprogrammable chips containing compilers for several kinds of authoring languages and of replaceable read-only memory chips for the easy modification of system software will "solve the problem of transferability that has hindered for so long the propagation and popularity of CAI" (Attala, p. 61). Chambers and Sprecher[11] recommend the development of a nation-wide, standard high-level CAI language for complex CAI development which incorporates authoring aides, computational capability, graphics capability, multisensory input/output controls, and prescribed documentation standards. They believe that such a language should be easy to use and should be capable of running on large, mini-, and microcomputers. Because the development of such a language would be in the national interest, they argue that it should be funded by the federal government with the impetus coming from the educational sector and possibly incorporating a cooperative venture with the private sector.

The second major impediment, and considered by some to be the most serious, is the lack of a sufficient quantity of high-quality courseware. The problem of portability of software and courseware which restricts the market, the copyright problem, the tremendous amount of time required to develop materials, and the need for experienced and qualified educational and computer professionals are factors working against a solution to this problem. As discussed above, the problem of the portability of courseware could possibly be solved through the development of a standard CAI language or through hardware advances which may also solve the copyright problem.

But the problems associated with the amount of time needed to develop materials and the difficulty in finding qualified and experienced instructional designers and computer programmers still exist. Gleason[21] warns educators that contrary to what they may have been told, courseware development is not easy:

> It involves careful specification of objectives, selection of programming strategies, detailed analysis of content structure and sequence, development of pretests and posttests, preliminary drafts, revisions, trials, validation,

and documentation. This is a very time-consuming and expensive process, well beyond the capability and resources of individuals and even small groups of teachers (Gleason, p. 12).

He points out that at the present time there is no comprehensive, systematic or effective organization to prepare good programs, and although there are thousands of programs being written, "most are virtually devoid of any instructional value and in most cases are acting as deterrents to widespread acceptance of CAI" (Gleason, p. 12).

Chambers and Sprecher[11] found that the majority of courseware that is available has largely been written in a machine-dependent language and is undocumented and therefore difficult to share. They report that in "The ABC's of CAI" project,[47] over 4000 CAI programs written in BASIC were reviewed, and about 3-4 percent were found to be acceptable by faculty in the fields concerned (Chambers & Sprecher, p. 338). In short, they are in agreement with Bork who argues that, "The notion that computer-based materials can be produced by anybody, completely by themselves, is an archaic concept" (Bork, p. 20).

A team approach employing two or three content area specialists, an instructional design specialist, and a computer programmer has been suggested as the only reliable way of ensuring the development of courseware that will be acceptable to faculty and students. Further, it has been found that direct financial reward was not a motivator in involving faculty in developing materials. Rather, as Chambers and Sprecher report, studies have shown that recognition and acceptance by one's peers for courseware development and sharing of such materials, release time, and acceptance of courseware development by peers and by administrators as equivalent to research publications for promotion and tenure, appeared to be the most important incentives in involving faculty members in developing courseware (Chambers and Sprecher, p. 339).

Hallworth and Brebner, in their report to the Department of Education in Alberta,[23] support the idea of field development of courseware. They argue that "there is a need for a coordinated effort within the Province to build effective CAI curricula with many groups contributing and exchanging materials, but with no duplication of effort on any topic because of the exceptionally large numbers of work hours involved" (Hallworth and Brebner, p. 215) and they believe that the only way this can be done is through the leadership and support of the Department of Education. They recommend that the Department:

1. Facilitate the development of courseware by teams of teachers and other persons having

experience in CAI, by appropriate financing including, for example, release time for teachers;

2. Monitor such courseware development to ensure continuity of curricula and prevent duplication of effort;

3. Set up mechanisms for disseminating information on developments;

4. Set up a mechanism for facilitating exchange of courseware, both within and outside the Province; and

5. Retain all rights within the public domain (Hallworth & Brebner, pp. 215-216).

There is also evidence that the major publishers of educational materials are becoming increasingly interested in developing CAI materials and with their resources, experience and organization it will likely not be long before there is a substantial number of acceptable CAI programs commercially available. In addition, there are large number of small companies and organizations which have entered the courseware development market. A number of these have not survived a second year in the market, but many are on a second major revision of their materials and have shown themselves to be very willing to listen to the suggestions of teachers and to modify their programs to bring them in line with teachers' expectations. Not only has the quantity of commercially available programs increased dramatically over the past two years, but the quality has improved to such an extent that what was considered to be good a year ago is now considered to be average or below average. New benchmarks in quality are constantly being set and the rest of the market gradually works to that standard until a new level is set.

Thus, if teachers and educational organizations constantly monitor what is commercially available and continually evaluate its applicability to the curriculum, they will be in a position to use what is acceptable in the commercial market and to be able to determine areas where support is needed for local development. Dence[17] has argued for the importance of doing more studies on areas where CAI has an advantage over traditional instruction and why it is more effective, and the results of these studies can be used to help educators plan courseware development efforts. This opinion is supported by researchers who argue against "financing an army of CAI authors." A better way, they say, would be to find the areas in which CAI is most effective, and then devise some effective tool for creating and testing good courseware addressed to those areas (Sugarman, p. 29). This argument seems to be supported by the fact that of the approximately 16,000 hours of CAI related materials created for Plato, requiring from 500 [thousand]-800 thousand

hours of writing, only 4000 hours are used regularly Sugarman, p. 29).

It would seem that, in the future, a combination of public and private resources will be concentrating on the courseware development problem. By constantly monitoring and evaluating what is commercially available, educators can direct their efforts only to those areas that are not being adequately addressed by the marketplace; and by concentrating their efforts on areas where the research has demonstrated that CAI is more effective and more cost effective than traditional instruction, educators can avoid the time and expense wasted in developing courseware that could have been purchased more cheaply than developed or that is not effective in the instructional setting.

The need for organizations that will provide independent evaluations of programs and professional advice as to the quality of commercially available programs is argued throughout the literature and is a reflection of teachers' need for support in this new and intimidating area of education. As Aiken and Braun[1] argue, "teacher acceptance is the biggest challenge facing us today" (Aiken & Braun, p. 13).

This appears to be corroborated by Chambers and Bork's study[13] which found that teachers' lack of knowledge about CAI and computers was considered to be a major impediment to the implementation of CAI in the schools, second only to funding. Similarly, Hallworth and Brebner argue that, "CAI will not succeed in any environment where it does not have the full understanding and backing of teachers" (Hallworth & Brebner, p. 216[23]); and Clement[14] reports that "Poor attitudes on the part of instructors have actually resulted in covert and in some cases overt sabotage to the computer-aided learning process" (Clement, p. 28). Teachers need information and knowledge and CAI needs teachers in order to be successful.

Clement believes that "changing most instructor attitudes is a matter of educating them on the adjunctive value of the computer in the learning process" (Clement, p. 30), and he suggests pointing out that the computer is capable of taking over the routine, information giving and drill-and-practice tasks, and the clerical tasks while freeing the teacher to facilitate learning through one-to-one and small-group interactions.

Hallworth and Brebner[23] argue for the importance of educating teachers and providing information, and suggest that demonstration projects, sponsored and supported by the Ministry of Education and in cooperation with an established research center, be set up by teachers who are already knowledgeable about CAI and who can demonstrate the benefits to other teachers. They also recommend that the Ministry not only financially support and publicize the demonstration projects and provide encouragement and high professional status for teachers who demonstrate competence in CAI, but they should also require that new teachers have some knowledge of the use of computers in education. They encourage the Ministry to make computer literacy courses available to teachers at a number of different levels and recommend that such courses be made compulsory.

Aiken and Braun[1] recommend that courses and programs be provided for students training to be teachers, and point out that a way must be found to train the thousands of teachers who are already in the school system. They recommend the approach that the French have taken in training a small nucleus of teachers who are then used to teach others. However, they admit that whatever method is used, it is going to be expensive and a slow process that may require the use of video tape and videodisk as cost-reducing training media (Aiken & Braun, p. 13).

Henderson[25] is more specific. He argues that all teachers and educational administrators should complete a minimum of two courses in computer science as a general requirement for certification. He adds that all elementary teachers should complete one additional course covering the use of CAI materials for the elementary student, and secondary teachers should complete two additional computer science courses covering the use of computer-oriented materials and CAI materials designed for the secondary student and the development of computer-related materials. Administrators, according to Henderson, should be required to take two additional courses relating to the use of the computer in school operations and planning (Henderson, pp. 41–42).

CONCLUSION

A search of the literature regarding the instructional use of computers has revealed that for the most part, researchers are generally optimistic about the future of the computer in education. They feel that the hardware problems are being dealt with and that future advances in technology can only result in what Hirschbuhl terms "Education's Dream Machine." However, it is also generally accepted that the problem of ensuring an adequate supply of quality courseware and of training teachers how to use the computer in an effective manner will continue to impede the widespread integration of computer technology into the school system. It is also generally accepted that solving these problems is going to be expensive.

Until the research can be more specific, it seems reasonable that the resources of institutions, schools and ministries should concentrate their efforts on areas where CAI has proven itself to be both effective and cost effective. In their recommendations to the Alberta Department of Education, Hallworth and Brebner recommend that:

> ...those students who will benefit most from CAI are those for whom the patience and repetitiveness of the computer are of great assistance in their learning, those who require individual attention, those who for some reason have failed to learn in the regular classroom environment, those who feel inadequate and inferior and do not seek help from a teacher for fear of displaying their ignorance, those who do not have ready access to schools, and those studying subjects in which the computational and information processing power of the computer enhance learning (Hallworth & Brebner, p. 218).

Further, they argue that CAI must be given time to evolve while courseware builds up and irrational fears of computers are overcome. In this way, they believe that "computers should naturally find their place in the educational system."

REFERENCES

1. Aiken, R.M., & Braun, L. Into the 80's with Microcomputer-Based Learning. *Computer*, 1980, 13(7), 11–16.
2. Atkinson, R.C. Futures: Where Will Computer-Assisted Instruction (CAI) Be in 1990? *Educational Technology*, 1978, 18(4), 60–63.
3. Attala, E.E. Futures: Where Will Computer-Assisted Instruction Be in 1990? *Educational Technology*, 1978, 18(4), 60–63.
4. Bitzer, D. Futures: Where Will Computer-Assisted Instruction Be in 1990? *Educational Technology*, 1978, 18(4), 60–63.
5. Blaschke, C.L. Microcomputer Software Development for Schools: What, Who, How? *Educational Technology*, 1979, 19(10), 26–28.
6. Bork, A., & Franklin, S.D. The Role of Personal Computer Systems in Education. *Association for Educational Data Systems Journal*, 1979, 13(1), 17–30.
7. Bork, A. Machines for Computer-Assisted Learning. *Educational Technology*, 1978, 18(4), 17–20.
8. Braun, L. Computers in Learning Environments: An Imperative for the 1980's. *Byte*, 1980, 5(7), 6–10, 108–114.
9. Brebner, A., Hallworth, H.J., McIntosh, E. & Wontner, C.J. Teaching Elementary Reading by CMI and CAI. *Association for Educational Data Systems*, 1980, Convention Proceedings.
10. Bunderson, C.U. Futures: Where Will Computer-Assisted Instruction (CAI) Be in 1990? *Educational Technology*, 1978, 18(4), 60–63.
11. Chambers, J.A., & Sprecher, J.W. Computer Assisted Instruction: Current Trends and Critical Issues. *Communications of the ACM*, 1980, 23(6), 232–243.
12. Chambers, J.A. College Teachers: Their Effect on Creativity of Students. *Journal of Educational Psychology*, 1973, 65(3), 326–334.
13. Chambers, J.A., & Bork, A. *Computer Assisted Learning in U.S. Secondary/Elementary Schools*. Center for Information Processing, California State University, Fresno CA Research Report No. 80-03.

14. Clement, F.J. Effective Considerations in Computer-Based Education. *Educational Technology*, 1981, 21(4), 28–32.

15. De Laurentiis, E. Learning by Interactive Programming: Microcomputer Applications. *Educational Technology*, 1980, 20(12), 10–14.

16. Deignan, G.M., & Duncan, R.D. CAI in Three Medical Training Courses: It Was Effective! *Behaviour Research Methods and Instrumentation*, 1978, 10(2), 228–230.

17. Dence, M. Toward Defining a Role for CAI: A Review. *Educational Technology*, 1980, 20(11), 50–54.

18. Eisele, J.E. A Case for Computers in Instruction. *Journal of Research and Development in Education*, 1980, 14(1), 1–8.

19. *Academic Computing in Saskatchewan: A Status Report.* Exploratory Committee on the Academic Uses of Computers in Saskatchewan, 80 01 12.

20. Gershman, J., & Sakamoto, E. Computer-Assisted Remediation and Evaluation: A CAI Project for Ontario Secondary Schools. *Educational Technology*, 1981, 21(3), 40–43.

21. Gleason, G.T. Microcomputers in Education: The State of the Art. *Educational Technology*, 1981, 21(3), 7–18.

22. Hallworth, H.J., & Brebner, A. CAI for the Developmentally Handicapped: Nine Years of Progress. *Proceedings of the 1980 Conference of the Association for the Development of Computer-Based Instructional Systems*, 1980, 260–265.

23. Hallworth, H.J., and Brebner, A. *Computer Assisted Instruction in Schools: Achievements, Present Developments and Projections for the Future.* Calgary: Faculty of Education Computer Applications Unit, 1980.

24. Haugo, J.E. Management Applications of the Microcomputer: Promises and Pitfalls. *Association for Educational Data Systems*, 1981, Convention Proceedings, 129–132.

25. Henderson, D.L. Educational Uses of the Computer: Implications for Teacher/Administrator Training. *Educational Technology*, 1978, 18(8), 41–42.

26. Hirschbuhl, J.J. Futures: Where Will Computer-Assisted Instruction (CAI) Be in 1990? *Educational Technology*, 1978, 18(4), 60–63.

27. Hirschbuhl, J.J. Hardware Considerations for Computer-Based Education in the 1980's. *Journal of Research and Development in Education*, 1980, 14(1), 41–56.

28. Holznagel, D.C. MicroSIFT: A Clearinghouse for Microcomputing in Education. *Association for Educational Data Systems Monitor*, November 1980, 16–17.

29. Kearsley, G.P. Some 'Facts' About CAI: Trends 1970–1976. *Journal of Educational Data Processing*, 1976, 13(3), 1–11.

30. Kniefel, D.R. & Just, S.B. Impact of Microcomputers on Educational Computer Networks. *Association for Educational Data Systems Journal*, 1979, 13(1), 41–52.

31. Lavin, B.F. Can Computer-Assisted Instruction Make a Difference? An Analysis of Who Benefits. *Teaching Sociology*, 1980, 7(2), 163–179.

32. Luehrmann, A. Computer Literacy: A National Crisis and a Solution For It. *Byte*, 1980, 5(7), 98–102.

33. Luehrmann, A. Computer Literacy: What Should It Be? August, 1980.

34. Magidson, E.M. Issue Overview: Trends in Computer-Assisted Instruction. *Educational Technology*, 1978, 18(4), 5–8.

35. Molnar, A.R. The Next Great Crisis in American Education: Computer Literacy. *Association for Educational Data Systems Journal*, 1978, 12, 11–20.

36. Molnar, A.R. Understanding How To Use Machines to Work Smarter in an Information Society. National Science Foundation, November 1979.

37. Moursund, D. Microcomputers Will Not Solve the Computers-in-Education Problem. *Association for Educational Data Systems Journal*, 1979, 13(1), 31–39.

38. Moursund, D. Personal Computing for Elementary and Secondary School Students. *Point Paper for National Computer Literacy Conference.* December 1980.

39. Norris, W.C. Via Technology to a New Era in Education. *Phi Delta Kappan*, 1978, 58(2), 451–453.

40. NCSM National Council of Supervisors of Mathematics Position Paper on Basic Skills, January 1977.

41. Paden, D.W., Dalgaard, B.R., & Barr, M.D. A Decade of Computer-Assisted Instruction. *Journal of Economic Education*, 1977, 9(4), 14–20.

42. Pamphlet, Deltak Inc., Oak Brook, Illinois, 1981.

43. Rawitsch, D.G. Implanting the Computer in the Classroom: Minnesota's Successful Statewide Program. *Phi Delta Kappan*, 1981, 62(6), 453–455.

44. Sandals, L.H. Computer Assisted Learning with Handicapped Children and Adolescents and Those Students with Learning Problems. *Proceedings of the Third Canadian Congress of the Council for Exceptional Children*, 1978, 225–230.

45. Splittgerber, F.L. Computer-Based Instruction: A Revolution in the Making. *Educational Technology*, 1979, 19(1), 20–26.

46. Sugarman, R.A. A Second Chance for Computer-Aided Instruction. *IEEE Spectrum*, August, 29–37.

47. *The ABC's of CAI*, Fourth Edition, California State University, Fresno, California, 1979.

48. Travers, J.G. Development of a Microcomputer Implementation Model; An In-Situ, Adaptive Research Paradigm. Master's Thesis, University of Alberta, 1981.

49. Van Dusseldorp, R. Alaska On-Line Resource Information Bank. *Association for Educational Data Systems*, 1981, Conference Proceedings, 263–266.

50. Watt, D.H. Computer Literacy: What Should Schools Be Doing About It? *Classroom Computer News*, 1980, 1(2), 26–27.

51. Watt, D.H. Education for Citizenship in a Computer-Based Society. Invited Presentation at a Conference Sponsored by the National Science Foundation: National Goals for Computer Literacy in 1985, December 18–20, 1980, Reston, Virginia.

52. Watts, N. A Dozen Uses for the Computer in Education. *Educational Technology*, 1981, 21(4), 18–22.

WHAT'S YOUR OPINION?

1. CAI program writing differs greatly from textbook writing.

2. Teachers will use the computer as a tool to control knowledge.

3. In a teaching situation, I would rather see a human face than a machine.

4. With the aid of a computer, the teacher becomes more of a decision maker because the computer

can keep track of records much more efficiently.

5. Computer instruction is too much a rote-learning situation.
6. The computer encourages rote learning.
7. The child can better pace his or her own learning with a computer.
8. Educators should avoid using computers only for drill-and-practice.
9. LOGO's greatest advantage is that it develops a new way of thinking in the child.
10. Most of today's CAI simply reproduces the programmed-learning textbook.
11. Adventure games are educationally good because they force kids to process and reprocess information in a step-by-step fashion.
12. No teacher could expect the learner to pay as much attention to an adventure game as they pay to a computer.
13. A computer can give a child more attention than a teacher can.
14. A child will pay more attention to a computer than to a human teacher.
15. Educators who use a computer must be more cognizant of the ways in which students learn.
16. When using a computer, students cannot be passive as they can be in a regular classroom.
17. A child engages in more active learning with CAI than with a regular teacher.
18. In a few years the novelty of CAI will wear off, and students will become bored with it.
19. Because setting up simulations in a classroom is a tremendous amount of work for the teacher, it is easier to use the computer instead.
20. Working on CAI in pairs or in groups is preferable to working individually because group work develops social skills.
21. Until educators get together with computer programmers and graphics specialists, most CAI will be garbage.
22. There is no place for sarcasm in good CAI.
23. Well designed, tightly controlled evaluative studies of the use of CAI are rare.
24. Low-aptitude students profit more from the use of CAI than either average or high-aptitude students.
25. A major impediment to the widespread use of CAI is the lack of a standard, high-level, complex CAI language that is machine-independent.
26. The most critical issue in CAI today is the development and sharing of quality CAI materials.
27. The idea that good computer-based materials can be produced by an individual working alone is a mistaken concept.
28. Computers will be used to emphasize facts over concepts and principles, to condition acceptance of political doctrines, and to dictate personal philosophies.

29. Initial efforts to fund CAI should be made by the federal government because such a development would clearly be in the national interest.
30. All school districts should appoint a coordinator to acquire relevant information and to assist in the implementation of pilot computer-assisted learning projects.
31. Education by machine should not train people in skills that are better performed by machines.
32. The goal of CAI designers is not to figure out how to get the computer to play the role of a teacher but to have it serve as much as possible as a resource for students.
33. Drill-and-practice should be essentially asocial.
34. Drill-and-practice diminishes the student's ability to learn how to learn.
35. CAI is more capable than teachers of accommodating to specific learner needs, although it is perhaps less capable of detecting them.
36. Unless teachers can use CAI easily, it will end up sitting on shelves like filmstrips and videotapes.
37. In each state or province, computer consortiums should be implemented that hire programmers to program CAI material in the areas teachers want.
38. Most computer programmers don't know how to put lessons together in teachable ways.
39. Computer-assisted instruction provides the richest and most highly individualized interaction between student and curriculum of any method of instruction yet developed.
40. Microcomputers provide a drill-and-practice approach which children find motivating, which can be tailored to each child's needs, and which provides immediate feedback.
41. College courses taught strictly by computer would have a higher dropout rate than conventionally taught courses.
42. Computer-based instruction denies students the opportunity to act as teachers, to theorize, to reason with others, and to explain in their own words.

EXERCISES

1. How can we avoid the problems of reproducing the textbook in CAI development?
2. What can a computer teach that a human being cannot? What can a human being teach that a computer cannot?
3. Why does it take an average of 100 hours of preparation to produce 1 hour of student CAI contact-time at a terminal?
4. Is CAI worth the cost?
5. How would you set up a team of people to construct instructional CAI? Explain.

6. What factors inhibit College of Education faculty members from developing quality CAI, and what could be done to counteract these inhibitors?

7. How might a peer-review procedure work toward the development of quality CAI?

8. How well will existing print-oriented instructional design techniques work with CAI?

9. What is meant by the following statement: "Judgment of CAI should be made on the basis of what is expected of the program itself relative to the quality of the total learning environment."

10. Differentiate between tutorial, drill-and-practice, dialogue, and programmed-instruction forms of CAI.

11. What are the differences between computer simulation and gaming?

12. Do you believe that the use of the computer as an electronic page-turner to present programmed learning is a waste of valuable resources? Explain.

13. State the differences among CAI (computer-assisted instruction), CAL (computer-assisted learning), and CMI (computer-managed instruction)?

14. Identify the advantages and disadvantages of using CAI for remedial work or drill-and-practice in a classroom setting.

15. What are the advantages and disadvantages of using computer-generated simulations in your subject area?

16. Why are computers particularly well suited to scoring multiple-choice tests? Do you believe multiple-choice items serve well for analyzing student progress?

17. Investigate the kinds of courseware available in your subject area. If possible, test some of the programs on approval.

18. Describe types of courseware you would like to see developed for your subject area.

19. Give an example of a program that could incorporate learning techniques.

20. List three characteristics of computers that allow classroom activities which would otherwise not be possible.

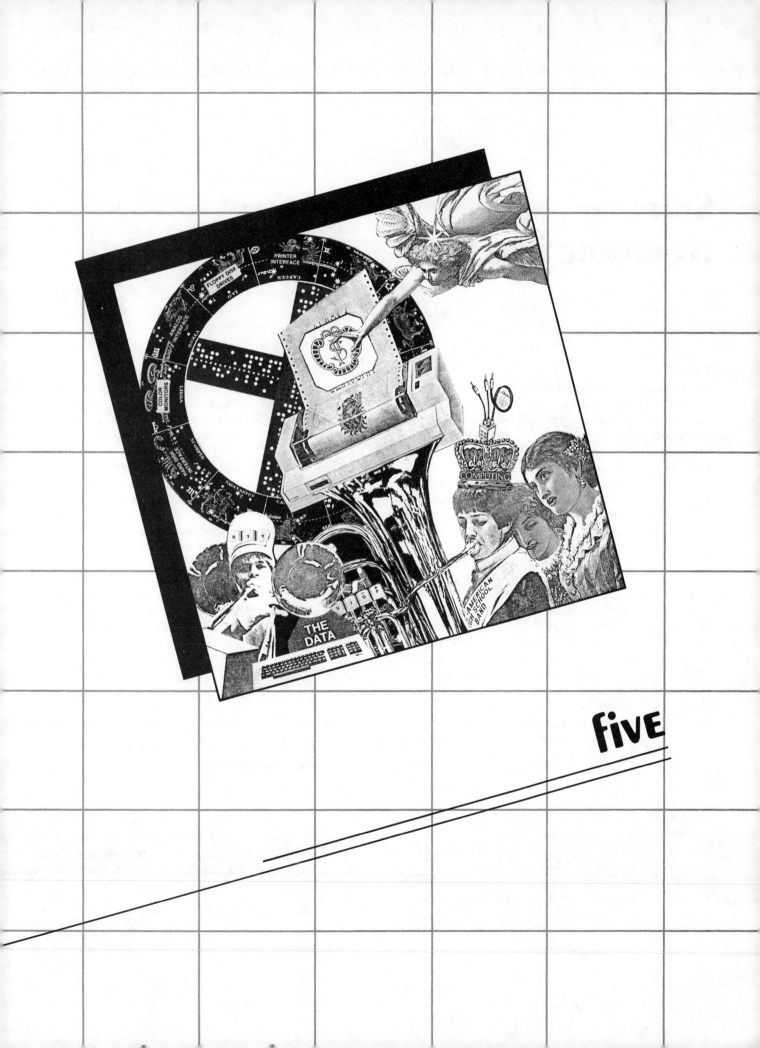

five

Software and Hardware Selection

As the number of educational computer programs continues to grow, appropriate guidelines to evaluate their worth become increasingly important. All too often courseware is lacking in quality: missing or inaccurate documentation, inflexibility, inappropriate terminology, mishandled input errors, and poor programming techniques are typical user complaints. Frequently, programs are written by noneducators who understand much about programming but little about how people learn.

We welcome the time when educators will become involved in courseware development, if not at the programming level, then in the design stage before the lesson is committed to the computer. Any computer-literacy program for teachers profits from the inclusion of discussions regarding what functions the computer is capable of and how to evaluate potential classroom materials. This is not to suggest that all teachers must become expert programmers. Certainly, however, they are better equipped to do their jobs if they are aware of basic programming techniques and how to apply them to various situations in order to produce the desired effects on the learner. In this chapter the articles by Wade and Potts present relevant principles of learning and lists of appropriate characteristics in instructional software, along with a justification for, and evaluation of, computer games.

The task of selecting the machinery most appropriate for a school situation is perplexing. Skilled educators who describe their experiences in choosing equipment advise that one should first determine the various functions the machinery will be expected to perform. Next, thoroughly investigate available software to determine whether the necessary activities can be accomplished using existing "canned" programs. Finally, the actual selection of hardware should be based on knowledge of existing and anticipated software for each product line, taking into account such factors as available funds, personnel, and unique local requirements. Thomas and McClain compare several computer systems on the basis of cost/computing power and offer a detailed analysis of popular makes. Staples gives a practical example of how one educator approached the question, while Braun details a method of assigning an "importance value" to various hardware criteria to determine the best choice for meeting one's particular needs.

Unfortunately, few educators at the classroom level are being invited to participate in the process of deciding which hardware should be purchased. Because teachers will be the ultimate users of the equipment selected, however, they should be familiar with the process of intelligent hardware choice and be prepared to offer informed opinions and proposals.

Evaluating Computer Instructional Programs and Other Teaching Units

T.E. Wade, Jr.

Evaluation implies standards. Evaluating an instructional program implies knowing the characteristics of a "good" program. But good for the goose may not mean good for the gander, particularly in an instructional process which has a wide variety of

From "Evaluating Computer Instructional Programs and Other Teaching Units," by T.E. Wade. In *Educational Technology,* November, 1980. © 1980 by Educational Technology Publications, Inc. Reprinted by permission.

generally acceptable learning outcomes and strategies from which to choose. Although we cannot list specific characteristics which every "good" teaching unit must have, we can suggest general principles to apply, thus helping the evaluator systematize a product evaluation.

In this article, we review some relevant principles of learning and develop a list of characteristics which might be expected in any overall learning program of which the computer program or other teaching unit is a part.

EVALUATION BY INSPECTION OF THE MATERIALS

Evaluation of instructional programs falls naturally into two categories. On the one hand, it is desirable to judge programs as they are being *developed* and to make initial choices of extant programs. This judgment is based on inspection of the materials themselves and of information about them. On the other hand, it is also desirable to evaluate programs as they are *used* to determine how well they actually succeed in helping students achieve the intended objectives. This article focuses on the former: evaluation as a process of guiding initial program development or as selection of already prepared materials, specifically computer-assisted instructional programs. Of course, in the final analysis, the latter evaluation process is the most valid, since programs are good only as they are good for students. But because time, energy, financial resources, and student specimens are not available in infinite supply, it is important to be able to make intelligent judgments of programs on initial contact with them.

The purpose of instruction, in general, is to facilitate learning. Gagne and Briggs[1] have identified "instructional events" which describe how instruction is accomplished. These events or components of instruction can provide a framework for classifying characteristics of instructional programs:

1. Gaining attention
2. Informing the learner of the objective
3. Stimulating recall of prerequisite learnings
4. Presenting the stimulus material
5. Providing "learning guidance"
6. Eliciting the performance
7. Providing feedback about performance correctness.
8. Assessing the performance
9. Enhancing retention and transfer

Not all of these events are necessarily found in every instructional program. Sometimes students are expected to provide part of the conditions for learning on their own, and often certain events are already present in the total learning environment outside the particular program or module in question. A brief computer program, for example, may be used as part of a larger learning unit. Its specific purpose might be only motivation, testing, or drill.

RELEVANT PRINCIPLES OF LEARNING THEORY

Gagne and Briggs identify six factors affecting the learning event. Three external factors are contiguity (or the time relationship between stimulus information and elicited response), repetition, and reinforcement. Three internal factors are availability of required information, either from memory or externally provided, intellectual skills (abilities to manipulate the information), and cognitive strategies (the ability to process or interpret input into meaningful information).

Newell and Simon[2] have described three information-holding functions of the human cognitive process. Outside information is sensed and held for about a second in the *visual, auditory, or tactile register* while being formed in a *short-term memory*. The short-term memory may hold information for half a minute or so while being coded for storage in the *long-term memory* or while being considered or used to activate the output.

Hestenes[3] has pointed out from this cognitive theory several implications for instruction. (1) The short-term memory should not be overloaded because it can hold only one piece of information at a time, and because a certain amount of time is required for coding for permanent storage. (2) More time than normally allowed is needed for thoughtful responses because information is retrieved and processed slowly from the long-term memory. (3) Good control of the short-term memory, achieved by writing, rehearsing, and similar activities, is important in communicating and learning. Intelligence may depend more on the processes set up in the brain for handling information than on the amount of information stored.

Instruction should take into account certain characteristics of individual learners. One of these learner characteristics is reasoning ability. Even some otherwise mature people have not achieved the facility to reason abstractly at what Piaget[4] calls the "formal operational" level. Rita and Kenneth Dunn and others[5,6] report that the optimum learning environment (determined by background sound, presence of other people, lighting, time of day, etc.) varies with individuals. Also, the most efficient sensory input mode (visual, auditory, or tactile) is different for different people.

Even the degree of interest in a topic or in the illustrations used to present it is obviously not the same for every student. The adaptation of instruction to take best advantage of learner characteristics is relatively difficult in classroom teaching. By comparison, computer instructional technology is more capable of accommodating specific learner needs, although perhaps less capable of detecting them.

McCombs, Eschenbrenner, and O'Neil[7] have proposed that the instructional process be optimized for individual learners using computer-based instruction. They cite several studies and papers which indicate that learning occurs best when conditions are controlled to enhance epistemic (or knowledge-seeking) curiosity and to reduce anxiety.

CHARACTERISTICS OF A GOOD LEARNING SITUATION

A learning situation is considered here in the sense of the totality of factors which create the learning of a particular module of instruction. These basic factors would be more or less the same no matter what techniques were responsible for the major burden of instruction, whether lecture, computer program, an independent trip to the museum, or whatever. Good learning situations have five fundamental characteristics: the learning must be right; the learner must be ready; learning needs to be managed or facilitated; assimilation must be practicable; and learning must be efficient.

The learning must be right

A segment of instruction may teach very well, but unless it is in harmony with the philosophy supporting the instructional system and helps achieve the general goals of the course of study of which it is a part, it would not be considered of value. This is probably a subconscious criterion but one, nonetheless, that must not be violated. It is also important to check learning materials to be sure they are accurate, and it is important in most cases that they be up-to-date. The learning to be presented must also be sufficiently complete to achieve its purpose.

The learner must be ready

Success in learning probably depends more on the readiness of the learner than it does on the materials used. Readiness is a function of the intellect, the emotions, and the physical condition. The *intellectual readiness* of the learner is probably the most obvious necessity. The intellectual skills and cognitive strategies already mentioned determine intellectual readiness. *Emotional readiness* would include the learning theorist's concept of reinforcement. Achieving in the learner a high degree of epistemic curiosity while maintaining low anxiety has been mentioned as an important factor. Helping

the student develop a sense of self-worth and the whole somewhat nebulous concept of motivation also are elements in the learner's emotional readiness. Factors in *physical readiness* would include freedom from physical needs, alertness, a healthy nervous system, and often strength and endurance. The instructional materials and even the immediate learning environment seldom have an effect on the physical readiness of the student. Yet, the physically unprepared learner surely cannot expect success.

Learning needs to be managed or facilitated

This characteristic and the two which follow dealing with assimilation and efficiency are of most obvious and direct concern for the program writer or the one who designs instruction. Several educators have suggested specific techniques which characterize quality computer instructional programs.[8,9,10]

To a certain degree the elements of learning management or the instructional tasks, as we have already identified them, are implicit in some of the other characteristics of a good learning program. And, although learning could occur without all of these elements, their presence does indicate a type of systematic instruction which is generally desirable.

Assimilation must be practicable

Making assimilation practicable is putting learning within the student's reach. One of the most obvious elements necessary in a good learning program is the availability of information. The development of skills, attitudes, and the simple storage of information must depend on both the information available and what the learner already knows. Information should be presented in a logical order. The long-established concept of contiguity would fit into the logic of presentation. The importance of repetition has been well established. Control mechanisms—or student learning skills—such as facility in note-taking are important for aiding the short-term memory. The availability of related knowledge as well as sufficient time is needed for encoding information to be stored in the long-term memory and for decoding information at the time of retrieval. Care must also be taken not to overload the short-term memory.

Learning must be efficient

A learning program may be successful in terms of reaching its objectives, but if it is not efficient, it is not likely to be considered of great value. Taking into account the characteristics of individual learners is obviously important in maximizing learning efficiency. This is related to the idea that the student's time should be used conservatively. Also, the financial cost must not exceed that of other programs of equal merit,[11] and an efficient use should be made of the teacher's or facilitator's time and energy.

EVALUATING INSTRUCTIONAL PROGRAMS

The characteristics of good instructional programs discussed in this article can be used as a *checklist* to help identify strengths and weaknesses of particular learning programs such as those written for computer-assisted instruction (CAI). Computer instructional programs are never intended as completely self-contained units to provide all the elements of a good learning situation. Judgment should be made on the basis of what is expected of the program itself relative to the quality of the total learning environment.

Visualize three columns on a checklist. The first is for identifying *expectations* of the instructional package in question. The second is for marking those expected characteristics which are actually found in the package (or the computer instruction). And the third is for verifying that the other characteristics are accounted for in the rest of the learning environment. If a numerical value is considered desirable, 1's and 0's can be used in the boxes. Or, the characteristics can be weighted by writing various numbers for the "expectations" in the first column and comparing the characteristics found to the ideal on that basis. However, any "measure" is highly subjective and is proposed only as an aid to the overall evaluation.

CONCLUSION

It appears to be unwise to establish specific standards for the evaluation of programs at all educational levels in all subject areas which use a particular medium such as the computer. However, an examination of general principles of successful learning can lead the evaluator to a balanced view and help him or her avoid overlooking important aspects of good instruction.

NOTES

1. R.M. Gagne and L.J. Briggs. *Principles of Instructional Design.* New York: Holt, Rinehart, and Winston, 1974.
2. A. Newell and H. Simon. *Human Problem Solving.* Englewood Cliffs, New Jersey: Prentice-Hall, 1972.
3. D. Hestenes. Wherefore a Science of Teaching. *The Physics Teacher,* April 1979, 235–242.
4. J. Piaget. *The Language and Thought of the Child.* New York: Humanities Press, 1959.
5. R.S. Dunn and K.J. Dunn. Learning Styles/Teaching Styles: Should They ... Can They ... Be Matched? *Educational Leadership,* January 1979, 238–244.
6. B.B. Fischer and L. Fischer. Styles in Teaching and Learning. *Educational Leadership,* January 1979, 238–244.
7. B.L. McCombs, A. Eschenbrenner, Jr., and F. O'Neil, Jr. An Adaptive Model for Utilizing Learner Characteristics in Computer Based Instructional Systems. *Educational Technology,* April 1973, 57–61.
8. A.M. Bork. The Computer in Learning—Advice to Dialogue Writers. *Journal of Educational Data Processing,* 9(3), 1972.
9. H.L. Schoen. CAI Development and Good Educational Practice. *Educational Technology,* April 1974, 54–56.
10. C.D. Spitler and V.E. Corgan. Rules for Authoring Computer-Assisted Instructional Programs. *Educational Technology,* November 1979, 13–20.
11. R.J. Seidel. It's 1980: Do You Know Where Your Computer Is? *Phi Delta Kappan,* March 1980, 481–485.

The author acknowledges the valuable counsel of Dr. Henry Heikkinen, Associate Professor of Chemistry, University of Maryland.

Smart Programs, Dumb Programs

Michael Potts

Many schools find themselves at a crucial point in the decision to bring computers into the classroom. It's a tough area to enter because it's so complicated, and there's such an apparent confusion of paths and advice. Like the legendary firm in England whose directors debated three hours whether to build a shed for the workers' bicycles (for 18s6d), then deliberated for seven minutes the proposal to completely requip the mill (at a cost of several hundred thousand pounds), too many administrators are looking at the wrong problem.

When you compare a minimal useful configuration, all of the small computers that can make it in the classroom are remarkably similar in price, capability, and reliability. I don't think it's possible to make a wrong decision here. (Although my conclusions apply to any classroom computer, my examples all run on the most popular machine, Radio Shack's TRS-80.)

Software, the marching orders the computer gets to do its educational thing, is the tough nut to crack. I've seen too many computers sitting, dusty and forlorn amidst a welter of battered program tapes, in the back corners of classrooms. When I ask "Why?" I'm inevitably told, "teachers overworked ... tape loading problems ... (mumble mumble) ... kids lost interest." One local school keeps its TRS-80 (and both program tapes) in a cupboard because none of the teachers will take it on. Twelve miles south, in another district, three TRS-80s hum away six hours a day every day, with little or no intervention from the teachers. What's the difference? Appropriate software.

Too often teachers, reading the woeful wails of hobbyists about "not enough memory," blow their whole budget on the machine, and find themselves software poor. It takes time to learn to program well enough that kids will enjoy running your programs . . . and anyway, it's tough to learn to program in a vacuum, with no one else's work to bounce off of. I've helped a few teachers through the lonely first years, and I'd like to share what I've learned.

Computer-Aided Instruction (CAI) and computer games have come to be treated as one-and-the-same. Programmers—usually amateurs and hobbyists with ambitious programming aims but marginal literary and educational skills—have discovered that children need to be entertained to stay with the machine, so Klingons have captured much of the available territory. Programmers fall victim to the TV spinoff syndrome: we've got a compelling subject here, guys, so let's change the story a bit, and write another program . . .

Heaven forfend that we re-open the Great Games Debate. Games are super. Anything that gets a child to relate to symbols with glee is super! Children—and big people too—require novelty and entertainment in their activities. Surprise, humor, and enlightenment make a program, or a novel, movie, whatever, successful if present, boring if absent. Examples: Battleship, the classic coordinate-based seek-and-destroy game, is a natural for the 6- to 10-year-old set, but the record-keeping involved in playing it well with paper and pencil is too complex for this notoriously scattered age group. People's Software Project (Box 158, San Luis Rey, CA 92068) offers several collections of programs, strewn amongst which are a few fine educational games. Tapes 5 and 7 ($8 each) are best for our purposes. Their version of Battleship (on tape #7), written by Harley Dyk, uses the computer to solve the record-keeping problem in an exemplary way: it's a real teaching program. It contains suspense (Will TRS-80 get me?), surprise (Haha! I hit the Battleship!), and the chance to polish strategy and see immediate results. Many children are intimidated by machines, and so a screening for bad input should be gentle; this program's universal response to user error is a loving "You goofed!" Well done, Harley.

My favorite pigeon among crummy "games" is one of the various versions of States: what is the capitol of Maine? etcetera . . . Programmers find it attractive because it presents a neatly-bounded data base with a simple relationship between elements—Dover always goes with Delaware, and vice versa. Teachers seem to like it because it purports to teach a frustrating subject without much teacher effort. So then what's the problem? It isn't much fun to run; kids get bored before they get much out of it; an atlas with pictures does the job better. Another loser is the oft-rewritten "pre-school math program," presenting math facts (3 + 4 always equals 7), then testing comprehension. Radio Shack's pathetic little phallic rocket in their Math 1 package makes my kids laugh in pity . . . right before they walk away. Robert Purser proposes "Hangman" as a candidate for an award in this category: "Here is a simple game which is better suited to pencil and paper than a computer. For the lack of anything better to do, over a hundred people have written and are selling their own computerized version of this game." Give all these guys a 1 for entertainment. (The People Software tapes have two different versions for your edification, plus a couple of versions of States and one or two elementary math testers.)

A near miss at relevancy: The Bottom Shelf's Addition program from "100 Programs." The program has been designed to do addition like a kid, adding from least significant to most. That's a wrinkle I'm ashamed to say I left out of my adding program. But a nice feature does not a great program make: it's still a testing program, and the kids walk away after a few problems. TBS's "100 Programs" is largely useless educationally; the few useful concepts are aimed at adults, not children, and need drastic revision.

A Key to good CAI is "repeat business": if a program challenges and intrigues, the student will come back for more. Repetition leads to mastery; it also saves the teacher repetition of program directions. In some ways—the presence of surprise, engaging fantasy, and the like—repeatability is related to entertainment. But I find the program's built-in attitude is important, too.

Even the most forbearing teacher has bad days, grumbles at students, and picks on wimps. One of the incredible qualities of the computer is that it can be programmed for infinite patience. Gentleness is a necessity: the customer is always delicate.

Star Trek is entertaining, but it's horribly frustrating for most children below age thirteen. Usually many hours are required to get good enough (and lucky enough) that you don't leave the computer depressed because you've been demoted to cabin boy, leaving 26 Klingons to destroy the Galaxy. Reinforcement value, nil. Battleship, which teaches much the same material (coordinate geometry), is much more compact and machine-efficient—although undeniably less challenging. At the age level where this lesson is most appropriate, Battleship will suffice; the more sophisticated student will consume vast hunks of computer time mastering Star Trek for an arguably marginal educational gain. The People's tapes have two versions of Star Trek, plus a few other Klingon games for your enjoyment.

The Adventure games are in a class by themselves. In these games the player conducts the computer on a quest using two-word directives like "ENTER BUILDING" or "OPEN DOOR." Periodically, malevolent dwarfs and other added distractions throw axes and knives . . . but it all takes place on the computer's display as narrative: interactive literature. The children it appeals to most are generally the non-readers, who get sucked in and end up reading despite themselves. The games are incredibly time-consuming, but the value is obvious. The granddaddy Adventure is Microsoft's version (originally run on the DEC PDP-11 mainframe computer, it's been rewritten to run on a 32K disk-based S-80, costs $30). Scott Adams' reprises of the formula are engaging, too, and run nicely on a minimal 16K machine (Adventure International, Box 3435, Longwood, FL 32750, $15 each and also available from Creative Computing Software.) A significant part of the appeal is the marked difference between the verbal exchange of these games as contrasted with the numerical preoccupation of commoner computer games. Adding an Adventure to your library increases the flexibility of your computer twofold.

Simulations bridge the gap between games and pure education, depending on the material and the program-writer's sense of humor. "Tai-pan" is a near-perfect example of the potential for education offered by simulations: author Art Canfil has translated his own obvious love for the potential for adventure in the China trade of the 1800s into an exciting trading game, complete with marauding pirates, Wu the moneylender, and officials bent on seizing your opium. To win, the trader must parlay a modest stake into a million; the memory and calculation required are incidental to the enjoyment of the game. "Hammurabi" is a classic along the same line: the player rules a pre-Biblical realm in the fertile crescent, deciding annually how much the peasants eat, how much land is bought or sold, how much grain is planted; on these few decisions hangs the welfare of the State. Both of these games have the added attraction that big people like them, too. Games like these provide a jumping-off point for broader classroom units on trade, history, or whatever the teacher's imagination decrees; the children should note an increase in their playing skill as their grasp of the concepts improves. These programs are usually written by teachers with just this effect in mind; making the lessons real.

At the far end of the spectrum are the programs (and packages of programs) which make comprehensive use of the computer as a drill-and-practice tool. Radio Shack's new K-to-8 Math Package attempts to provide such an instrument for the full range of Elementary math. This powerful series of programs —arrayed as a horizontal grouping of general number skills—150 lessons for Kindergarten through third grade (6 programs by grade level)—and a vertical array of operations program—70 addition, 70 subtraction, 50 multiplication, and 37 division lessons (4 programs, one for each operation) offers a reasonably broad range of individual competence within each program, making it easy to load and shuffle students through the program, while broadly challenging students across the full spectrum of the four operations up to eighth grade. The programs tread a thin line between gentleness and insult: if the child takes too long answering, she is prompted to "Try another" —a nice touch—or reprimanded—"Don't fall asleep." I was concerned that children might be offended when needled by the computer, but the machine's timing seems superb: the "Don't fall asleep" message comes along about the time the child needs a giggle. The package is expensive ($200), but it is comprehensive, providing all by itself justification for a computer lab for the math department. True: drill and practice is dull. But test results indicate it's reasonable to expect that most children will attain concept mastery two or three times faster than conventional workbook drills given adequate practice with this series of programs: it's an elegant use of the computer to solve a tough problem. A foundation package like this is an absolute necessity in any well-integrated computer program.

Finally, your software library needs to start out with the ability to "bootstrap load" (a computer term for bringing a system—in this case a human—from a state of total ignorance to usefulness) the teachers and students with enough computer knowledge to use the system. Computers have the unique and amazing ability to teach absolutely anything, including themselves. Using such a system, a receptive teacher can dedicate an afternoon a week, or a few weekends, to the task of learning to program to her own specifications, and succeed handsomely in a surprisingly short time. Radio Shack's Basic self-instruction tapes offer this capability at a modest price. It could have been done with more style and spirit, but this is a workmanlike effort.

Two last details: subscribe on your school's behalf to a computer magazine or two, and encourage the parents of a couple of your "computer heroes" to do likewise. CLOAD Magazine (P.O. Box 1267, Goleta, CA 93117, $36/year) sends monthly program tapes which will flesh out your games department, but don't count on them for much educational material. Purser's Magazine (P.O. Box 466, El Dorado, CA 95623, $12/year) consists of reviews of educational programs, and will save you the price of admission in lousy software. You'd be wise to set aside a few dollars for the right program when you see it. Given the solid foundation library you've established by following my advice, you'll be able to pick and choose.

This "shopping list" for a minimal TRS-80 software library undertakes to make two points. First: if your computer had the pick of these programs, you'd be able to settle back and let the programs come to you, confident that your computer could earn its keep educationally for at least a year. At year's end, you can expect to spend some time weeding out inferior programs in order to keep your library manageable. Second, and more important: exercise careful judgment in getting and keeping programs. Children have a tendency to play what's available: if it's Star Trek or Hangman, your computer program is being ill-used. If, on the other hand, you provide a bouquet of valid, challenging, and engaging programs to embellish a solid back-bone of instruction (like the Radio Shack K-8 Package), you have a viable computer program which will justify by any objective measure your school's expenditure and your energy.

Selecting Microcomputers for the Classroom

David B. Thomas and **Donald H. McClain**

Microcomputers seem to be everywhere. They are found in automobiles, ovens, sewing machines, televisions, and most recently in electronic games. Microcomputers may be seen in department stores, stereo shops, and computer stores. Advertisements for inexpensive systems appear in *The Wall Street Journal,* Sunday editions of metropolitan newspapers, and in-flight magazines. Microcomputers have been featured in the *ABC Evening News.* Micros are now available at the consumer level and have entered our consciousness.

From "Selecting Microcomputers for the Classroom," by David B. Thomas and Donald H. McClain. In the *AEDS Journal,* November, 1979, by the Association of the Educational Data Systems. Reprinted by permission.

Teachers have discovered microcomputers, and may see micros as an inexpensive means to develop computer literacy and provide computer-assisted instruction to students at a cost lower than that of time-sharing systems. Many have rushed to buy one of the systems which are now available; some number of these recent purchasers will find, unhappily, that the system they have bought will not continue to meet their needs. Others may find that their instructional needs are not well served by the system they have purchased.

Selecting an instructional computer system from the large number and variety of microcomputers now available can be a challenging venture even for an individual knowledgeable in instructional computing. It can be a dilemma for the administrator or teacher not knowledgeable about computing, given the quantity or the quality of most information being distributed by computer vendors. A problem arises from the large discrepancy between the price of a basic system quoted by the company in its advertisement and the actual cost of a minimum system configuration capable of easily and efficiently supporting instructional computing.

The key to the successful selection of a microcomputer lies in the careful analysis of the instructional problem, the determination of instructional requirements, and the specification of the required computing capability. Once the computing capability has been determined, the potential buyer can survey the marketplace for systems satisfying the specified needs. The final task is the selection of the microcomputer system that satisfies all the predetermined criteria.

This paper strives to guide the educator in the selection of a computer system, especially a microcomputer system, that will be used primarily to enhance the instructional process. We have attempted to outline a model which will help teachers perform the prerequisite activities necessary for the specification of a microcomputer system which will meet present and future instructional computing needs.

The importance of performing an analysis of the instructional needs and anticipated uses of the computing resources cannot be overemphasized. The assumption that a microcomputer will permit the same varieties of instructional computing as are available on existing large systems (or on mini computers) is simply incorrect. The faulty assumption is compounded when the user attempts to extend use of the micro to applications beyond those initially intended. The extensions are sometimes not feasible. Microcomputers can be valuable additions to an instructional program, but careful planning is necessary to avoid disappointment which might ensue with the selection of an inappropriate system.

THE MICROCOMPUTER SELECTION MODEL

All too often, one begins with the purchase of a computer/terminal intended for instructional use, then attempts to determine what applications should be implemented with the new computer/terminal. We suggest that this approach is backwards and that one ought to begin by identifying instructional problems for which various forms of computing may offer solutions. A five phase model, depicted by Figure 1, provides a systematic approach to the selection of a microcomputer which will meet both present and anticipated instructional needs. (Note that many of our analyses inevitably lead to the selection of microcomputers. Obviously, neither all instructional problems nor even most of them will lead to computer solution.)

Identify instructional problem

Individualized instructional problems require that the teacher spend time with diverse student ability groups in the classroom. Some students may work on vocabulary, while others work on grammar, mathematics facts, chemical symbols, or spelling. Others need the opportunity to recite, to explain, or to ask questions. We believe that the computer has much to offer the former, freeing the teacher to concentrate on the latter more frequently. *It is important that the specific learning activity and a*

SELECTION PROCESS

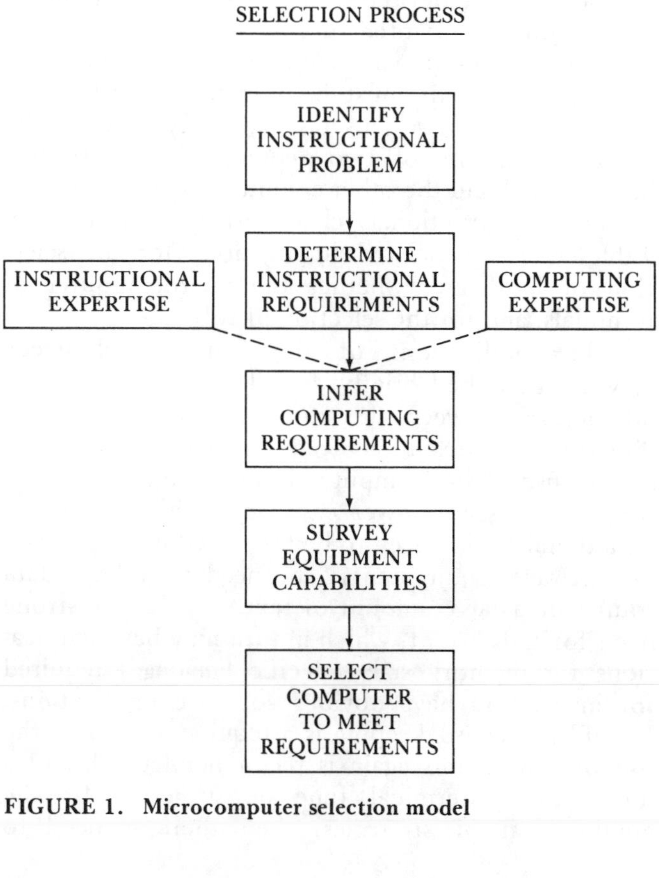

FIGURE 1. Microcomputer selection model

potential computer application be identified early in the selection process. The computer is, after all, a tool which amplifies the teacher's effectiveness. *But the teacher, as the responsible professional, must recognize the unique instructional problem for which a computer solution is available.* The teacher who realizes that a group of students will profit from interactive drill on punctuation skills, for example, has completed the first step in the microcomputer selection process. Problems associated with the application of rules, or verbal associations, or concept learning would also serve as examples. The teacher's problem identification process likely would identify many areas where computing could provide help with the learning process. Selecting the appropriate computing tool to solve the problem will yield more satisfaction than fitting the problem to the tools already selected.

Determine instructional requirements

Having identified an instructional problem, the teacher is best able to select a strategy for teaching the skills required of the student. We have identified *11 instructional activities* or strategies for which microcomputers might be used. These strategies, although not exhaustive, represent the bulk of applications for which computers have been used in instruction (purely administrative applications have been excluded).

Drill represents a form of interactive computer-assisted instruction in which the student responds in a rather quick fashion to brief items or questions under a "flash card" format. The computer provides feedback as to the correctness of the student's answer and may adapt to the individual student by varying the number of items or the frequency of the stimuli as a function of the student's responses.

Tutorial programs provide paragraph-like material, interspersed questions, and response-sensitive branching. These programs are usually characterized by an abundance of textual material.

Problem-solving programs typically help the student in the learning of principles or rules by harnessing the power of the computer to eliminate the need for each student to complete complex calculations or engage in the manipulation of multiple logic states. These programs are usually short algorithms for which the student repeatedly supplies data to be manipulated according to the rule or principle being taught.

Programming involves the use of a computer language to provide the proper instructions which control the computer. Perhaps the major single use of computers in instruction is in the teaching of computer programming.

Simulations model phenomena of an often very complex nature in which random events are introduced to add realism to the interaction. Simulation is a valuable strategy when one needs to compress time (as in an explanation of radioactive decay) or avoid dangerous phenomena or use of expensive equipment.

Testing by computer permits the educator to exercise options not available with traditional testing mthods. Items may be administered contingent upon prior responses to improve test reliability: diagnostic tests may be collapsed into short testing sessions; tests may be scored instantaneously.

Computer-managed instruction (CMI) is characterized by the collection of student data and the transmission of learning prescriptions following objectives-referenced tests.

Data analysis involves the activities for which computers are most widely known. The use of standardized statistical analysis programs, list processing programs, and similar programs are a central topic in many disciplines.

Information retrieval is a much used application in the social and physical sciences as well as in the humanities. In this application, the computer is used to select information from a large storage medium according to certain predefined rules. Typical applications are literature searches, selective mailing lists, and fact-finding.

Word processing provides an environment whereby the computer permits easy manipulation of text for reports, essays, and other paragraph material. This strategy may facilitate the student's preparation of essays by permitting easy insertion of text, correction of spelling, or reorganization of presentation without the necessity of completely rewriting the material.

Computer literacy represents the use of a computer itself as a demonstration of computer hardware and data processing capabilities. The ten strategies previously described also may be employed in this context.

Each of these 11 activities or teaching strategies has associated characteristics which in part define the instructional milieu. For example, interaction is a necessary characteristic for drill but not for data analysis; large amounts of text are typical requirements for tutorials, but not for problem-solving programs. Eleven characteristics have been identified which describe the 11 strategies defined above. These characteristics are not exhaustive, but represent the major instructionally oriented concerns associated with the activities mentioned.

The 11 characteristics of the instructional "contact" and the 11 strategies may be formed into an Instructional Requirements Matrix as shown on Table 1. The intersection of a strategy and a charac-

teristic indicates a requirement which subsequently will be translated into a computing requirement. The problem-solving strategy may be illustrative; neither high student terminal time nor significant interaction typically take place within a problem-solving program. *Graphics may be necessary* for some applications, such as where the shapes of mathematical functions are being studied. It should be noted that the entries in Table 1 are intended to be illustrative rather than prescriptive.

The Instructional Requirements Matrix provides the information needed to develop a requirements list. By selecting the strategies which will be employed in the classroom, and collapsing across strategies, one obtains a list of instructional needs which the computing equipment must satisfy.

In identifying strategies it is important to take a fairly liberal view, considering the relative frequency of use of the various strategies and the strategies which will be employed in the future. This analysis, by its very nature, is quite subjective, but will provide one with weightings for the various computer system characteristics. These subjective weights are used during a subsequent phase of the selection procedure where specific computing requirements are developed.

Infer computing requirements

Previous phases in the selection process represent a needs assessment. The problem was identified and a solution devised which resulted in a set of instructionally oriented needs as expressed by a collapsed Instructional Requirements Matrix. These instructional needs must be transformed into computer requirements. This task typically requires the combined talents of two people, one representing instructional and the other computing expertise.

Each instructional characteristic indicated in Table 1 has associated implications for the selection of hardware, whether the microcomputer or terminals, and for the selection of software.

The implications of the instructional needs may be described briefly as follows. The extent of interaction between the student and the terminal directly translates to a need for the assessment of ease of use of the computer system and its software. Requirements for lower case or graphics in the instructional setting need to be translated into hardware or software requirements. The need for a large data source of a large amount of text suggests the strong need for a disk unit, which in turn may have implications for memory size. Specific languages required for instruction have obvious software implications. If student record keeping is a requirement, then the use of a disk unit again is recommended. Should a high student terminal time be suggested by the combination of strategies, then there is need to

TABLE 1 **Instructional requirements matrix**

Strategy/ Characteristic	Drill	Tutorial	Problem Solving	Programming	Simulation	Testing	CMI	Data Analysis	Info Retrieval	Word Processing	Computer Literacy
Interaction	X	X			X	X	X	X	X	X	X
Lower case		X			X	X				X	
Graphics		X	X		X	X		X			
Large Data Source		X			X	X	X		X	X	
Specific Language			X	X							X
Multiple Languages				X							
Student Record Keeping/ Testing	X	X				X	X				
High Student Terminal Time		X		X	X					X	
Large Amount of Text		X		X	X			X	X	X	
Hard Copy Printed Output			X	X	X	X	X	X	X	X	X
Packaged Statistical Programs			X					X	X		

consider the number of terminals or microcomputers necessary to assure that student waiting periods are not excessive. For the applications where hardcopy printed output is required, one needs to be cognizant of a microcomputer's ability to support printers or that of the terminals being surveyed. Finally, if packaged statistical programs are assumed necessary to the instructional application, both the availability of the package and the usability of the package on various systems need to be considered.

A crucial decision at this stage is whether one ought to be investigating a microcomputer or a large system. Table 2 shows four levels of computers and recommendations for the kinds of instructional computing which are appropriate for each. The mix of applications, their complexity, and their use-frequency will determine the appropriate system size. From this point forward, we assume that the instructional needs and computing capabilities which have been analyzed have resulted in the decision that a microcomputer is to be selected. The phases completed thus far provide the information needed to focus attention on the microcomputers which are appropriate for meeting identified needs.

The following narrative describes the general capabilities or options of microcomputers that are believed to be essential in the consideration of an instructional computing system. These capabilities will be related to the various instructional activities or strategies. A survey of a range of microcomputers with different features will follow, as well as a list of points to keep in mind when making the final selection.

TABLE 2 **Computer capabilities by size**

VERY SMALL	–	(KIM, SYM, ELF, Single Board)
	–	Programming
SMALL	–	(PET, TRS-80, APPLE II)
	–	Drill
	–	Problem Solving
	–	Programming
	–	Simulation
	–	Testing
	–	Data Analysis (Small)
	–	Information Retrieval (Small)
MEDIUM	–	(PRIME, HP2000)
	–	Tutorial
	–	Data Analysis
	–	Information Retrieval
	–	Other Modes
LARGE	–	(IBM 360, 370, CYBER)
	–	All Modes
	–	Programming
	–	Data Analysis
	–	Information Retrieval

Capabilities of microcomputers

At the heart of every microcomputer is the microprocessor, the part of the system that manipulates all data and performs all calculations. Each of the different processors has sufficient power, speed, and precision for most instructional applications, making the brand name less important than some of the other features. However, one processor characteristic that some individuals believe makes a difference is whether it uses an 8- or 16-bit word length. The 16-bit processor might have faster speed, more efficient instruction and data handling, and greater precision. High precision might be necessary for some applications such as data analysis or simulations; but in most instructional strategies, greater precision is not necessary to aid students in understanding concepts or in practicing rules.

The instructional program and data being processed by the microcomputer are stored in the memory unit. Memory is a vital resource of a microcomputer, and the size of the memory is a very important factor in determining the types of instructional computing that can be undertaken. There are two kinds of memory in most microcomputers, read only memory (ROM) and random access memory (RAM). ROM, as the name implies, can be read but not changed, making it non-accessible as user memory. ROM contains code which may not be modified, such as system programs. In some microcomputers, the programming language software is in ROM. However, in most systems, part of all of the programming language software and even some of the system utilities are loaded into RAM along with the instructional programs. Therefore, the number which should be of concern is not the total memory, but the amount of memory available for the instructional materials. For example, on one 16K microcomputer, where 1K represents approximately one thousand characters, the disk operating system and other system software take up almost 12K, leaving less than 4K of usable RAM. 16K of RAM sounds sufficient but the actual 4K is not enough for the majority of applications. Often the minimum amount of memory listed for a microcomputer is not enough, and additional memory needs to be acquired. Also, the maximum amount of memory that can be supported by the microcomputer should be considered, giving room for expansion. Memory is a very important and relatively expensive resource, but advances in the technology are lowering its cost, making larger quantities possible.

Another capability that should be considered is the character set. Many microcomputers have only uppercase letters and it is desirable for most instructional applications to have both uppercase and lowercase. Almost all of the other learning materials

that a student utilizes make use of both; an educator should not settle for less when doing instructional computing. Further, the size of the characters should be noted along with the availability of special characters. The ability for the user to design an alternate character set might be an asset in certain applications and should be kept in mind.

In conjunction with the character set, the number of characters per line and the number of lines per display should be factors weighed in the selection process. The number of lines is dependent upon the display unit used by the system. A display unit of some kind (hardcopy or video) is required, and if the number of display lines is too small, it can be a limiting factor on the type of instructional application. Also, the number of characters per line can limit what can be presented in an efficient and readable manner. A recommended size is 64 to 80 characters per line and 24 lines per display for video terminals.

Every instructional system must have some external storage device for keeping the curriculum materials and associated programs. Typically, this storage medium is either a cassette tape or a floppy diskette. The cassette tapes used are the typical audio tapes and their contents are input into the computer through a regular tape recorder. The floppy diskette is a thin, circular magnetic recording surface enclosed in a square envelope which has an exposed recording area. The diskettes come in two sizes, 8-inch or 5-inch. To confuse matters, the two diskette sizes can also come in double density which holds approximately twice the amount of information of the regular single-density diskette. The information on a diskette is read into the computer's memory by a disk drive. Microcomputers may have either single or multiple disk drive capability. If students are utilizing several different programs during a session, a disk capability is recommended over the tape recorder. Tape recorders are inexpensive but are very slow and sometimes unreliable, taking several attempts before successfully loading a program. It is further recommended that at least one microcomputer in a cluster be equipped with a dual-disk drive for backing-up the system and creating copies of courseware.

Many microcomputers have graphics capability integrated within the system. In some systems, this feature even includes colors, ranging from four to fifteen different hues. In selecting a microcomputer with graphics, the buyer should consider one with a resolution of 128 by 128 addressable points for a minimum. The ability to display graphical representations can be extremely useful in many types of instructional computing.

Two other features that might be necessary in some instructional applications are the existence of several programming languages and the ability to utilize the microcomputer as a terminal to another computer. Some microcomputers have available other programming languages, such as FORTRAN, PASCAL, or a CAI language, PILOT. The addition of other programming languages can be necessary in the teaching of computer science. The ability to utilize the microcomputer as a terminal to a larger computer system can be an asset, in that it may permit the development of programs on the larger system and then the transfer of the resulting code to the memory of the microcomputer. Also, the systems could be used in an hierarchical arrangement where the micro-computer is utilized as a stand-alone system for most computing, but when more resources are required, the larger system could be employed. In an environment where the user has access to other computer systems, it is recommended that the microcomputer be equipped with a communication interface, permitting its use as a terminal.

The last capability of microcomputers to be dis-cussed is the ability to directly connect peripherals, expanding the system's potential. Peripherals that would be extremely beneficial in instructional com-puting are printers, plotters, graphic input tablets, music boards, speech synthesizers, speech recognition systems, random access audio devices, random access slide projectors, and video-disk players. A microcomputer with the flexibility to permit connec-tion of a good selection of peripherals should be viewed favorably. When comparing peripherals, make sure software is available to support them

on the particular microcomputer and that their addition does not require a major revision of existing courseware. The addition of other media to your instructional computer applications can greatly enhance effectiveness.

Table 3 shows the capabilities of a micro-computer which are believed to be essential for each of the various instructional strategies. However, a particular application, even though classified within one of the strategies, might require capabilities other than those listed. The educator should compile a set of computing requirements, using the Instructional Requirements Matrix and employing Table 3 as an aid.

Several microcomputers having a range of capa-bilities are described in the survey in Table 4. During the final phase of the selection process, a potential buyer would want to create a similar survey, match-ing the capabilities and systems that satisfy the computing requirements generated previously.

In completing the selection process, the following questions should be asked of each of the possible microcomputers:

a. Is it *flexible and easy to use*?
b. Does it have *good documentation*?
c. What is the *manufacturer's reputation*?
d. Does *courseware* exist for it?
e. Can it be *expanded*?
f. What are the *service options*?
g. How long is the *warranty*?

TABLE 3   Micro requirements per instructional type

	Drill and Practice	Tutorial	Problem Solving	Programming	Simulation	Testing	Computer Literacy	Other
Usable Memory (RAM)	4-8K	16-32K	8K	8K	8-32K	16-32K	4-8K	16-64K
Lowercase Characters		Y			Y	Y		Y
Cassette (C) and/or Disk (D)	C	D	C	C	D	D	C	D
Graphics		Y	Y		Y			
Hardcopy		Y		Y		Y	Y	Y
Decimal (Non-Integer) Arithmetic			Y	Y	Y			Y
Other Programming Languages				Y				Y
Files		Y			Y	Y		Y
Communication Capability		Y		Y	Y	Y		Y
Number Lines Display	12	24	16	24	24	16	12	24

TABLE 4   Comparison of microcomputer systems

	PET	TRS80	APPLE	SORCERER	COMPU-COLOR	TI 99/4	HEATH H 89	TERAK	ORION	CROMEN-CO S-2	OHIO SCI C2-8P	PDP 11/03
PROCESSOR	6502	Z80	6502	Z80	8080	TM9900	Z80	LSI 11	8080	Z80	6502	LSI 11
MEMORY MIN/MAX	8/32	4/48	16/48	8/32	8/32	16/16	16/48	28/56	16/56	32/512	4/36	32/56
LOWER CASE	Y	OPT	OPT	Y		OPT	Y	Y	Y	Y	Y	Y
DISPLAY	Y	Y	NI	NI	Y	Y	Y	Y	Y	NI	NI	Y
CASSETTE OR DISK	C/MD*	C/MD*	C*/MD*	C*	MD	C*MD*	MD	D	DMD	DMD	C/D*	DD
GRAPHICS RESOLUTION		124x48	280x192 40x48	512x240	128x128	123x256		320x240	512x512	128x128	256x512	
TEXT (LINESxCHAR)	24x40	16x 64/32	24x40	30x64	16/32 x84	24x32	25x80	24x80	32x64	TD	32x64	TD
COMMUNICATIONS		Y	Y	Y	Y	Y	Y	Y	Y	Y	Y	Y
DOCUMENTATION	Y	Y	Y	Y	Y	Y	Y	Y	Y	Y	Y	Y
MULTIPLE LANGUAGES		Y	Y	Y			Y	Y		Y		Y
COURSEWARE	Y	Y	Y	MAYBE	UNK	SOME		SOME	SOME	Y	UNK	Y
SPECIAL FEATURES	Char Graphic		4/15 Colors	Memory Cartrid.	8 Colors	16 Colors	Cursor Addr	16 Bit	Touch Slides Plasma	S-100 Quality Control	6 & 9 Digit (Fast)	16 Bit Multi Users
COST	795	698	1195	895	1495	1150	2295	6615	10295	3990	799	10500

NI – Not Included   DD – Dual Disk   TD – Terminal Dependent   OPT – Optional item not usually from manufacturer
MD – Mini Disk   DMD – Dual Mini Disk   Y – Yes   *Extra Cost
UNK – Unknown

Individuals who own microcomputers are a ready source of valuable information. Additional sources are the various personal computing magazines which periodically evaluate micros, and computer store dealers who offer more than one manufacturer's product. In the area of service, a buyer can choose from purchasing a service contract, sending the system to a factory representative, or switching boards or chips. If several microcomputers of one kind are purchased, it may be advantageous to purchase several boards or chips and do your own servicing.

The selection of a microcomputer which will be responsive to the needs you have identified and to the requirements you have generated now follows. You should be more confident in your selection when you implement the model proposed. A system which is congruent with your present and future needs will do much to assure a successful instructional computing experience.

Van Helps Schools Select the Right Computer

Betsy Staples

Which is the best computer? Which software should we buy? What can we actually do with a computer? How can we teach people to use it? Who will fix it when it breaks?

These are only a few of the questions that confront a school system when it first begins to consider the purchase of a small computer or computers for classroom use. Sometimes the questions are never answered adequately. Sometimes teachers and students are unhappy with computer hardware and software chosen in a haphazard fashion.

What seems to be needed is a systematic approach to the selection of hardware and software for classroom use. The Pennsylvania Department of Education offers just such an approach to almost 500 schools in the Commonwealth in the form of the Multi Media Training Van, a vehicle which provides information and training in everything from writing to photography to computers. The van, staffed by Media

Specialist Shirley Douglas, travels around the state visiting various school districts which have requested its services. The project is currently a joint effort of the Pennsylvania Department of Education and a Title IV-C project at the Colonial Northampton Intermediate Unit, Nazareth, PA. The program is coordinated through the state's Intermediate Unit Instructional Materials Service department.

In addition to the normal array of audio-visual paraphernalia, the training van carries a Bell and Howell Apple, a TI 99/4, and a TRS-80. When a school system decides to investigate the benefits of computers in the classroom, teachers and administrators may request copies of "A Guide to Microcomputers" and "A Guide to Instructional Microcomputer Software," both compiled by Ms. Douglas and Gary Neights, Coordinator of the Instructional Materials Service Programs in the state. These booklets provide information on computer literacy and guidance in developing purchase criteria.

The district may also request one of the "In-Service Programs" offered by Shirley in the van. Her introductory half-day course is entitled "Microcomputers," and assists participants in developing the criteria and purchase specifications mentioned in the booklets. It offers hands-on experience as well as discussion and demonstrations.

In "A Guide to Microcomputers," prospective purchasers are urged to identify the specific uses to which the new computer will be put. A list of "Projected Uses" (Figure 1) serves as a guide during this initial phase of the selection process.

FIGURE 1. Projected uses

I. Initially determine curriculum areas of use and possible other uses.

Subject Areas	*Other Uses*
___ math	___ guidance
___ science	___ library science
___ social studies	___ media
___ health	___ management
___ industrial arts	___ computer literacy
___ home economics	___ other _____
___ reading	_____
___ language arts	
___ foreign language	
___ business education	
___ physical education	
___ other _____	

II. If the microcomputer is to be used as an instructional tool (i.e., math, art, music, etc.) the next step is to determine the microcomputer's utilization by the classroom teacher and the student.

Classroom Teacher Application	*Student Application*
___ curriculum (subject area teaching)	___ discovery learning
	___ problem resolution
	___ graphics development
___ computer operation and programming	___ musical exploration
	___ computer programming
___ computer literacy instruction	___ computer awareness
	___ counseling and guidance
___ testing	___ other _____
___ classroom management (teacher's record keeping)	
___ other _____	

III. If the microcomputer is to be used beyond that of an instructional tool, the following applications should be considered.

Media	*Library*
___ program development	___ instruction
___ inventory	___ book location
___ utilization and maintenance records	___ card file
	___ inventory
___ budget	___ budget
___ video	___ circulation control
___ circulation control	___ other _____
___ graphics generation	
___ other _____	

Management	*Support Services*
___ attendance	___ word processing
___ letter file	___ teacher assignment
___ class registration	___ student assignment
___ student scheduling	___ other _____
___ bus routing	_____
___ fiscal and budget control	
___ inventory control	
___ other _____	

Guidance	*Buildings and Grounds*
___ student tracking	___ security
___ occupation selection	___ maintenance schedules
___ college selection	___ other _____
___ confidential student files	
___ other _____	

IV. From the varied uses indicated, more than one *microcomputer system* may be necessary. The potential locations of these systems will be an additional factor to consider and thus determine the quantity of microcomputers necessary to meet the potential needs.

LOCATION:

Classroom

___ a. permanent location
___ b. shared (mobile between classrooms)
___ c. estimate number needed:
    ___ permanent
    ___ shared

Other

___ school office
___ library
___ TV studio
___ media office
___ business office
___ administration building
___ guidance office
___ other _____

_____

Once the uses have been defined, the people who will use the machine are asked to consider such criteria as cost, flexibility, mainframe interface, keyboard layout, execution and loading speed, memory capability, system expansion and many others. A tally sheet lists 17 of these criteria; the prospective user assigns a number between one and ten to indicate how important he or she considers each feature. If the school plans to use the computer in more than one area, or for more than one application, all prospective users should assign "importance factors" based on their individual needs.

When importance factors have been assigned, individual computers can be considered. Based on promotional literature, information provided by sales people, or experience with one of the machines in the van, a "Comment Sheet" can be completed. Figure 2 shows a comment sheet for the mythical Spacetron 007.

On the final tally sheet, users are asked to consider again the 17 criteria and assign a value between one and five for the computer in question. "If the cost is high, give it a 1. If it is easily movable and compact then flexibility may be a 5." These "single rankings" are then filled in on the tally sheet and multiplied by the importance factors to produce a rating for each criterion. (See Figure 3.) When the ratings are totalled, the user has a number which can be compared to the totals for other machines or for the same machine in other departments. While obviously not infallible, this technique provides a method of quantifying what might otherwise be left to someone's gut feeling. The instructions conclude by cautioning: "Color of the case, unnecessary extras or the salesperson's personality should not affect the choice."

When evaluating a microcomputer, use the comment sheet. Write notes about that particular model and brand. The notes on the comment sheet will be translated into numbers on the tally sheet.

FIGURE 2.   Comment sheet

CATEGORY	BRAND: SPACETRON MODEL: 007	BRAND MODEL
1. Cost—Total	795-16K 995-32K	
2. Flexibility	reg. power source no spec. environ. controls NASA portability tested	
3. Mainframe Interface	none	
4. Keyboard Layout	standard w/calculator	
5. Additional Ports	5 ports uses RAM	
6. Execution Time and Loading Speed	L.S. - 5 sec 1.2 sec E.T.	
7. Memory Capability		
8. System Expansion	48k	
9. Editing	none	
10. Input and Output Devices	printer, plotter, disk	
11. Software	5 programs math manuals	
12. Graphics/ Characters	Hi Resolution	
13. Color	14 color stand. TV monitor	
14. Voice Command and Voice Generation	no	
15. Music Generation	no	
16. Servicing	none	
17. User Training	none	
18. Totals	N/A	

Software selection

Once the computer system has been selected, the problem of which software to purchase may be overwhelming. Very few manufacturers are willing to send sample programs, and it may be difficult to find educational software in the local computer store. Here comes the van again.

QUESTIONS TO ASK ABOUT A COMPUTER SYSTEM

1. **Cost:** This is a factor to be considered. Micros generally range from $500 to $3,000 to establish a system. This cost is to be with all peripherals needed to operate.
2. **Flexibility:** (Size, portability, cords and modules, environment) Depending upon needs, can the unit

On the tally sheet, using a scale ranking (1–5), assign a rank value for each category from the comment sheet. If the cost is high, give it a 1. If it is easily movable and compact, then flexibility may be a 5. If no service is available, category (16) is assigned a 0, etc. When all categories have been assigned a scale ranking, multiply them by the importance factor you originally assigned. The end results are added together. The highest total (18) will indicate the microcomputer best suited for your uses and needs. Be as sincere as possible to get an unbiased evaluation. Color of the case, unnecessary extras or the salesperson's personality should not affect the choice.

FIGURE 3. Talley sheet

CATEGORY	IMPORTANCE FACTORS	BRAND: SPACETRON	
		SCALE RANKING	RATING
1. Cost—Total	5	1	5
2. Flexibility	5	5	25
3. Mainframe Interface	10	0	0
4. Keyboard Layout	3	5	15
5. Additional Ports	10	4	40
6. Execution Time and Loading Speed	10	3	30
7. Memory Capability	10	2	20
8. System Expansion	8	5	40
9. Editing	10	0	0
10. Input and Output Devices	9	3	27
11. Software	10	2	20
12. Graphics/ Characters	8	5	40
13. Color	5	5	25
14. Voice Command and Voice Generation	5	0	0
15. Music Generation	3	0	0
16. Servicing	10	0	0
17. User Training	10	0	0
18. Totals	—	—	297

be readily moved? Is it necessary for the unit to be moved? Is it sturdy and reliable to survive moving around? Has it been tested for durability? How much does it weigh? Is it necessary to be near an outlet or telephone lines? Do the learners have to be brought to the unit or does the unit have to be taken to the learners? Can the unit be accessed other than being right at the micro-computer itself? How many cords are necessary to operate the micro? Is there a need for special environmental controls, i.e., temperature, humidity, dust? (Protection from exterior electrical interference, i.e., other computers, static charges, another electromagnetic field.)

3. **Mainframe Interface:** Does the unit have the ability to interface with available mainframe computers to function as a smart terminal?

4. **Keyboard Layout:** Most micros come with a standard typewriter layout. If the unit does not, will it fit your needs? Does it have a calculator layout on it? Is a calculator layout necessary or can the standard typewriter numbers fulfill the calculation needs?

5. **Additional Ports:** Can other peripheral devices be connected to the unit, i.e., printers, plotters, phone lines, disks, etc.? Are there sufficient ports to substantiate your operational needs? Do these ports use memory (RAM) that would otherwise be available?

6. **Execution Time and Loading Speed:** How long does it take the microcomputer to execute an operation? How fast can information be loaded into the unit? Is the execution time, problem, operation or loading of a program too long for student attention spans?

7. **Memory Capability:** How much ROM memory is the unit capable of? How much RAM memory can be taped? RAM is found in varying forms. If strictly for running of prepackaged materials, then usually 16K will suffice but generally self-generated programs will take more bytes of memory (RAM).

8. **System Expansion:** Can the system be expanded easily? What are the limits of the expansion? What peripherals are available? Are peripherals needed? With the current state of advances new items for purchase are always being developed, such as light pens, graphics, tablets, voice synthesizers, etc. Maybe even keys for the blind or some other new advances are in the making.

9. **Editing:** Can editing take place immediately as mistakes occur? Is editing simple? After the program is completed, can editing be done? Can changes in the program to suit needs be done? Will the unit identify specific program errors?

10. **Input and Output Devices:** As specified for purchase, what input and output devices are included in the package, i.e., cassette, disk, TV monitor, printer, plotter, graphics tablet, light pen, voice synthesizer?

11. **Software:** Are there sufficient manuals, reference and program material available to support the microcomputer? Are there programs suited to the user's needs? Have outside companies (other than the original designer) made additional software programs? Is there enough software available to fulfill needs? Can programs be made to fulfill the user's needs? Have the programs been vali-

dated (field tested with students)? Cost of prepared programs? Ease of self-generated programs?

12. **Graphics/Characters:** Is the unit capable of low or high resolution graphics? How many characters per line are available on the micro? How many lines on the CRT are visible? What is the screen size? Graphics tablet? Light pen?

13. **Color:** Is color necessary for your operations? If color is necessary, does the CRT monitor have to be a special monitor?

14. **Voice Command and Voice Generation:** Does the unit have voice synthesizers, to generate voice? Does it have or can it be adapted to accept voice commands?

15. **Music Generation:** Is there music capability? Does it have an internal speaker or separate speaker system for sound?

16. **Servicing:** What are the warranties available? Can the unit be serviced at its home base? Is on-site servicing necessary? Can local technicians make necessary repairs? For additional cost, will the unit be updated for the next year as new developments are made? Length of time for service including transportation to and from service facility? Service cost including transportation?

17. **User Training:** Will vendors provide on-site user training? At what cost? How many hours? For how many people?

Shirley purchases single copies of educational programs from many different vendors and makes them available in the van to educators who want to consider them for adoption. If a teacher decides to adopt a given program or package, it must be purchased through his or her school district. Software carried in the van may not be copied.

The software evaluation form (Figure 4), found in "A Guide to Instructional Microcomputer Software," is designed to assist in the selection of software. First an instructional objective must be stated. Then the objective is compared to the features of the program with regard to grade level, validation, correlation with text, instructional strategies and instructional design features. It also includes room for a description of the program and an overall evaluation.

After hardware and software are chosen, teachers may avail themselves of a second in-service program which deals with "Microcomputer Classroom Applications." During the full-day course, participants learn to operate the computer, run programs, and even write a short program in Basic.

Other services

The van staff has taken special care to reach administrators, since they are most frequently in decision-making positions. The Microcomputer Ad-

FIGURE 4 Microcomputer instructional software evaluation form

Instructional Objective Desired: _____

Desired Instructional Needs	Program Title _____ Producer _____ Cost _____
A. Objective (Above)	A. Objectives Met: ___ Yes ___ No Content: ___ Good ___ Fair ___ Poor
B. Grade Level ___ C. Validation	B. Grade Level ___ C. Number of Times Tested ___ Number of Times Revised ___ Students Tested: Number ___ Grade Level ___
D. Current Text in Use: _____	D. Correlated With: _____
E. Instructional Strategies Needed: ___ Drill and Practice ___ Simulation/Gaming ___ Inquiry and Dialogue ___ Problem Solving ___ Information Retrieval ___ Tutorial	E. Instructional Strategies Employed: ___ Drill and Practice ___ Simulation/Gaming ___ Inquiry and Dialogue ___ Problem Solving ___ Information Retrieval ___ Tutorial
F. Instructional Design Features: 1. Student Instructions ___ Audio ___ Written 2. Built-in Clock ___ Yes ___ No 3. ___ Linear ___ Branching 4. Student Progress ___ Daily ___ Cumulative 5. Prescription or Homework Assigned ___ Yes ___ No	F. Instructional Design Features: 1. Student Instructions ___ Audio ___ Written 2. Built-in Clock ___ Yes ___ No 3. ___ Linear ___ Branching 4. Student Progress ___ Daily ___ Cumulative 5. Will the program prescribe study assignment or develop homework? ___ Yes ___ No

Description of the Program:
Recommended for _____
(Include grade level, course and student ability level)
Overall Evaluation:
___ Excellent ___ Good ___ Fair ___ Poor ___ Unacceptable

ministrators Days Workshops, in which administrators get an overview of small computers in education as well as specific information on hardware specifications and evaluation and software evaluation, have reached over 50% of the school district administrators in the state.

Perhaps the most innovative program in this innovative program was the repair seminar conducted in March 1980, in which Bell and Howell Apple personnel trained approximately 20 of the state's Instructional Materials Service Technicians to repair their computer. Negotiations are under way with several other computer manufacturers to provide similar sessions.

Shirley points out the participants in these and other courses and services provided by the van are expected to be "multipliers." Key personnel are trained to train others in the school or district. The van enables one person and a few pieces of audiovisual and computer equipment to serve many people and many school districts all over the state.

Help!!! What Computer Should I Buy???

Ludwig Braun

The plea in the title of this article has been made to me hundreds of times in the past three years by educators and administrators all over the United States. These people are bewildered by the technology and its capabilities, by the large number of companies marketing microcomputers, by the rapid rate of new developments in microcomputer technology, and by the wide range of models and peripherals available.

Computer companies perceive the education market as lucrative. As a result, they direct slick TV ads and very persuasive salespeople at educators.

Faced with pressures of staff, students, parents, and school boards to get their schools into computing, educators seek advice from any quarter about which machines to buy. Salespeople usually are more interested in making a sale than they are in meeting the needs of their customers. Because many educators have no competent, objective person to give them the help they need, they turn to the salespeople for advice and sometimes buy computers that do not meet their needs. The result is frustration, disappointment, and, frequently, disenchantment with the entire concept of computers in education.

Properly chosen and properly used, computers can make important contributions to the learning environments of children. The purpose of this article is to assist educators to make good decisions about equipment for their school systems.

Purchasing computer hardware and software may be compared to purchasing automobiles. On our roads we see a wide range of automobile models with different-size interiors, different engine power, front- or rear-wheel drive, manual or automatic transmissions, two or four doors, and so on. Some people buy Fords, some Chevrolets, and some Toyotas. The automobile owner uses a variety of criteria—some objective and some subjective—to make a decision about the automobile to buy. The diversity of cars on the road indicates that there is no single automobile that is the best—just as there is no single microcomputer that is the best in every educational situation. I will not tell the reader which computer to buy or which to avoid. I *will* suggest a set of criteria that is useful as a guide in making the decision and a rational way of applying these criteria to all computers under consideration.

A FEW BASIC GUIDELINES

There are some guidelines that I consider basic to the decision-making process and that are more important than the size of the memory, the language features, and other criteria that people usually apply. These guidelines follow.

a. Get the most entry ports that your budget permits. This is so obvious that it shouldn't need to be said; however, there are educators who buy a single computer costing many thousands of dollars rather than five, or even ten, simpler computers for the same total. Whatever the capability of the expensive machine, the educator has the fundamental responsibility to maximize the educational impact of every dollar he or she spends. The basic question here is, Does the powerful, but expensive, computer produce more educational "bang" than a group of simpler, but less costly, computers?

Primarily for this reason, the Compucolor, the micro PLATO, and the Terak computers will not be considered here, even though they are excellent computers with capabilities not available on the computers that will be considered in detail.

b. Do not choose a particular computer unless there is a body of users of that computer in your region. Most educators do not have a great deal of expertise concerning computer hardware or software. There is great value in joining a community of users. Such communities frequently form clubs for exchange of programs, ideas for application, and other experiences—good and bad. In a group it is likely that you will find someone else who has had (and solved) your problem—no matter what. If you are the only user of the XYZ computer in your region, you will be dependent on the manufacturers for help; and that has not proved to be a good source of help in at least some cases. For this reason we will consider in detail only the Apple, Commodore PET, and TRS-80 computers even though Atari, Heath, Ohio Scientific, Texas Instruments, and other companies make fine computers.

c. Buy from a local dealer. There are some computer dealers who advertise nationally and who offer computers at prices that sometimes are somewhat better than those of local dealers. Local dealers, however, provide local service and local maintenance and frequently will loan you a computer while yours is being repaired.

Educational institutions frequently are required to purchase from the low bidder. This may be a mistake when maintenance and machine availability are factored into the decision process. Sending a computer out of town for repair usually takes a month because of shipping delays. Such a hiatus will make the teacher and students unhappy and may jeopardize the computer program in the school.

d. Buy peripherals with care. There are many peripherals available for microcomputers. There are printers, disc drives, music generators, analog-to-digital converters, and light pens, to name just a few. Each peripheral you buy enhances the capability of the computer to which it is attached, but it also takes away money from the purchase of computers (cf. item *a*).

Probably the most valuable peripheral is a printer. There are times when hard copy is valuable for the student (e.g., to provide a listing in a programming course). Further, sending children home with a printout of what they did on the computer will convince many parents to support computers in their schools.

A disc drive is also useful because program loading is much faster (seconds compared to minutes) and more reliable.

It is possible to use a single printer and a single disc drive for ten or even twenty computers by cabling all the machines together and ensuring that only one student at a time accesses the printer or disc drive.

Other peripherals may be useful in special circumstances (e.g., music generators for music instruction and experimentation), but they should be purchased with item *a* in mind.

I have one final caveat for the educator. *Don't wait for computer developments (price reductions or hardware improvements) to settle down.* If you "wait till next year," you will wait forever. The three best microcomputers for classroom applications are the Apple, the PET, and the TRS-80, all of which were introduced in 1977!

A BASIS FOR DECISION MAKING

In 1979, I proposed an approach for comparing computers that permits each educator to factor into the decision-making process the uniqueness of her or his environment and individual assessments of the extent to which each computer under consideration meets the educator's goals. The approach involves a three-step procedure.

1. *Identification of a set of capabilities of importance to the individual.* Table 1 includes thirteen capabilities that I consider to be important in my environment. A teacher who is interested in music instruction may wish to add music-generation capability to this table. Others may not be interested in connecting external video monitors to the computer and may want to drop item 7 from the table. Any capabilities may be added to or subtracted from this table to suit the individual situation.

2. *Assignment of an importance value to each of the capabilities in Table 1.* The importance of a specific capability may be chosen (arbitrarily) to range from 0 to 100, with 100 considered to be very important and 0 considered to be unimportant. My assignments of importance are shown in table 2. I chose the set of importance values so that they total 100.

3. *Assignment of a quality value to each of the capabilities of table 1 for each of the computers under consideration.* My assignments of quality for the Apple II, the Commodore PET, and the Radio Shack TRS-80 Model III are shown in table 3. In this table there are two columns for the Commodore PET—one for the basic computer and one for the computer with vector graphics capability. Each quality value is in the range 0–10, with 10 being the highest value.

The set of importance values assigned in item 2 (table 3) may be represented by a vector with elements $I(n)$, and the set of quality values assigned in item 3 may be represented by a vector with elements $Q(n)$. The worth of a specific computer is the sum of products of the elements $I(n)$ and $Q(n)$. Mathematically,

$$\text{Worth} = \sum_{n-1}^{M} I(n) \times Q(n),$$

where M is the number of capabilities included in table 1.

It is of the utmost importance for the reader to be aware that the specific capabilities that are included in table 1 and the importance and quality values assigned in tables 2 and 3 *were selected by me to fit my situation and my subjective interpretation of that situation.* Each person who uses this approach must choose a set of capabilities and sets of importance and quality values that correspond to her or his unique situation.

In table 2, for example, I gave the most weight to the importance of computer cost (in line with guideline *a*, mentioned earlier) and next most importance to graphics resolution, because mathematics teachers need high resolution to permit drawing of geometric figures and graphs of functions. I am not convinced of the value of color in most learning situations and assigned zero importance to it in table 2. The other values in table 2 were chosen on similar judgmental bases.

Some explanation of the quality values in table 3 is in order so that the reader can understand the approach. These values were chosen for the following reasons (in the order in which they appear in table 3).

1. *Cost.*

$$Q = \frac{\text{lowest cost}}{\text{cost}} \times 10.$$

2. *Portability.* The value here is based on the concept that more pieces mean less portability.

3. *Memory.*

$$Q = \frac{\text{memory}}{\text{largest memory}} \times 10.$$

4. *Cassette reliability.* The Apple and TRS-80 computers use standard audio cassette recorders and, depending on settings of volume and tone controls, can be unreliable—whereas in the PET a special cassette recorder is used without such controls and is more reliable.

5. *Execution time.*

$$Q = \frac{\text{fastest time}}{\text{time}} \times 10.$$

TABLE 1   Capability vector for several personal computers

Capability	Apple II (Note 1)	PET 4001-16N	PET 4001-16N Plus Graphics (Note 2)	TRS-80 Model III
1. Cost (note 3)	$1560	$759	$1209	$959
2. Portable	moderately (3 modules) 27 pounds	very (single unit and cassette) 37 pounds	very (single unit and cassette) 37 pounds	very (single unit and cassette) 25 pounds
3. Memory				
a. ROM	12K	14K	14K	14K
b. RAM	16K	16K	16K	16K
c. Expandable to	48K RAM/24K ROM	32K RAM/26K ROM	32K RAM/26K ROM	48K RAM/14K ROM
4. Cassette reliability	moderate	high	high	moderate
5. Execution time of computation (note 4)	4.0 sec	4.5 sec	4.5 sec	7.4 sec
6. Program loading speed	730 bits/sec	410 bits/sec (note 5)	410 bits/sec (note 5)	500 or 1500 bits/sec (note 6)
7. Composite video or rf signal	composite video (note 7)	neither (note 8)	neither (note 8)	not available
8. Editing capability	moderately powerful	very powerful	very powerful	moderately powerful
9. Graphics resolution	280 × 190 (note 9)	160 × 100 (note 10)	320 × 200	48 × 128 rectangular blocks
10. Screen size (characters × lines)	40 × 24	40 × 25	40 × 25	64 × 16 or 32 × 16
11. Colors available	15 (low-resolution mode)	black and white only	black and white only	black and white only
12. User-definable graphics characters	yes	no	no	no
13. Keyboard				
a. Layout	good	excellent	excellent	good
b. Size	full size	full size	full size	full size
c. Number of keys	52	73	73	65

Notes for Table 1

1. Apple II Plus with 16K RAM, 9-inch black-and-white monitor, and audio cassette recorder.

2. This configuration is the PET 4001-16N plus the MTU Visible Memory Module graphics package, which adds $450 to the system cost. It adds vector graphic capability to the PET's character-oriented graphics.

3. These costs are the net costs to educators in spring 1981. The PET cost reflects the three-for-two sale in force at Commodore; the Apple price includes a 5% educational discount; and the TRS-80 price includes an educational discount of 10%. Depending on quantities and the specific dealer, better prices may be possible.

4. Execution time is time to execute the program:

```
10 X = 0
20 FOR I = 1 TO 1000
30 X = X + 1
40 NEXT I
50 PRINT X
```

5. The effective loading speed is 410 bits/sec rather than the published value of 810 because of redundancy and error checking.

6. The loading speed is user selectable at either 500 or 1500 bits/sec.

7. rf modulator available for $30.

8. Plug-in unit with video output available for $38.

9. The Apple II has a high-resolution mode (280 × 192) with six colors or a low-resolution mode (40 × 48 blocks) with fifteen colors.

10. The resolution of the PET is difficult to specify. The screen has 1000 screen positions (40 characters per line × 25 lines). Each character is defined by an 8 × 8 dot matrix, so that the potential resolution is 64,000 dots. Because only 128 graphic characters have been defined, the resolution was chosen as a compromise between 1000 and 64,000 on the basis that the average number of dots per character is 16.

11. Frequently a teacher will want to display the computer output on a large screen so that a group of students may see the computer screen simultaneously. This may be accomplished in two ways: (a) by using a video monitor or (b) by using a TV set. In the former case, a video signal (called a *composite video signal*) is required; whereas in the latter case, a signal (called an *rf signal*) from the computer must be connected to the antenna terminals of a TV set.

TABLE 2 Importance vector for capabilities of Table 1

Capability	Importance Value
1. Cost	25
2. Portability.	10
3. Memory	0
4. Cassette reliability	5
5. Execution time	5
6. Program loading speed.	10
7. Composite video or rf signal.	10
8. Editing capability.	10
9. Graphics resolution.	15
10. Screen size.	5
11. Colors available.	0
12. User-definable graphics	0
13. Keyboard	5
Total	100

6. *Program loading speed.*

$$Q = \frac{\text{rate}}{\text{highest rate}} \times 10.$$

7. *Composite video or rf.* Apple has built-in composite video, the PET has a port to which an inexpensive adapter can be attached, and the TRS-80 has no capability for such a signal unless the user makes internal modifications.

8. *Editing capability.* The PET has excellent, easy-to-use screen-editing capability, which makes it simple to correct errors in program statements; the Apple has screen editing, but it is somewhat difficult to use; the TRS-80 has no line-editing capability, except by retyping a line.

9. *Graphics resolution.*

$$Q = \frac{\text{pixels}}{\text{largest number of pixels}} \times 10.$$

A pixel is a picture element. The PET with graphics, for example, has $320 \times 200 = 64{,}000$ pixels.

10. *Screen size.*

$$Q = \frac{\text{number of screen characters}}{\text{largest number of screen characters}} \times 10.$$

11. *Colors available.* Only the Apple has color capability.

12. *User-definable graphs.* Only the Apple has user-definable graphic characters.

13. *Keyboard.*

$$Q = \frac{\text{number of keys}}{\text{largest number of keys}} \times 10.$$

If we use the worth equation with the importance and quality vectors of tables 2 and 3, the computers that we have considered are ranked as follows:

Computer	Worth
PET with graphics board	778
PET without graphics board	758
Apple II	669.5
TRS-80 Model III	594

If one accepts the values chosen in tables 2 and 3, the choice is clear—almost. The PET with graphics and the PET without graphics have worths that are almost identical. The essential differences between the two are in price and graphics resolution. To choose between the two requires changing emphases on these two capabilities.

CONCLUSION

It is my hope that the approach proposed in this article will help educators to make the difficult decisions wisely and to avoid the traps inherent in sales promotions.

The hardware decision already is difficult. As we learn more about the Commodore VIC color

TABLE 3 Quality vectors for computers of Table 1

Capability	Apple II	PET 4001-16N	PET 4001-16N Plus Graphics	TRS-80 Model III
1. Cost	4.9	10	6.3	7.9
2. Portability	6	8	8	8
3. Memory	9.3	10	10	10
4. Cassette reliability	6	10	10	6
5. Execution time	10	8.9	8.9	5.4
6. Program loading speed	4.9	2.7	2.7	10
7. Composite video or rf signal	10	7	7	0
8. Editing capability	5	10	10	5
9. Graphics resolution	8.4	2.5	10	1
10. Screen size	9.4	9.8	9.8	10
11. Colors available	10	0	0	0
12. User-definable graphics	10	0	0	0
13. Keyboard	7	10	10	8.9

computer for $300, the Radio Shack color computer for $400, and the Sinclair ZX80 for $200, the decision will be even more difficult; but just think—a decade ago educators who used computers had almost no decisions to make, except whether to buy yellow or white paper for their teletypewriters. We are much luckier than they were. Our choices are exciting ones!

BIBLIOGRAPHY

Braun, Ludwig. "How Do I Choose a Personal Computer?" *AEDS Journal* 13 (Fall 1979):81–87.

WHAT'S YOUR OPINION?

1. Few educators employ systematic decision making in the selection of microcomputers.
2. The best method for teachers to detect flaws in courseware is to observe students using microcomputers for instruction.
3. By using students as guinea pigs to evaluate inferior software, we are doing them more harm than good.
4. Trained educators are far more capable of writing software that looks at the broad issues of curriculum than are other software producers.
5. Most available educational computer software should not be offered for sale.
6. A school should delay purchase of computers as long as possible because improved models are constantly being introduced.
7. The computer's ability to handle a wide range of jobs gives it the potential to ease the money crunch on education.
8. All the small computers that can make it in the classroom are remarkably similar in price, capability, and reliability. It is not possible to make a wrong decision here.
9. Hardware manufacturers should be required to standardize much of their equipment to make software more transportable.

EXERCISES

1. Find out why most programs written for one type of computer can't be run on another manufacturer's machine. What recommendations would you have for (a) computer manufacturers and (b) software developers and programmers?
2. What constitutes software documentation? How important is software documentation to the user?
3. What is the difference between internal and external documentation? How important is each to the user?
4. Software suppliers often refuse to allow schools to duplicate courseware for protection purposes and backup. Should educators oppose this policy? What alternatives would you suggest?
5. Discuss methods which schools could use to protect software and data against theft, accidental loss, damage, or unauthorized use.
6. Suggest procedures for protecting the software and data files of a microcomputer system that uses cassette and floppy diskettes.
7. Obtain copies of programs in as many different computer languages as possible. To what type of computer application is each best suited?
8. Should one get the largest number of computers that the budget can provide or go for fewer, better-quality machines?
9. Describe the meaning of "built-in-attitude" in computer software.
10. To what extent does the powerful, more expensive computer produce more educational profit than a group of simpler but less costly computers?
11. List the names, uses, and approximate costs of common input and output devices.
12. Define the term *analog*. What types of analog devices can be connected to a computer? Predict what other common analog devices might be interfaced to a computer in the future.
13. Compare cassette tape storage to "floppies" in terms of their advantages and disadvantages.
14. Compare cassette tape to magnetic tape reel storage in terms of their methods of recording data.
15. Define *microcomputer, minicomputer,* and *maxicomputer.* Are there precise lines separating the three types? Draw a chart comparing the three on the basis of price, speed and accuracy of calculating, memory capability, typical auxiliary storage, and common types of applications.
16. Make a chart comparing the prices and capabilities of four of the popular brands of microcomputer systems. Then investigate and compare the quantity and quality of courseware available for each system.
17. The Minnesota Educational Computing Consortium initially promoted the statewide use of APPLE microcomputers in elementary and secondary schools. Subsequently, however, MECC purchased a large number of ATARIs for use in the schools. Find out why the switch was made, and list some of the problems this change might create. Will courseware that MECC developed for the APPLE be capable of running on the ATARI?

six

Classroom Applications

Chapter 6 presents several examples of computer uses in classes from kindergarten through grade 12. Teachers share their experiences in using microcomputers for instructional applications and offer helpful suggestions to those seeking a practical introduction. The grass roots advice contained in this section provides invaluable assistance to those just starting out.

Burns offers practical examples to prepare fourth- to eighth-grade students for developing appropriate thinking skills, while the Carrs outline a multi-disciplinary program for seventh and eighth graders. Brisson reports on one school's switch to microcomputers from terminals, calculators, and mini-computers, and Larsen outlines another school's experience with a third- and fourth-grade program. Stone discusses computer use at an alternative school; Behmer describes a story-analogy approach; finally, D'Ignazio describes his success using a fantasy-adventure story for preschoolers. Often teachers discover on their own initiative many applications for the equipment after they have used it for a while, and educationally oriented newsletters frequently carry articles describing new classroom techniques.

GETTING KIDS READY FOR COMPUTER THINKING: THOUGHTS FOR TEACHERS, GRADES 4–8

Marilyn Burns

It's true that computers have invaded everyone's lives. But it's not true that they've become an active part of many of our elementary classrooms. That has begun to change. In some elementary schools there are small computers in resource centers and in classrooms. This is not yet the norm, but waiting for computers to appear in the classroom before including computer learning in the curriculum isn't necessary. It is possible to do something now, without costly equipment, to give children experiences with the kind of thinking that is needed to deal with computers. And it's possible to do this in ways that even a computer-shy teacher can handle.

Kids don't seem to have any difficulty interacting with computers. They take to them effortlessly for recreational games when they have the opportunities. But children also need to understand that computers are basically problem-solving machines that serve people in a variety of ways. Computers do jobs you want done when they have instructions they can follow. Giving computers instructions requires thinking in special ways.

To use a computer as a problem-solving tool, programming skills are needed. Programming a computer to do a task requires defining the task so the computer can understand its job. A computer does only what it is told to do and exactly when it is told to do it—and only when told in a language it can understand. There are two basic aspects to programming computers: learning the

From "Getting Kids Ready for Computer Thinking—Thoughts for Teachers, Grades 4–8," by Marilyn Burns. In *The Computing Teacher*, September, 1980. Reprinted by permission.

167

suitable language and learning to express ideas precisely and in a logical sequence. The first aspect is similar to learning a foreign language, and is useful when starting to interact directly with a computer. That's not the focus here. The second aspect, expressing thoughts precisely and organizing them sequentially, requires some problem-solving skills of a special order. It's in this second aspect that teachers can help to develop students' thinking, in ways that need not rely solely on mathematical prowess but will be useful to the goals of the elementary curriculum in several ways.

Some underlying concepts of how children learn structures follow: First, children learn best by being actively involved—doing, not just sitting and listening. Secondly, children relate best to things in their real world. These two principles are at the base of including educational experiences that might better prepare children for developing working understandings of computer thinking. The notion is this: Use children's real experiences as the basis for helping them develop the kind of thinking that uses the problem-solving skills necessary to program computers.

Here's a first sample of how to do this, described in some detail so that it can serve as a model for the additional ideas that follow. The content for this sample: Peanut Butter and Jelly Sandwiches. As a writing assignment, ask kids to write directions for making a peanut butter and jelly sandwich. Have them do this individually. Collect them and read through the directions to choose one or two to use for a class demonstration. What you do is actually bring to class what's needed to make a sandwich: bread, peanut butter, jelly, a knife, etc. Explain to the class that you're going to try some of their directions. Do it this way. Give the directions you chose to the student who wrote them. That student is to read the directions to you, stopping after each one so you can do exactly what is said. The student may not embellish on the directions; they should be read verbatim. You may not ask questions and no comments may be made from the class.

Your job as teacher is to follow the directions accurately, though in an unconventional way if possible. Here's an example. I did this in a class of fourth graders. Below are the directions that were read and what I did for each.

"Take two slices of bread."	(I did this, removing them from the loaf.)
"Open the jar of peanut butter."	(I did this.)
"Spread peanut butter on one side of one slice of bread."	(Here was my first chance to follow the directions, but not as they were intended. I reached my hand into the jar and scooped out some peanut butter, smearing it onto the slice of bread with my fingers. No knife was specified and I chose not to use one. The kids' eyes got very big.)
"Now open the jar of jelly."	(I did this—but not before licking the peanut butter off my fingers.)
"Spread jelly on one side of the other slice of bread."	(Back to the hand routine, a sticky mess, but a small sacrifice for demonstrating the possible consequences of imprecise directions.)
"Put the two slices of bread together."	(I did it, putting the sides smeared with the peanut butter and jelly facing out, and handed it to the reader to eat.)

I did another, more for fun than for necessity. The kids got the point about how fuzzy directions can produce results that are both unexpected and unwanted.

Next, return all the papers to the kids and organize them into small groups so they can do some collective thinking. Each group task is to write a set of foolproof peanut butter and jelly sandwich making directions.

When this is done, have each group choose someone to read his/hers out loud. Discuss with the class the various solutions to the task. Encourage students to share, when they can, how they arrived at their ideas, and what ideas they discarded and why. Generate opinions as to whether the directions indeed will work, or can be tampered with "legitimately" as you did initially.

Most likely, kids will have written their directions in a paragraph. Once each group has verified that their directions are sound, show how they can be represented in another form—a numbered list.

Most computers today need to receive their directions in a list of specific instructions that are numbered in order. Show the class how you could write the peanut butter and jelly sandwich instructions this way:

1. Get 2 slices of bread.
2. Put them on a plate.
3. Get a jar of peanut butter.
4. Get a knife.
5. Open the jar.
6. With the knife, spread a thin layer of peanut butter on one side of one slice of bread.
7. Get a jar of jelly.
8. Open it.
9. With the knife, spread a layer of jelly on one side of the other slice of bread.
10. Put the 2 slices of bread together with the peanut butter and jelly sides both on the inside.
11. Eat it.

After writing your directions, you might notice a problem, something you left out. For example, there's no provision for closing the jar of peanut butter or the jar of jelly, or for washing the knife after using it for the peanut butter so you don't mess up the jelly in the jar. Adding those directions would necessitate renumbering some of the other directions. List these new instructions, and have the class decide where they should be inserted and how the list would now need to be renumbered. Here are some additional instructions to include:

Put the top back on the peanut butter jar.
Wash the knife.
Put the top back on the jelly jar.
Clean up.

There's no one way to add these, and there might be others that your students feel should be included. The following shows one way to add the extra instructions listed and renumber the list:

1 Get 2 slices of bread.
2 Put them on a plate.
3 Get a jar of peanut butter.
4 Get a knife.
5 Open the jar.
6 With the knife, spread a thin layer of peanut butter on one side of one slice of bread.
7 Put the top back on the peanut butter jar.
8 Wash the knife.
9 Get a jar of jelly.
10 Open it.
11 With the knife, spread a layer of jelly on one side of the other slice of bread.
12 Put the top back on the jelly jar.
13 Put the 2 slices of bread together with the peanut butter and jelly sides both on the inside.
14 Eat it.
15 Clean up.

Seem simple? I hope so. Learning doesn't need to be hard to be valuable. But you may be questioning whether it's educationally valuable to include peanut butter and jelly sandwiches in the curriculum. Consider these benefits from what's been presented so far.

1. Children have had reinforcement of writing skills.
2. Children have had opportunities to work both independently and with others.
3. Children have had the chance to solve a problem that invites both different solutions and different ways to reach those solutions.
4. Children have experienced a task that demanded precise and sequenced thinking—essential for dealing with computers.

5. The activities basically focused on direction giving and following, often an area of contention in the classroom.

Peanut butter and jelly were not the essence of these experiences. That content was chosen because children have had actual experience with it. The focus was on the process leading to expressing precise and sequential thoughts. It makes much more sense not to complicate the focus with unfamiliar content. Because computers are seen to be basically an extension of the study of mathematics, it doesn't mean you need to limit yourself to what's traditionally considered math. Start with the children's real experience.

Continue to develop this skill in other activities. Games, for example, lend themselves well. Start this with a small group assignment. Have each group list all the two-player games they can think of. Then have them sort their games into two groups by putting a star next to the games on their list that they think are suitable for the classroom. Compile a class list of the starred games. Discuss and make sure you agree each game is indeed a game for two players and is suitable for the classroom.

Place the class list somewhere where children can put their names or initials next to the games they know how to play. Do this by taping the list on the chalk-board or by making a graph on butcher paper. You can then use the information from the graph to form groups of students so that everyone in each group knows at least one game in common.

In their groups, students write directions for playing a game as a numbered list. It's useful to introduce this assignment with a sample. Make a numbered list of directions for playing Tic-Tac-Toe. When writing directions, it's helpful to leave space so you can insert other directions later. Some computer programmers find it best not to number any directions until they're satisfied with the completed list. The numbers are necessary, however, for a computer to know the correct order of the instructions. Other computer programmers prefer to number as they go along, but skip numbers so they have room to insert other directions later. As long as the numbers go up, even if they're not consecutive, the order is specified. Computers don't mind if there are skips between the numbers; they just go to the next larger number each time. Kids can get used to this, too. The instructions for Tic-Tac-Toe are numbered by 10's. If you do this for the class, you can show how extra directions can be added with in-between numbers. Notice that this list has a new kind of hitch. It circles back in directions 60 and 70 with the "GO TO" instruction. That's a computer short-cut for not having to write directions over and over. They're called loops and are essential to much of programming.

How to Play Tic-Tac-Toe

10 On a piece of paper, draw a playing board as shown. There are 9 playing spaces, each marked with a dot. Don't put dots on yours, but make it big enough so you can write a letter in each space.
20 Decide which player will be X and which will be O.
30 Decide who goes first.
40 The player whose turn it is writes their [sic] letter in an empty playing space.
50 Check to see if there are 3 of that letter in a row, horizontally, vertically, or on a slant.
60 If Yes, the game is over. Player with 3 of their [sic] letters in a row wins. Go to 10.
70 If No, then the next player plays. Go to 40.

Ask your students for other directions that might need to be added. For example, you might want to tell that this is a game for two people, and that each person needs a pencil. Those could be added without renumbering the others:

3   This is a game for 2 players.
5   Each player needs a pencil.

Some kids' rules are that after a game the player who lost goes first in the next game. See if kids could fix the directions so that when a game ends, the loser goes first for the next time.

When students write their own directions, it doesn't matter if they number the list by skipping numbers as with the Tic-Tac-Toe example, or if they merely leave spaces and number when they're done. Leave that choice up to them, but the skipping numbers strategy is useful whenever you number to allow for additions or improvements. A side benefit for your class from using games as the content is that you can then offer kids the opportunities to teach mini-courses, with kids teaching games they know to other students who don't know how to play them.

There are many other projects that also get students thinking in this mode of precise and sequenced directions. Here are some suggestions:

Write directions for how to get from one place to another, like from home to school, or from one place in school to another.
Write directions for making familiar things, like cooking a hamburger, scrambling an egg, or making a paper airplane.
Write a numbered list that shows what you do before coming to school in the morning.
Construct a numbered list for someone to use who has never eaten at a fast food restaurant.
Create a numbered list as a tour guide for someone to use who has never visited your town or city before. This could tie into a social studies unit on the community. Maps could be used (or made) first. Students could write annotations for each direction offering historical or current information about points of interest.
Following directions in textbooks often poses a problem. Students ignore them; teachers harp. Try having students write numbered lists for some of those types of directions.
Classroom rules sometimes get muddy. Have a committee make a poster-size numbered list for a common procedure, like collecting lunch money, or the procedures for checking a book out of the library.
Create pictorial solutions for problems such as those inspired by Rube Goldberg and Edward de Bono. Problems can be like these: "How to Stop a Dog and Cat from Fighting," "How to Make a Sleep Machine," "How to Weigh an Elephant," etc. Problems like these also serve to make art in the curriculum a useful problem-solving tool. Kids can convert their drawings into numbered lists.

After students have had success learning to use numbered lists as a way to communicate, it's possible to have them construct a set of task cards for each other to use as reinforcement. Children, individually or in pairs, make lists for something of their choice. But they purposely put an error in it so the list doesn't work perfectly. They write the numbered list on one piece of paper; they explain the flaw on another. When you collect the lists, number them and put them in a file folder. Number the error sheets correspondingly and put them in a second file folder. Make a class record sheet so students can record when they've found the error in someone else's work. They do this by entering the date under the name of their sheet. Put all this in some accessible storage place to use as tasks. If a student disagrees with the creator's opinion, they [sic] have to discuss it with him or her and come to you with the resolution of their differences.

You may be wondering when and how all this will begin to relate to computers—or at least to math. Be assured, it does relate to both. You can use content directly from the math curriculum if you prefer. Students can write directions for individual story problems and then have kids exchange with other kids to see if they produce the correct results. Kids can write numbered lists for how to solve a particular kind of arithmetic operation, like two-place multiplications. These are fine exercises, but are one step removed from the child's active, familiar world, and therefore don't make the best starting places. Besides, the onus of mathophobia has hit a goodly number of kids (and teachers, too) and the ideas presented here attempt to sidestep that current phobia. Making numbered lists, regardless of the content, is a form of math thinking that is useful and essential for computer work. You don't need to muddy the math thinking with other than very comfortable content at the beginning.

Follow up these experiences with more direct computer contact if you can. Invite a computer programmer in to talk with your class. Check to see where the nearest microcomputer is—many are appearing these days. Call distributors to find out. If you're feeling particularly plucky yourself, get a book on Basic, the language used for most microcomputers today. You may choose to extend what's here into more formal computer work. But if not, you've given your students some first-hand experience with a useful kind of thinking. It used to be considered thinking for the future. But the future is here; there's no more time to waste.

Computer Survival Course for Kids

Everett Q. Carr and Claire J. Carr

"If you're going to teach seventh and eighth graders computer programming, what are we supposed to teach them when they are freshmen?" We heard this lament from three different school administrators: a high school principal, the dean of a two-year college and the math and science department head of a liberal arts college. The answer to all three questioners is to the point, "It's a matter of survival—theirs and yours."

INTRODUCTION

Seventh and eighth graders are at the age—according to the eminent child psychologist, Piaget—when they can deal simultaneously with the abstract concepts, the cognitive content and the interactive environment provided by microcomputers as an instruction medium and a tool in a student's skill kit. Still, it is difficult to communicate the extent of the changes computer power can effect in the present school curricula. Revamping the mathematics education system is just one example.

Pencil and paper routines used to teach children arithmetic are neither fundamental nor efficient. They are just rote methods of getting the right answer . . . unfortunately, not all the time because the arithmetic is actually an additional rote mental process. The pencil applied to paper is merely the scoreboard of the process.

Furthermore, this fundamental approach fails almost totally, beyond obtaining square roots, unless

log and trig tables are available. Most microcomputers have log and trig functions built-in to a precision and in-use reliability far better than the average school tables.

STAYING ALIVE

The crux of the matter is survival. The kids are eagerly grabbing the first generation of full-feature appliance computers. Parents ask, "What use is there for a computer?" Teachers question, "How do I teach programming when I don't know how to program myself?"

But survival is chancy. For certain, the future is almost never a linear extrapolation of the present—more people, more cars, more jobs, more of everything that we have now. Change is exponential and explosive. Worse yet, it is unpredictable and virtually uncontrollable. Hard as one may try to predict the future and its limits, the unknowns are often just beyond current knowledge.

Consider the last two years, during which the number of people learning to program computers increased by a factor of 100 times. Until 1977, the rank of computer programmers was limited by the high cost and low availability of computer systems. Even in 1979, universities were awarding master's degrees in computer science to graduate students who had never actually had a computer to operate. They had been trained to program with pencil and paper and sometimes even to operate a Hollerith card punch, which was fed by an operator when machine time became available. There was no interaction between the person and machine.

Low-cost computers changed that, and the interactive programming process allows people of entirely different personalities to program computers. The sheer number of programmers now in training with high-level languages on so many computers creates an incredible societal change in itself. Low-cost computers have already made programming a hobby—even a pastime—and removed it from the realm of the industrial-media complex.

CLASSROOM COMPUTERS

In the spring of 1978 it was difficult to obtain delivery of any of the big three appliance computers designed for volume production. By our school district definition, an appliance computer was a complete functioning system, preferably self-contained, operating in a standard BASIC in ROM. By the spring of 1979, the big three—the Radio Shack TRS-80, 16K; the Commodore PET 2001, 8K; and the Apple II, 16K—were readily available.

Our school system had selected, tested and found the Commodore PET satisfactory. In our area, the

TABLE 1 Computer survival course for seventh, eighth and ninth grade students

Course Objectives

1. To learn the fundamental principles of BASIC programming with a microcomputer.
2. To apply BASIC programming techniques in the high school curriculum, extracurricular activities and to personal requirements.
3. To supply a student with a sufficient base to proceed independently in programming study and application.

Course Outline

Hours: 8:30 AM to 12:30 PM

Day 1	8:30– 9:30	Parents Meeting—Program Director
		Student Orientation—Staff
	9:30–12:30	The PET Computer
Day 2	8:30– 9:30	The Elements of Algebra
	9:30–12:30	CAI BASIC
Day 3	8:30– 9:30	The Elements of Algebra
	9:30–12:30	CAI BASIC
Day 4	8:30– 9:30	The Elements of Geometry
	9:30–12:30	CAI BASIC
Day 5	8:30– 9:30	The Elements of Trigonometry
	9:30–12:30	CAI BASIC/Text Assignments
Day 6	8:30– 9:30	Applications—Graphics
	9:30–12:30	CAI BASIC/Text Assignments
Day 7	8:30– 9:30	Application—Problems in Geography
	9:30–12:30	Text Assignments—Sports
Day 8	8:30– 9:30	Applications—Simulations in Sociology
	9:30–12:30	Text Assignments—Astronomy of the Sun
Day 9	8:30– 9:30	Applications—Space Travel
	9:30–12:30	Text Assignments—Mars Flight Simulation/Planetarium
Day 10	8:30– 9:30	Computer Careers
	9:30–12:30	Applications in High School

"CAI-PET BASIC Compleat," *The Paper,* Box 43, Audubon PA 19407.

Text: Thomas A. Dwyer, Margot Critchfield, *BASIC and the Personal Computer,* Addison-Wesley Publishing Co., Reading MA 1978.

school system had begun in 1978 with two PET computers for a teacher orientation and a classroom lending program. On this base, and with the addition of a third unit, 17 teachers had each received 14 hours of individual instruction with the PET. Every participating school had a loan computer for a minimum of 20 school days. Each of more than 600 students had access to a computer for at least ten hours. The result was that school administrators, teachers and an enthusiastic group of students wanted to move forward.

To demonstrate the idea that schools should think in terms of filling a classroom with computers,

we sought and obtained a small grant for an experimental intensive summer course for gifted/talented seventh, eighth, and ninth graders. Twenty students selected by participating schools would have access to 20 PET 2001 computers for about 40 hours. In this grade span it was necessary to cover the fundamental principles of algebra, trigonometry and geometry.

But the course was intended to be multidiscipline, and the necessary mathematics base was integrated in computer program applications in geography, astronomy, space travel and a simulated round trip exploration of Mars. A set of computer programs simulated landings and takeoffs as well as the interplanetary flight. The simulation took place in a planetarium where the special-effects projectors and a mock-up of the interplanetary vehicle-array added realism to the exercise. The course outline is given in Table 1.

In our 15,000-student school system, we had forecast that in this, the second year, there would be 20 computers for the children at the secondary level. There will actually be 42 computers in the system. The five-year forecast is for 756 computers in this system on the basis of full school use—through the elementary grades for computer-aided instruction; in the middle schools, with a fundamental course in program integration with a mathematics and science curriculum; and in the high school, with advanced courses in programming with a wide range of multidiscipline applications.

Ambitious? No. It's a matter of survival in a new age.

Making the Grade at Keene High School

Dennis Brisson

Keene (NH) High School increased its enrollment last fall by 13. That's the number of TRS-80 microcomputers the school brought into the classroom for its computer-programming classes. Although the use of desk-top computers for individualized instruction is in its infancy at the school, computer use and instruction is not a new idea. Indeed, Keene High was one of the first public schools in New Hampshire to make use of computers.

If KHS can be credited with breaking new ground in the computer-education field, then its principal trailblazer is Charles Tousley, math department head, who has taught programming at the school for the last 13 years. During that time, he has seen the

From "Making the Grade at Keene High School," by Dennis Brisson. In *Kilobaud Microcomputing,* June, 1980. © 1980 by Wayne Green, Inc. Reprinted by permission.

school experiment with various computers. It was his pioneer spirit that recently prompted KHS to board the microcomputers-in-education bandwagon.

Tousley was well tutored in the fundamentals of computer programming. He notes with some pride, "I learned BASIC from the man who invented the language, Dr. John Kemeny." As part of a contingent of representatives from Vermont and New Hampshire public schools, Tousley studied the time-sharing system at Dartmouth College under the direction of Kemeny in 1967. Having learned the intricacies of programming, he operated the high school's time-sharing terminal, which hooked into the Dartmouth system. But this arrangement for teaching programming was expensive. "It cost $6000 a year just to rent the equipment," explains Tousley.

In 1972, Keene High discontinued this system and purchased programmable 8-bit calculators for its computer classes. In 1976, the students learned programming on a PDP-11 minicomputer, which the Cheshire Vocational Center, adjoining the high school building, purchased.

Advances in the computer industry produced other, less expensive, alternatives. The microcomputer had arrived, making individual use by students a practical means of teaching programming. Tousley's eyes brighten as he recalls, "Two years later, along came the TRS-80."

PROBLEM OF FUNDING

Early on, Tousley recognized the value of microcomputers in education as effective in increasing student achievement and in motivating students. However, finding people who shared his enthusiasm proved difficult at first. One such person who shares his vision of future school uses of micros is John Amstein, head of the science department at the school, and instrumental, together with Tousley, in setting up the school's microcomputing program.

Whereas Tousley learned BASIC just two years after its development, Amstein is a self-taught programmer and a relative newcomer to computers. Despite these divergent backgrounds, the two are working together toward a common goal: establishing microcomputer use at the school for all subjects. Tousley explains: "John, who hadn't done any work with computers at all until this year, at least has the enthusiasm I've got; he recognizes the importance of them." He adds, "We are always dumbfounded when we can't find the same enthusiasm in the people who control the drawstrings on the purses."

Obtaining funds for innovations in education, particularly microcomputers, is difficult at best, as Tousley, who follows closely the latest develop-

ments in computer education and the problems of other schools, is well aware. With school boards and administrators grappling with the rising costs of running a school, they are reluctant to defend the initial investment for computer equipment. They question, too, the cost-effectiveness of microcomputers as compared to the more traditional teaching aids.

Tousley sees this thread of thinking running throughout the nation. "We all run into the same problem: administrators and school-board members went to school when there weren't any computers. So trying to convince them that computers are a necessity in the curriculum is a heck of a hard job," he laments.

Tousley feels that the schools' money couldn't be more wisely spent. On this point, he is as persuasive as he is determined. Approaching the school board for the OK on this year's microcomputer expenditure, Tousley was armed with a convincing statistic he derived while thumbing through the help-wanted ads in a Boston Sunday paper: over 75 percent of the employment opportunities required some knowledge of computers or a related math background.

The previous year, the school board approved the purchase of two TRS-80s, which "proved so satisfactory in the classroom that we went to the board again the following year to ask for more money."

He got the money—not the $10,000 he requested from the school board, but $9000 the board allocated from a special school source, the Academy Fund. This year he's going after more money to purchase more computer equipment. He's seeking $4000 from the Academy Fund and a federal government Title IV three-year grant for $40,000. He modestly explains his success: "Basically, I recognized the importance of computers and their place in school, and I just kept after people until we got the money to get them [the microcomputers] into the classroom."

EDUCATORS' REACTIONS

Getting computers into the classroom is one thing; convincing others of their teaching potential is another. Tousley has been instrumental in encouraging and aiding area schools to establish microcomputer programs. But he has encountered obstacles. He has run up against educators who are reluctant to accept computers, to experiment and explore the potential of computers as a teaching tool. He cites administrators who dislike the prospect of curriculum changes involving computers because "it means changing all the methods they've developed over the years."

Even more myopic are math teachers "who are serious when they can't even think of any uses for computers. They can't imagine why computers are anything other than toys," Tousley says in disbelief.

Through the education of the people involved, the trend is changing, according to Tousley. "We're fighting a constant battle with people who are entrenched in the old way of doing things. Hopefully, this will gradually change. I know it will," he adds optimistically.

Today's students, born in the computer era, will reap the benefits of an advanced technology that has resulted in computer-assisted instruction. But today's teachers in the high schools, and even in the grade schools, face a challenge: how to deal with the influx of microcomputers in the classroom.

At Keene High, Tousley sees a positive reaction among the teachers. He is quick to point out that the Keene High administration has been supportive of the microcomputing program, and inquisitive teachers have borrowed the TRS-80 manuals and units ("admirably suited for self-learning") to learn programming at home in order to better understand the educational value of these machines.

Next year he plans to initiate workshops for the teachers about computers and their potential for classroom teaching. His enthusiasm for, and belief in, computers is catching . . . particularly among his students.

USES IN THE CLASSROOM

Tousley's students need no supervision, nor anyone to tell them to begin class. Computer programs allow the students to practice and learn on their own, with immediate feedback on their progress. When not in use by the programming classes, the micros are in operation by the students during their free periods.

The purchase this year of the 13 Level II 16K TRS-80s was a joint project of the school's math and science departments. As presented by Tousley and Amstein to the administration, the microcomputing program involves three phases.

The first phase seeks student involvement—to familiarize the students with the fundamentals of programming and introduce them to all the capabilities of the microcomputers. Tousley has found that the best way to introduce students to computers is through hands-on experience. He concentrates on the graphics capabilities of the computers and relies heavily on computer games to spark student interest.

Game playing is a fundamental first step in learning the use of computers. But for most students, the game-playing stage lasts briefly before they realize the potential for more constructive uses and become eager to write their own applications. The school even boasts its own computerized radio station where the

DJs can call up information on the latest Top 40 hits or recording star on the station's TRS-80.

"The first year of the project, we're trying to get as many people acquainted with the computer as possible. We want to mass-produce enthusiastic students," says Tousley.

As students use the computers more and as teachers become more involved, Tousley and Amstein predict that ideas for applications in the classroom will blossom. Outside of the programming classes, the computers see limited use in computer-aided instruction (CAI). The school uses some CAI programs to drill students on the concepts of algebra and basic math. CAI programs are also used in science: genetic cross-breeding, population growth and diet-calorie analysis programs for biology. A student who was in Tousley's computer-programming course last year and is a physics student in Amstein's class this year converted a sun-tracking program into TRS-80 BASIC.

Tousley's programming classes include about 32 sophomores and juniors. As seniors, with the knowledge of BASIC programming, they will be expected to write their own applications in the physics and science classes, an idea particularly appealing to Amstein, who ranks the computer as valuable a tool as the microscope to teach science.

Phase two of the microcomputing program involves creating applications programs and expanding the school's collection of science and math program tapes. Teachers would probably prefer plug-in software, but the KHS program calls for the students to write their own, thus expanding the learning process involving computers.

Although the amount of software on the market is growing, Tousley and Amstein cite the general lack of educational programs. They realize that computers as educational tools are only as effective as the programs written for them. So they plan to develop their own; the students will write their own applications for use in advanced math, geometry, calculus, physics, chemistry and biology. Compiling a library of good program tapes will take time.

In the third phase, Tousley and Amstein want to see the widespread use of computers throughout the school in all subjects. As Amstein explains, the school's immediate future goals include equipping a complete computer classroom, installing a computer in each of the school's 18 classrooms, and making computers available to students in the library during their free time.

"By the third year of the program, we should have a large supply of program applications. We want people to realize that computers are not just tools for math and science, but for English, foreign languages and who knows what else," explains Tousley.

CHOOSING THE TRS-80

After investigating the various microcomputers on the market, KHS opted for the TRS-80 over the PET ("tiny keyboard design was a major mistake") and the Apple ("twice the price"). From the outset, Tousley was convinced that the TRS-80 was the computer for the job at KHS. "I can't see how anyone is going to compete against the TRS-80. It's the best one for the job. It isn't the best computer in the world, but for its price, and for what we want to do with it in school, there's no other competing model."

Quality and low cost were the two main features of the TRS-80 that prompted the school's selection. The availability of nearby service and the maintenance support offered by a local Radio Shack store also appealed to the school, as did the unit's portability, which allows it to be transported from classroom to classroom. The trigonometric-functions capability was also attractive.

Next year the school plans to buy several more TRS-80s, line printers and the Radio Shack Network System, which allows up to 16 microcomputers to use the same disk drive. The classroom setup at present features a large, modified TV-screen monitor from which Tousley can instruct the entire class. Each computer is comfortably situated on its separate desk-top area, with a place for keyboard, cassette recorder and monitor, as well as a CLOAD and CSAVE switch modification constructed by Tousley.

CLASS DISMISSED

Many educators, such as Tousley and Amstein, believe that computers are destined to have a profound influence on the way we educate our children. More educators are investigating the impact of computers on the education process—not just as tools for teaching, but to prepare the students for post–high school education and for a world increasingly influenced by and dependent on the use of computers. Their place in the classrooms at Keene High has been assured by the enthusiastic reception by students and faculty.

After a brief period at the computers, the students are anxious to begin computer applications programs. Quiz and data programs, storage for foreign-language vocabulary and other data-storage uses are several applications the students are working with.

While no student has yet developed a program to replace the teacher in the classroom, the day is fast approaching when a computer in every classroom will become a reality.

Kids and Computers: The Future Is Today

Sally Greenwood Larsen

Computer dealers in Racine, Wisconsin aren't surprised any more when an eight year old in overalls, a striped T-shirt, and bumper tennis shoes strolls into the store, sits down at the keyboard of a TRS-80, and writes a computer program for the drive-up window of a McDonald's restaurant. Or a program to print out all the even numbers from 1 to 100, in four columns, with a half-second delay in between. Or a graphics program for a birthday cake, complete with blinking candles.

Jefferson Lighthouse Grade 3 Computer Programming Students

These third and fourth graders are students at the Jefferson Lighthouse School, a program for gifted and talented children, where I teach BASIC programming as part of their mathematics classes. With an average of 45 minutes a week of group instruction over the past year, students in these classes have mastered the concepts covered in introductory college courses in programming, and have become adept in the use of the school's microcomputer. In an area where a strong math background has been a customary prerequisite, it is amazing to realize that most of these children are just learning to multiply and divide!

Our microcomputer is in use from the minute school opens in the morning until the last child leaves in the afternoon, and the only games they play on the machine are those they have written themselves. It's exciting to watch, and even more fun to teach. For a society which will be computerized beyond our imagination by the time these children are adults, it is sad to see the majority of elementary schools using their affordable, portable microcomputers only for computer-assisted drill-work, or playing guessing games. Children can easily learn

Flowchart "How to Get a Date with Amy Carter"

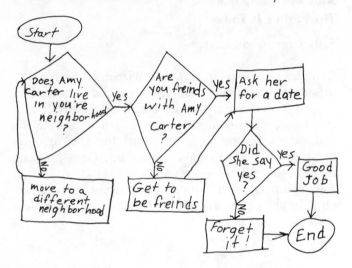

to write their own programs. However, the elementary teacher who wants to teach programming to kids faces the problem of finding materials which take into account their conceptual development and reading levels. Finding relevant examples is also not an easy task. Physics problems and checkbook balancing simply will not do.

I dealt with this problem by writing my own materials, building the lessons on the following framework:

1. What is a computer?
   A perspective on why computers came to be, what they are used for, and what kinds of jobs they are and are not capable of doing.
2. How does a computer carry out your instructions to get a job done?
   An explanation of simple linear logic, using flowcharts.
3. How do you communicate your instructions to the computer?
   The BASIC language.
4. How do you put together a program which is both efficient and creative?
5. What uses do we make of computers? What new uses can we invent or forecast?

Children have funny notions about machines in general, and especially computers. They need a mental picture of what goes on inside a computer, and its purpose.

WHAT IS A COMPUTER?

When a caveman had work to do, he had no tools or machines to help him. He had to do it all by himself.

Man has since invented many tools to help him with his work.

Instead of pounding with his hands, he now uses a hammer. The hammer lets him pound harder and longer than he could with his hands alone.

Man invented the telescope so that he could see farther into space. He can now see stars he did not know existed before he had the telescope to help his eyes.

Using his brain, man can remember information and solve problems.

Man wanted to invent a tool so that he could extend the use of his brain, so he invented the COMPUTER.

Just as a hammer can't do work without a person to hold it, a computer cannot do work without a person to run it, and tell it what to do. This person is called a PROGRAMMER.

Even the best hammer cannot do all the different things our hands can do.

And even the best computer cannot do everything our brains can do.

A computer cannot feel emotion. It cannot feel happy or sad, as we can.

A computer can't combine ideas like our brain can. It can't put two ideas together and take the best parts of each one to make a brand new idea.

BUT . . .a computer can do some of the simpler jobs our brains can do. And it can do some of them even faster than our brains can!

A computer can remember many more things than most of us can with just our brain, especially things like long lists of names or numbers. Information stored in a computer is called DATA.

A computer can compare data, to see if one thing is bigger than another, or smaller, or the same. It can also put things in order.

A computer can sort lots of pieces of information and put together the things that are alike.

And a computer can recall the information a computer programmer wants, and print it out for him on a video screen or a sheet of paper.[1]

Once the children have an overview of the function of a computer, they need to see graphically how a computer program breaks down a task into small steps, and progresses in linear fashion from one step to another. Simple flowcharts, showing an activity with which the children are familiar, produce an easy to digest and sometimes hilarious picture.

Now the children are ready to see that the way in which we communicate with a computer must be standardized, and we need a particular language for this purpose, and a set of rules for typing in statements on the machine. After group instruction in operating the keyboard, and statements dealing with the execution of the program, such as CLS, BREAK, NEW, LIST, RUN and END, the children can do a surprising amount of experimentation with the simple PRINT statement and its variations.

[1] From "The Apple Corps: An Introduction to the Apple II for Children," by Sally Greenwood and Dr. Donald Piele, 1978.

HOW TO SCARE YOUR MOM WITH AN ELEPHANT

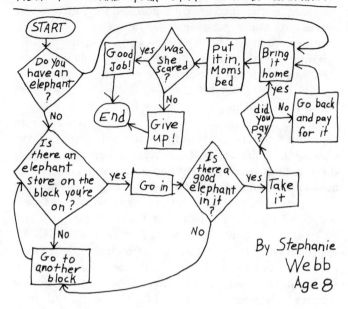

By Stephanie Webb Age 8

PRINT "My name is Jerry DeMaio. I love computers."
PRINT "RIGHT"
PRINT "LEFT"
PRINT
PRINT "8-4"
PRINT 8-4
PRINT "*?&$#%)"

It is essential to schedule all the children on the computer at least once a week, so they practice what is learned in group instruction. Pairs of children seem to work best, for one child alone gets "stuck" too often, and three or more argue over who will type on the console.

Allowing the children, especially the youngest groups, to use prepared game programs at this point is a serious mistake. It kills their desire to put in the effort required to learn BASIC since canned programs are so much less work. It is interesting to note that when game tapes are made available to children who are already fluent programmers, they will typically play them once, LIST them and see if they can pick up any programming tricks and then abandon them.

Worksheets to check the children's progress and provide practice are helpful, especially when machine time per child is limited.

To build the complexity of their programs, the children now need to learn the concept of a **variable**, and GOTO statements. Trying to teach variables to children who have had no algebra frightens many teachers unnecessarily. The simple picture of a series of mailboxes, all labeled with a name or a letter, and holding different numbers as specified, works beautifully.

COMPUTER PRACTICE
30 OCT. 78
NAME _____

Simulate these computer runs. Show your "printout" on the screen.

```
10 CLS
20 PRINT "BIG"
30 PRINT
40 PRINT "YELLOW"
50 PRINT "BLUE"
60 END
```

```
10 CLS
20 PRINT "THE ANSWER"
30 PRINT 30*2
40 PRINT 30+2
50 PRINT "30-2"
60 PRINT "THE END"
70 END
```

Here is a program and "printout." Find and fix the mistakes in the programs so a run will produce what is shown on the screen.

```
10 CLS
20 PRINT 20+6
30 PRINT 30+4
35 PRINT
40 PRINT "60-3"
50 PRINT 10-10
60 PRINT "HELLO"
70 END
```

```
26
34
57
0      HELLO
```

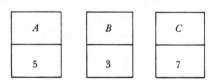

A	B	C
5	3	7

If the "mailboxes" are drawn on the chalkboard, a simulation of a program can be traced carefully, and most children will have no trouble understanding how a memory works. In this case, they have an advantage over the algebra student, in that eight year olds see nothing peculiar about the statement

$$X = X + 1$$

With the addition of INPUT and RND functions, the student now can produce quite a wide range of programs. To complete a beginner's course in text programs, the more difficult IF-THEN and FOR-NEXT are taught in a very concrete fashion.

The children picture themselves as "traveling" through their own programs, doing each of the statements in turn, and imagining they see this sight when they reach IF-THEN:

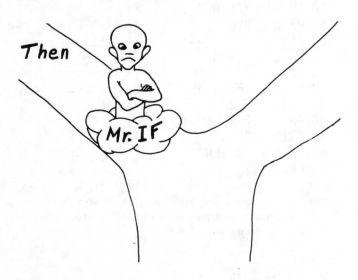

Mr. IF will only let them pass to THEN if they meet his test. Otherwise they must proceed down the open branch of the path. When deciding on the test to go on to THEN, they must figure out who Mr. IF wants to go down his path, or who he wishes to exclude.

FOR-NEXT statements are best saved until last, and shown as a shortcut method for accomplishing a more complex list of simpler statements.

```
 5 X = 1            5 FOR X = 1 TO 4
10 PRINT X         10 PRINT X
15 IF X = 4        15 NEXT X
   THEN GOTO 30    20 END
20 X = X + 1
25 GOTO 10
30 END
```

The basic tools of the graphics program, SET and RESET, along with the other function statements covered earlier, enable the children to make their own initials on the screen (always a big favorite), draw pictures of objects, and design a myriad of programs, using horizontal and vertical lines, as well as individual points.

Numbered graph paper, along with much practice on naming coordinates of a point, contribute to the success of these programs. On a system with color graphics, such as the Apple, beginning with graphics programs, rather than starting with PRINT statements, is a natural. But either approach works well.

Once the children are able to write a program without consulting their notes for statement meanings, and are able to conceptualize a program from beginning to end without the use of written flowcharts, they are ready to evaluate their work under the headings of **efficiency** and **creativity**. The teacher must stress that there are many ways to write the same program, just as there are many ways to express the same idea in English, but some of the ways are awkward, or have extraneous steps, or could be approached better from a different view of the problem. As can be imagined, it takes a great deal of work before an elementary school programmer reaches this point, and some never will until they become older.

The last portion of the teaching framework, looking at new uses for computers, can vary from collecting information on existing systems and research, to inventing new systems of their own. This is a natural place to discuss hardware and software, and form opinions on whether computers can "think."

Soon after the children are able to write their own programs, prepare yourself for the following events:

1. If you want to use your school's computer, you'll need to make a reservation a week in advance.
2. Parents will call you and want to know why their child is suddenly speaking a foreign language, with words like "do-loop" and "glitch."
3. Santa Claus will be having a few choice words with you.

I have found computer programming to be an exciting way of teaching thinking skills, mathematics, and problem solving. It is highly motivating for children whose abilities range from average to very bright, who have enough reading and number skills to operate the keyboard. It gives young children a view into their future, while at the same time seeing the present in a new light.

I am anxiously awaiting the day when these kids are college freshmen, and they walk into their computer science course with **ten years** of programming already under their belts at age eighteen. The implications for their futures and ours stagger the imagination.

Computers at an Alternative School

Deborah Stone

High Valley is a small private tutorial school in rural Dutchess County, New York, founded in the 1940s by Olga and Julian Smyth.

High Valley is an old farm, and our school buildings are old farm buildings. Our students have animals to take care of and a great deal of space (almost 120 acres) to explore.

The main features of High Valley which distinguish it from other schools are as apparent to the eye of the casual visitor as to those of us who know it best. It does not look like a school. An old farmhouse is our center, and the old barns and other outbuildings of the farm have been converted to form inviting classrooms.

There are only twenty students here, almost half day students and the rest five-day boarders. Some of our students are here because they have done badly in school, some because their parents think other schools have done badly by them. The students range in age from eight to eighteen.

The staff roles are extremely fluid, especially for the four of us who live here. We all assume disparate and shifting roles as needed; each of us is available to be the special friend or port in a storm to any student, regardless of whether we are that student's assigned teacher.

The upper-middle-class orientation and style of most other private schools is lacking. Private schools tend to have a strong emphasis on conventional standards of academic achievement, while High Valley's group is so diverse that the focus instead is on the development of each pupil's potential and learning style, with achievement for each individual meeting his or her own idiosyncratic needs and abilities. This is a pervasive ethic, as can be seen in the free and understanding personal relationships between students of obviously different abilities on a conventional scale. Thus the school introduced the practice of mainstreaming long before it was fashionable or indeed had a name.

The High Valley approach to teaching is built around caring relationships and personal attention. As a community we hold a morning meeting, take meals together, and do chores around the farm. As individuals all students are given challenging work, whether they are at an advanced academic level or at a more formative, foundation-building stage. There are no grades, as these introduce mean-

ingless standards of comparison. Our approach does not mean that things degenerate into hanging around until you find yourself. Children are less likely to find themselves through introspection than through finding honor in doing something well.

Our contact with computers began casually. One of the boys' fathers brought, at different times, Sol and Sorcerer computers for the kids to play with. Response was enthusiastic. "Lunar Lander" on the Sol was a popular program, and one of the kids found out how to make it harder or easier. Some were especially interested in the graphics, and one boy invented lovely patterns in very much the same way he liked to noodle around with music on the piano or guitar. We could see in all this the kind of independent, mischievous thinking that we are always so glad to encourage in our students.

Though getting our own computer seemed to be the thing to do, we circled around the decision for a long time. With the help and advice of a few parents, and the kids who had been most involved, we narrowed our choices down to the Apple, the Sorcerer, and the Radio Shack TRS-80.

After mulling it over we chose the Apple, for the completeness of its package, its high-level facilities, and its legendary reliability. The original purchase (in February '79) was a 16K Apple II without disk, to be used with cassette storage and a black-and-white TV. Contributions from a number of enthusiastic parents helped make the purchase possible. Since that time it has been upgraded to 32K, with a disk and color TV. Our next step will be to get the full 48K of memory and a printer.

We have been very happy with the choice. One repair was needed after a year and a half—we think that's pretty good. (A friend of the school later gave us a TRS-80. This unit is underutilized, partly because we don't have a disk drive for it yet. As a result, however, our two computers give us a computer-to-student ratio of one to ten—a rather high figure, we understand.)

Due to the delicacy of the equipment, we have had to exercise some caution about access to the machine. Our computer center is a lockable room (shared with our photographic darkroom equipment); some of the students have permission to go there alone and some must go in the company of others.

One of the charms of the situation has been that the faculty knew absolutely nothing about the computer, and weren't even too interested. Aside from the one parent who got us started, who would drop by every few weeks and ask how it was going and give the kids pointers, teaching about the machine has by default, been left to the students who understood it; the kids have been free to do it on their own. They had no guidelines from us about what you're supposed to do with a computer, because we didn't *know*.

Games were the first things that the kids tried on the computer. They loved Breakout, which came with the original cassette configuration. As a game, it gave us an immediate sense of the computer's approachability. It also provided a gradual transition to more serious use and understanding of the computer. Creating modified versions of Breakout by changes in the program created much enthusiasm, and provided indirect programming insights to students who were not yet interested in learning to program. The Animals game, which is supplied with the disk system, has also been very popular among students at all levels.

The Animals game is a simplified data-base system which gives considerable insight into the nature of stored information. The program tries to guess what animal the player is thinking of, by asking about the animal's traits in a "twenty question" yes-or-no format. If the animal you are thinking of is not yet in the data base, the computer asks you how to distinguish that animal from the one it already has stored which is most nearly like it. Your present animal is then stored along with all the rest, and thus joins the computer's repertory.

The thing that's interesting about Animals as played at High Valley is that some kids put wrong information in it inadvertently. Confusion has arisen over the question "Does it give milk?" which for some kids signifies Cows, for others Mammals, and by others is seen as excluding males. Thus a large and somewhat inconsistent data base has evolved which I suppose has educational value even in its inaccuracies.

Some kids played Star Wars and Breakout until they were able to knock down all the bricks, then lost interest entirely. But always there have been others who are interested in working with the computer.

They have had all kinds of different reasons. One wanted to hang out with our two experts. Another had an older brother who was involved with computers. Two other boys enjoyed learning programming.

Several of the students have written their own programs. Two of them have become real pros. (One boy has already bought his own Apple computer, with his parents' help, and has found work as a professional computer programmer and consultant in addition to his high school studies.) Another student has begun saving for an Apple.

Our computer has turned out to be like everything else around here that we use—it figures in our personal relationships and our learning experience. For instance, one boy wrote a story in which the computer came alive and spoke to him when he was trying to play Breakout. In response to his story, one of our experts programmed the computer so that the next time the boy went to play Breakout, the computer greeted him with exactly the words he himself had written in the story. He loved it.

Having the kids teach themselves and each other has in general worked out very well. There has been no formal attempt on the part of the staff to use the computer in our teaching, but our two hotshot programmers did make some teaching programs for fellow students who were having trouble understanding fractions.

However, the arrangement has left something to be desired in terms of the amount communicated to the students who don't put themselves out to learn about it. For our first year and a half of experience, however, we are very pleased.

HOW IT FITS IN

The way we work with our children is based on a humane respect for children's dignity and worth, and an awareness of and a readiness to meet children's emotional needs.

I am beginning to suspect that while having learning difficulties in regular school may reveal weakness, vulnerability and inadequacy, it may also betoken a kind of integrity and strength to resist that which is not of oneself. The cost to the bright conformers of moving successfully through the school years without having a chance to develop their own ideas or work for their own reasons is probably very high in terms of loss of creativity, originality and strength of inner-directedness. Many kids who won't do well in school are secret computer geniuses, because there nobody is telling them what to do.

There are teachers who are not afraid to renounce the safety, the predictability of a method in which they are the imparters of prescribed information to docile, uninvolved, anonymous minds. It has been my good fortune to work in a school where children are allowed freedom to learn. We hope that more people who are as truly themselves as they can be will go into teaching, or will start schools that will let other people—children—learn to be themselves also.

Computers can be a part of this. Our experience with computers at High Valley has been positive and enjoyable, and has shown the adaptability of computers to the alternative-school setting.

Explaining Microcomputer Information Storage to Children

Daniel Edward Behmer

The general population has a tendency to personify computers, so it is not surprising to discover this tendency among elementary school children. Science fiction movies and books have led many to believe that a world full of wonders is available NOW if only they believe it is possible. That sense of wonder and belief is a marvelous attitude in children, but if not channeled properly it becomes counter-productive as they interact with the real world of men and microcomputers. Fantasy can either promote or obstruct a solid understanding of how microcomputers operate. Teachers must learn to channel the fantasies of children so that they lead to a more accurate correspondence with reality.

Most of us who work with microcomputers have been guilty of making statements such as "The computer says," or perhaps, "When the computer asks your name, type it on the keyboard." Of course we know that the computer cannot in fact ask anything; that it is the program that calls for a response. I think that it is important to be as accurate and truthful in this small instance as it is for parents to tell their children eventually that there is no Santa Claus. The personification of a microcomputer may be charming in its innocence, but counterproductive in its effect upon a child's understanding. In the long run it will block the development of real understanding within elementary school children.

A case in point is the way that we teach children how a microcomputer stores and retrieves information. If it is difficult to convey an accurate notion of this process to adults, how much more difficult it is to accomplish the same task with children. Their lack of experience with technology, limited vocabulary, and short attention span would suggest to teachers that the concept be taught in a different and possibly non-technical manner.

One approach would be to capitalize in a positive way upon the willingness of children to use their imaginations! The challenge for a teacher would be to balance the use of imagination with sufficient scientific facts so that the children would be led to a more accurate analogy—a view of the microcomputer that would both communicate and inform. Too often teachers settle for a use of imagination which leads only to entertainment. I believe that the joy of using the imagination and the joy of learning are not mutually exclusive. The art of teaching involves learning how to adapt teaching procedures to the characteristics of the learner. Indeed, adult learners would be aided at times if they could approach learning with the wonder and imagination of children.

In order to illustrate this point I have written a brief story-analogy which attempts to teach children how microcomputers store and retrieve information. It is a fundamental concept, and one that is difficult to teach at every level.

From "Explaining Microcomputer Information Storage to Children," by Daniel Edward Behmer. In *The Computing Teacher*, December, 1979. Reprinted by permission.

The target audience for the story is children who are in the third through the fifth grades. It could also be used with older students, but in that event the vocabulary and approach should be adjusted to fit their maturity.

The story presumes that the teacher has either brought an actual microcomputer into the classroom, or at the very least has given children an opportunity to see pictures of one which are on display around the classroom. The best preparation for the story-analogy would be for the children to have an actual hands-on experience with the microcomputer by means of a math or language drill. From such an experience could emerge questions which NEED to be answered such as: how does a microcomputer remember a child's name, or how does it record a child's answers.

The story-analogy should be read to younger children, making allowance for them to interrupt and comment on their personal experiences with the microcomputer. With older children it might be more effective to assign the story for silent reading and use a follow-up discussion to develop and clarify their notions about how a microcomputer accomplishes storage and retrieval tasks.

I have attempted to make the story-analogy both simple and accurate. That is difficult to accomplish, and I would appreciate hearing about the experience of those who use it with their pupils. I expect that modifications will be appropriate. In addition, it is my hope that elementary school teachers will begin to design more appropriate methods for aiding children to use and understand microcomputers.

THE SECRET OF THE NUMBER WAREHOUSE
(A secret you can tell)

Somewhere in your classroom is sitting one of the strangest warehouses in the world. It is strange for two reasons:

1. It contains more storage rooms than any other warehouse in the world; and
2. Most of the warehouse storage rooms are empty most of the time!

Some warehouses store furniture, while others store bicycles or clothing. This warehouse is different, however; it only stores numbers! The numbers are very long, and only one number can be stored in any storage room. Can you imagine how hard it is to remember where all the numbers are stored in the warehouse if each has its own storage room? It helps to put an address on the door, just like an address on someone's house. In that way, the storage room can easily be found again.

Even your school has a number on each room so that pupils and teachers can find one another easily. Most schools contain less than 64 rooms. Just imagine: a number warehouse can contain up to 64,000 storage rooms. That is a very great number—a thousand times more rooms than are in your school! How was it possible to build so many storage rooms? One way was to make them very, very small. They are so small in fact that you cannot see them with your eyes. They are so small that 4000 storage rooms can fit on half of an ordinary postage stamp. That is small indeed!

The warehouse has so many storage rooms that they are counted by the thousands. For example, one warehouse can contain as many as 64K (64,000) storage rooms. Other warehouses contain 32K or maybe only 4K—that is, 4000 rooms.

Now the mystery really deepens. The number warehouse is sitting right in your classroom today. Do you know where it is? Here is a description that will help you find it. Most of the warehouses look exactly the same on the outside no matter how many storage rooms are on the inside. For example, a number warehouse with only 4000 storage rooms (4K) is about the same size as a warehouse with 64,000 rooms (64K). So, if you want to find such a warehouse, do not expect to recognize it by its size alone. Most look like a small breadbox. They have a typewriter keyboard in front so that numbers can be entered, as well as a television screen which shows what has been typed.

Now what have we said about the number warehouse so far? It is shaped like a small breadbox; it has a typewriter keyboard in front; it has a small television screen which shows what is typed; it has up to 64K storage rooms for numbers but they are so small that they cannot be seen. Finally, the number warehouse is somewhere right in your classroom!

Have you guessed where it is yet? Of course I have been talking about a MICROCOMPUTER! Your teacher either has one in your classroom, or has shown you a picture of one. A microcomputer is a number warehouse which can contain up to 64K (64,000 storage rooms). Each of the rooms has a number address. In those rooms are stored words and instructions in the form of numbers.

When someone types on the microcomputer keyboard, you will see words appear on the television screen. The microcomputer is able to store all the words and show them to you many times. That is possible because all the words are changed into numbers, and those numbers are stored in separate storage rooms within the warehouse. If you know the address of the room where a number is stored, you can find it again and turn it back into a letter, a word, or other information.

Your teacher will probably show you an interesting game or other activity on the microcomputer. First, your teacher must give the microcomputer a list of instructions called a PROGRAM. The program instructions are stored at many addresses in the number warehouse. If the program has 50 instructions, then the program may occupy thousands of storage rooms. Just one instruction may occupy 50 addresses or more. One by one, each of the storage rooms is found by means of its convenient address, and the numbers stored inside cause the microcomputer to do wonderful things: play games, help you with your lessons, or even play computer music!

When the electricity to the microcomputer is turned off, it is a completely empty number warehouse! Only when the electricity is turned on and your teacher types instructions on the keyboard are some of the storage rooms filled. It is important to remember that the microcomputer can only do what you or your teacher instruct it to do. Without those instructions, the microcomputer is unable to do anything but wait, and wait, and wait.

The final secret of the number warehouse is that it can follow instructions with the speed of lightning! It sometimes takes hours to type the instructions on the keyboard, but the microcomputer can follow all those instructions in only seconds. It is like a magician whose hands move so quickly that you do not SEE him hide a coin, and so it seems to vanish into the air. When the microcomputer follows the instructions of a program just as quickly, you are fooled into believing that the microcomputer was able to think all by itself.

Now you know the secret of the number warehouse called a microcomputer. It stores words and other information in the form of numbers in any of its 64,000 storage rooms. They are easy to find again because each room has its own address. As long as the electricity is turned on, the microcomputer is completely empty. It remains that way until you or your teacher put something into that number warehouse.

So the secret of the number warehouse is a secret you can tell your friends. Together with your teacher you can use the magic of the microcomputer to help you learn more and have fun at the same time.

The World Inside the Computer

S. Frederick D'Ignazio

Kids use personal computers to play games. What are these games? Often, they are *simulations* or *models*. In creating computer games, kids are learning to build

From "The World Inside the Computer," by D. Frederick D'Ignazio. In *Creative Computing Magazine,* September, 1980. Copyright © 1980, Ziff-Davis Publishing Company. Reprinted by permission.

miniature replicas of the universe—models of the real world and worlds of fantasy woven from the threads of pure imagination. As personal-computer technology evolves, and as the child becomes a more knowledgeable and sophisticated model-builder, his or her models will become increasingly life-like, dramatic and enchanting. Volcanoes will roar, thunder and belch black plumes of ash and smoke. Fire-breathing dragons will appear unexpectedly along dark and slimy, mazelike corridors. Heroes and heroines will arrive on the scene, accompanied by the child's personally composed epic music.

Consider for a moment, the youngest children —the preschoolers and the primary-school kids. These children are to be envied. Their inquisitive minds, their natural inventiveness, and their unbridled imaginations are perfectly suited for the personal-computer devices—"the mind tools"—that lie just around the corner.

The question arises: "How should we introduce the computer to these kids?" Certainly we should abandon the approach followed in the past. At that time computers were often pictured as rows of boxes connected by skinny lines and arrows. To the young child the computer was a curious hodgepodge of *memory* boxes, *processor* boxes, *input* boxes, and *output* boxes.

Then, with theory out of the way, the child was shown pictures of a real computer: stark, black-and-white photographs of hulking, whooshing tape drives, squat card readers laden with stacks of punch cards, and huge switchboard panels teeming with tiny blinking lights. And who did the child see working with these machines? Solemn, silent people servicing the machines, feeding them and communicating with them. Everyone was well-dressed. It was a lot like church.

Obviously, a new approach is needed to introduce the new, personal computers to the youngest children. Of course, within only a few years, this will cease to be an issue at all. Then, home computers will be so common that even the youngest child will first learn about computers by watching his or her mom and dad or older brother or sister. Shortly after, she, too, will be talking and listening to the computer, making it play musical tones, and painting pretty pictures on the computer screen with her light "brush."

But for now, an alternative approach is needed. One method has been recently tried and been proven effective, and I'd like to briefly describe it to you. This method consists of introducing computers to young children using my picturebook, *Katie and the Computer*. The book is a fantasy adventure story, but one with an important twist: each episode in the story parallels the functions of a real computer as it processes a real program. The program itself

isn't an "adult" program, producing business-like and adult results. Instead it is a *FLOWER* program that produces something interesting for the child: a pretty picture and an attention-grabbing sound.

Introducing computers to children via an adventure story accomplishes many objectives. First, it captures children's interest. And, in becoming interested, the children identify with and become personally involved with the adventures of the heroine in the story as she journeys through the computer. Second, it establishes an important connection between computers and drama, color, imagination, action and excitement. And last, unobtrusively, yet deeply and effectively, the adventure story familiarizes the child with the key words associated with computer components and with the major processes occurring within a computer. The components are metaphorically realized as landmarks in *Cybernia,* the world inside the computer. The processes appear as episodes in the story.

KIDS, MEET KATIE AND THE COMPUTER!

Katie's father was waiting for her when she got out of school. He was very excited. "Katie," he said, "our computer came!"

"Oh, boy!" said Katie. "Can I play with it?"

"Sure," said her father, and they rushed home.

Katie and her dad arrive home. Her dad types the word "PARROT" on the computer, and a bright green parrot appears on the screen and says, "SQUAWWK!"

Katie wants to make something, too. Her father has her type the word "FLOWER" to make a picture of a flower.

As Katie typed "flower," she leaned closer and closer to the picture screen. Then she lost her balance and fell forward. But instead of bumping her nose on the glass, she went right through it and began spinning and falling, just as if she'd tumbled off the top of a tall mountain.

So begins Katie's adventure with her magical computer. On her whirlwind trip through the world of *Cybernia* inside the computer, Katie bobsleds down the vertical face of a mountain, parachutes from an airplane, slides down a slippery brass pole, gets fired from a cannon, and comes face to face with a monster robot spider.

She also meets a variety of characters in Cybernia. There's a fiery *Colonel,* "a curious-looking man in a fancy soldier's uniform." There are the *Flower Bytes,* each with a letter from "flower" painted on his or her uniform. There is the *Table Manager,* "a frail, frazzled looking man with fists full of paper scraps." There are the *Flower Painters* "who grab buckets of gleaming paint" and who "move like whirlwinds." And there is the "mean and tricky" program *Bug,* perhaps the most memorable character of them all.

The Origin of Katie and the Computer

Catie's nose banged into the computer picture screen. "WAAHHH!" she howled.

I leaned forward, grabbed her under the arms, and took her into the kitchen to her mother. "She's done it again," I complained. "Bounced forward on my lap, right into the computer. She keeps this up, and she's going to break her nose on the screen."

"Or maybe go right through," my wife mused.

"Go right through? And get tangled up in wires or get a blast from a hot cathode?"

"Not at all," Janet said, smiling. She wiped away our daughter's tears. "Catie wouldn't find wires or cathodes. She'd find adventure and zany characters, just like Alice did when she fell down the rabbit hole into Wonderland. Only this wouldn't just be a "land," it would be a whole world, a world inside the computer."

Janet loves children's books. It was just like her, taking something complicated and technical, like a computer, and turning it into a fairy tale. "But once Catie fell into the computer, how would she get out?" I asked.

"You're so anxious to write a children's book," Janet said. "Here's your chance. Write about Catie's adventures to teach little kids how a computer really works."

"But I still don't know how she gets out," I said. I imagined a bizarre scene in which Janet and I used cranes and pulleys to rescue two-year-old Catie from the electronic bowels of the computer.

"You'll think of something," she said.

And she was right. We were on the interstate just outside South Hill, Virginia, in the middle of a long trip back from Pennsylvania. Caught between the monotonous boredom of the road and hyped up on coffee, I began seeing an animated cartoon of "Catie and the Computer" right inside my head.

I pulled off the road and drove up to a Pizza Hut. "I'm starving," I said. "And, besides, I've got to write this down."

Without explaining, I hopped out of the car and dashed into the restaurant. When Janie and Catie walked in, a moment later, I had already accumulated a stack of paper napkins, and I was busily scribbling—blotting blue marker and tearing the paper, but capturing the story as it flowed from my brain.

When we left the restaurant, I carried my precious napkins with me in a tight little wad. We finished our drive back home to Chapel Hill. The next day I called my friend Stan Gilliam, a local artist. Stan and I had gotten together several times trying to figure out a kid's picturebook we might collaborate on. "I think I've got an idea," I told Stan. I rushed out to his place, a tiny log cabin nestled against a forested hillside south of town.

When I got to Stan's I began telling him the story. I stood up, paced around the room, and gestured wildly as I talked. We both became excited. Stan reached for his drawing pad. Swiftly, nimbly, he began sketching scenes from the book as I described them. "Here's the Colonel," he said, "and Catie, and the mean and awful Bug."

(continued)

I had never worked with an artist before. I couldn't believe my eyes. It was like magic. My words were being turned into pictures, even as I talked. This is going to work, I thought. We've got ourselves a book!

Well, not quite. First, I had to write the words down. (Up until then, all I had were scribbled notes on an untidy stack of Pizza Hut napkins.) Second, Stan and I began endlessly revising the pictures and the words, to get them to work together harmoniously and dramatically.

We attended an evening course on children's literature and presented our story to the class on its final meeting. I told the story in spite of a bad case of laryngitis. And a sudden downpour threatened to wash away Stan's watercolor illustrations as he pulled them out of the trunk of his car and made a frantic dash to our instructor's front porch.

While we revised our words and pictures and attended our course, Stan and I conducted a literature search for other children's picturebooks about computers. After an exhaustive search, we only managed to turn up two titles in over ten years, and both books were completely different from ours.

We began sending our proposals: to ten publishers, twenty, forty, eighty, a hundred. Finally, almost a year after the fateful visit to the South Hill Pizza Hut, and after three false starts with other publishers, we sold our book to *Creative Computing.*

Now the real work began. Stan started turning out page after page of original, full-color illustrations. Meanwhile, with guidance and help from Burchenal Green, our editor at *Creative,* I revised my manuscript another dozen times. I cut the story's voluminous descriptive passages and relied on Stan's pictures to visually convey each scene. I had to throw out most of my big words in order to make it possible for a second or third grader to read the book herself. And there was the balance to strike between the book's two main goals: *entertainment* and *education.* I had to walk a swaying tightrope and make the episodes metaphorically parallel the functions of a real computer yet keep them action-oriented, dramatic and exciting.

Finally, the story and illustrations were ready. At the last minute, we changed the name of our heroine from "Catie" to "Katie," to avoid mispronunciation. We persuaded our editor, Ms. Green, to retain the story's villain, the Bug, who we felt, though scary and evil, was a dramatic highpoint of the book, and still (on many occasions) metaphorically accurate. We suffered through endless delays with the book's printer and binder. But the book was finally ready. On December 20, 1979, on Catie's fourth birthday, she and I drove up to New York City and jointly autographed the first copy of *Katie and the Computer.*

What does Katie do inside the computer? She tries to get the computer to paint a picture of a flower. Is she successful? Does the flower get painted? Does Katie escape from Cybernia and return to the real world?

Over four thousand children have "met" Katie and the computer, and have heard me tell the story through to its climactic conclusion. The kids' ages range from 3 to 11. I've told the story at a day care and at a dozen elementary schools. Over time I've developed three different approaches to telling the story, depending upon the age or grade-level of the children.

Inside the computer it was snowing

With the youngest kids (the kids at the day care and the five- and six-year-olds), I concentrate on the story as an *adventure* rather than as a *technological metaphor*. I tell the story on my feet, acting out the parts and adopting voices for each of the characters. For example, when the Table Manager talks, he has a quivering, squeaky falsetto. But when the huge and horrible Bug appears, my voice deepens into a gravelly, threatening roar.

As I talk, I pace back and forth in front of the kids, waving my arms, leaning from side to side. I try to dramatize each of the story's major episodes. In one episode, the Colonel smacks the Table Manager with the flat part of his sword to get the Table Manager's attention. In expressive pantomime, my arm and my imaginary sword arc high in the air, then swoop down. My hand loudly slaps the back cover of the book, giving the Table Manager a resounding "SMACK!" on the bottom.

Later in the story, Katie and the Flower Painters hop aboard a Cybernian Bus and leave RAM Tower, the Flower Painters' home. Just as the bus begins rolling, the Colonel arrives and makes a giant leap onto the bus' tail end. Playing the part of the Colonel, I back up, then run forward and jump high into the air. I close my eyes and make believe I'm Mikhail Baryshnikov hurtling gracefully across an opera stage. But like the Colonel landing on the bus, I come crashing down onto the schoolroom floor, puff noisily and holler, "Head to the CPU, then on to the Tube for some fireworks!"

As I'm telling the story, I punctuate it with numerous sound effects, just like those in the book. Katie lands "FLUMPFF!!" in a bank of feathery snow. The Flower Bytes' bobsled pulls up in front of the CPU with a "SHHHUUUUPPP!" And the cannons roar "BOOOM!! BAROOOM!! BOOOM!!" as they "belch colorful clouds of fire and smoke into the nightime sky."

Also, I try to get the children to participate in the story as much as possible. For example, I point to illustrations in the book, and have the kids call out: "R-O-M!!" "C-P-U!!" and "R-A-M!!" As Katie races through her adventures, I have the kids constantly spelling out "flower." And when I reach the part of the story where the Flower Bytes line up in the CPU and call out their letters to the Table Manager, I get six eager volunteers to stand up, stick out their chests, hold their heads high, and yell out their letters: "F!" "L!" "O!" "W!" "E!" "R!"

At the end of the story (which takes around twenty minutes to tell), I pop out of the fantasy and remind the children that Katie's computer wasn't real, it was magic. But I make it clear that real computers are *almost* magic. I tell the kids about integrated circuits that keep getting smaller and smaller. I talk about whole computers that fit inside a paper clip, million-byte bubble memories smaller than a kid's thumbnail. I talk about the computer's amazing speed—how it can do thousands, millions and someday billions of things in a single second. Then I answer the kids' questions and make sure to get the kids talking about what computers mean to *them*.

The parts of the book that I use with this youngest group are the story itself, of course, and the magnified image of the computer chip that appears at the end of the book. Also, I tell the kids that a real computer doesn't have little people running about; that, instead, the computer is powered by tiny bursts of electricity zipping about at a fantastic speed. I show the kids the page that says, "MEET THE FLOWER BYTES." Pointing to the Flower Bytes, I tell the kids that each byte is made up of charges of electricity, whizzing single file along the computer's wires. I remind the kids how the bytes themselves, all in a row, bobsledded down the mountain to the CPU.

Half magic

The next group of kids are the seven- and eight-year-olds, kids who are in the second and third grade. From experience, I've learned that the book's fact and fantasy mix together just right for these kids. They're at the tail end of the picturebook age, and they still have a great appreciation for magic and fantasy. Yet they are old enough to understand the computer concepts introduced in the book.

I enjoy telling this group about some of the applications for small computers, including robots, computer music and computer "paintbrushes." We talk about such things as computer *animations, movies* and *cartoons*. I ask the kids what kinds of movies and cartoons they might create, what kinds of sound effects they might use. We talk about composing theme music and creating computer graphics for computer games, and about animating characters on the video "stage." On occasion, Stan has appeared and enriched this discussion with the ideas and techniques he used to illustrate *Katie and the Computer*.

With this group, too, I begin by telling the story,

complete with characters' voices, bounds, leaps and frantic arm waving. Also, I often bring along a small computer, like a *PET* or an *Apple II*. After I tell the story, I open the computer up to show the kids the electronics inside. But there is a problem. The element of fantasy becomes so real for these kids that when they crowd around the computer they want to know where the characters from the story are—*especially the Bug!* "Let's see the robot spider!" they cry. "Where does he live?"

So I've developed a response, a way to make a clean break between the real and fantasy sides of the book. Now, as soon as I've read the story, I walk over to a table and grab a chair. "You have just heard a story about Katie's magic computer," I begin. "If you want to see a real computer, go to a shopping mall and visit a Radio Shack. Radio Shack stores have a computer known as the TRS-80."

"Let's pretend that I'm in a Radio Shack right now." I point to an empty spot right in front of the chair. "Let's say I've just entered a Radio Shack and walked over to a TRS-80 computer sitting in front of this chair. Say I've read the story of *Katie and the Computer,* and I want to be like Katie and somehow get into Cybernia, the magic world inside the computer.

"I look all around. I want to be sure no one is watching. Good. The coast is clear. Real quietly, I step up onto the chair. Then, before anyone can stop me, I fold my hands together, and, like the Table Manager in the book, I dive like an eagle—right into the TRS-80 computer!"

In the classroom or library, with the kids' mouths wide open and the teachers looking amused or perplexed, I crouch down low on the chair, then spring high into the air, and come crashing to the floor with a loud "THUMMPP!!"

I run over to the kids, eyes squinting, a serious look on my face, and ask, "If I really did dive into a computer, would I r-e-a-l-l-y fall inside, just like Katie?"

Usually, I've looked so absurd and ridiculous that the kids' sense of realism takes over, and they all cry, "Noooooo!"

"What would *really* happen?" I ask.

"You'd crash into the glass!"

"You'd break the computer!"

"You'd get all tangled up in the wires!"

One third grader, blessed with a vivid imagination, had a more elaborate answer: "You'd fall into the computer, but you'd blow up and be splattered all over and be all around. And then you'd be electrocuted!"

After that one, I had little worry about some gullible kid trying to mimic Katie and jump inside a real computer. At least I knew *I'd* never try it.

Binary numbers, adventure games and robots

When I tell the story, the most charming kids are the ones in the first two groups. They get thoroughly wrapped up in the fantasy, yet, with a little prompting, they easily make the leap back to the world of real computers.

When I talk to the third group, the kids nine years old and older, things are different. These kids are past the picturebook age, and they look at picturebooks as babyish and beneath them. Also, they're more skeptical than the younger kids and more likely to resist the strong element of fantasy in the story.

The real pleasure I get with the older kids comes after the story is finished. Then I can use the entire book as it is meant to be used: as a teaching aid. I use the factual section at the end of the book to teach the kids about computer *hardware* and *software*. I use the "Pictorial Outline" in the front of the book to show the kids how a real computer would process a "FLOWER" program and display a color image of a flower on the picture screen. And I teach the kids about *binary numbers* and *computer translation* with a scene where the computer's operating system, pictured as the blustery, imperious Colonel, summons the Flower Bytes:

> *"This is where the Bytes live," the Colonel said. "Each Byte has a letter or number that's all his own." The Colonel reached for his bugle. "I use this to summon the Flower Bytes," he explained. "It only plays two notes, but I can arrange them into a special song for each Byte. Listen, and you'll see."*
>
> *"BLEEETT!" burped the bugle. "BLAATT! BLEEETT! BLEEETT! BLEEETT! BLAATT! BLAATT! BLEEETT!"*

I flip to the page called "MEET THE FLOWER BYTES." As the book does, I tell the kids about high and low electric charges and how a "BLATT!" from the Colonel's bugle means a high charge or a *one*, and a "BLEEETT!!" means a low charge or a *zero*. I stand at attention, like the Colonel, and begin loudly blowing my imaginary bugle. I play a special song for each Flower Byte. At the end of each song, I get the kids to use the *ASCII* table in the book (illustrated with cartoon pictures of each Byte) and tell me which Byte's song I just played.

I especially like telling the older kids about *adventure* games. We get into a discussion of model-building and simulation—of real worlds and worlds of fantasy. When I have time, I mix computers and creative writing. First, I have each child write up the script for a simple adventure game. Second, we read the scripts out loud. Last, we discuss how the games might be implemented on the computer, and we try to come up with enhancements to make the games more exciting.

One of the most popular parts of my presentation

deals with computer-controlled robots. Kids love them! A lot of articles have recently appeared in kids' periodicals about young inventors who are building robots in their folks' basement workshops, in their bedrooms, even in their apartment-house kitchens.

At the beginning of the discussion, I make up an imaginary robot whom I call *Humphrey*. Humphrey looks like a cross between a lawn mower and a garbage disposal, but he's a lot smarter: he can beat me at backgammon and chess, he's great at bluffing, and he has an endless repertoire of wisecracks and one-liners.

What's more, he's pretty silly. And using Humphrey's silliness to lighten the discussion, I introduce several basic computer concepts and techniques, including *programs, bugs, loops* and *recursion*. For example, I turn to the page in the book where the Bug lassoes Katie and the Colonel's yellow airplane with his sticky bubblegum rope. Katie and the Colonel hang on for dear life as the monster swings their little plane round and round in a loop, "like a merry-go-round gone crazy."

I tell the kids about bugs and loops in real computer programs, then I describe a short *LOGO Turtle* program.[1]

```
TO LOOP :SIDE :ANGLE

10 FORWARD :SIDE
20 RIGHT :ANGLE
30 LOOP :SIDE :ANGLE

END
```

Together, the kids and I work through the program and "discover" that it makes Humphrey go around in a circle (or loop). We talk about how the program works and about loops and recursion. Then I play the part of Humphrey executing the program—with input values of 10 centimeters for SIDE and 15 degrees for ANGLE. I goosestep swiftly through one loop, then another, and another, and another. After awhile I become so dizzy and uncoordinated that I collapse in a heap in front of the giggling teachers and kids.

In talking about programming, I like to touch on the computer's literal-mindedness: How a computer only does what you tell it—nothing more and nothing less. How you may not know exactly what you told it. And how this produces results that are sometimes humorous, sometimes alarming, but always unpredictable.

I talk about bugs and how they creep into programs unexpectedly. I illustrate this problem with another performance from Humphrey. This time Humphrey's mischievous young inventor programs him to play a prank on his big sister. Humphrey is to go barging through the bathroom door, unannounced and uninvited, and surprise the kid's big sister in the middle of her bubble bath.

Unfortunately for the kid (and his big sister), there is a bug in Humphrey's program. The kid told Humphrey to do only one thing: go FORWARD :SIDE. But he set SIDE equal to four meters, and it is only 3½ meters to the bathtub. Humphrey enters the bathroom. Accompanied by horrified shrieks from big sister, he paces forward four meters, bangs into the tub, and does a front flip, landing on big sister's lap and burying himself in pink bubbles.

I'm not sure the teachers appreciate this example, but the kids love it. It always provokes an animated discussion about robots, programs, bugs and big sisters in bathtubs.

SPRINGBOARD TO THE FUTURE

Katie and the Computer is a picturebook adventure that acts as a powerful aid in introducing computers to young people of widely varying ages. The book's color, action and exciting story have served to stimulate children's interest and imagination, making the factual discussion following the story lively and productive.

Admittedly, the story is a fantasy based on magic. But consider the remarkable fantasies children are already spinning on small computers. Consider, too, the fabulous pace at which computer technology is advancing. In this light, *Katie and the Computer* can be seen as a springboard to a *real* future that is waiting only for kids and small computers to grow up—*together!*

WHAT'S YOUR OPINION?

1. Educating by computer is more cost-effective than by traditional teaching aids.

[1] This example was inspired by *Turtle* robot "Micro-World" programs. The programs, written in LOGO, were found in Ellen C. Hildreth, "The Creation of Design: An Exploration in Art, Mathematics, and Creativity," Cambridge, Mass.: LOGO Project, September 1977.

2. Computers are chiefly classroom toys.
3. Teachers should rely initially on graphics and computer games to spark student interest.
4. The computer can be as valuable a tool as a microscope is in teaching science.
5. With an average of 45 minutes a week of group

instruction over a one-year period, third and fourth-grade students can master the concepts covered in introductory college courses in computer programming.

6. The best games for students to play on the computer are those they have written themselves.
7. When children are programming at a computer, pairs seem to work best. One child alone gets stuck too often, while three or more argue over who will type on the console.
8. Allowing students to use prepared programs kills their desire to learn a programming language to develop their own software.
9. Teaching the concepts of variables in BASIC to children who have had no algebra should not frighten teachers.
10. Games give an immediate sense of the computer's approachability.
11. Having kids teach themselves and one another about computer programming generally works out very well.
12. Using fantasy can promote a solid understanding of how microcomputers operate.
13. It is possible for educators to teach programming when they themselves don't know how to program.

EXERCISES

1. When children enter their first college computer science course with ten years of programming experience behind them, how will this influence the course content of the college class?
2. A computer-awareness class often has students who own a computer. Discuss ways of making productive use of these students in the classroom.
3. List three common experiences of childhood that could be used as the basis for helping children to develop the kind of thinking that uses the problem-solving skills necessary to program computers. (Refer to the "peanut butter and jelly sandwich" presentation by Marilyn Burns.)
4. Answer the question posed in the reading "Computer Survival Course for Kids": "If you're going to teach seventh- and eighth-graders computer programming, what are we supposed to teach them when they are freshmen?"
5. Would you allow your students to play computer games in class? After class? Why or why not?
6. What are the advantages and disadvantages of keeping student records (test scores, attendance) on file in a computer?

7. How might computers be used in the future to help individualize classroom instruction?
8. Following are three hypothetical situations followed by a list of considerations to be taken into account when dealing with each. Use the background you have gained from this book and from class discussion to outline your proposal.

(a) The board of education has allocated $7500 for the first year to initiate a computer-literacy program for gifted students. You have been asked to implement the program. There are approximately 30 eligible students (grades one-six) in your school.

(b) You have been asked to design an experimental pilot project to see how computers could be beneficial to a district's 6000 students in three high schools, three junior high schools, and 11 elementary schools. The board has allocated $20,000 for this program. What projects would you suggest? Consider:

    (1) projects in various schools
    (2) project in one school
    (3) bus students to one school
    (4) move project from school to school
    (5) others

(c) The district has asked you to organize a computer in-service day at the local fairgrounds for the district's 210 teachers. All teachers would have the day off to attend this professional development session. Consider:

    (1) what learning activities would be available
    (2) student participation
    (3) teacher participation
    (4) vendors (hardware and/or software)
    (5) length of day
    (6) workshops
    (7) speakers
    (8) committees required

9. For all three parts above, consider the following:

    (1) resource people
    (2) location
    (3) needed personnel
    (4) curriculum (programming, CAI, games, tutorials, literacy, and so on.)
    (5) hardware (which model, storage devices, peripherals)
    (6) software and books
    (7) future considerations
    (8) class logistics
    (9) overall validity of the project

SEVEN

Computers in the Arts and Humanities

Computer-literate educators are finding increasing applications for computers in the fields of English, art, music, social studies, and other nontechnical subjects. Teachers who have had no prior exposure to computers often express pleasant surprise at discovering the "friendliness" of personal computers. The use of authoring languages is more common in these applications, and other software techniques such as word processing are frequently employed.

Unfortunately, although some of the more interesting and innovative software is to be found in the arts and humanities, teachers of culture-oriented courses are often the last to realize how beneficial the computer can be to their programs. As teacher-oriented computer-literacy courses become more common, however, it is expected that a wider range of teachers will be exposed to the advantages of microcomputers in the classroom. In Chapter 7, Jones reports on this relatively new area of computer application. Ettinger and Rayala discuss the interfacing of computers and art education.

Computers in the Arts and Humanities

Beverly J. Jones

Avant-garde artists and musicians as well as educators working in universities and experimental facilities have been exploring the various ways that computers can be used in their tasks. They have written computer programs which assist them in composing visual, musical and literary forms, programs which perform stylistic analyses of these forms, and programs which retrieve information from or about them.

Educators in universities, experimental facilities and public schools are studying and experimenting to discover methods for utilizing computers in precollege education in the arts and humanities. These projects have included using the computer as (I) an instructional device to teach basic concepts; (II) a compositional medium; and as (III) a device to help students analyze and criticize. Instructional analysis and management programs have also been written. This paper will describe a few of the projects which are being conducted by those working in the arts and humanities as both practitioners and educators. An attempt will be made to derive implications for the future of computer applications in precollege education from the results of these projects.

I. INSTRUCTION IN FUNDAMENTALS

Within each of the arts it is presumed that students will receive instruction in certain fundamental concepts and skills. The ability to recognize the basic

From "Computers in the Arts and Humanities," by Beverly J. Jones. In *The Computing Teacher,* February, 1981. Reprinted by permission.

structural components and perform simple tasks using these components is usually included in instructional goals. To effect these instructional goals, several computer assisted instruction (CAI) programs have been created and tested in music, visual arts and the humanities.

Music

Programs for teaching music fundamentals to various age groups have been developed at a number of facilities. Among these are the Minnesota Educational Computer Consortium, PLATO projects, at University of Illinois and the University of Delaware, Ohio State University, University of Georgia, University of Iowa, Stanford, and State University College at Potsdam. Both Stanford University and the University of Delaware have developed systems for instruction and research in ear training. Drill and practice and game-simulation strategies are used to teach pitch and interval recognition, dictation of melody, chords, harmony and rhythm. Exercises to assist the student in sight-reading and instrumental methods have also been developed. Studies which have been conducted on groups of students using these instructional programs indicate that the computer assisted instruction is as effective or more effective than conventional instruction. A system which has been developed at the University of Delaware Plato Project called GUIDO is designed so that the instructors using the system can study individual differences among students as well as group tendencies.

A glance at Table 1 indicates the range of programs for teaching music fundamentals available at some institutions. This table is not meant to be all inclusive, but indicative of the commonalities and differences between instructional programs in music fundamentals.

Humanities

Within the humanities there are a variety of approaches to teaching fundamentals. Pauline Jordan lists in an index of community college English lessons computer-assisted-instructional units on "capitalization, composition, editing, grammar, poetry, punctuation, research, spelling, usage, vocabulary and miscellaneous." These seem to reflect a concern with the basic structural elements of language and some of the concepts necessary to successfully combine those elements. Language instructors in French, German, Spanish, Latin and ancient Greek are using computers to teach vocabulary, grammar and translation skills. At a higher level of difficulty, but still essential to a fundamental understanding in humanities, are programs which assist the student in identifying key ideas in their reading of literature and philosophy.

M. Miller at Pacific University in Washington has developed programs which attempt this task. He has designed a series of computer assisted instructional units which aid students in identifying key concepts in their assigned readings in philosophy. The skills necessary to understand the basics of language—spelling, vocabulary, grammar, the structure of literary forms—and the more complex skills of understanding and interpreting these forms have all been taught using computer assisted instruction.

Visual arts

The identification and manipulation of the components of visual design may be considered fundamental to an understanding of the visual arts. Further, a conceptual grasp of the varieties of visual combinations and interpretations these components may evoke is also fundamental to a basic understanding. There are fewer individuals and institutions involved in the study of computer uses in teaching visual arts fundamentals than there are in music or humanities. However, among those active in this area are the computer research group at Ohio State University headed by Charles Csuri. Recently this group has incorporated the techniques developed by June McFee and Rogena Degge for teaching fundamentals of perspective and the depiction of three dimensions on a flat surface in a computer assisted instructional program for elementary school students. At the University of Delaware, Raymond Nichols has developed a number of lessons in art fundamentals for the PLATO system. These include "Composition Using Grey Scale Tones, Design Aesthetics and Creation and Letter Spacing" among others which stress the computer as a medium rather than as an instructional device for basic concepts. According to Nichols, his program, unit design, provides a solution to four distinct problems which occur with beginning students in the foundation courses in visual design:

1. The restriction which is placed on the visual presentation of the student's ideas resulting from the level of the student's basic technical (hand) skills;
2. The final solution having been dictated not by the student's aesthetic tastes but by the fact that it is easier to change one's tastes than it is to change the actual design;
3. The difficulty involved in the instructor's evaluation due to the different mixtures of technical and conceptual skills of the students, making it hard to separate the two areas for discussion or criticism; and
4. The difficulty for the instructor in presenting an effective criticism to the student (given that the

UNIVERSITY OF IOWA	
Grand Staff	Primary & Secondary Triads
Ledger Lines	v^7 Chord
Ascending Intervals	Primary & Secondary v^7 Chords
Descending Intervals	Secondary 7th Chords
Major & Minor Scales	Primary & Secondary Diminished 7th Chords
Scale Keys & Signatures	Neopolitan 6th Chord
Triads	Augmented 6th Chords

UNIVERSITY OF GEORGIA

Notes & rests
Time Signatures
Complete the Measure
Keyspinner Game
Keyboard Notation

STATE UNIVERSITY COLLEGE AT POTSDAM

Clefs
Intervals
Tetrachords
Scales and Modes
Key Signature
Trichords
Triads
Progressions

MECC APPLE

Music Theory—Vol. 1, Version 1
Introduction
Name the Note
Enharmonics
Keysigs
Terms
Musicai
Staffint
Note Types
Counting
Music Theory—Vol. 2, Version 1
Wrong Note
Missing Note
Rhythm
Rhythm Play
Whole-half
Find-the-Half
Scales
Triads
Sevenths

C.A.I.

THE OHIO STATE UNIVERSITY

Grand Staff
Ledger Lines
Octave-Transposition Signs
Intervals
Triads
Seventh Chords
Placing Chords in Keys
Altered Chords
Modulation

UNIVERSITY OF ILLINOIS (PLATO PROGRAMS)	
Tests & Measurements in Music Education	Micro-Teaching in Music Education
Instruments Methods Series (wind & percussion instruments)	Critical Incidents in Music Education
Percussion Terminology	Hand Signals for Music Teachers
Violin Fingering Drill (elementary school level)	Elementary Music Fundamentals
Viola Fingering Drill (elementary school level)	Part-Writing
Instrument Recognition (elementary school level)	Jazz Chording

Table showing programs for computer-assisted instruction in music fundamentals. *(Information derived from: Hofstetter, Fred T. "Foundation, Organization, and Purpose of the National Consortium for Computer-based Musical Instruction." Moursund, D. (Ed.) "MECC Apple Software," The Computing Teacher, Volume 7, No. 3)*

experiences and tastes which the instructor uses for his/her evaluation are not the same experiences and tastes that the student uses in receiving and evaluating the criticism) which makes a clear understanding between the instructor and the student quite difficult.

The program does this by reducing the technical skill necessary for the execution of the design and by providing all students with the same range of choices which may be implemented with equal ease so that any evaluation on the part of the instructor will not have to take into consideration the manner in which the design was done but only the compositional success of the design. Other programs in the PLATO system at the University of Delaware include work in typography, basic illustration, advertising design and portfolio preparation.

Both Aaron Marcus at UC Berkeley and Kenneth Knowlton at Bell Labs have developed courses which utilize the computer as a graphic tool for developing visual concepts and graphic design. The content of these courses presents a promising approach to teaching not only art fundamentals but the programming skills necessary to implement designing on a computer graphics system. Ken Knowlton has developed a computer language called EXPLOR for the teaching of computer graphics and computer art. A smaller version of this language will run on mini-computers. It is called MINI-EXPLOR and requires only 8 to 16K of core memory storage. It would appear that courses such as these would be useful to instructors who wish to learn to use the computer in creating computer assisted instructional materials in the visual arts.

Implications

What general concepts may be derived from an examination of some of the diverse projects related to instruction in the fundamentals in the arts and humanities? It would appear that many of the repetitive aspects of teaching fundamentals are quite ably handled by computer assisted instruction. This may permit students to have greater control over their learning process in several ways. They may repeat a task as many times as necessary to achieve success without incurring the impatience of their instructor or slowing the progress of other students. Not only may their individual learning rate be varied but the level of material presented may be varied with greater ease than in a conventional classroom so that greater instructional flexibility results.

Even so, utilizing the computer in an instructional mode which dictates the range of student choices causes some educators to question its appropriateness. Certainly, if this were the only instruction available it would be questionable. However, if several alternative programs are available and the instructor is also present, it would seem these programs could contribute to the quality of an instructional package. The instructor may be freed from the continual repetition involved in teaching such topics as pitch detection, sentence construction, or optical letter-spacing and may concentrate on assisting individual students utilize the knowledge and skills acquired while interacting with these computer assisted instructional lessons. The extent to which the use of this type of instruction is appropriate is a question which each person developing curricular packages needs to consider. Too great a use of drill and practice type materials will lead to the charge that the computer is being used to program students, limit their choices and concepts.

II. COMPOSING WITH THE COMPUTER

Visual artists, musicians, dancers and a few poets have experimented with the computer as a device for creating artistic forms. Usually they have attempted to emulate traditional artistic forms using the computer as a designing or composing device. However, some are interested in exploring the unique qualities of the computer as media.

Music

Computer instruments available for composing and performing music range from small handheld musical calculators to the elaborate facilities of the Center for Computer Research in Music and Acoustics (CCRMA). Computers have been used to control or emulate traditional and electronic instruments as well as serving as unique digital musical instruments or controlling unique musician-built devices. A January 1980 report from the Center for Computer Research in Music and Acoustics states:

> As a musical instrument the computer system is possibly the most flexible of all instruments. To speak of it as a conventional musical instrument, however, is somewhat misleading because the system is capable of simultaneously producing a large number of independent voices having arbitrary timbral characteristics. It is much more general than a conventional musical instrument in that it can generate any sound that can be produced by loudspeakers, modify and transform real sounds entered into the system by means of microphone and digital-to-analog converters, remember and modify articulated musical input and simulate the location and movement of sounds in a variety of illusory reverberate spaces.

and later:

> Using the most powerful synthesis and programs, all developed at CCRMA, faithful replications of natural sounds are synthesized for the manipulation of perceptual data in the psychoacoustical research, for musical composition based on the natural sound, and for composition where natural sound is a rich point of departure for new and novel sounds.

Studies conducted at the Center examined the way in which sounds made by conventional musical instruments are constituted. The information gained from these studies allows a computer controlled musical synthesizer to emulate the sounds made by the conventional instruments. Thus, a person using the computer controlled synthesizer could hear a composition played by a simulated violin, clarinet, oboe, and cello, by a single instrument, or by a simulated full orchestra. The space in which the sounds are played may be varied also. For example, the reverberations achieved in a large concert hall or in an intimate drawing room may be simulated. Several universities have facilities which allow music students to utilize some of these capabilities.

Lief Brush at the University of Iowa is one of the avant-garde musicians or artists interested in the unique qualities of the computer as a musical instrument rather than as a device to emulate the sounds made by conventional musical instruments. The "instruments" which he has created are unconventional and sometimes blur the distinctions among musical instrument, sculpture and conceptual performance piece. An example of his work is the Riverharps structure. This instrument consists of four concrete steel beams forty feet in height which are anchored and serve as supports for five layered banks of fifteen wire strands, each spanning a river.

The wire strands emanate from ten wooden trestles, five located on each side of the river. There is also a master control booth on the river bank and three modules which comprise a floating performance barge. The wire strandage is designed to respond to ambient sounds and sounds resulting from direct contact with the wires from both natural and man-made sources. Thus the sounds absorbed for transformation by this "instrument" would include such diverse sources as thunder, insect and bird voices, wind, raindrops, and human-made sounds such as performances by poets, instrumental musicians, vocalists and dramatists performing on the barge surfaces.

Within the control booth the composer using the Riverharp decides which audio resources, qualities and combinations are desired. The use of electronics and computer control is essential to the success of experimental instruments of this type.

In addition to emulating conventional instruments and acting as a control mechanism for unconventional instruments, computers are sometimes used as a control to conventional instruments. For example, David Ashton reports the development of a project using a computer controlled organ in conjunction with a graphics scope. Children aged four to twelve, as well as adults, used the equipment to compose music and to manipulate compositions presented to them.

Humanities

Fewer projects using the computer as a compositional device have been conducted in the humanities than have been conducted in visual art or music. The computer has been used to experiment with poetic composition. Early work along these lines made extensive use of the random selection from a set of programmed alternatives. Programs of this sort are frequently used in elementary schools to compose haiku or cinquain.

Students input a series of alternatives for each section of the poetic form, then use the computer to compose alternative poems using the input in various combinations.

More recent work involves the use of programs used in stylistic analysis. These make it possible to compose within stylistic rules controlled by the programmer rather than by random selection. Several complex experimental programs have been devised to generate poetry and study the writing of poetry based on analytical research.

Some poets and artists interested in the visual qualities of poems are constructing concrete poems using the computer as a graphic designing tool. The results of these experiments blur the distinction between the literary and visual arts. Aaron Marcus is among the graphic designers experimenting with computer generated concrete poetry. Programs intended primarily for computer graphics such as those which select and generate symbols and typographical forms which then alter their size, slant, or location are suited to the development of concrete poetry.

Visual arts

There are some interesting parallels between the projects developed in music and in the visual arts. Artists are using the computer to emulate and facilitate conventional processes. A few are also interested in developing artistic forms which can only be created with the aid of a computer. Some conventional art processes have been radically altered by computers. Most notably graphic design, industrial design, advertising art and film animation have been affected. Many of the examples of these visual images which we see today have utilized the computer as a designing tool or have used it to facilitate the process in some way. Similarly, those involved in the design and execution of woven textiles frequently rely on computer assistance for some phase of their work. Artists working in fine arts areas such as sculpture, printmaking, drawing and painting are experimenting with the computer as an aid to design or execution of their work. The speed with which designs can be created, manipulated and stored in a computer graphics system contributes to its desirability of use by artists.

The line between the arts is blurred by individuals who use the computer to create unique instruments (i.e. the Riverharp). Bonacic and Ihnowitz are among those artists who have created their own computer controlled sculptures which are responsive to changes in their environments such as alteration in light, sound and movement. Other artists are trying to create responsive environments which change their shape, color, lighting, air movement and temperature in response to a variety of inputs from the artist or from the participants in the environment.

Implications

Since much of the current curriculum focus in both music and visual arts is on performance and production, it seems appropriate for those developing curriculum to consider the potential for change which these projects offer. Several questions appear to be raised. For example, in the work of avant-garde artists, musicians and poets there is a blurring between the arts. Is this appropriate to introduce in an early phase of a child's education? Also, a student may, with the aid of computer controlled synthesizers, listen to a full orchestral rendition of a simple theme just composed. The hours spent in learning to perform on a single instrument or to conduct an orchestra do not need to precede this event. Similarly, a student who has little knowledge of the craft of weaving can see examples of a newly designed woven tapestry displayed on a color television. In short, the technical aspects of the arts which absorb much time and are a primary source of learning in the current curriculum would be subordinated to the conceptual aspects of the same tasks. The number of experiments which students may attempt in the same period of time could be vastly accelerated. Certainly this could affect the design of the scope and sequence of a proposed curriculum using computer assisted composition.

The computer as a controller of other mechanical and electronic devices is a major source of inspiration for quite a number of contemporary artists. In education, some science instructors have begun to use the computer in this way. At MIT a computer scientist, Seymour Papert, has been allowing children to experiment with the interface of various devices with the computer. These have included a plotting (drawing) unit, music boxes, lights and electric motors. Students who have access to a laboratory situation of this type would have a much greater chance of understanding the work of artists described as well as being afforded the opportunity to explore concepts of industrial automation.

III. ANALYSIS, CRITICISM, AND INSTRUCTION

Researchers in the arts and humanities have made use of computer programs which store and analyze large quantities of information. The potential this has for students to analyze artistic forms and their own preferences and for teachers to analyze their instructional performance is only beginning to be explored.

Music

David Ashton has designed an educational environment with a computer-controlled organ. This system can display musical information in a graphic form for use by elementary school age children. This allows them to see a graphic visual representation of the correlation of parts of a musical score. Children may redraw parts of the score and hear the effect of the change on the sound of the music represented by the line drawing. The interaction of students with the system could be recorded so that analysis of instruction effectiveness would be facilitated.

Researchers have analyzed music of various periods and composers to understand structural differences. The information gained from these studies has allowed them to simulate these styles and create Bach-like music, for example. Students who have access to information gained from these stylistic analyses could experiment by composing within the structural limits set or by selectively departing from them. From individualized experimentation like this an understanding of musical structure and style could emerge that would appear difficult to achieve using other instructional methods.

Humanities

Stylistic studies in the humanities are revealing structural relationships within an author's work. This is used by researchers to attribute authorship to questioned passages. By studying the factors revealed in these statistical measures, such as richness of vocabulary and interesting patterns of word usage, students may derive a deeper understanding of the stylistic characteristics differentiating authors and periods in literature.

A course developed by Bruce Jones at California State College at Bakersfield provides a model for assisting students in developing skills in analysis and criticism. Using computer assisted instruction, his course in religious studies teaches a theory of biblical authorship, provides practice in literary criticism and elicits judgments about the theory. These exercises are intended to help students develop skills of interpretation, of analysis and in making and defending critical judgments.

Another course, conducted at Vassar, teaches students to use the computer as an analytical tool to discover patterns in literature and then test possible interpretations of these patterns. Students within this course have analyzed such diverse data as the literary language of Milton's *Paradise Lost* and the live communications of Watergate testimony.

Visual arts

Some studies have been done which attempt to analyze and simulate artistic style in the visual arts. The studies of Michael Nolls and Frieder Nake are the most well known of these. Nolls conducted an experiment involving simulation and preference testing of the work of Piet Mondrian. Nake attempted to simulate the artistic styles of Paul Klee and Hans Hartung. Although less developed, these experiments may be compared with the simulations of Bach in music or the simulations of Shakespeare in literature.

In a 1980 dissertation study, Thomas Linehan at Ohio State University explored computer assisted analysis of visual preferences. His work has great potential for developing teaching models of art criticism which allow students to explore their own critical judgments and compare them to those of others.

Implications

Common among the analytical programs described for the arts and humanities is the process of finding what appears to be reliable patterns in data and then testing possible interpretations or limits to these patterns. This would appear to foster an unusual problem solving approach to the subject matter of the arts and humanities. It is up to those developing curricular models whether they believe this would provide a valuable adjunct to the current curriculum.

IV. FURTHER IMPLICATIONS AND RECOMMENDATIONS

This paper has described a number of projects in music, humanities and visual arts which utilize the computer to teach fundamentals of the discipline, as a compositional aid, and as an aid in analysis and criticism of musical, literary and artistic production. Implications for educators were drawn within each of these sections. Most of these projects have been conducted in universities or experimental facilities, although a few have utilized public school settings.

Precollege arts educators should begin examining these studies in order to determine the directions their use of computers may take in the future. As the availability of small personal computers in elementary and secondary schools increases, it seems likely that their usage by all instructors would increase. Awareness of projects which utilize these devices and appropriate peripherals in successful instructional settings is essential to the development of good precollege programs. By reading studies and obtaining hands-on experience with a variety of hardware configurations and software systems, precollege arts instructors will develop their abilities to make appropriate decisions regarding purchase of hardware and software for their classrooms. This will also develop their critical perceptions of existing studies so they may build on them with materials appropriate to the age level which they teach. Without these experiences, their ability to weigh the benefits and limitations of specific types of computer assisted instruction, composition and critical analysis would be severely diminished.

As instructors become more knowledgeable regarding the implementation and design of instructional systems using computers as a key element, questions of selectivity and curricular suitability may be addressed. Questions such as, "How do the unique characteristics of the computer change the way subject matter may be approached?" may be asked. In some instances within the arts and within other subject matters, the worst aspects of conventional instruction have been automated. For example, the computer has been used as an electronic page turner. Instructors should consider making use of computer capabilities to store and search large bodies of information, to repeat a single task with slight variations without tiring, to provide many branches within instructional, compositional or analysis programs, to keep accurate records of student interaction, to provide dramatic examples of sound and graphics in conjunction with essentially static lessons and to provide students with the opportunity to experience in a direct way links between the arts and between the arts and sciences.

This latter computer capability appears to me significant as a factor in contributing to the unification of subject matter experiences in precollege education. Instructional sequences which allow students to program or experiment with computer hardware, perhaps creating unique output devices like those described in this article, create meaningful links between the arts and sciences within the student's immediate experience. Instructors may also consider creating projects which encourage overlap in instruction between physics and the arts as students study video or musical synthesis. Opportunities to visit research facilities such as Stanford's Center for Computer Research in Music and Acoustics or the electronic studios in the Chicago Arts Institute would be beneficial to either arts or science instruction in a secondary school.

Another project which has the potential for suggesting interdisciplinary curricular directions is the graphic communication project of Aaron Marcus, "Visualizing Global Interdependencies." In this project, data from the social sciences and physical sciences are combined to show their global human significance using a dramatic graphic treatment. The computer as a powerful tool for synthesis of information and communication across disciplines is displayed in this project. Students working on a similar type of project would rapidly become aware of the interrelationships among the isolated facts which they learn in various classes.

Although this brief article can only indicate in a cursory way some of the current projects and their implications for precollege educators in the arts and humanities, it is hoped that it will heighten awareness, interest and spark experimentation in innovative and appropriate computer usage for instruction, composition and critical analysis.

REFERENCE NOTES

Allvin, Raynold L. Computer-assisted music instruction: a look at the potential. *Journal of Research in Music Education*, 1971, 19, 131–143.

Alonso, S., Appleton, J.H., and Jones, C.A. A Special Purpose Digital System for the Instruction, Composition and Performance of Music. *Proceedings of the Sixth Conference on Computers in the Undergraduate Curriculum,* 1975.

Ashton, David M. Design of an Educational Environment with a Computer-Controlled Organ, Intermountain Regional Medical Program, Salt Lake City, Utah, 1973.

Brush, Lief. Terrain Instrument/Riverharps Affiliate, *Numus West,* Vol. 2, No. 1, pp. 47-50, 1975.

Chowning, John M.; Grey, John M.; Moorer, James A.; Rush, Loren; Smith, Leland C. January 1980 Report from Center for Computer Research in Music and Acoustics, Stanford University, 1980.

Della-Piana, Gabriel M. The Development of a Model for the Systematic Teaching of the Writing of Poetry. Final Report. Utah University, Salt Lake City Bureau of Educational Research, August 1971.

Diehl, N.C., and Ziegler, R.H. Evaluation of a CAI Program in Articulation, Phrasing, and Rhythm for Intermediate Instrumentalists, Council for Research in Music Education, 31, 1-11, 1973.

Eddins, J.M. Random Access Audio in Computer Assisted Music Instruction, *Journal of Computer Based Instruction,* Vol. 5, No. 1-2, 22-29, 1978.

Gilbert, Betsy. The Computerized Artist, a Graphics Unit for Artists Who Aren't Programmers, *Interface Age,* December, 1979.

Heller, Jack J. and others, Graphic Representation of Musical Concepts: a Computer Assisted Instructional System. Final Report, Connecticut University, Storrs, April, 1971.

Henkels, R.M., Jr., and Egea, E.R. Using a computer-generated concordance to analyze and document stylistic devices in Robert Pinget's Fable, *Computers and Humanities,* Vol. II, No. 6, 325-8, 1977.

Hofstetter, Fred T. *Fourth Summative Report of the Delaware PLATO Report,* University of Delaware, 1979.

Hofstetter, F.T. GUIDO: An Interactive Computer-based System for Improvement of Instruction and Research in Ear-training, *Journal of Computer Based Instruction,* 1, 100-106, 1975.

Hofstetter, Fred T. Instructional Design and Curricular Impact of Computer Based Music Education, *Educational Technology,* 18, 4, 50-53, 1978.

Jones, Beverly J. Instructional Potential of the Computer in Visual Arts Education, ES3 Report, February, 1980.

Jones, Bruce William. Religious Studies as a Test Case for Computer Assisted Instruction in the Humanities, Conference on Computers in the Undergraduate Curricula, Claremont, California, June, 1973.

Jones, Morgan John. *Computer assisted Instruction in Music: A Survey with Attendant Recommendations.* Doctoral dissertation, Northwestern University, 1975.

Jordan, Pauline, and others. Community College English Lesson Index. Computer Based Education Laboratory, Illinois University, Urbana, 1976.

Lefkoff, G. Computers and the study of musical style. *Computer Applications in Music,* West Virginia Library, 43-61, 1967.

Linehan, Thomas E. *A Computer Mediated Model for Visual Preference Research with Implications for the Teaching of Art Criticism,* Doctoral Dissertation, Ohio State University, 1980.

Malina, Frank J. (editor). *Visual Art, Mathematics and Computers.* Pergamon Press, London, England, 1979.

Marcus, Aaron. New Ways to View World Problems. *East West Perspective,* Vol. 1, No. 1, 15-22, 1979.

Misek, L.D. From Poetry to Politics: Vassar Freshman Concord Watergate, Conference on Computers in Undergraduate Curricula, Fort Worth, Texas, 1975.

Moorer, James A., and Gray, John. Lexicon of Analyzed Tones: Part I-a Violin Tone, *Computer Music Journal,* 1, No. 2, 39-45, 1977.

Moorer, James A., and Gray, John. Lexicon of Analyzed Tones: Part II-Clarinet and Oboe Tones, *Computer Music Journal,* 1, No. 3, 12-29, 1977.

Moorer, James A., and Gray, John. Lexicon of Analyzed Tones: Part III-The Trumpet, *Computer Music Journal,* 2, No. 2, 23-31, 1978.

Noll, A.M. *Human or Machine: A Subjective Comparison of Piet Mondrian's Composition with Lines (1917) and a Computer Generated Picture,* James Hoss (ed.), Penguin Books, Inc., Baltimore, Maryland, 1969.

Paisley, W.J. Identifying the unknown communicator in painting, literature and music: The significance of minor encoding habits, *Journal of Communications,* Vol. 14, p. 219-237, 1964.

Paisley, W.J. The Museum Computer and the Analysis of Artistic Content, Conference on Computers and Their Potential Applications in Museums, 1968.

Papert, Seymour, and Solomon, Cynthia. *Twenty Things to Do with a Computer,* Artificial Intelligence Memo No. 248, Massachusetts Institute of Technology, Cambridge.

Peters, G. David, and Eddins, John M. Research: A Selected Bibliography, *Journal of Computer Based Instruction,* Vol. 5, No. 1-2, 41-44, 1978.

Ray, D., and Killam, R.N. Melodic Perception Development and Measurement through CAI, Proceedings of NECC 1979 National Educational Computing Conference, 329-34, Iowa City, 1979.

Vaugn, Arthur Clarence, Jr. *A Study of the Contrast between Computer-assisted Instruction and the Traditional Teacher/Learner Method of Instruction in Basic Musicianship,* Doctoral Dissertation, Oregon State University, 1977.

The Two Cultures and Computer Science

Beverly J. Jones

The cultural split between scholars in the sciences and those in the arts and humanities has been discussed extensively. C.P. Snow's description focused attention on this problem in 1959. However, there seems to be little alleviation in spite of the time that has passed. A new section of *The Computing Teacher* invites educators in the arts and humanities to discover how they may participate and contribute their expertise to an area of the sciences—computer science.

This area seems particularly appropriate for the interface to occur for several reasons. Foremost is the unique quality of computer science as a discipline. Computer science has a specific body of

From "The Two Cultures and Computer Science," by Beverly J. Jones. In *The Computing Teacher,* December, 1980. Reprinted by permission.

knowledge which is unique to it. However, because it deals with information processing, it also has applications to all other disciplines. Current speculation on the extent of these applications has been likened to speculation on the extent of applications of electricity which occurred at the beginning of this century. Because of this, two areas of concern for educators in the arts and humanities present themselves. First, and most frequently cited, is the development of computer applications within their disciplines. These include computer assisted and managed instruction, research and computer assisted composition, design and artifact creation. Secondly, and less frequently cited, is the development of techniques for examining and directing the potential effects of proliferating computer applications on the quality of human life. Some computer scientists such as Joseph Weizenbaum have expressed concern regarding this second area. However, few, if any, people trained in the study of human values, particularly aesthetics and ethics, have turned their attention to this concern. Most of the individuals in the arts and humanities who have written about the larger problem of the impact of technology on the quality of human life have taken an anti-technological stance based on problems inherent in mechanical technology. Their literature reveals very little knowledge of electronic technology, particularly computers.

The failure of educators in the arts and humanities to attempt to study the direction and impact of computers on the quality of human life seems a significant omission. It appears that those most directly concerned with developing computer applications are also failing to examine and evaluate the potential range of choices and their long-reaching effects.

The cultural split between the arts and humanities and the sciences has opened a societal crack through which factors important to the quality of human life are slipping. Surely those trained in the study of human values should contribute time and effort to repairing this chasm. While recent developments in computer science are not the only scientific developments creating unexamined societal effects, it is an area deserving attention.

The tendency to use a new technology in the mode of a previous technology is a theme familiar to those in the arts and humanities. Historical artifacts tend to support the idea that we use new techniques and materials in ways which reflect the technique or material being supplanted. Examples include ancient Egyptian stone columns in the form of earlier bound papyrus stem columns; the first McCormick reapers with the molded metal bull's head on the front; and plastic furniture which imitates lathed wooden forms. In a similar vein, we are now tending to use the computer, a manifestation of electronic technology, in a fashion suitable to the mechanical technology with which we are more familiar. Recent efforts to automate some aspects of education and industry reflect this. Concepts valued for mechanical technology as manifested in mass production (efficiency, standardization, exact repetition, depersonalization of the final product, centralization) are accepted with little question as being suitable criteria for developments in electronic technology. It is no longer necessary that every item on a production line look alike or that every student receive the same instructional sequence.

The task of individuals trained in the arts and humanities is to ask questions about the nature of the new technology and its relation to human needs and values to determine appropriate modes of development and application. Questions such as, "What should be done? How does the new technology alter existing concepts?" may supplant, "How may this be done more efficiently?" Questions regarding who should control the technology and in what manner, need to be raised. This involves not only large-scale but small-scale decisions; such as, in a given instance of computer-assisted instruction, who should control the construction of the program: the student, the teacher or an expert? Questions such as "Should the computer be used to program the student?", "Should the student learn to program the computer?", "Should instruction utilize both of these techniques?", or "Is it appropriate to use the computer at all?" logically follow this line of inquiry.

Exposing some aspects of life to examination, inevitably revealing the unexpected, has been the task of artists and philosophers. The language, procedural sets and metaphors of computing increasingly permeate the language and literature of other disciplines. As this occurs, questions need to be raised regarding the way these concepts change the way people think of themselves and view the world. Mass media and popular literature use metaphors; such as, the human mind is a computer. It is also frequently pointed out that the computer can solve certain types of problems with much greater rapidity and accuracy than humans. The inference that the human mind is "less than a mere machine" may lower the regard in which people hold themselves. This is in marked contrast to the regard for the mind held by those computer scientists who are attempting to simulate aspects of human intelligence and abilities. The difficulty and complexity involved in simulating seemingly simple human behaviors is evidenced in the literature of artificial intelligence. Simulating human use of natural language and visual perceptual systems has proved especially difficult. Developing the critical abilities of students so they may analyze the subtle messages about technology embedded in popular magazines and television as well as providing them with accurate information is a task for all educators.

M. Maruyama, in an article titled "Toward a Cultural Futurology," raised the questions: "Does cultural change have to follow technological change? Can people generate cultural goals ahead of technology? Cannot technology be directed toward serving generated cultural goals?" Questions like these must be considered by those who have studied human values, and who also have some understanding of the potential and limitations of specific aspects of technology. To educate students capable of raising and addressing such questions is the shared responsibility of educators in the two cultures.

COMPUTERS IN ART EDUCATION

Linda Ettinger and Martin Rayala

This article describes the interface of computers and art education in the near future. Some readers will think this is speculative science-fiction, while others will recognize that developments similar to those described here have already appeared over the last twenty-five years.

It is likely that some elementary and secondary school art classes will increasingly reflect the influence of computers on our visual environment and include lessons about computer graphics as well as hands-on, computer graphic experiences for students. Teachers may find increasing value in using computers to assist in teaching art concepts, helping to manage records and art supplies and as a ready resource for art information.

In some ways, this article in itself is an indication of the growing interface between computers and school art. The first part of this article will describe some of the implications computers have for the nature of art and the second part will discuss the use of computers in teaching art.

COMPUTERS IN SCHOOL ART CLASSES

There appear to be few elementary or secondary school art classes in which computers are discussed or used as a regular part of the curriculum, but there are three ways in which computers are likely to surface in art classes in the near future:

From "Computers in Art Education," by Linda Ettinger and Martin Rayala. In *The Computing Teacher*, December, 1980. Reprinted by permission.

1. Computers are actively present in our environment already and we are exposed to their effects whether or not we are aware of it.
2. Art teachers will begin showing examples of computer art and talking about it with their classes.
3. Teachers will begin using computers as a medium for doing art projects in the classroom.

Computer art as part of our environment

The first of these areas reflects the fact that computers are already part of our visual environment, even though we may not be aware of it. Designers for ads in magazines and television commercials rely heavily on computers. A recent issue of *Print* magazine, which is directed at professional graphic designers, pointed out that the single most influential development shaping the look and production of visual design is the computer. Some styles of images and lettering have been created especially for the requirements of computers, and "computer-look" lettering and image style is often used even when it is not produced by a computer.

Some football stadiums are equipped with large display boards operated by computers which can produce anything from the word "Touchdown!" to an animated picture. This same technology is used by some retail businesses in the form of computerized signs which present changeable messages.

Movies and television shows, especially space adventures, often have sequences which were created with the help of computers. Many cartoon shows use computers for the laborious animation process. Popular video games are really computer games and have helped make people familiar with some of the types of images which can be created with a computer. An art program which would hope to make students more aware of their visual environment could hardly be complete without at least acknowledging the role computer images already play in our lives.

Computer art as a topic in art appreciation

Computers may also appear in art classes as a topic in the curriculum along with painting, composition, sculpture and perspective. Beverly Jones, professor of art education at the University of Oregon, has compiled a slide set entitled *Computer Art* with a cassette and script, published by Oregon Mathematics Education Council, 1976. This slide set is available through the Oregon State film library for out-of-state use and through ESD's for in-state use. There are some books about computer art which provide information about major developments in computer art over the past quarter-century. One of the earliest comprehensive descriptions of the interface between art and computers appears in Gene Youngblood's 1970 book *Expanded Cinema*. Youngblood gives examples, descriptions, and explanations of computer films, television experiments and holographic laser images which were recognized for their aesthetic potential ten years ago. Many of the computer images still reproduced in books and articles today are from that period. In the 1960's, these images were produced on large and expensive computers owned by companies and universities, but today many of these can be simulated on microcomputers, such as the Apple II.

Three other good sources for historic and general information about computers as a visual medium are Franke's *Computer Graphics—Computer Art* (1971), Ruth Leavitt's *Artist and Computer* (1976) and Jasia Reichardt's *The Computer in Art* (1971).

A public television series called *Fast Forward* is one of the best opportunities for students and teachers alike to see a wide variety of examples of computer graphics. This series, produced by TV Ontario, covers a broad spectrum of computer concepts with actual examples.

Television is a particularly appropriate medium for showing computer graphics because, unlike reproductions in books, TV can show the movement associated with many computer images. In addition, since the computer's CRT is actually a television set, the reproduction is especially faithful to the original. In some ways it could be argued that the two are identical.

It is useful to make a distinction between computer graphics and computer art because many articles and books about the visual capabilities of computers refer to generating graphs, diagrams and flow charts which are usually of minimal interest as aesthetic objects. While they are produced for utilitarian purposes, these images can be so novel and visually stimulating that they evoke an aesthetic response in the viewer. Computer art, then, loosely refers to images created for their visual effect without necessarily including regard for their utility.

Reichardt makes the interesting observation that computer art may be one of the first visual art forms which has not yet produced any acknowledged master artists or major works of art, but is profoundly influencing the boundaries and definitions of art as a whole (Reichardt, 1971).

Perhaps it is more useful to compare computer images to craft forms, such as weaving or quilting. Much computer art that we see today is similar to quilting, for example, in that the formal requirements of the medium are attended to and the patterns are often passed on from artist to artist. Quilting has its Lone Star pattern and computer art has its kaleidoscope program!

Computers as media in the art class

The third impact of computers in art classes will be in hands-on media experiences for the students. Computer manufacturers are already producing graphic packages that have some interactive capabilities for use on microcomputers. This means that the user has some control over what the image looks like, although so far it is within tightly limited parameters.

Mitchell Waite's 1979 book entitled *Computer Graphics Primer* may be an example of the kind of material that is most useful to microcomputer users at the present time. Unfortunately, some of the programs do not work as printed and average readers may have difficulty in detecting and correcting the errors on their own. Waite's book includes about two dozen actual programs that microcomputer users can type into their home computer to make and manipulate pictures. In one of the programs in the Waite book, for example, the instructions result in a line drawing of a bird that can be made to glide across the screen.

Although this type of material sounds like a rather simple-minded activity, this is a common way to learn computer programming. By using a program someone else has written, one can learn to alter the program in some way and finally try to write one's own.

Computer games and canned programs provide the user with some understanding of the capabilities of computers and introduce the basic elements of computer graphics. One of the first elements, for example, is the horizontal and vertical line restrictions. Diagonal and curved lines can only be simulated by creating a stair-step effect of small horizontal and vertical lines. On low resolution graphics, which use larger steps, the effect is very obvious, but is minimized in high resolution graphics which reduce the size of the steps. This is not unlike the limitations found in weaving and the etcha-sketch toys children have for drawing. Some microcomputers have only alpha-numeric graphics, such as the PET, or only low resolution graphics, such as the TRS 80.

Typing instructions into the computer is not the only way to make computer images. Many companies sell a device called a graphics pad with an electronic stylus for drawing very much as one would with a ball-point pen. Graphics pads and the other items mentioned below are called *peripherals* because they are not part of the basic components of a computer but instead are added on. A variation of the stylus is a little circle with cross hairs which can be used for tracing a picture. This stylus is sometimes called a *mouse*. Another peripheral for computer graphics is a light pen similar to the stylus but used on the face of the computer's display screen. Wherever you touch the display screen with the light pen, the computer will make a mark visible on the screen.

A more elaborate way to get an image into the computer is to use what is called a digitizing camera which is a variation of a small television camera. You have probably seen this device used to make computer portraits at fairs and shopping areas.

These are some of the ways to put pictures into the computer (called INPUT devices) and there are a variety of peripherals for getting the images back out of the computer (OUTPUT devices). The CRT (cathode ray tube) is one of these and is probably the most popular for computer graphics. Since most computer users still work with words and numbers, however, the line printer is still an often used computer output device. It is the machine that produces the well-known computer "print-out" that looks like a typed page. The computer photographic portrait outfits use a CRT to show you the portrait before having it output in "hard copy" on a line printer.

Another peripheral, especially suited to making line drawings, is called a *plotter*. It involves an inked pen for outputting architectural and engineering drawings as well as charts and graphs. All of these devices are referred to as hardware and can only work with the programs, or software, the user puts in.

In most cases these devices were developed for technical drawings and are not well adapted for aesthetic purposes. Most of the people who have made the difficult attempt to switch from computer graphics to computer art are not generally artists, but have come from the more technical side of computer science. To date, not many artists have taken the time to learn the technology of the computer as a graphic medium.

It is fashionable in some circles to adapt an anti-computer, anti-technology posture. Artists have traditionally been highly involved in many areas of technology, however. Blending oil pigments, casting bronze sculptures, printing photographs, firing clay pieces, etching metal printing plates with acid and designing buildings are but a few of the activities of artists which require a high degree of specific technological knowledge and skill. Artists have been proud of their ability to suggest broader applications of technologies previously used in restricted and unimaginative ways. Computers are another example of technology which could benefit from artistic input.

THE EDUCATIONAL COMPONENT— CURRICULUM IMPACT

Next, we shall focus upon the learning situation and the potentials and limitations of the computer as an instructional aid in the classroom. Relationships of the computer to education will be divided into three main areas which include: (1) computer assisted instruction or CAI; (2) computer managed instruction or CMI; and (3) information retrieval. When these three divisions are compared to the traditional roles in an educational system, a parallel can be seen to the (1) teacher; (2) administrator; and (3) researcher.

Computer assisted instruction

Computer Assisted Instruction, or CAI, refers most generally to two broad approaches of classroom instruction: one which supplements the learning situation (teacher aid) and one which substitutes for other modes of instruction (tutorial). Instructors of art should find valuable uses for general types of CAI through software presenting both teacher-controlled programmed information designed to teach fundamental concepts, and student-controlled programming for experimentation with concepts.

"Projections for 1980–85 indicate computer assisted learning will be used by more school districts than any other type of computer application. Usage is anticipated to rise from 54% of the districts to 74%. Microcomputers are anticipated to play an increasingly significant role in computer assisted learning usage in the school district" (Chambers and Bork, 1980).

Perhaps the most widely accepted value of CAI is that it actively involves the individual in the learning process. Whether the student interacts with a predetermined canned program designed by someone else, or directly with the computer when experimenting on his own, it is impossible for the student to be totally passive in the situation. Another specific value is the ability of the learner to proceed at his or her own pace.

The use of computers in this manner frees the teacher from the repetitive aspects of teaching to devote more time to personal, human considerations of their students. The teacher in the art class may find access to a computer exists only on a shared basis with the actual terminal located in some other area of the school. If this is the case, it will affect the kinds of CAI programs the teacher selects to use. David Moursund, professor of Computer Science at the University of Oregon, states that the problem of access should no longer be a stumbling block to the classroom teacher because computers are no longer a scarce resource.

Current examples of applications of computer assisted instruction in learning situations other than art include experience with problem solving, text manipulation, simulation, drill and practice and complex tutorial systems. A look at instruction in art reveals curriculum models which include elements relating to the roles of the artist, the art critic, the aesthetician and the art historian. When we compare these traditional role models in art to the applications of computing in other learning situations, a number of distinct relationships become apparent. In an article entitled, "Instructional Potential of the Computer in Visual Arts Education," Beverly Jones explores several examples. "Teachers," she says, "can utilize CAI to aid students in understanding and/or emulating the role of the artist. Similarly, the role involved in an educated response to art works, i.e., the critic, the aesthetician and the art historian, can be illuminated for students via CAI" (Jones, 1980).

Tom Linehan and Charles Czuri of the Ohio State University have designed a computer assisted instructional package which utilizes interactive computer graphics to teach concepts associated with perspective drawing to elementary school students. To assist in describing the project, an eight-minute videotape has been made showing a third grade student interacting with a graphics terminal. By working with the terminal keyboard, the student is able to manipulate the images presented in the program until the concepts are understood.

Current software programs available from microcomputer manufacturers provide limited examples of microcomputer graphics capabilities. However, Beverly Jones is currently developing (through a grant from the Apple Computer Company) two introductory computer programs investigating microcomputer applications in art education. These two programs will demonstrate how the microcomputer can provide instruction in the arts and also be used as an artistic device to create art. Tom Linehan has been studying computer assisted analysis of visual preferences. His work has the potential for aiding students in understanding the structure of their own art preferences and relates to the teaching of art criticism. Studies also exist which analyze and simulate the work of specific artists, such as Paul Klee, Hartung and Mondrian.

Computer managed instruction

The computer as an information processing device is capable of manipulating symbol sets of many sorts, including the visual, auditory and verbal. As such, the computer holds great potential as an aid in record keeping and evaluation in the art classroom.

In traditional forms of student evaluation, i.e. the test, the computer can be used to calculate an item analysis of each test question. For example, a statistical program used on the computer can determine which questions were answered correctly most often, thereby representing primitives for the students; and which items were answered incorrectly most often, suggesting a need for further consideration. In addition, the computer can be used to store data banks of test items and for automatic test generation. The computer can hold class rosters, individual student records, including grades, attendance, assignments, interests, etc., and compute final grades. Teachers can use the computer to maintain an up-to-date inventory of art supplies at any given time.

Many art teachers are concerned that students learn to criticize and evaluate their own art work and responses to art as an important part of the complete problem solving process. With the computer, students can store, review, expand, modify and compare their own work and responses in a wide variety of ways. This kind of personal student interaction with the computer allows for immediate feedback and the construction of a developmental historical record.

Information retrieval

The computer as an aid to research doesn't just augment our accessibility to information; it *changes* it. Information retrieval refers to a branch of computer science relating to techniques of storing and searching large quantities of information in order to retrieve specified parts of that information. Such a system affords access to large networks of information and resources through the connection of several computers. Connections can be hardwired or made with existing telephone systems. Researchers currently use information retrieval through libraries to access large data banks of information, such as ERIC, Psychological Abstracts and Dissertation Abstracts. A computerized literature search provides rapid access to bibliographic materials in a large variety of subject disciplines. In a computer search, a list of keywords expressing the specific subject interest is compared to words in the titles, subject headings and abstracts of the bibliographic citations. Those materials that match the description given in the search strategy can then be displayed. With the use of such a system, the computer can be used to help develop curriculum based on the teacher's particular interests or the specific class need. But this is only the beginning of the potential of the computer as an information processor in art education. In a recent paper entitled, "Computer Assisted Research: Measurement, Meaning and Metaphor in Products, Process and Discourse," Beverly Jones presents a comprehensive look at many of the other important uses of the computer in art education research. For instance, researchers and teachers interested in studying art products made by children could use the computer to create a data base of stored images and related verbal and numerical data, such as dialogue of subjects while creating art products, their verbal responses to art works of others, verbal reactions of judges, personal data about subjects, etc. Through information retrieval, it would be possible to share this information among interested researchers and teachers. Images existing in the form of microfiche, holograms, videotape and video disk are also machine retrievable. Researchers interested in the analysis of art products will find recent research in picture processing and analysis programs of interest.

Jones states, "Computers cannot formulate research, synthesize research, or interpret research. However, they can assist researchers by performing complex comparisons, by searching long lists of data and by accumulating and manipulating symbolic material in a precisely controlled manner" (Jones, 1980c).

A computer search was conducted for this article in ERIC via the bibliographic Retrieval Services, Inc. We wanted to see comparative figures for ERIC listings concerning the use of computers in various disciplines. The results show 439 titles under the heading of mathematics education and computers; 598 under science education and computers; and 10 under art education and computers. Although these figures reflect a limited data base search, they do point out the dearth of attention to the potential applications of the computer in art education.

BIBLIOGRAPHY

Benthal, J. *Science and technology in art today.* New York: Praeger, 1972.

Billings, K. and Moursund, D. *Are you computer literate?* University of Oregon, 1977.

Burnham, J. "Systems esthetics." *Art Forum,* September, 1968, 30–35.

Chambers, J. and Bork, A. "Computer assisted learning in U.S. secondary/elementary schools." *Computing Teacher,* Vol. 8, #1, 1980.

Chambers, J. and Sprecher, J. "Computer assisted instruction: current trends and critical issues." *Communications of the ACM,* 23, 6, June, 1980, 332–342.

Csuri, C. *Computer graphics and art.* Proceedings of the IEEE, 62, #4, April, 1974.

Davis, D. *Art in the future.* New York: Praeger, 1973.

Florman, S.C. *The existential pleasures of engineering.* New York: St. Martin's Press, 1967.

Frampen, M. and Steitz, P. Ed. *Design and planning 2.* New York: Hastings House, 1967.

Franke, H.W. *Computer graphics, computer art.* London: Phaidon Press, 1971.

Gilbert, B. "The computerized artist, a graphics unit for artists who aren't programmers." *Interface Age,* December, 1979.

Graham, N. *The mind tool.* St. Paul: West Publishing Co., 1980.

Jones, B. *Computer art,* a slide set with cassette and script published by Oregon Mathematics Education Council, 1976. Available through the State Oregon Film Library.

Jones, B. "Initial report of art, music and humanities task group." *ES3 Report,* September, 1979, 16–17.

Jones, B. "Instructional potential of the computer in visual arts education." *ES3 Report,* February, 1980, 11–17.(b)

Jones, B. "Computer art and art related applications in computer graphics: a historical perspective and projected possibilities." *Proceeds of the Second West Coast Computer Faire, Palo Alto, California,* 1980.(a)

Jones, B. "Computer assisted research: measurement, meaning and metaphor in products, process and discourse." A paper delivered at the National Symposium for Research in Art, University of Illinois at Urbana-Champaign, October, 1980.(c)

Leavitt, R. Ed. *Artist and computer.* New York: Harmony Books, 1976.

Linehan, T. "A investigation of criteria for evaluating computer art." *Computer Graphics and Art.* May, 1976.

Linehan, T. "A computer-mediated model for visual preference research and implications for instruction in art criticism." Unpublished dissertation, Ohio State University, 1980.

Lourie, J. *Textile graphics/computer aided.* New York: Fairchild Publishers, 1973.

Moursund, D. *Basic programming for computer literacy.* New York: McGraw-Hill, 1978.

Noll, A.M. "The digital computer as a creative medium," IEEE. *Spectrum,* October, 1967.

Reichardt, J. *The computer in art.* London: Studio Vista, 1971.

Solomon, R. Guggenheim Museum. *On the future of art.* New York: Viking Press, 1979.

Waite, M. *Computer graphics primer.* Indianapolis: H.W. Sams and Company, 1979.

Youngblood, G. *Expanded cinema.* London: Studio Vista, 1970.

WHAT'S YOUR OPINION?

1. Art-related CAI provides the potential for studying a student's work by viewing the whole process rather than only the finished product.
2. The individualized experimentation available in music-CAI can result in an understanding of musical structure that would be difficult to achieve using conventional instructional methods.
3. Classroom teachers must have an opportunity to become acquainted with studies in their subject matter areas, experiment with existing computer programs, and have some hands-on experience with a variety of combinations of computer equipment.
4. Overlap in instruction would be possible between physics and music or art as students study musical and video synthesis.
5. The computer can be a powerful tool for synthesizing information and communication across disciplines.

6. The impact of computers on quality of human life should be an important issue to educators in the arts and humanities.

7. The cultural split between the arts and humanities and the sciences has opened a societal schism into which factors important to the quality of human life are being lost.

8. Must cultural change necessarily follow technological change?

9. Can people generate cultural goals ahead of technology?

10. The computer is the single most influential development shaping the look and production of visual design.

11. Contemporary artists must learn the technology of the computer as a graphic medium.

EXERCISES

1. List five goals that an art teacher could profitably pursue by using a computer.

2. List five goals that a music teacher could profitably pursue by using a computer.

3. Describe the difference between computer graphics and computer art.

4. How might word-processing equipment (or a micro with a word-processing option) benefit students in an English composition class?

5. Contact the music department of a local university or high school to determine whether computers are used in the teaching of music. If they are used, interview students taking the course on their reactions to computers.

6. Investigate the types of software available in noncomputer subject areas.

7. Who should control program construction: the student, the teacher, or an expert in instruction and computing?

8. Can technology be directed toward serving generated cultural goals?

9. List five unique characteristics of computers that should alter the conventional approach to presentation of subject matter.

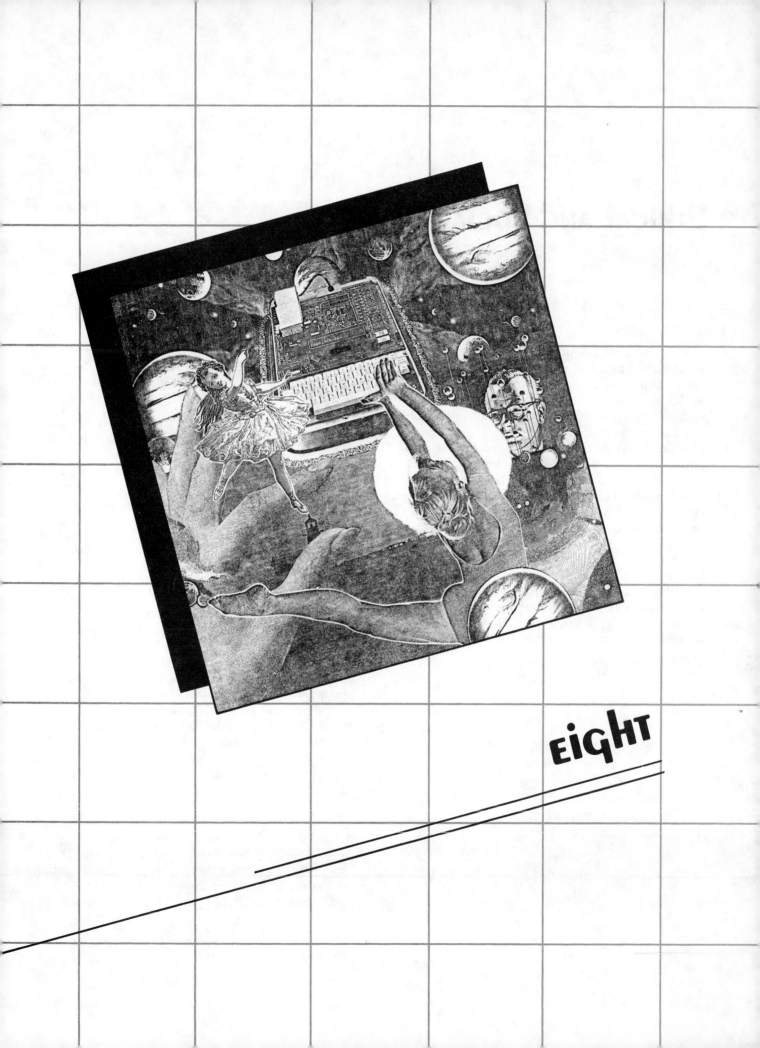

eight

Ethical and Social Issues

The extension of computer use into everyday life raises far-reaching and pervasive social issues which we are at present ill-equipped to comprehend and unable to solve. School personnel should take immediate responsibility for educating both teachers and students in order to ensure a future generation capable of making critical decisions regarding computer use. A computer-literate society must deal with fundamental questions of privacy, human rights, moral and legal obligations and restraints. The very course of modern society's existence would seem to lie in the outcome of such issues.

In Chapter 8, East's report to the ACM outlines his group's efforts to collect, organize, and disseminate relevant information to educators. Thought-provoking examples are provided, and appropriate organizations are urged to begin serious discussion of social and ethical issues. Tinker discusses the problems computers raise for women and ethnic minorities.

Ethical and Social Concerns

Philip East

Reflecting an increasing awareness among scientists of the ethical and social aspects of their disciplines, ACM has taken a clear position in favor of including ethical and social concerns in the college level computer science curriculum. Adopting a similar stance, this task group recommends that ethical and social issues related to computers be integrated into computer literacy programs and computer science instruction at the secondary level as well.

The major focus of this task group is to both encourage and assist teachers in dealing with ethical and social concerns relative to computers. To accomplish this, we must first provide justification for including these issues in the curriculum. Then, information about topics, methods and materials must be made available to teachers.

While the above tasks are the major focus of the group, we would be remiss if we did not urge a more extensive discussion of ethical and social concerns within the professional computing community. We believe that the extent of our success will depend upon the support and leadership from professionals in industry, in research institutions, and in educational institutions.

JUSTIFICATIONS

One obvious justification for considering the ethical aspects of computing is to prevent criminal activity within the field. While the extent of computer crime and/or abuse can only be surmised, estimates are that

From "Ethical and Social Concerns," by Philip East. In *Topics* Association of Computing Machinery (SIGSCE, SIGCUE), January, 1981. Reprinted by permission.

the reported cases comprise only a fraction of the whole problem. However, an even more important issue is that students are known to engage in behavior of questionable ethics. When an instructional account has its allocated resources depleted, students sometimes use other accounts to complete work. Some students have made a game of swapping access codes and breaking codes for other accounts. Many students have been known to use limited computer resources for playing games. While such behavior, in and of itself, is not terribly frightening, the potential unethical behavior of these students as professionals is.

Another major reason for a community-wide discussion of computer values is the newness of the technology. Society has not yet had enough time to deal with the issues of computers. Many people are directly affected by computers. Yet few people actually understand them, and many stand in awe of them. Ordinary citizens are often at a loss when told "the computer made an error." Computer professionals are often required to make ethical decisions without any prior understanding of the values that may impact them.

TASKS

To develop such a curriculum in ethical and social values, we suggest that several tasks need to be completed. The first is to create the documentation necessary to justify such a curriculum. Second, we must provide methodological assistance to this course of study in addition to discussion topics. Then guidelines must be developed for both establishing the ethical questions as well as the research methodologies for exploring them. Last, research that has been conducted should be monitored and evaluated. Below is a more detailed discussion of each of these task areas.

Document justification

A first task is to compile documentation for the justifications listed above and to develop a bibliography. News stories, opinion articles, books, research papers, congressional hearings, and personal anecdotes are examples of sources for such documentation.

Provide methodological assistance

Almost all areas of human endeavor have questions related to values associated with them. As computer use becomes more prevalent, these endeavors will also have questions about computer values associated with them. Thus, it is important to deal with computer values in an educational setting. To do so, two critical aspects of values and ethics must be recognized. First, every individual has a sense of

values, but it is not always developed or used in a conscious manner. Second, a sense of values is not acquired through being taught what is right, but instead is molded by one's experience and the models of ethical behavior the individual is exposed to.

Since specialists in the field of moral education are divided in their opinion of "the" method for enhancing values systems of students, the best course of action for teaching values appears to be the open discussion of social and ethical issues. This technique is a generally accepted teaching method and has an abundant research base.

Discussions of social and ethical issues related to computers can be conducted in almost any class at any grade level. Teachers should search for issues that are applicable to their particular classes. Since issues often arise naturally in the context of a class, teachers should seize upon them when they occur. To do so, it is imperative that teachers have insight into issues in the computer field, possess skills in leading discussions, as well as have knowledge about some theory of moral or values education.

Proposed guidelines for such a discussion are discussed in the paragraphs that follow. First, present situations with social, ethical, or values considerations. Ideally, such situations should arise out of subject matter, student experiences, or actual happenings in society. Begin the discussion by stating questions that ask "what should be?" or "what would you do?"

Allow students to interact freely as long as their discussion remains on the issue or is intended to clarify the issue. The values generally held in society and formal codes of ethics are expected to be relevant to the discussion. Activities of individuals or organizations may be put forth as models of ethical or unethical conduct. Assignment of responsibility will likely be an issue, also.

Maintain control of the discussion enough to avoid arguments that become personal. Remember, however, that the purpose of the discussions is to examine student beliefs and to expose students to the beliefs and attendant rationales of others. Teachers' beliefs are relevant to the discussion, but not as "answers" to ethical questions.

The purpose of the exercise is to discuss issues, not to arrive at a solution or to come to a consensus. Thus, while consensus may occur, it is expected that discussions normally will end without any formal resolution.

Discussions of this type are expected to serve several purposes. The exposure to, and discussion of, the beliefs of others and of professional ethics should enhance the values systems of students. The identification of issues with values considerations should be made easier. When students begin making decisions relative to computers, the social and ethical aspects of problems are less likely to be overlooked and more likely to be considered an integral part of the information upon which to base decisions.

Provide discussion topics

This task group sees itself as a clearinghouse for information on ethical discussions. While the examples below are meant to provide some insight into the types of topics that can be used as a basis for values discussions, actual topics used and data concerning student responses would be appreciated. Other extensive lists of similar issues have been compiled elsewhere.

Example 1

A high school science teacher decides to replace all lab work with computer simulations. Is this appropriate? Will students learn the subject matter as well (perhaps better) using simulations? Is there some "hidden curriculum" in the physical performance of labs that will not be included in the simulations? Are individual teachers, regardless of background, the appropriate decision makers in cases such as this?

Example 2

A junior high school computer-literacy class is discussing social and ethical concerns. One student asks, "Why do we have to talk about ethics? Don't computer programmers belong to some organization like doctors and lawyers, where ethics are set up by the group?" Is this true? What are the professional ethics for programmers, computer researchers, etc.? Can ethics be legislated? If so, how effectively can they be enforced?

Example 3

A student tells her teacher, who is knowledgeable about computers, that her (the student's) father has been overcharged by some company that says their computer system hasn't made a mistake. Is there an ethical question involved? Does the father have any recourse? What are the rights and responsibilities of consumers in cases involving computers?

Example 4

Students in a high school algebra class are studying logarithms. The teacher presents the topic from the point of view that logarithms are mainly useful for computation, e.g., extracting roots, raising numbers to powers, multiplication, and division. A student asks, "Why learn this stuff, since computers can do all of these things quickly and easily?" Why should they? Are there areas other than math where the content is being transformed by computers? What does it mean to "know" a discipline?

Example 5

A professional programmer has been asked to write a program to perform a task she considers to be ethically questionable. When she notifies her superior of her feelings, she is told that upper echelons have made the decision and that pursuing the matter will cost her her job. What should she do? Is there any source of assistance for professionals in such circumstances? How do professional ethics address this situation?

Example 6

A majority of students either own or have free access to a computer and extensive data banks, which they are permitted to use in their schoolwork. The few students without such access are advised to use library facilities, for which there is a nominal fee. Is this fair? Should the library charge for use of computer facilities since it is publicly supported? Will computer access become a right for future citizens?

Developing ethics guidelines

Another major task of this group will be to gather information about ethical behavior in relation to computer use. The computer science profession and individual computer scientists have generally served as good models of ethical conduct and have been sensitive to the public's welfare in their work. However, as the number of people who either work with computers or are directly affected by them increases, the need for a well defined moral code also increases. Therefore, this task group will collect and disseminate codes of ethics of various professional groups. By referring to these manuals, students will be able to keep abreast of what the computing community is doing in the area of ethics and how it compares with other disciplines, in addition to using the codes as models for their own values.

Along with the collection of this information will be a sustained effort to prod the computing community into developing social and ethical policies or guidelines which will consider the following items:

To demonstrate, possibly by examples, what constitutes ethical and unethical conduct for computer professionals.

To define what is meant by "misuse" of the computer.

To provide possible recourses for professionals and consumers who feel they have no place to turn with their computer-related ethics questions.

To establish the responsibilities of computer professionals in relation to those they interact with, e.g., employer, client, fellow professionals, members of the public (or society in general), and themselves.

To determine the rights and responsibilities of members of society relative to computers and uses of computers.

Establish research guidelines

Recommendations about guidelines for scientific research are made with reservations. Historically, scientific research has been considered to be amoral. The developments of nuclear power, of various drugs, etc., and new research techniques (recombinant DNA, for example) have caused the attitudes of many, both in and out of scientific fields, to be altered. An example of such guidelines can be taken from the work of Kraemer and Colton, where the discussion of a broad spectrum of issues is advocated when considering the new computer application, electronic funds transfer.

It does seem appropriate, if not imperative, to be asking not "Will it work?" but instead "Should it be done at all?" Thus, part of the information this task group would like to disseminate is the dialogue generated by the discussion of what constitutes an appropriate use of computers. An interesting method of formalizing and mandating such discussion can be borrowed from the current practice of preparing environmental impact statements. Conducting "societal impact" studies prior to the introduction of computer technology into various segments of society is a concept that deserves consideration by the professional community.

Monitor educational research related to computers

A significant amount of research has been conducted relative to the use of computers in education. The primary emphasis of research to date has been the effectiveness of computerized instruction and student attitudes toward such instruction. While effectiveness research is important, several critical questions remain to be answered.

How will students be affected when they spend significant amounts of time interacting with computers, both at school and at home? What role will students assign to computers; to teachers; to their peers? How will the human interaction process of students be affected? What hidden curriculum is included in a highly computerized educational system?

It is hoped and expected that computers will have few if any deleterious effects on students, but not expecting such effects is no longer an acceptable excuse for not looking for them. Television was not expected to have any effects on viewers. Our society

and environment are very complex, as are the human mind and psyche. Changes that may affect them should be implemented carefully, with a constant vigil for the development of unforeseen consequences.

SUMMARY

This task group considers its primary purpose to be the collection, organization, and dissemination of information. This process is intended to encourage and assist computer knowledgeable educators to begin discussing with their students a wide variety of social and ethical concerns relative to computers in society and in education. Some examples of topics for such discussions have been given as have some guidelines for conducting them. It is expected that current activities of organizations of computing professionals will be used as a model for guiding students in establishing their own values systems. The possibility that this model will be inadequate has led us to urge such organizations to begin a serious and ongoing discussion of their policies relative to social and ethical issues.

GUEST EDITORIAL

Robert F. Tinker

The rapid introduction of microcomputers into education raises important equity issues. Unlike other educational innovations, the trend toward increased use of microcomputers is proceeding not from the top down but through a grass-roots movement stimulated by parents, teachers and students who perceive the vocational, educational and social importance of computers. While this process of introduction allows microcomputer use to be expanded quickly, there are two side-effects of this grass-roots implementation that should concern us all.

One side-effect of this mechanism of introduction is that microcomputers are most likely to appear in communities which already possess both knowledge and affluence. A related feature is that when implemented in poorer schools, computers tend to be used chiefly as tools for drill and practice in basic skills, while in more affluent schools, students learn programming activities designed to give them computer literacy. Dan Watt, former research associate for the MIT Logo Group and current editor with Byte Books, suggests that, "Affluent students are thus learning to tell the computer what to do, while

From *The Computing Teacher*, January, 1982. Reprinted by permission.

less affluent students are learning to do what the computer tells them!"

A second side-effect is that the number of male students who are learning how to use computers far exceeds the number of female students. Teachers who have observed students with computers in the classroom have noted persistent inequities in male/female use of computers. Most of the teacher computer buffs who first introduce kids to computers are male. An equally common occurrence is that fathers bring a computer home to show it to their sons and teach them how to use it. Also, because the number of computers in a school is limited, access to the computer is often tied to stereotypically male-style aggressive and competitive behavior, an obstacle to the female who doesn't know how to vie with *any* crowd for computer time, let alone an all-male crowd.

In addition to the inequality caused by the manner in which computers are being introduced into education, a more subtle level of inequality may also be operating. Most leaders in the field of education and computers are middle-class men who were trained in traditionally male professions, particularly physics and math. The content, evaluation criteria, and teaching style used throughout computer education reflect their values. For example, there are implicit assumptions contained in computer programs which utilize sterotyped sex roles and depict military settings which require aggressive, war-oriented strategies. Similarly, software often utilizes language and situations which draw upon the experiences of suburban, middle-class children, and not the experiences of poor or urban children. Whether or not these assumptions lead to biases are made explicit, so that schools can knowingly choose among alternatives, depends upon the diversity of the creators and evaluators of software.

The plethora of math-related software, the paucity of material to support learning literature or interpersonal relations, the absence of practical, job-related software, and the prevalent assumption that programs for handicapped and disadvantaged students should be drill and practice are also evidence of a middle-class male bias. There are obvious historical reasons for the predominance of math-related software. Computers were initially seen as calculators, so it was natural to apply them chiefly to mathematics, and to teach programming using arithmetic problems. In the schools, moreover, it is often the male math teachers who introduce computers into the classroom. Thus, though it is understandable that there is a plethora of math software, it is time to act on the knowledge that computers have enormous educational potential in other areas as well; namely sciences, reading and writing, and the arts.

Before suggesting what might be done, however, perhaps we should try to reach a better understanding of the mechanisms which may be generating these cultural and sexual stratifications. A teacher computer specialist recently looked at a brochure advertising the games of a major computer manufacturer and noticed that all of the figures but two drawn on the screens were men. Of two women, one was a buxom blonde and the other wore a shirt bearing the words "Kick Me." When asked why the company used such advertisements, a representative of the company replied, "Ninety percent of our users are white, college-educated males, so we're catering to our audience."

Ninety percent is a figure which cannot be ignored in an open marketplace. A figure such as this opens the way to severe tension between market strategies and social structural realities. Computers are usable and useful in equal measure by male and female, affluent and less affluent alike; yet figures such as 90% put irresistible pressures on suppliers to support the most viable market.

It is important for us to work toward reversing the economic and sexual bias caused by micro-computer implementation. First, microcomputers are valuable tools which can help *all* students develop reasoning and problem-solving skills, logical thinking and creativity—in math and science as well as in reading, writing, music and art. In order to pursue goals of equity, all students—girls, boys, low-income, learning-disabled—should have equal access to the best teaching tools we have to offer.

Second, the prevalence of computers will force society to make critical decisions which will be influenced and understood by those who understand computers. Examples of these decisions are: how will microcomputers be used in a given school—for drill and practice or for teaching programming skills?—for math and business education, or for social science and language as well? Will there be any deliberate effort to bring females into computer courses? Larger political decisions may force us to answer questions such as: How much personal information will the government store on computers? What rights will the individuals possess? What if that individual is a welfare recipient, or a social activist? Will the federal government allot funds to researching how computers can be used in education and health, or in missile guidance systems? As more of these questions arise, uneven access to computers and the exclusion of certain groups from gaining computer literacy will have far-reaching impact on social and educational equity.

Educators and planners should not be content with the current laissez-faire mechanism of introducing computers into the classroom. We should establish a voice in determining who introduces students to computers in the schools, what teaching methods they will use, and the content of curriculum and software. Female students may need to learn more math in order to gain access to computer skills; teachers may need to speak out to manufacturers and publishers if they are not satisfied with the roles and teaching styles inherent in the design of the software and hardware they are finding in their classrooms. Built-in financial pressures should be resisted by government and unbiased purchasers. If we are going to strive for educational excellence with equality of opportunity, for democratic citizen participation in decision-making and governing society, then educators should begin to assess the effects of increased use of computers in the schools, to articulate equitable social goals, and to formulate intentional policies to reach those goals.

WHAT'S YOUR OPINION?

1. Increasingly, computers will become the private property of individuals, thus gradually returning to the individual the power to determine patterns of education.
2. Americans should expand the Bill of Rights to include freedom of computation, empowering the government to legislate computer availability for everyone.
3. The inference that the human mind is "less than a mere machine" may lower people's self-regard.
4. All educators are responsible for developing students' critical abilities so that they can analyze the subtle messages about technology embedded in popular magazines and television.
5. It is virtually impossible to stop software piracy in the schools.
6. Software piracy is a short-term problem because future technology will alleviate it.
7. Software piracy is both morally and legally wrong.
8. Copying software in education is like photo-copying from books.
9. Teachers who illegally copy software set a bad example for students.
10. Because it is impossible for teachers to spend the time necessary to develop their own software when the economic situation facing the schools is critical, they are forced to copy software illegally for the benefit of students and the nation's future.
11. Once a school district has paid for a piece of software, it is OK to make multiple copies for use by the district's teachers.
12. Given today's high costs, there is no way a district can legally acquire all the educational software needed for a broad educational program.
13. Software manufacturers should increase prices to compensate for piracy.
14. Vendors' high prices encourage software piracy.
15. All software should be accessible only from a national data base, with each customer paying for this access.
16. The preponderance of males in computing should be turned around in the elementary schools because girls tend to be higher achievers at this age.
17. In secondary schools, computers are dominated by in-group boys.
18. Many articles on computers in education (including some in this text) use sexist language. To guard against this, editors should thoroughly screen each article before publication.
19. To encourage more female participation, schools should offer computer-related curriculum in subjects other than math and science.
20. Because hand-held computer games are geared toward males, boys grow interested in electronics and computers but girls do not.
21. The lack of software for Spanish-speaking and French-speaking people is a major cause of poor minority participation in the computer revolution.
22. Schools cannot afford to produce software relevant to minority populations.
23. People who write software are from upper-middle-class backgrounds and tend not to consider the interests of minorities when producing software.
24. It is important to deal with computer values in an educational setting.
25. As the number of people who work with computers increases, the need for a well defined moral code becomes critical.
26. Educators should consider conducting "societal impact" studies before introducing computer technology into the educational system.
27. Computers are likely to replace teachers in a majority of learning situations by the early 21st century.
28. Military dictators in developing countries will not allow computers into education because of their possible effect on the common citizen's knowledge level.
29. Women will have fewer opportunities for jobs in the future if they do not become computer-literate.
30. Many difficulties that we face today are a result of blindly trusting technology to find solutions to our problems.

EXERCISES

1. Actors and musicians often make millions of dollars per year for their work even though much of their material is copied (videotape and recorders). What prevents programmers from making millions even though their work is being copied?
2. What percentage of the people who illegally copy software would you expect to be convicted? (Can you find any statistical evidence in this area?)
3. What can be done to make it profitable for programmers to produce good software?
4. Name some of the advantages of buying an original copy of software as opposed to pirating a copy.
5. Compare the industrial revolution to the current technological revolution.
6. Isaac Asimov's "Rules for Robots" suggests that (a) robots should not cause humans to come to harm; (b) robots must obey orders from humans as long as these orders do not violate rule 1; (c) robots must protect their own existence as long as this protection does not violate rule 1 or 2. In July 1981 a Japanese factory worker was killed by a computer-controlled robot. Should the factory abandon the use of robots?
7. Define "future shock." (See Toffler, A. *Future Shock*. New York: Random House, 1970.) To what extent do computers in education contribute to future shock?
8. Read Orwell's *1984* (Orwell, G. *1984*. New York: Penguin, 1949). How accurate has Orwell's prediction of today's world been so far?
9. If you were a writer of science fiction attempting to depict the way of life in the year 2000, what would you predict about education?
10. Under which of the following circumstances is it permissible to copy a copyrighted disk?

PERSON	PROGRAM
• High school math teacher	Algebra program
• Parent	Game for your child
• Head Start program	Reading readiness CAI
• College student	Word processor
• College student	Video game
• Child	Video game
• Child	Math CAI
• Education minister of a developing country	CAI
• Superintendent of schools	Back-up copies of CAI
• Elementary school teacher	Back-up copy for student
• Elementary school teacher	Typing-tutor
• College professor	CAI for class demonstration

11. List five methods software vendors might use to market their goods.
12. How can schools and software vendors best work together for their mutual benefit regarding software piracy?
13. What can educators (e.g., U.S. Department of Education, state office, county, local, graduate schools of education, teachers' organizations, PTA) do to ensure that computers enter the schools in such a way as not to encourage discrimination against women and ethnic minorities?
14. The advent of the computer age will bring an end to religion as we know it today. Discuss.
15. How can educators ensure that the social aspect of education is not lost through the increased use of computers in education?
16. If we can predict anything about the future on which to base educational policy, it is that change will be basic to 21st-century living, but problems will exist and people will exist. What have computers to do with these predictions?

NINE

Exceptional Students

One of the great advantages of having micro-computers in the classroom is the opportunity they afford to assist the student whose abilities lie outside the norm. Too often teachers are forced to aim lessons at the "mediocre middle," while students toward either end of the scale tend to suffer. Bright kids quickly become bored; slow learners soon fall behind and either drop out or become "problems." The computer enables the teacher to provide meaningful remedial work or new challenges through supplementary assignments, as well as to reach handicapped or special students on an individual basis. Although the computer is not intended to replace the teacher, it does offer a valuable extra hand in appropriate situations.

In this concluding chapter, Williams, Thorkildsen, and Crossman report on the use of computers for mentally and physically handicapped persons, while Kolstad and Lidtke outline an ACM report on the use of computers to assist gifted/talented students; two specific programs are also detailed. In addition, Weir and Watt describe a LOGO project to help learning-disabled students in grades five through eight. Kleiman, Humphrey, and Lindsay look at the use of computers in assisting hyperactive children.

LOGO: A Computer Environment for Learning-Disabled Students

Sylvia Weir and Daniel Watt

I. INTRODUCTION

This paper describes a project designed to provide an innovative computer-based learning environment for learning-disabled students in grades 5–8. The students will learn LOGO, a computer language for elementary school students, and will engage in a variety of computer programming activities designed to enhance basic skills and to develop problem solving abilities. They will learn to use a computer text-editor for creative writing. The project will provide extensive training and support for teachers of learning disabled students, and will develop a set of curriculum materials and a teacher methodology which will allow these methods to be successfully implemented in other schools. The project will provide a model of a computer-based learning environment which can be adapted to a variety of student populations.

The LOGO computer language and associated activities have been developed by the MIT LOGO Group over the past twelve years. Significant learning gains have been observed among students who have had the opportunity to participate in these activities, gains which we attribute to a variety of factors. The prestige associated with learning to program a computer leads to an increase in motivation for most students. The LOGO learning environment operates best when children are allowed to decide the content and pace of the activities they undertake and this

From "LOGO: A Computer Environment For Learning-Disabled Students," by Sylvia Weir and Daniel Watt. In *The Computing Teacher*, January, 1981. Reprinted by permission.

control of their own learning has a strikingly beneficial effect on their self-confidence. Programming in an interactive computer graphics situation lends itself to an emphasis on *process* rather than *product,* in that the typical tasks are structured to enable direct feedback on the intermediate steps during the solving of a problem. A discrepancy between what is intended and what actually happens is thus more readily available to both teacher and learner than is usually the case, and such an error or "bug" becomes a source of insight into the learning process, into the problem solving process.

Typical beginning LOGO tasks in Turtle Geometry (see Appendix) mobilize and help to cultivate skills in spatial reasoning often not otherwise utilized in the conventional curriculum and this fact can be an advantage to those whose gifts lie in this direction. In the process of exploring problems in Turtle Geometry, students gain concrete mathematical experience which provides a foundation for more abstract mathematical subjects such as algebra, geometry and trigonometry. In addition, they develop skills in reading, spelling and typing in the process of inputting their programs and in deciphering the computer messages; the availability of a text-editor enhances this experience and provides motivation and a practical tool, allowing some students to make dramatic progress in creative expression.

All of the above remarks apply most especially to any learning-disabled students participating in LOGO activities, and following some promising preliminary results with this group, it was decided to set up a project specifically directed at this area of special educational need.

A central goal of the project concerns the need to help teachers of learning-disabled students develop the skills and confidence required to integrate computer use into students' individual education plans. The project will also provide documentation, curriculum materials and assistance to other schools seeking to adopt the methods developed.

II. BACKGROUND

Karl is a tall, awkward boy who has severe learning disabilities. In sixth grade, his general academic achievement was at approximately a second grade level. His attitude toward school seemed to be one of hostile resignation. At this point Karl was given the opportunity to program a computer, during the course of which he overcame severe typing and spelling difficulties to learn LOGO. Working over a period of thirty-six hours, Karl demonstrated skills and understandings in geometry, non-verbal reasoning, organization and logical problem solving, that had not been previously evident to his classroom teachers or his learning disabilities tutor. (See Appendix II for a sample of Karl's work.)

In an interview following the conclusion of the classes, Karl was asked to solve the problem of finding all the possible different arrangements of a group of blocks of four colors. Rather than lay out all the blocks and compare arrangements—the strategy used by most students—Karl slowly calculated that there were twenty-four possible arrangements. When the interviewer confirmed this solution, he picked up the microphone of her tape recorder, and speaking directly into it said, "I'm a brain!" (Papert, et al., 1979)

Karl's story is a dramatic example of what can happen when a learning-disabled student is provided with a new kind of learning opportunity—one which allows him a measure of control over his own learning, and one which enables him to make use of skills which have not been developed in his prior school experience. In the remainder of this section we shall discuss the nature and extent of the learning gains illustrated here. First we provide some general background information.

LOGO—A computer language and learning environment

The work proposed here is directly linked with a series of research and development projects carried out at MIT and elsewhere during the past twelve years. The computer language, LOGO, was originally developed as a computer-based learning environment in which children could learn computer programming, problem solving and mathematical thinking. The LOGO learning environment is based on the developmental psychology of Jean Piaget as well as an approach to the design of computer languages as problem solving tools developed in the study of Artificial Intelligence. (Feuerzeig, et al., 1969; Papert and Solomon, 1971; Papert, 1971) In the late sixties, the developers of LOGO chose to base their learning environment on computer systems that would not be available to the general public for ten to fifteen years. Predicting a rapid decline in computing costs, they spent that time developing and exploring the kinds of learning environments that would be possible when there was general public access to inexpensive computers.

Under the guidance of MIT Professor Seymour Papert, the working philosophy of LOGO's developers has been "No threshold, no ceiling." Any student should be able to learn in a LOGO learning laboratory and the gifted student could exploit the open-ended possibilities made available in this environment. During the past twelve years, researchers at MIT and elsewhere have worked with hundreds of elementary and middle school students of a range of ages, interests and abilities. They have developed activities which have the dual attributes of capturing and holding a child's interest and providing a rich intellectual environment to further the child's learning. While students as young as five and six have successfully learned to use aspects of LOGO, the usual starting age has been about eight or nine, the age when most students can begin to be comfortable with a computer keyboard. At the other extreme, LOGO has been used with extremely bright high school and college students. As a programmer gains experience with LOGO, s/he can carry out complex programming projects, just as with any other high level programming language. (Papert, 1973; Abelson and diSessa, 1976).

During the past several years, the LOGO group at MIT, part of MIT's Artificial Intelligence Laboratory and its Division for Study and Research in Education, has been concerned with facilitating the use of these methods by educators and by the general public. In 1977–78, a computer laboratory was established at the Lincoln School in Brookline as part of a research project sponsored by the National Science Foundation. (Papert, et al., 1977) All of the school's sixth grade students were given the opportunity to learn LOGO during twenty to thirty-six hours of individual computer access. The learning experiences of sixteen of the students representing a full range of ability, were carefully documented and formed the basis for the final report of the project. (Papert, et al., 1979) The report details both the subject matter learned by the students, and the individual learning paths of each of the sixteen students. *It was a major finding of the report that the LOGO learning environment had had significant impact on the education of exceptional students at both ends of the spectrum of ability. In particular, learning-disabled students made dramatic growth in both skills and motivation.* Karl, described above, and Tina were the prime examples:

> Tina is another severely learning disabled student who participated in the research project as a sixth grader. Tina expressed a persistent interest in using the computer as a typewriter, rather than in programming it. She was given the opportunity to use a simple text editor, which allowed her to write letters and stories, by typing them on the computer keyboard. If she made an error in her typing she could go back and rub it out, editing her work as she saw fit. When her work was complete, she used the computer to make as many printed copies as she wanted, each one looking like a professionally typed document. Starting with a two line letter to her mother, Tina gradually increased her output until she was spending an hour at a time on a story, and writing stories that powerfully reflected her interests and feelings. (See Appendix III for a sample of Tina's work.)
>
> When the computer teacher sought samples of her creative writing from her classroom teachers and her learning-disabilities tutor, he found that Tina had not done any creative writing during the entire school year,

and was extremely resistant to school work in general. Using the computer, Tina was not only writing, but was proud of her work, making many copies of each story and distributing them to her family, friends and teachers. Tina's blossoming as a writer has continued even after the computer classes terminated. During the following two years she has continued to think of herself as a writer, and has written and illustrated several small books. (Papert, et al., 1979).

III. A TEACHER'S PERSPECTIVE

Clearly, something important is happening here. In the year and a half since the end of the research project, the Brookline Public School System has been conducting its own Pilot LOGO Project at Lincoln School. Two computers have been placed in various classrooms, and children have been allowed access to computers on an individual basis. Because of the original success of learning-disabled students with LOGO, one of the classrooms involved in the Pilot LOGO Project has been the school's Learning Center. In June, 1979, Karl and Tina's Learning Center teacher, Ellie Shacter, submitted the following report to Jeff Resnick, Brookline's Special Education Supervisor:

Use of the LOGO computer in the learning center

The LOGO computer was designed so students could do their own computer programming. Students control the computer, decide what to do and then carry it out; they are in charge and can make things happen.

They are able to succeed without having to rely on building up deficient academic skills.

In learning to program the LOGO Computer, students are:

- learning an approach to thinking which will eventually allow them to program other computers;
- gaining understanding which, at least, enables them to live more comfortably in a technological age;
- developing logical (mathematical) thinking and problem solving;
- using strategy and variables;
- gaining information about symmetry, design, angles, geometric forms;
- learning to develop and test their own theories.

Personal characteristics such as the ability to take independent action, the ability to sustain interest in a project, increased self-esteem, and greater self-knowledge about their individual, personal ways of exploring are fostered.

Students can develop a sense of being empowered as they are able to make decisions about this particular "educational environment."

Deficit skills can be remedied within a pleasant, challenging environment (and in conjunction with use of the computer rather than as separate problems to be solved).

- Fine motor skills are improved (through the typing).
- Near point reading (of CRT screen messages) is encouraged.
- Short-term memory is developed (while students learn to use a typewriter keyboard and the various logging in and programming procedures).
- Students learn to spell the commands.
- Students learn to receive error messages as informational messages that help them reach their chosen objectives, i.e. they experience "making mistakes" without "punishment" and gain information which enables them to move a step closer toward reaching their goal. Students can compose, edit, and print-out multiple copies of letters and stories they have. written at the computer keyboard.
- Students develop direction-giving and direction-following skills.
- As they gain skill and experience in the use of LOGO, students can move from concrete to more abstract levels of thinking.

IV. A THEORETICAL PERSPECTIVE

From a theoretical perspective we would like to raise the following issues in considering the impact of LOGO activities on learning-disabled students:

1. It may be that we just hit it lucky—that this is a very localized phenomenon peculiar to the few individuals studied so far. It is important, therefore, to ascertain just what proportion of the learning-disabled population responds to this computer-based learning experience; i.e., to gauge the *extent* of the phenomenon.

2. It may be that the felicitous effect observed flows largely from the fact that *working with computers is seen to be a prestigious event* which in itself spurred the children involved to achieve in ways that had previously been impossible for them. If this should turn out to be the case, that would not necessarily be an argument against using computers for this population. Rather, it would incline us toward their use, while at the same time forcing us to carefully document and constrain any claims we may want to make as to the role of the LOGO computer environment in contributing to student success.

3. In searching for reasons why learning takes place in some particular situations, we recall that *learning is a complex process,* and the learner will have had to achieve, at the least,

(a) the mastery of new facts
(b) mastery of new procedures and operations connected with those facts
(c) knowing when and where to use (a) and (b) in solving a problem; i.e., the relevance of knowledge

(d) knowing that s/he knows (c); i.e., the self-confidence to use knowledge.

The LOGO work claims to have particular virtues in regard to (b), (c), and most especially (d), flowing from the *nature* of the system; i.e., the interactive graphics and the explicit decomposition of problems combine to give rather *transparent feedback* to promote the acquisition of this kind of knowledge. Because of the record automatically available during the course of this activity, many of the information processing steps involved in the task are explicitly available for scrutiny by both the student and his teacher. (The student is learning and the teacher is learning about learning.) Using this system, component skills can be tested out and particular hypotheses about rasoning strategies can be probed in a relatively straightforward way. (For an example of this see Weir, 1979.)

4. All this should aid in the analysis of just what is going on. LOGO activities can be both *diagnostic* and *interventionist*. There is a good deal to indicate that the learning-disabled comprise a heterogeneous category (summarized in Weir, 1979). Briefly, the suggestion is that the development of spatial reasoning and linguistic ability do not necessarily go hand in hand. For example, subjects weak in linguistic skills can have relatively unimpaired or even highly developed spatial intelligence. The latter is rarely engaged in the usual school subjects, and the children whose strengths lie in this area go unrewarded (until they show their aptitude for mechanical drawing or industrial arts in the non-academic area). LOGO has the virtue of exploiting such spatial skills, allowing their owners to shine among their peers and to turn such skills to an *academic* (mathematical) purpose. On the other hand, for some children, the learning problem may lie in exactly this area, *viz* in an impaired spatial sense to the point of affecting the scrutiny of letter strings. Thus the performance on LOGO tasks promises to be of diagnostic aid in the process of establishing subtypes of learning disability by providing one basis for a functional specification of such subcategories.

In addition to the development/documentation project described here, we will be seeking funding for a research oriented project to be carried out among the same population of students and teachers. If funded, the two projects will function in a mutually supportive manner, providing a collaborative setting in which fundamental research and innovative educational development can inform and support each other.

An important thread of LOGO research during the last five or six years has been the use of LOGO with students who have physical, psychological and functional handicaps. In 1976, one of us (Sylvia

Weir), then affiliated with the Edinburgh LOGO Group in Scotland, documented the successful use of LOGO with an autistic child (Weir and Emanuel, 1976). Since June of 1978, Weir has co-directed, with Professor Seymour Papert of MIT, a research endeavor exploring the effect of LOGO on students with cerebral palsy. (Papert and Weir, 1978; Weir, 1980). This work seeks to remedy some of the deficiencies in the learning environment of a cerebral palsy victim due to communication difficulties, and to the lack of concrete manipulative experiences available to normal children. With a suitable computer language, and with appropriate interface devices to reduce typing difficulties, it is hypothesized that a computer-based learning environment such as LOGO can provide both a medium of communication and a source of concrete learning activities for the student. Initial results, with students at the Cotting School for the Physically Handicapped in Boston, have been extremely encouraging, as well as providing much new data about the specific developmental deprivations of cerebral palsied students. (Weir, 1980). Of special interest is the development of diagnostic tests run on a computer graphics screen, thus making it possible to test the *performance* ability of severely physically handicapped children, something which has been notoriously difficult to do.

V. A METHODOLOGY FOR SUPPORTING INNOVATION

At the core of this project is a complex learning experience for the teachers involved. We would like to suggest that the teachers' learning can be compared metaphorically to the process of learning to skate. A beginner skater goes through three significant stages. The first is "hand-holding." A friend, parent or instructor goes out on the ice with the learner, providing her literally with the direct support she needs to gain confidence, along with specific instructions and feedback. The second is the "watch me!" stage. The new skater ventures out on the ice alone, but under the watchful gaze of her teacher, to whom she can return for support when necessary, and from whom she can get specific feedback and suggestions. The third stage is "free skating." Now the learner is truly on her own, skating freely without outside support. From time to time she may seek instruction in special areas, or work to perfect a particular skill, but she is essentially free to pursue additional learning at her own rate and in accordance with her own interests and desires.

We believe that this metaphor is applicable to the process of integrating a new learning environment such as LOGO into the ongoing practice of a Learning Center teacher. Our project plan provides for a significant amount of direct support to teachers, especially during the first year of their participation. In addition to working closely with each teacher during the "hand-holding" stage, the project will create materials for teacher use and eventual dissemination, and will build a supportive network for the project within each school, and within the community at large. We believe that these three aspects of our plan—direct teacher support, development and dissemination of materials, and the building of a support network—are all vital in establishing and sustaining the innovation.

The project is designed to initially involve learning centers in five schools. During the second year it will expand to serve about 140 special-needs students in all eight Brookline elementary schools. The successful provision of services to students depends on successful training and support of the Learning Center teachers. During the first year, our activities will focus most strongly on training teachers, providing the teachers with supportive services and materials, and documenting student and teacher learning. As teachers gain experience in project activities, the project staff will gradually shift its major focus from training and support of teachers, to preparation and dissemination of project documentation. By the third year of the project, the first five teachers should be functioning independently, the second group of three teachers in their second year of participation will need less support, and the project staff will be devoting most of its energy to writing project documents and disseminating information about the project to interested schools.

Training and support for teachers will be provided in a variety of ways.

1. Training:

A two-week summer workshop at the start of the project will provide teachers with an understanding of the philosophy and methods of the project, as well as training in the LOGO computer language and activities. By focusing on their own learning during the training, teachers will be better able to understand their students' learning experiences. The relationship between LOGO activities and the needs of learning-disabled students will be thoroughly discussed. Additional training will be provided in a series of monthly workshops throughout the year.

2. Materials:

The project staff will provide materials for teachers and students. Many of these materials already exist or can be adapted for special-needs students. Others are currently being developed by the MIT LOGO Group. Additional materials will be developed by the project staff, tested by the teachers and students, and revised by the staff. These materials will be an important part of the dissemination of the project's methods to other teachers.

3. Direct support:

During the first year of a teacher's participation, regular support will be provided by a resource teacher and by an instructional aide. The resource teacher will visit classes, observe students and meet with the teachers to discuss the overall progress of the project and help with planning for individual students. The instructional aide will provide teachers with release time from regular tutorial duties so that they can participate more fully in project activities. The amount of support for *experienced* teachers will decrease during the second year as new teachers are added to the project. During the third year, it is anticipated that the original teachers will be functioning independently, with only occasional assistance from the project staff.

4. Project meetings:

Teachers will be released from regular duties for one half-day per month to attend project meetings. At these meetings they will receive additional training, discuss the progress of the project in their own classes, share and analyze successes and problems with individual students, and participate with the staff in ongoing project planning.

5. A support network within the school and the community:

The instructional aides and student teachers who make up each Learning Center team will be provided with training so that they can participate more fully in project activities. School personnel such as classroom teachers, pupil support personnel, the school principal and guidance counselor, will attend at least one orientation workshop offered by the project staff. Parents, who play a major role in supporting each child's Learning Center program, will be invited to an orientation meeting and encouraged to visit classes. Parents who wish to volunteer as tutors will be able to receive additional training from the project staff. An Advisory Council will be established to help the project maintain contact with various groups within the school system and in the community at large. Information about the project published in local, regional and national media will help provide support to the project, as well as informing a wider public, as part of project dissemination.

VI. GOALS OF THE PROJECT

In summary then, the goals of the project are as follows:

1. Student Goals: To help mildly to moderately learning-disabled students, grade 5-8, who receive remedial services in school Learning Centers, make gains in the areas of motivation, self-confidence, basic skills in math, reading, spelling and punctuation, creative writing, typing, logical problem solving, and computer literacy.

2. Teacher Goals: To help teachers of learning-disabled students develop competence and confidence in educational uses of computers, and the understandings necessary to integrate those uses appropriately into each student's individual education plan.

3. Dissemination Goals: To securely establish the innovative methods of this project in a supportive context within participating schools; to make other schools and school systems aware of the project; and to provide documentation, training and technical assistance to help them make use of the methods developed here.

VII. EVALUATION OF PROJECT OBJECTIVES

Since the project stresses flexibility of approach, and the integration of computer activities into individual education plans, all students will not be expected to meet all objectives equally. An important aspect of the project will be the development of the best possible integration of individual student needs, and project activities in order to meet particular objectives. The project staff and teachers will make use of ongoing evaluation of each child's work to make the best possible match between student needs and project objectives. For example, some students may make extensive use of the text-editor, with reduced emphasis on computer programming. For others the reverse may be true. The overall evaluation will need to take these individual differences into account.

The evaluation design, to be developed by the project staff and an evaluation consultant, will make use of previously developed standardized measures whenever possible. In other cases, non-standard measures will have to be found or developed. Since some of the student objectives involve indirect effects of the experience (such as increased self-confidence), or types of learning that are not routinely measured in schools (such as computer programming skills or problem solving abilities), the development of the evaluation design will be a critical task to be addressed early in the project.

A unique form of evaluation data available to this project will come from "dribble files" kept automatically by the computer. These are detailed, keystroke by keystroke records of a student's interaction with the computer. They are invaluable in the understanding of problem solving strategies, mathematical and logical reasoning, and frequency and duration of computer use. These will be used by project staff and teachers in ongoing assessment of student progress and to contribute to the overall evaluation and documentation of the project.

VIII. THE POTENTIAL SIGNIFICANCE OF THE PROJECT

We believe that the success of this project could have a significant impact on the use of computers in the education of special-needs students, and on instructional uses of computers in general. We use technology to create a teaching/learning environment which goes far beyond the common concept of a computer as a tutorial or record keeping device. We do this by reversing the usual order of things: whereas conventional Computer Assisted Instruction systems have a "clever" computer program teaching a "dumb" student, our students develop an intelligent self-image as they learn to teach a "dumb" computer. By stressing learner choices within a range of possible activities, we seek to remedy the problem of alienation experienced by many special-needs students, and to accommodate a variety of individual needs and capabilities. Finally, with our stress on the process of teacher training and the development of teacher and student materials to integrate a new methodology into an ongoing program, we hope that this project will provide a model for the incorporation of computers into educational programs at all levels, and for a variety of student populations.

IX. BIBLIOGRAPHIC REFERENCES

Abelson and diSessa, "Student Science Training Program in Mathematics, Physics and Computer Science." Artificial Intelligence Laboratory Memo #393, LOGO Memo #29, MIT, 1976.

Feuerzeig, Papert, Bloom, Grant and Solomon, "Programming Languages as a Conceptual Framework for Teaching Mathematics." Report No. 1889, Bolt, Beranek and Newman, Cambridge, Mass., 1969.

Papert, "Teaching Children to be Mathematicians vs. Teaching about Mathematics." Artificial Intelligence Laboratory Memo #249, LOGO Memo #4, MIT, 1971.

Papert, "Uses of Technology to Enhance Education." Artificial Intelligence Laboratory Memo #298, LOGO Memo #8, MIT, 1973.

Papert, Abelson, diSessa, Watt, "Assessment and Documentation of a Children's Computer Laboratory." Artificial Intelligence Memo #460, LOGO Memo #48, MIT, 1977.

Papert, diSessa, Watt, Weir, "Final Report of the Brookline LOGO Project. Part II, Project Overview and Data Analysis. Part III, Individual Student Profiles." Artificial Intelligence Laboratory Memos #545 and #546, LOGO Memos #53 and #54, MIT, 1979. See especially Part II, Chapter 3, "The Experience of Exceptional Students," and Part III, Chapters 10, 15 and 16.

Papert and Solomon, "Twenty Things to Do with a Computer." Artificial Intelligence Laboratory Memo #248, LOGO Memo #3, MIT, 1971.

Papert and Weir, "Information Prosthetics for the Handicapped." Artificial Intelligence Laboratory Memo #496, LOGO Memo #51, MIT, 1978.

Weir, "The Use of LOGO for the Diagnosis of Children's Abilities in Areas of Spatial Reasoning, and the Use of LOGO for Remediation." Internal working paper, MIT LOGO Group, 1979.

Weir, "Evaluation and Cultivation of Spatial and Linguistic Abilities in Individual with Cerebral Palsy." Artificial Intelligence Laboratory Memo #570, LOGO Memo #51, MIT, March 1980.

Weir and Emanuael, "Using LOGO to Catalyse Communication in an Autistic Child," Department of Artificial Intelligence Memo #15, University of Edinburgh, Edinburgh, Scotland, 1976.

APPENDIX I
INTRODUCTION TO LOGO

To provide a context for "learning by doing," we link up various devices to a computer so that a child can, via a computer, "command" an output device to carry out an action. One device we have used is a mechanical "turtle" capable of moving forward or back in a particular direction (relative to itself) and of rotating about its central axis. It has a retractable pen on its underside which can be in two states called PENUP and PENDOWN.

The mechanical turtle can be replaced by a △ on a display screen, and this is made to "act" by typing commands. At any one time the turtle is set at a particular place and facing a particular direction.

FIGURE 1

If the pen is down, then as the turtle moves around, it leaves a trace, and so arbitrarily complex patterns can be drawn. For example, the following commands will cause the turtle to draw Figure 2.

```
PENDOWN
FORWARD 100
LEFT 120
FORWARD 100
LEFT 120
FORWARD 100
```

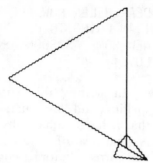

FIGURE 2

There are many paths to take from this point depending on the individual characteristics of the learner (and of the teacher). For example, the set of instructions required to draw a triangle can be wrapped up into a bundle as a PROCEDURE and given a NAME. Different sizes and orientation of triangle can be drawn by introducing a variable parameter for the procedure. This immediately leads to the *discovery* that other polygonal shapes can be drawn by selecting appropriate values for the input variables.

```
TO TRI :ANGLE :SIDE      TO POLY :ANGLE :SIDE
10 FORWARD :SIDE         10 FORWARD :SIDE
20 LEFT :ANGLE           20 LEFT :ANGLE
30 FORWARD :SIDE         30 POLY :ANGLE :SIDE
40 LEFT :ANGLE           END
50 FORWARD :SIDE
END
```

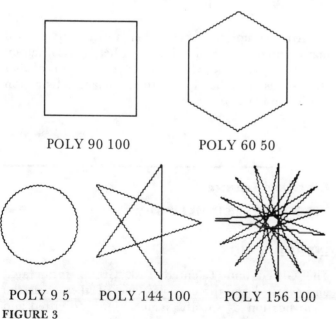

POLY 90 100   POLY 60 50

POLY 9 5   POLY 144 100   POLY 156 100

FIGURE 3

Notice that in addition to learning computer programming, the student is learning *mathematical*

ideas—he is exploring the notion of ANGLE, POLYGONS, RECURSION and so on.

Problem solving

Repeated calls of the same triangle procedure were named by children in a LOGO class in the Brookline public school system as:

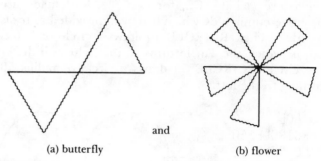

and

(a) butterfly   (b) flower

FIGURE 4

Complex patterns can be seen as consisting of familiar parts. For example a house can be broken into:

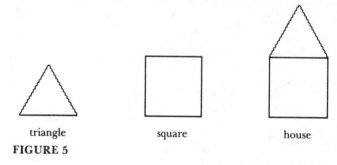

triangle   square   house

FIGURE 5

This introduces a basic PROBLEM-SOLVING heuristic, i.e., break up a complex problem into its subparts. The HOUSE procedure can be built up out of a TRIANGLE sub-procedure and a SQUARE sub-procedure. Putting together these procedures produces an unexpected result.

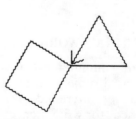

FIGURE 6

This is because when the triangle was completed the turtle was left facing in the direction of the arrow. So this introduces the idea of a BUG, which can be easily fixed or DEBUGGED because it is so easy to follow what is happening—*the relation between the action and its consequence is very explicit.*

APPENDIX II
AN EXAMPLE OF KARL'S WORK

Karl, a learning-disabled student referred to in the body of this paper, engaged in a number of programming projects in which he was able to make use of and develop his geometric understanding, organizational skill and reasoning ability. In the procedure called ACE, for example, Karl made use of circle commands which had been provided as tools by his teacher. RCIRCLE 50 draws a circle of radius 50, in which the Turtle turns to the right as it draws the circle. LCIRCLE 50 draws a circle of radius 50 turning to the left.

```
TO ACE
1 RCIRCLE 50
2 LCIRCLE 50
3 FORWARD 100
4 BACK 200
5 RCIRCLE 50
6 LCIRCLE 50
7 FORWARD 100
8 FORWARD 100
9 RCIRCLE 50
10 LCIRCLE 50
END
```

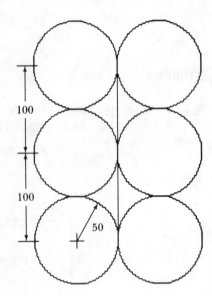

FIGURE 7

The geometric organization of ACE is shown in Figure 7. In drawing his design, Karl made use of right/left and forward/back symmetry and made creative use of the relationship between the radius and diameter of a circle.

APPENDIX III
EXAMPLES OF TINA'S WORK

Tina's pattern of computer use was unique among sixteen experimental subjects in the Brookline study in that she was not interested in Turtle Geometry and never learned to write her own LOGO procedures. On the other hand, Tina established an intense, personal relationship with the computer, and, using the computer as a text editor and word processor, wrote a series of stories that represented a major achievement in the area of creative writing.

The letter, HELEN, is representative of Tina's first two attempts to use the computer for writing:

```
DEAR HELEN HOW ARE YOU IN YOUR NEW HOME.
I AM GOING TO GET YOU SOMETHING FOR YOUR
NEW HOME AS SOON AS I GET MY MONEY.
LOVE TINA
```

In writing this letter Tina regularly asked for spelling and punctuation help. She was concerned that it be grammatically correct, and in proper form. A great deal of time was spent making sure each line was correct, before going on to the next.

Once she shifted from writing letters to stories, Tina became less concerned with spelling and grammar (although she continued to ask for help in these areas). Instead, she was more concerned with the details of the story: the names of the characters, the places they lived, the sequence of events, and the feelings of the characters involved. Tina had deep feelings about her subject matter. Her story, SONNY, is typical of her style and intensity of feeling.

```
SONNY IS A LITTLE BOY HE LIVES WITH HIS
AUNT HELEN IN CALIFORNIA   HE HAS BEEN LIVE
WITH HER FOR 9 YEARS. HE IS GOING TO A
HOME FOR LITTLE WONDERS 4 WEEKS AFTER THAT
TO COUPLE A ADOPTED SONNY HE WAS THE
HAPPIEST BOY THAT YOU EVER SEEN. I GUESS
IF THAT WAS ME I WOULD BE HAPPY IF SOME
ONE WOULD ADOPT. BUT SEE I AM NOT ADOPT I
HAVE MY ON MOTHER AND I AM GLAD THAT I
HAVE MY ON MOTHER BECAUSE THE KIDS THAT
HAVE FEELS REALLY BAD. THAT'S WHY ALL THE
KIDS IN THE WORLD SHOULD BE GRATEFUL TO
THEIR PARENTS. THE END.
```

After completing each of her stories, Tina printed many copies to be distributed to her friends, family and teachers. The widespread distribution of her stories was an indication of the pride and satisfaction she felt in her work.

Gifted and Talented

Rob Kolstad and **Doris Lidtke**

INTRODUCTION

The Gifted and Talented Task Group formulated and worked on three goals. One of them was the identification of specific issues related to gifted and

From "Gifted and Talented," by Rob Kolstad and Doris Lidtke. In *Topics,* Association of Computing Machinery (SIGSCE, SIGCUE), January, 1981. Reprinted by permission.

talented students along with documentation of working gifted and talented courses. Specific problem areas were to be identified and proposed solutions were to be sought. A bibliography of relevant information was to be prepared.

SURVEY

A survey distributed to task group members identified the perceived needs in this area and also identified the current status of programs across the United States.

The responses to the question concerning needs can be grouped into roughly three categories: curriculum development, liaison, and software/project exchange. A few miscellaneous replies extended beyond these categories.

Curriculum development
    Develop guidelines and teach computer enrichment topics.
    Suggest guidelines for developing new programs.
    Make a general suggested curriculum.
    Find good software activities for the elementary school curriculum.
    Provide resource lists to local schools of: guest lecturers, field trip sites, local industries that will support computer education.
    Find out what new abilities gifted and talented students exercise due to computers (e.g., creative art and music composition).
    Document obvious uses by gifted and talented students: problem solving, game creation.

Liaison
    Set up an apprenticeship program providing gifted high school students with on-site experience in ACM members' shops.
    Establish an "equipment for education" pool.
    Establish a "services for education" pool (these pools would donate equipment, services, or time to computer related projects).
    Find volunteer mentors and consultants.
    Cooperate with NCTM and NSTA.
    Involve university personnel in designing a thorough college prep course.

Software and project exchange
    Disseminate computer programs from student-made contributions.
    Provide an exchange.
    Determine what programs exist and make descriptions widely available.
    Develop software using currently available microcomputers for use in the classroom.
    Establish a clearinghouse to keep track of what is available and where.
    Compile information on projects currently operating.

Miscellaneous
    Publicize support of gifted and talented use of computer.
    Provide vocational education for computing.
    Provide instruction so that teachers will be able to use the computer.
    DON'T do boring CAI.

It can be seen that several respondents were very enthusiastic about a formalized gifted and talented curriculum or project management guide. They also wished to establish interfaces with the community and other sources of computing experience. The recurring theme of "provide a software exchange" rings out of this survey. The miscellaneous comments speak for themselves.

There are many ongoing projects. Among these are: (1) NSF and independently sponsored Saturday Institutes which typically provide experiences for teachers (and highly motivated students). These sessions meet on weekends and provide teachers with experiences in new technology areas along with graduate credit. (2) Summer programs sponsored by universities offer one to eight week courses in computer science for talented high school students. When not supported by the NSF, these courses generally serve as a recruiting and interest-building vehicle for the institution. (3) The Junior Engineering Technical Society (JETS) (a high school engineering club) has chapters throughout the United States. Their activities include local speakers and interest-building meetings in addition to local and regional engineering "competitions" in various fields. (4) Boy Scouts of America supported Explorer Posts: 271 explorer posts offer career and enrichment activities to 7,341 high school students in the area of computer science. (5) Universities as resource centers. A small cadre of elite high school students tend to obtain access to and use of computer facilities at most universities (though not necessarily in an organized fashion).

Daniel Keating states that "the creative thinking experiences necessary for gifted kids must have (at least) three components:

1. possibility of use of divergent thinking
2. familiarity with a subject so as to be at its frontier
3. need for judgment and evaluation of performance."

Use of a computer allows all of these to be done—perhaps better than any other vehicle. "However, kids will need careful guiding in #3 [above] and this task group should address that. Also, there is a little evidence to show that bright kids will start writing educational programs to teach other kids, thus impinging on the teacher's realm."

Other respondents asked the following sets of questions:

> What special uses do computers have for the mentally gifted? What special problems can be expected? What are the potential vehicles or methods used for the gifted? Where are exemplary programs of this type located? What priority does a program of this type occupy in a general program of computer usage?

> How much structure is appropriate to computer education of the gifted? What type? Will gifted students benefit more by developing programs or by using them? What languages give the gifted student the greatest opportunity for interaction? What languages best help the gifted student to organize his thoughts while he writes programs?

From the survey results, it can be seen that the respondents want software for their computers (although it is not completely clear what to do with it), information and guidance both for the teachers and students, and a curriculum for gifted and talented (and other) students. No mention was made of problems pertaining to equipment acquisition. Only slight mention was made of guidelines for producing programs of high quality for gifted students.

The survey pointed up that our respondents come from a broad variety of backgrounds and a broad variety of experience with computing. Most seem very interested in having special programs for gifted and talented students, though the criteria for identifying such students is not addressed.

PROBLEMS AND SOME SOLUTIONS

The survey pointed up several different problems: some specific to gifted and talented students, and some general to all precollege computing programs.

Probably the most requested and biggest problem for gifted and talented programs is the creation of a curriculum or project list for such students. Unfortunately, no such list has appeared. It appears that the kinds of projects that are appropriate need almost be tailor-made to environments and current fads. (Current projects for precollege programmers at the University of Illinois include creation of different kinds of games and parts of games. The problem of "gaming addiction" for PLAYING the games was ultimately solved here, but creation of certain kinds of games seems to provide the right kind of stimulus: implementation of advanced fantasy simulation (dungeon) games requires advanced data structures and algorithmic concepts. There is currently a keen competition among local precollege and some college programmers to see who can implement the best simulation game. It is interesting to note that many of these same programmers continue to carry high GPA's and part-time employment.)

The problem of a curriculum for gifted and talented students carries with it the problem of implementing such a curriculum. It is a very rare group of gifted and talented students whose interests range uniformly and develop at the same rate. Self-paced programs allow the most interested students to proceed at a breakneck pace without being held back by other students who prefer to concentrate at some particular level. Evaluation of accomplishment within the curriculum must be judged individually since individual goals and interests vary. A clearinghouse (as suggested) for projects and sample curricula could be established, but maintenance time for such a library could be high.

Local resource lists for lecturers, tour sites, and local industries are something which must be acquired at the local level. How does a school create such a list? First, check with the closest local ACM chapter. Its members would be informative and helpful. Local universities can almost always help, but many cities have no universities. Well trained teachers or informed parents can sometimes contribute. Perusing the yellow pages can lead to finding a helpful industry which may be the key to many varied activities. Again, acquisition of this necessary data must be done by volunteers. Coordination could be possible through the "clearinghouse."

Apprenticeship and liaison programs seem universally to revolve around one central person in the liaison organization. The stereotype of this person is a worker who has an interest in youth and an ability to persuade his management that such an interest is of value to the industry and community. Typically these mentors are involved in computing at work or have a strong hobby interest. It is unfortunate that caution must be extended about some enthusiastic hobbyists: the training required to guide a gifted and talented student through advanced technical material is extensive. It is often a good idea to let the student research his/her own solutions. Standards of excellence do exist for precollege students in computing: one goal of all gifted and talented programs should be achievement of that excellence.

DESCRIPTION OF TWO PROGRAMS

This describes two fundamentally different gifted and talented programs in central Illinois: (1) a voluntary program in Urbana-Champaign, and (2) a more formal program in Danville (partially supported by federal funds). One major component of both of these programs is the University of Illinois's PLATO computing system. The programs are compared and contrasted with comments on the success of various components.

Urbana-Champaign

The extensive use of computers in Urbana-Champaign is partly due to the University of Illinois's early establishment of a computer science department and partly due to the high availability of PLATO. The Computer-based Education Research Laboratory (CERL) has a long-standing commitment to the support of precollege programmers. Some of the precollege programmers in the early days of PLATO eventually became system programmers and have since moved on to other industrial employment.

In 1972, a pilot computer-based math education program placed several terminals in elementary schools in Urbana-Champaign. The small number of terminals was initially used to test acceptance by the school system. A year later, many terminals were added to the classrooms and were used extensively for math CAI. Self-selected (but interviewed) gifted students from grades 4 through 6 (and possibly others) were instructed in production of CAI programs in the hope of ultimately increasing the available CAI libraries. Unfortunately, this age group was unable to sustain the level of literacy and quality required to produce usable computer programs. One student was able to produce a quiz program for math facts and presentation of a multiplication table. Insurmountable difficulties were encountered by the students in programming. However, some students were able to significantly increase their motor skills. Typical skill gains for elementary gifted students were in the areas of manipulation rather than abstraction and creation. Elementary students became masters at this art of understanding and bending prepackaged programs to their will. Some students were spending 20 hours/week on terminals, but devoting 95 percent of their time to playing games.

By 1975, a more formal program for learning programming had evolved for gifted junior high school students. This program was self-paced and attempted to encourage these students to increase their software skills. Some of their efforts, though unsophisticated, were marketable and are still in use today. This program evolved into a program known as the "yprog" group, which is the direct ancestor of the current "jpr" group.

Gaming was a major activity of the precollege programmers. The amount of terminal time spent on recreational activity increased at a great rate until restrictions were placed on its use.

Currently there are at least 100 precollege students using the PLATO system as a means of learning programming. These students are spread throughout many groups with varying purposes and degrees of supervision. The University of Illinois lab school supports many of these students as part of its commitment to computer science education. The initial computer science course teaches BASIC using PLATO. Subsequent courses, some of which are individual study, teach PLATO's native language, TUTOR.

Some students are supported by the "jpr" facilities. These students are given resources to learn programming. Occasional short courses are taught, but most instruction is self-paced and learned through peer group interaction. These students can continue to use the PLATO facilities as long as they demonstrate "progress", i.e., learning to program, learning to type, or gaining expertise in any of the different computer science activities available. A marked lack of "progress" for a month or two results in loss of privilege of using PLATO. The number of students in "jpr" varies from 15 to 40 depending on the season of the year.

Danville

The Danville gifted program is a relatively new one and was started two years ago when a group of four students (who had been using TRS-80s) asked to learn PLATO usage. An aptitude test was given to the 60 junior high school students interested in learning about PLATO and approximately 30 were selected for the "vikings" program. The first year included about five 1.5 hour lectures and two hours terminal time per week for each programmer. Parents supervised the terminals to avoid damage to the terminal room, but, of course, provided little programming expertise. A 50 percent dropout rate after the first year allowed an expanded usage of four hours per programmer per week in the last year at Danville. The Danville programmers have succeeded (among the current 12 of them) in producing a simple game and have spent the last three months or so "testing" it, though this does not yield a skill increase in programming. The original four programmers in Danville have maintained their skill superiority and are marginally good high school programmers. Only one member of the new group has achieved significant success and progress when compared to the "jpr" in the previous section.

The Danville administration also instituted a program this year for gifted students to use the CAI facilities on PLATO. Any "gifted" student could use PLATO for two hours per week for nine weeks and choose any CAI program to study. Usage statistics show that almost one-third of the time spent on PLATO was in the only remotely recreational activity in their catalog. Most of the students were bored within two weeks of their first usage. Danville's funds for PLATO will soon be diverted to the usage of microcomputers for CAI.

In summary: terminal access and supervision are two essential qualities in establishment of a precollege computing program. The development of a core group of programmers can relieve some of the burden of the supervisor, but programmers must still be accountable for the time they consume resources. Those programmers who had reasonably well qualified instructors and supervision have become competent coders; only a handful of the unsupervised are able to exhibit skill in problem solving and software. To start a new program, at least one skilled supervisor must be available to guide the new programmers. Once a routine has been established, the programmers can police themselves with only minimal outside supervision, though accountability must always be maintained.

SUMMARY

It is difficult to specify precisely what a gifted and talented program should include. Different communities with different interest and talent levels will require different kinds of instruction and projects. The availability of suitable teachers (an absolute necessity for full development of a gifted and talented student's potential) is crucial. Equipment necessary for a successful gifted and talented program usually exceeds initial expectations. A TRS-80 or Apple microcomputer typically provides a very pleasing initial experience with computing—but once ten students wish to spend two hours each per day on the computer, not only are more computers necessary, but within a few months the students find their programming appetites desire far more than the microcomputers can offer. Memory and secondary storage requirements typically grow most quickly. Access to larger computing systems for exceptional students is one solution (if such resources exist). Otherwise, a more theoretical education can help students with limited resources learn to utilize them to their fullest extent.

REFERENCES

Abelson, H. and DiSessa, A. *Student Science Training Programs in Mathematics, Physics, and Computer Science.* Cambridge, Mass.: AI Lab, 545 Technology Square, Cambridge, Mass. 02139 ($1.90), EC 113 748.

Cooke, G.J. Scientifically gifted children. *G/T/C*, March-April 1980, 17–18.

Gallagher, J.J. *Teaching the Gifted Child.* Boston, Mass.: Allyn and Bacon, 1975.

George, W.C., Sanford, J.C. and Stanley, J.C. *Educating the Gifted: Acceleration and Enrichment.* Baltimore, Md.: Johns Hopkins University Press, 1979.

Gifted—Programs, Teaching Methods, and Curriculum, 1977, Topical Bibliography. ED 146 734.

The Gifted and the Talented. Seventy-eighth Yearbook of the National Society for the Study of Education. Chicago: University of Chicago Press, 1979.

Ginsberg, G. and Harrison, C.H. *How to Help Your Gifted Child: A Handbook for Parents and Teachers.* New York: Monarch Press, 1977.

Glover, D. Computers—Are all dinosaurs dead? *G/T/C*, September-October 1978, 16–17, 46–50.

Gowan, J.C., Khatena, J. and Torrance, E.P. *Educating the Ablest* (rev. ed.). Itasca, Ill.: Peacock Publishers, 1979.

Hampton, C. Introduction to computers. *G/T/C*, March-April 1980, 44–45.

Henson, F. *Mainstreaming the Gifted.* Austin, Tex.: Learning Concepts, 1976.

Hopkinson, D. *The Education of Gifted Children.* Totowa, N.J.: Woburn Press, 1978.

Karnes, F.A. and Gregory, B. Saturday programs for the gifted. *G/T/C*, March-April 1980, 49–51.

Keating, D.P. *Intellectual Talent: Research and Development.* Baltimore, Md.: Johns Hopkins University Press, 1976.

Khatena, J. *The Creatively Gifted Child: Suggestions for Parents and Teachers.* New York: Vantage Press, 1978.

Laubenfels, J. *The Gifted Student: An Annotated Bibliography.* Westport, Conn.: Greenwood Press, 1977.

Pinelli, T. Utilizing community resources to encourage student scientific creativity in all grades. *Creative Child and Adult Quarterly*, August 1977, *2, 3*, 156–163.

Readings in Gifted and Talented Education. Guilford, Conn.: Special Learning Corporation, 1978.

Renzulli, J.S. *The Enrichment Triad Model: A Guide for Developing Defensible Programs for the Gifted and Talented.* Mansfield Center, Conn.: Creative Learning Press, 1979.

Renzulli, J.S. and Smith, L.H. *A Guidebook for Developing Individualized Educational Programs (IEP) for the Gifted and Talented.* Mansfield Center, Conn.: Creative Learning Press, 1979.

Sisk, D. Computers in the classroom: An invitation and a challenge for the gifted. *G/T/C*, January-February 1978, 18–21.

Stanley, J.C. and George, W.C. SMPY's ever-increasing D. *Gifted Child Quarterly*, Winter 1980, *24, 1*, 41-4-48.

Stanley, J.C. and George, W.C. (eds.). *The Gifted and the Creative: A Fifty Year Perspective.* Baltimore, Md.: Johns Hopkins University Press, 1977.

Stanley, J.C., George, W.C., and Solano, C.H. *Education Programs and Intellectual Prodigies.* Baltimore, Md.: Johns Hopkins University Press, 1978.

Stanley, J.C., Keating, D.P., and Fox, L. (eds.). *Mathematical Talent: Discovery, Description, and Development.* Baltimore, Md.: Johns Hopkins University Press, 1976.

Vail, P.L. *The World of the Gifted Child.* New York: Walker, 1979.

Vernon, P.E., Adams, G., and Vernon, D.F. *Psychology and Education of Gifted Children.* Boulder, Col.: Westview Press, 1977.

AGENCIES AND RESOURCES

American Association for Gifted Children
15 Gramercy Park
New York, NY 10003

The Association for the Gifted
1411 S. Jefferson Davis Highway
Arlington, VA 22202

Council for Exceptional Children
1920 Association Drive
Reston, VA 22091

Council of State Directors of Programs for Gifted
California State Department of Education
721 Capitol Mall
Sacramento, CA 95814

Gifted Child Society
59 Glen Gray Road
Oakland, NJ 07436

Gifted Education Resource Institute
Purdue University
West Lafayette, IN 47907

Metropolitan Council for Gifted
40 Seventh Avenue South
New York, NY 10014

National Association for Gifted Children
8080 Springvalley Drive
Cincinnati, OH 45236

National State Leadership Training Institution
on the Gifted and the Talented
316 West Second Street Suite PH-C
Los Angeles, CA 90012

Northeast Exchange
Educational Improvement Center
New Jersey Department of Education
207 Delsea Drive
Sewell, NJ 08080

Office of Gifted and Talented
Room 2100, ROB-3
7th and D Streets, S.W.
U.S. Department of Education
Washington, DC 20202

Office of Talent Identification and Development
The Johns Hopkins University
Baltimore, MD 21218

Study of Mathematically Precocious Youth
Department of Psychology
The Johns Hopkins University
Baltimore, MD 21218

Ventura County Schools
535 East Main Street
Ventura, CA 98009

Microcomputers and Hyperactive Children

**Glenn Kleiman, Mary Humphrey,
and Peter H. Lindsay**

INTRODUCTION

Recent advances in computer technology have made powerful microcomputers affordable for widespread use in schools. The overall aim of our research is to determine how best to capitalize on the potential benefits of these computers for hyperactive and other attention deficient children. This report is a brief summary of some pilot work and an initial experimental study conducted at the Child Development Clinic, Hospital for Sick Children. This research compared children's performance on arithmetic

problems administered by computer with problems given in a standard paper and pencil format.

The children in the project were referred to the Clinic for problems of hyperactivity. They participated in the computer study during their free time between scheduled appointments in which they were being assessed for drug effects on their hyperactivity. Since the evaluation of drug effects was not part of the computer study, all children were tested during times when they were not subject to effects of previous medication.

Seventeen children served as pilot subjects in the initial phase of developing the computer program. Observations and interviews with these children resulted in significant changes in the program, including a modification of the display to make it more readable, altering feedback timing, giving the child control of problem pacing, and adding special graphics and prompt messages. The detailed characteristics of the program are outlined below.

Eighteen children, ranging from 6 to 14 years of age, participated in the experimental study. Each child did addition problems on paper one day, and on a PET computer another day. The difficulty level of the problems was adjusted for each child, and was the same for the problems presented on paper and the computer. On each day, the child was asked to "do as many problems as you want and stop when you think you have done enough." The study compared the accuracy, number of problems attempted, and rate of problem solving in the computer format and the paper and pencil format.

THE COMPUTER PROGRAM

The computer program 1 used in this study had a number of characteristics that should be considered in the design of any program for children:

1) The level of problem difficulty could be individually tailored for each child (i.e., whether or not carrying was required, the number of addends, and the number of digits in each addend).

2) The display format on the computer was designed to be easily readable (e.g., extra spacing between characters; vertical problem format; prompt arrows).

3) The answer format on the computer was designed to be as similar to the pencil and paper format as possible. The answers were entered into the computer from right to left rather than the usual computer format of left to right; carrying could be marked above the appropriate column of numbers with a special key; another special key allowed the child to erase mistakes.

4) Problem solving was completely self-paced: When the child was satisfied with an answer, he or she could press a button to get the answer recorded

	# Problems done	% Correct	Avg. time to do problems	Avg. time between problems	Total time working problems
Computer	31.4	74	37.8 sec.	6.8 sec.	23.3 min.
Paper & Pencil	17.6	76	36.5 sec.	6.6 sec.	12.6 min.

and obtain feedback; when ready to proceed to the next problem, the child could press another key and the computer would proceed.

5) Motivational features were incorporated such as graphic displays and praise statements following correct answers. For incorrect answers, the message "Wrong, the correct answer is . . ." was given.

6) There were several built-in messages that were specifically related to the child's problem of hyperactivity—special messages appeared whenever a child answered incorrectly too quickly, took too long to respond, or simply made too many inappropriate button presses (i.e., "STOP IT!").

In addition to controlling all of the problem generation, the display and the feedback material, the computer automatically recorded the child's response, the time taken to make the response, the time taken to request another problem, the number of erasures, if any, and the occurrence of any special messages.

The problems for the pencil and paper test were generated by the same computer algorithm so that the difficulty levels of the problems would be comparable. During the paper and pencil sessions, an observer, located behind a one-way mirror, recorded the time the child spent on each problem.

RESULTS AND CONCLUSIONS

The results were very clear-cut. There were no differences between paper and pencil and computer work in the proportion correct, the average time to do problems, or the average time between problems. The differences appeared in the number of problems the children voluntarily chose to do in the two mediums. On the average, the same children working on the same level of problems did almost twice as many problems on the computer as they did with paper and pencil. The table above gives the average across the 18 children.

Apparently, hyperactive children are willing to spend significantly more time working problems on the computer, without any significant loss of accuracy or speed. The children spent an average of over 23 minutes working on the computer—an unusually long time for hyperactive children to voluntarily stay on one task. Informal interviews

with the children confirmed their strong preference for the computer. Among the comments they gave were that the problems seemed to be easier on the computer, it was nice not to have to write down the answers, and they liked the rapid feedback. Many were eager to return and wanted to know when they would have a chance to work on the computer again. None of them requested more paper and pencil drill.

These results are from a single study and need to be replicated and extended before strong claims can be made. Our current work investigates longer term effects of computer presentation on learning rates and changes in children's interest and confidence related to working with computers. However, the present results do encourage optimism as to the potential use of microcomputers as a classroom tool. Microcomputers provide a way of doing drill and practice which children find motivating, can do with minimal adult supervision, can be tailored to each child's needs, and provides immediate feedback. Well designed programs may be able to dramatically increase the time children with attention problems will spend on some school tasks.

A version of this program, revised for classroom use rather than data collection is available from Teaching Tools: Microcomputing Services, P.O. Box 12679, Research Triangle Park, NC 27709.

Application of Computers to the Needs of Handicapped Persons

Joseph G. Williams, Ron Thorkildsen, and Edward K. Crossman

INTRODUCTION

Computer technology has been applied to the problems of handicapped individuals for at least 12 years. The application began in 1969 with the deaf (Rathe, 1969a, 1969b) and has continued since then (Knutsen & Prochnow, 1979) with applications to other handicaps. The number and scope of applications are likely to continue to increase as computer technology becomes more readily available and the application of this instructional technology becomes more mature. This review aims to do the following:

1. Summarize the current applications of computer technology with special education, blind, deaf, and other physically disabled populations.
2. Suggest probable future areas of application within each of these populations.
3. Suggest needed areas of research, evaluation, and improvements in methodology.

Despite the widespread use of computer technology in society, education in general has been only slightly influenced, and handicapped individuals have hardly been touched by the technological revolution. In 1954, Skinner observed that the average American kitchen contained more in the way of technology than classrooms. Since that time, the classroom use of technology has changed very little, particularly with regard to education of the handicapped. Speaking of instructional technology in general, Withrow (1976) suggested that removing all such technology from American schools would have little impact on the educational process. Lance (1977) has suggested four reasons for the current disuse of computer technology with handicapped individuals in instructional settings:

1. The conservatism of education and the institutional inertia of an organization open to intense public scrutiny.
2. The fact that educators often perceive such technology as a personal threat, competing for their jobs as well as for the time they spend with students.
3. Too little investment in new technology since the costs for such innovation are high, and the average school spends less than 1% of its budget on all instructional materials, including printed materials.
4. Few groups or organizations promoting change among educators. In light of these problems and hesitancies, education can be seen as "an island unto itself" while technology is being used to an ever greater extent in the society outside.

Using business as their example, Gibson and Nolan (1974) list four phases of growth in computer technology within a given field: initiation, expansion, formalization, and maturity. Lance's explanations suggest that education is still in the initiation stage, though there are indications that entrance into the expansion phase will soon occur. Speaking of education in general, Jamison, Suppes, and Wells (1974) observe:

> The key to productivity in every economic sector has been through the augmentation of human efforts by technology, and we see no reason to expect a different pattern in education. We use the term augmentation deliberately here to set aside the notion of technology's replacing teachers; the purpose of the technology must be to make teachers more productive, not to replace them completely [p. 57].

Although heightened productivity is a desirable goal for education, the first widespread use of technology to improve productivity will probably occur outside traditional education in the area of industrial training. Indeed, Norris (1977) suggests that computer technology will eventually impact on education because of the demonstration of its efficacy in industrial training. Currently, such training is a huge undertaking, occurring at all levels of a corporation. The national expenditure on education, including the primary, secondary, and college levels, is $100 billion annually. Expenditures for training are at the same level, and, according to Norris (1977), an effective demonstration of the efficacy of computer technology in training could provide a powerful model for education.

Despite the current isolation of education, it seems likely that it, too, will experience the same pattern of increasing technological involvement. Certainly, an increasingly technological society will demand more and more technological skill. Finally, familiarity with technology on the part of educators should lower education's resistance to change and help to alter the present lack of technology in today's classroom.

General education aside, the impact of computer technology will be greater in the case of handicapped individuals for two major reasons.

1. Work with the handicapped is frequently labor intensive. There has been, and continues to be, a severe shortage of trained personnel to meet the educational needs of handicapped persons adequately (Cartwright, 1976; Education of the Handicapped Today, 1976).
2. Certain types of handicapped persons would benefit substantially from such prosthetic devices as communication systems for severely involved cerebral palsied individuals.

Hence, expansion of the use of computer technology with handicapped individuals is very likely. A later section will review the current status of computer technology with the deaf, special-education populations, the blind, and the otherwise physically impaired, indicating areas of needed improvement and future directions for research. Before proceeding, however, some definitions of terms are in order.

Computer Assisted Instruction (CAI). An instructional situation in which computer technology is used to present material, test for mastery of the material, and/or determine sequencing of material.

Computer Managed Instruction (CMI). An instructional situation in which computer technology is used to keep records, to keep tests, and to provide prescriptive information concerning proper sequencing of instructional material for the student.

...hysical equipment that makes up a
...em.

...O). The hardware used to enter data
...xtract data from, a computer system.

...I/O device linked directly to the
...y data lines; a device for communicating with a computer using a keyboard and an
alphanumeric printer or cathode-ray tube (CRT)
display.

Time-Share. A means by which one or more terminals can be connected to, and worked with,
one central computer system.

Microcomputer. Hardware composed of a group of
separate elements, including read-only memory
and random-access memory, microprocessor,
interface logic for I/O, and timing circuitry for
transmitting signals from one element to another.

Software. Generally, computer programs but also
used to refer to everything that is not equipment (hardware).

It should be remembered that the use of computer technology with handicapped populations is
in its early stages. Because much of the work that
has been done is exploratory, many of the reports
contain little or no evaluation data.

COMPUTER TECHNOLOGY AND THE DEAF

The deaf comprise the largest group to benefit from
computer technology. Although Watson (1978) and
Jones (1978) have reviewed this area, the present
review will update these and also elaborate various
directions for future research.

Von Feldt (1978) reported the results of a
national survey of schools and programs for the deaf
that made use of computer-assisted instruction (CAI).
The survey, conducted in 1976, showed that 11 of
the 50 states surveyed had implemented computer-
based instruction. There were 34 computer systems
with 408 terminals identified. Of these 34 systems,
28 were dedicated to CAI rather than being used
for other functions, indicating that CAI with the deaf
has passed beyond the experimental level and has
begun to touch substantial numbers of deaf students.
The impact of early federal funding is one of the
reasons why CAI has had such an influence on the
education of deaf. Projects located at the National
Technical Institute for the Deaf in Palo Alto (NTID)
and at Stanford University in California strongly
boosted the use of CAI with the deaf, and these
projects will be described below.

Early publications by Stuckless (1969), Behrens,
Clack, and Alprin (1969), and Rathe (1969a, 1969b)
signaled the beginning of interest in CAI with the
deaf, suggesting that CAI was an exciting new teaching
tool and urging educators of the deaf to investigate

its use. Behrens et al. reported on the initiation of a
project at Kendall School for the Deaf in Washington,
D.C., where a mathematics curriculum developed at
Stanford University was being used to teach math
skills to 107 pupils, ages 9 to 21. Although posttest
data were not yet available, reaction to the material
was very favorable by both students and teachers.

Rathe (1969a, 1969b) and Stuckless (1969)
described plans for using CAI at NTID. Later, Barnes
and Finkelstein (1971) reported on the development
and implementation of a CAI mathematics curriculum at NTID. Progress was considered to be
quite good, and students were using the curriculum
to remedy their deficiencies in mathematics. Lessons
were also being developed to teach English grammar
and a computer language.

Historically, the Institute for Mathematical Studies
in the Social Sciences (IMSSS) advanced CAI, with
the deaf in particular and CAI in general, during the
duration of the project's life (1970–1973). In a
project involving more than 4000 students from 15
schools for the deaf in five states, students received
CAI in a variety of areas, emphasizing elementary
school mathematics and language arts as well as
algebra, logic, computer programming, and basic
English (Fletcher & Suppes, 1973). In 1972–1973,
they reported that more than 180 terminals were
connected to the system. In discussing the results,
they state "The project demonstrated that CAI can
significantly benefit deaf students, that CAI can
support serious research in deaf education, and that
CAI is economically practicable" (Fletcher & Suppes,
1973, abstract).

Fletcher (1974) reported the results of three
studies conducted during the course of the Stanford
research. The experiments were conducted during the
presentation of a language arts curriculum to deaf
students. From three residential and five day schools
for the deaf, 138 language arts students were chosen
at random. These were randomly assigned to one of
two groups for each of the three experiments.

In the first experiment, one group received
correction messages that were tailored for specific,
anticipated wrong answers. Members of the second
group were told only that their incorrect answers
were wrong. No practical or statistically significant
difference in achievement was found between the
two groups.

A second experiment investigated the utility of
allowing students who had picked an incorrect
response alternative to make a second or third choice
in an attempt to select the correct alternative. To
investigate this question further, one group of students was allowed three consecutive trials per exercise
while another group was allowed only one trial per
exercise. Posttreatment tests showed significantly

greater achievement for the three-trial group over the one-trial group.

In the third experiment, each group was informed of the correct answer after an incorrect response. One group, however, was required to echo the correct response by typing it back in; the other was not. The former group showed greater achievement in post-treatment tests than did the latter. The success of the Stanford Project can be seen by the fact that 13 of the 15 participating schools elected to continue the project with their own funds after completion of the study (Culbertson, 1974).

Saunders, Hill, and Easley (1978) reported on a project that used computer technology to instruct the deaf in a novel way. A CAI program was developed to teach four deaf children to recognize tactile patterns that corresponded to sound played by an audio unit. This system would enable users to understand spoken words or words reproduced from tape or record. The commonly used method now is lipreading. However, this method is unsatisfactory in dim light, if the person speaking is not close to or facing the deaf person, or if the generator of the sound (such as a tape recorder or an audio record) is not a human being. The tactile patterns were reproduced by a vibrating surface the children wore on their abdomens. Results were said to be encouraging, but additional details were not given.

Zawolkow (1979) reported on a project in California which continued the work of the IMSSS project but utilized the Apple II microcomputer instead of a large time-share system. The program is located at California School for the Deaf, Riverside, CA, and it provides a regional center for cooperative development and dissemination of CAI programs for the deaf. No further details were given.

Dugdale and Vogel (1978) reported on the use of the modified PLATO (a trade name for a CAI system of the Control Data Corporation) terminal and the extensive PLATO CAI material to teach deaf students. The modification of the terminal consisted of the addition of a small red light which was illuminated after a student's response had been accepted by the PLATO terminal (for hearing students, a beep would have been used). No quantitative data were reported.

An innovative approach was reported by Galbraith (1978) who used a RAMTEK terminal and a NOVA 3/12 computer to teach manual and written language to deaf learners. The approach was innovative because it used the RAMTEK terminal (a color display unit with resolution of 512 by 256 individually addressed display points) to provide pictures of objects, words, and human hands performing manual signs. The system also took advantage of residual hearing by using computer-generated speech.

Myers (1979) has described still another system developed to assist in teaching the deaf. The system consists of a computer that is used to control a videotape machine. The videotape was displayed on a color monitor, and student responses were entered through a keyboard. One application of the system was added to aid the instruction of lipreading. Deaf students viewed video sequences of an instructor saying words, phrases, and sentences and were required to identify what the instructor said.

Although Myers gives no specifics, videotape systems have the drawback of affording slow access to distant portions of the tape. This means that on completing one instructional sequence, the learner must wait while the tape moves to the next sequence. This problem can be minimized by anticipating the sequence of video segments that students are likely to encounter and placing these segments as closely together on the tape as possible.

Suggesting the direction that instructional technology for the deaf may take in the future, Margaret Withrow (1978) reported on a computerized graphic system (developed by Charles Csuri at Ohio State University) which produces high-quality color animation in real time. The color animation is described as being equal or superior in quality to that commonly seen in TV cartoons. The graphics system can be programmed in a specialized command language which has features to adjust size, shape, color, lighting, and perspective, and the system can produce videotapes when desired. The capability to produce color animation easily and cheaply means that many more high-quality instructional sequences will be available. This system has tremendous potential for the education of handicapped as well as of normal learners.

In still another promising approach, the Media Development Project for the Hearing Impaired (MDPHI) at the University of Nebraska is using the videodisc player controlled by a microcomputer to deliver CAI to deaf learners. Videodisc technology is an important advance in CAI, particularly for the handicapped, because it allows presentation of true-to-life sound, motion, and color under computer control and quick access to all parts of the videodisc, making possible rapid instructional feedback and rapid branching to remedial sequences. The microcomputer accepts student responses and then directs the videodisc player to play appropriate sequences from the videodisc. The microcomputer also records and summarizes data.

Propp, Nugent, Stone, and Nugent (1980) reported that by the end of their project, they will have produced ten one-sided videodiscs. Those already produced include discs showing the typical life of a boy on a kibbutz in Israel; teaching finger spelling; demonstrating some of the applications of videodisc technology in the education of the hearing impaired; teaching high school-level literature; and showing hearing impaired students in typical everyday situations. Though quantitative data on instructional effectiveness are not available, the authors indicate that the material is effective.

The use of computer technology with the deaf has been reasonably widespread and is likely to increase with the development of technology that allows the presentation of visual material. Videotape and videodisc are likely to be increasingly used for the next 5 to 10 years. Following this, however, the quality of computer graphics will probably rival the quality of videotape and videodisc. The emergence of all these technological capabilities will enable educators of the deaf to teach their students more productively.

COMPUTER TECHNOLOGY AND THE MENTALLY RETARDED

The literature on CAI for educating the mentally retarded is somewhat meager, and the approximately 25 reports extant have tended to indicate the success of the individual project rather than to address broad issues. These issues include such factors as the optimal spacing of trials; the optimal number of trials in a session or for an individual problem; the best type, frequency, and timing of feedback; the efficacy of tailored feedback for incorrect responses versus standard feedback for wrong responses; and the effect of forcing a correct response. Although some of these issues may be settled with specific reference to the instructional situation (type of media, instructional content) and learner variables (IQ, age, physical handicaps) some generalizations exist which enable more effective instruction to be designed. Three of these generalizations (dealing with specific feedback, number of trials, and forcing correct trials) were addressed in studies utilizing the deaf and reported by Fletcher (1974); but these studies were initial investigations into an area in which much work remains to be done.

Knutson and Prochnow (1970) described an early project that utilized CAI with substantial numbers of the mentally handicapped. Involved were 38 students, of whom 21 finished the course. For various reasons, four students became unavailable and did not complete the course. Six students did not complete the course even though allowed an adequate amount of time to do so. Ages ranged from 12 to 18 years, and IQ ranged from 45 to 75. The CAI material was a program to teach making monetary change. Hardware included slide projectors and simplified keyboards (with fewer keys). Performance on pretests (given before undertaking the instruction), posttests, and a retention test (given after instruction) were analyzed statistically (t-test), and significant gains ($p < .01$) were found to have occurred.

Nelon (1972) reported on another early application of computer technology with the mentally handicapped. Twelve mentally retarded (MR) and 12 normal subjects were divided into a control and an experimental group, and the method of assignment was not given. The control group received a posttest only; the experimental group received CAI in English vocabulary followed by a posttest. The experimenter states that subjects' mental ages averaged around the first-grade level. In the experimental group, MR and normal subjects of similar mental age did not differ significantly in learning (F, $p = .25$), error rate (F, $p = .10$), or time necessary for completion (F, $p = .50$). The experimental group's posttest scores were significantly higher than the control group's as measured by a t-test ($p < .01$).

Nonspeaking autistic children (particulars such as sex and age were not given) have also benefited from computer-assisted instruction (Colby, 1973). This system provided up to 1000 different audio-visual sequences. Two examples of sequences were (a) pressing an "H" on the TV screen and a voice saying "H," and (b) pressing an "H" on the keyboard producing a running horse on the screen along with the sound of a horse's hooves. Colby reported that these "games," organized at various levels of complexity, were designed to show a child "how English is put together from sound and letters into words and expressions" [p. 225]. Visuals were displayed on a TV-type screen. Colby reported that 13 of 17 children began using some level of speech after use of the system; but he did not report on the permanence of this effect, and more specific information was not provided.

Elfner (1973) reported on a 3-year project in which the first year involved use of a computer as a direct instructional aid. Revisions were reported to have occurred in the instructional packages during the first year as a result of formative evaluation, but specific results were not given. The project served 40 emotionally and mentally retarded (EMR) children and taught reading. Computer-managed instruction (CMI)—i.e., using the computer to provide testing, diagnosis, and then suggesting instructional material for individual users—was the project's central feature.

Luyben and Brown (1973) used a CAI instructional package to examine the effects of pictorial representations of words on the acquisition of a slight vocabulary (the ability to recognize a word when shown it). Subjects were 27 emotionally and mentally retarded (EMR) students; two groups were used. The Word-Word group received a printed word and response alternatives consisting of other printed words. The Word-Picture group received a printed word and several pictures, one of which was a picture that corresponded to the printed word. The average ages for the students in the Word-Word and Word-Picture groups were 9.75 and 9.28 years respectively. Response choices were accepted by the computer, and students were given feedback. For each group, respective gains of 19.64% and 41.45% were recorded between pretest and posttest scores, indicating that both groups improved. Further analysis indicated that the gains for the Word-Picture group were significantly greater than those for the Word-Word group ($F = 9.09$, $df = 1,18$, $p < .01$).

Rosenkranz (1974) reported on a (CMI) project that provided special-education teachers with reports of reading skills mastered by students, skills not mastered, and appropriate instructional materials with their location for subsequent instruction. Students involved were 160 EMR, 347 disadvantaged, and 326 normal children. Reading gains for normal students changed from below average to above national norms, and EMR children made gains described as being equivalent or superior to other existing high-quality programs (non-CMI). Since no control group was used, the contribution of CMI to the gains was impossible to estimate.

Berthold and Sachs (1974) compared computer alone, teacher alone, and combined computer and teacher methods of tutorial instruction among six 9- to 11-year-old, special-education students. Instruction given was "multiplication, spelling, etc." [p. 122]. The authors reported that interest (as measured by eye contact with task) was high in all three conditions, but the teacher-alone and combined combinations were superior to computer-alone in terms of pretest-posttest gains.

Several factors must be noted about this study, however. Each subject was exposed to each condition for 2 consecutive days a week for 2 weeks for a total of 4 days in each condition. This seems a brief time to affect multiplication or spelling significantly. The order of conditions was not specified. The combined condition consisted of a student receiving teacher instruction for 1 day, computer instruction the next, and so on. In addition, it was not stated whether the material presented by the computer and by the teachers were equivalent. Finally, the pretest and posttest were reported as being identical and were given before and after each session, but no validity or reliability data were reported for these tests. In short, it is difficult to say what, if anything, this study showed.

St. Aubin (1975) reported on a project undertaken in 1975 by the South Metropolitan Association for Low-Incidence Handicapped (SMA) to provide handicapped children in the south suburban area of metropolitan Chicago with CAI learning opportunities. Students showing hearing, visual, mental, or other learning disabilities were placed in math, reading, or language arts programs prepared by Computer Curriculum Corporation. The type of computer system used was not identified, but 25 terminals were placed in various schools. Anecdotal data (obtained from a questionnaire) and objective performance data (consisting of improvement after an initial baseline period of the program) for 198 subjects were collected.

The author reported that both students and teachers reacted affirmatively to the project. Objective data indicated that gains of 3.8, 3.0, and 3.1 months were recorded (during the 4-month period the material was used) for behavior disordered, educationally disadvantaged, and EMR groups respectively. The absence of a no-treatment control group made interpretation difficult, but it was reported that such gains were not typically found in these populations. It was suggested that student progress was correlated with the amount of exposure to the program, but this suggestion was not elaborated.

Goeffrion and Bergeron (1977) reported on the CARIS system, which supplied computer-controlled animated reading instruction to handicapped children (handicaps included mental retardation, learning disabilities, deafness, and aphasia). No reading ability was assumed; the computer delivered pictures that acted out sentences constructed by the child. Several case studies were presented addressing the system's utility. The results of these case studies were quite positive in developing beginning reading skills. Because data are subjective, however, the effective use of the system must be regarded with skepticism.

Aeschleman and Tawney (1978) worked with a severely handicapped population using a time-share system. Placed in students' homes, special-purpose terminals were used to facilitate the instruction of visual discrimination and motor skills. In the area of visual discrimination, letter matching and brightness discrimination were examined. In the area of motor skills, programs aimed at increasing arm pulls, leg kicks, and visual tracking were used. Reinforcers, such as recorded music, were used on-site, and parents were involved in prompting responses. While specific data were presented for only one subject, the experimenters state that all children showed improvement.

Chiang (1978) described a larger scale project in a California school district in which 14 special education teachers and 200 students participated. The project attempted to use a larger time-share system to teach reading, language, and mathematics. Of the 200 students, about half were described as learning disabled, and the remainder were described as being evenly divided among educable mentally retarded, educationally handicapped, and severely oral-language handicapped categories. The ages ranged from 7 to 16 years. No control group was used. Though only half the subjects demonstrated gains, this may be attributable to the limited amount of time spent with the equipment (a half-hour per week). The gain itself must be regarded cautiously, however, because random factors could have accounted for it.

Sandals (1974, 1979) reported on the use of CAI among 875 variously handicapped children in several school districts in Canada. Equipment used included a large time-share system and a TRS-80 microcomputer. Subjects taught were basic mathematics and language skills. Results were not presented.

A 9-year project carried out by Hallworth and Brebner (1980) describes a project at the University of Calgary that emphasized self-help skills (such as money handling, nutrition, time sense, and laundry symbols) along with basic math and reading skills. The project has developed a number of programs described as being effective in teaching these skills to trainable mentally handicapped individuals. Hardware consisted of a time-share system with special terminals and keyboards to facilitate input from physically handicapped individuals. Slide projectors and cassette tape recorders provided audiovisual material. Again, however, results were not presented.

A videodisc player coupled with a microcomputer may have a substantial influence on the future of education of the handicapped. A videodisc player enables rapid access (using a laser to read data from a rapidly rotating disk) to audiovisual material. Rapid access follows feedback, remediation, and so forth to be given soon after a response, as well as keeping instructional "dead time" (time during which nothing is happening) to a minimum. Using the microcomputer to control the videodisc player allows appropriate sections of the videodisc to be played depending on the learner's response.

A somewhat similar system can be created by controlling a videotape machine from a computer. A significant disadvantage of videotape is that access times are longer than videodisc (speed is somewhat dependent on the physical relationship of segments on the tape). Another disadvantage is that still frames are frequently unclear, and the image is not stable with videotape. An advantage of videotape is that on-site filming can be followed immediately by field testing of the material. To use videodisc after filming the material, the film must be sent to a factory so that a videodisc can be produced.

A research and development project is currently being conducted at Utah State University's Exceptional Child Center in Logan, Utah to develop and investigate the effectiveness of a computer-assisted instruction system (coupled with a videodisc) designed for use with the mentally handicapped (Thorkildsen, Bickel, & Williams, 1979). The system utilizes the recently developed videodisc player (Disco-Vision PR-7820) interfaced with an Apple II microcomputer. Software for the computer (including programs to control the videodisc and programs to present instructional material) is being developed to utilize these new technological advances in hardware.

If evaluation shows the system to be both instructionally and cost-effective, it will offer a means for providing self-paced, individualized instruction to mentally handicapped nonreaders without direct attendance by the teacher. The system also provides an automated means of collecting, analyzing, and reporting extensive student data. During the first year of the project, instructional programs were developed in four areas: (a) discrimination between sizes, shapes, and colors; (b) time telling; (c) identification of functional words; and (d) identification of coins. Future packages being considered for development include a program to teach prepositions and a pre-reading program.

The use of computer technology with the mentally handicapped has been considerably hampered by the fact that, in general, mentally handicapped individuals cannot read. For this reason, CAI with the handicapped has had to await the development of technology to enable the presentation of pictures and preferably to present them rapidly. Insofar as the videodisc fills this requirement, educators of the mentally retarded are likely to take increasing advantage of this technology in the future. Videotape systems also make possible the presentation of instructional material to nonreaders, but slower access speed is a significant problem with individuals as easily distractible as are many mentally handicapped individuals.

COMPUTER TECHNOLOGY AND THE BLIND

Compared with other handicapped individuals, the blind have benefited very little from computer technology, and the reason for this is easy to understand. Traditional computer output devices provide either a printed copy or a display text on a TV screen, neither of which can be used by the blind. In the near future, however, the blind are likely to benefit very substantially from computer technology. This benefit will take two forms: (a) a computerized device to scan printed material and provide voice or tactile output to a blind person and (b) terminals which allow blind individuals to interact with computers using typing (utilizing standard keyboards) for input and using voice synthesis (using electronic components to simulate speech) for output. Both approaches are being investigated.

Ballenger (1979) is utilizing keyboard input and voice output to enable blind persons to interact with computers. The purpose of the project was to develop a terminal capable of being interfaced with a computer system, which would allow the blind to receive output from a computer through voice communication and to respond to the computer by means of a keyboard. The hardware was acquired and found to require no further design or engineering to function. This was important because it allowed the system to be easily duplicated from readily available components.

To enable the hardware to be used with the blind, computer programs (software) were written and lessons produced to teach the users to operate the system. These included keyboard training and speech intelligibility and student readiness testing. The second lesson allowed students practice in recognizing the computer-generated speech. Following completion of these lessons, students were exposed to lessons teaching basic accounting. Ballenger (1979) states that too few students had used the equipment and programs for adequate evaluation, although his description suggests that results were very encouraging.

Another report of a project allowing blind individuals to interact with a computer was given by Evans and Simkins (1973). This project used three terminals equipped with keyboards similar to those of typewriters and a time-share system to teach mathematics at a sixth-grade level. The approach was similar to Ballenger's (1979) except that Braille output was used instead of voice output. No data were reported.

Finally, another computer-based device, called an OPTACON, translates print into tactile simulation, enabling a blind individual to "read" by feeling the shape of a letter (Jaquiss, 1978). This system allows blind persons to read material designed for sighted persons, bypassing the need to translate the material into Braille.

The approach involving speech output and keyboard input would seem the most promising for use by the blind because of its speed and ease of use. Using this system, sight impaired individuals can communicate with a computer, an ability that will enable them to perform a great many jobs—among them, programmer and airline reservations clerk.

THE COMPUTER AS A PROSTHETIC DEVICE

The advent of the microprocessor with its diminutiveness and low cost has advanced the computer into a relatively new role—that of a prosthetic device.

Although many of these devices are still in the experimental stage, they show real promise in eventually diminishing the physical limitations experienced by handicapped persons. Scully (1978) gives a dramatic example of this. Robin, a girl with cerebral palsy, was unable to speak and was only somewhat able to control the movements of one knee, but this movement was sufficient for her to move a switch. Through the use of a microprocessor, a communication system was designed that enabled her to select words or letters from a list displayed on a TV screen. This in turn enabled Robin to communicate (with anyone watching the screen) for the first time.

Social programs have been set up to provide technical training for the severely disabled. Linthicum (1977) described a project that trained a number of individuals with mobility handicaps (cerebral palsy, stroke victims) to become computer programmers. Supported by industry, this large-scope project was successful in placing many individuals in jobs as programmers.

Nelson and Cossalter (1977) also reported a microcomputer-based communication system for the physically handicapped. A communication board containing either 256 or 512 Bliss symbols is upright and facing the handicapped person and his/her intended audience. A simple paddle switch enables the receiver to indicate his/her choice of symbols as the machine slowly scans through the symbols. Memory functions enable strings of symbols to be stored for later display. The authors described the system as being capable of interfacing with a speech synthesizer, enabling vocal communication to take place.

Communications technology may enable large numbers of handicapped persons to be gainfully employed at home (Overby, 1973, 1976). Overby (1976) suggests that two major factors will bring this about. First, growing numbers of people are engaged in information processing rather than in processing physical materials. By 1980, it was estimated, 51.5% of the labor force would be employed in white-collar jobs. Some industries, such as insurance and banking, are almost entirely information processing rather than engaged in the manipulation of physical materials. Second, as the use of computers has enabled information transmission to become increasingly commonplace, handicapped individuals can perform at home useful functions that would previously have been performed at a centralized place of work. This trend is accelerating among the general population as well, partly because the energy crisis has so greatly increased transportation costs and partly as a result of lower communication costs.

For the physically disabled, systems such as those described by Ciarcia (1980) allow a greater amount of control over their environment. One system, for example, provides for computer control of electrical devices throughout a house. Using computer-controlled devices, a bedridden person could turn any electrical device in the home on and off from a central location. Telephone answering devices and the existence of computer networks (networks formed by computers connected in such a way as to relay, and sometimes to store, messages) allow the physically disabled to send and receive letters, interact with computer programs resident on a larger system, or receive information from the UPI wire service (Craig, 1980).

Ciarcia (1979) has also described an input system utilizing EMG muscle potential to control a computer. This input system would allow even the most severely disabled persons to enter information into a computer, thereby opening for the user a tremendous potential for communication, instruction, and entertainment. Simpson (1980) has described a keyboard-controlled microprocessor system that generates speech for those severely afflicted with cerebral palsy. This system utilizes residual movement in hands and arms, enabling the handicapped person to communicate by operating a simplified keyboard. The system fits onto a wheelchair and is easy to learn to use.

In summary, the use of computer technology for prosthetic purposes seems almost certain to increase, largely because of the small size and low cost of microprocessors. People with handicaps that affect mobility will benefit from technological changes that enable them to work at home. Systems designed to facilitate communication, such as artificial speech generation, will also assist blind and cerebral palsied individuals in communications.

CONCLUSION

The use of computer technology in special-education settings is in its early stages. To date, the area of deaf education seems to have benefited most; the education of the blind to have benefited least; the mentally handicapped have benefited to a small extent and the motor handicapped slightly more. In the future, computer technology will almost certainly be used more generally and extensively but the areas of greatest impact may well be those of the blind, the physically disabled, and the mentally handicapped.

Substantial growth in educating the mentally handicapped may result from recent technological advances making the presentation of visual images a practical instructional technique (Thorkildsen, Bickel, & Williams, 1979; Withrow, 1978). The blind and physically disabled will also be likely subjects for expansion in the area of computer technology.

Approaches described by Ballenger (1979) and Overby (1976) suggest the probable future directions of these approaches.

It is to be hoped that the future will bring more quantification of results and research into basic parameters such as those investigated by Fletcher (1974). This information will enable special educators to make intelligent choices regarding this new technology. To be effective, however, this information must be communicated to special education decision makers. Currently, information sources in this area are widely diverse, making it difficult for information to be disseminated effectively. The present review may help to encapsulate some of this information, but that a more centralized, ongoing information source is needed cannot be overemphasized.

Despite the inevitability of increased technological utilization in special-education settings, this will be a slow process. Lance (1977) has discussed the inherent conservatism of educational institutions and the inadequate expenditures on all instructional materials. However, as computer technology becomes more ubiquitous in industrial training, in society, and in education in general, computers will eventually become commonplace in special education classrooms as well.

In reviewing this area, several clear impressions emerge. The first is that the amount of computer technology being used with handicapped populations is growing and will continue to grow for several reasons.

1. Computer technology is becoming more available in society at large because of more products, more companies, and greater applications.
2. The cost of computer technology is diminishing.
3. The advent of certain technical innovations, such as random-access videodisc and videotape, make computer technology more accessible to the handicapped population.

A second impression is that much more needs to be done in quantification of results. Study after study reports essentially that "everybody loved it," though no serious attempt is made to compare new and old methods of instruction. Only a few studies on the use of computer technology with the handicapped have reflected anything approaching adequate experimental control. To be sure, the work done so far is important in showing that computer technology can be applied with handicapped populations, but it has not shown that the use of such technology is superior to present practice.

Despite the paucity of empirical data, the beneficial application of this technology to handicapped populations remains a strong future possibility. It remains for future investigators, utilizing adequate control procedures, to demonstrate that such applications are effective in terms of both educational and cost benefits. Another crying need is the establishment of basic parameters. Such matters as the optimum spacing between trials, the effects of different methods of input, and the optimal speed of feedback have not yet been determined.

A third impression is the tremendous amount of positive impact that computer technology can have on handicapped populations. The capability of a computer to serve as a private tutor as well as a prosthetic device makes computer technology a valuable tool for the special educator.

Finally, in addition to developing systems for educational use, serious evaluation of each CAI system and each instructional program is now essential. This would not only allow a basis on which to establish basic parameters but would provide data for making decisions regarding the classroom use of technology. Investigations should include not only the results of a given instructional system but also details on program development and cost-effectiveness. It is difficult for educators to justify use of a system that seems costly, that offers programs insufficiently tested and evaluated, and the applications of which may be confined to a few programs for a limited population. Without such information, however, CAI will continue to be a toy and will not be regarded as a standard educational tool.

REFERENCES

Aeschleman, S.R., & Tawney, J.W. Interacting: A computer-based telecommunications system for educating severely handicapped preschoolers in their homes. *Educational Technology*, 1978, *18*(10), 30–35.

Ballenger, W.L. *A computer-assisted instruction system for the blind and visually impaired*. Paper published in the proceedings of the National Educational Computing Conference, University of Iowa, Iowa City, June 1979.

Barnes, D.O., & Finkelstein, A. The role of computer-assisted instruction at the National Technical Institute for the Deaf. *American Annals of the Deaf*, 1971, *116*(5), 466–468.

Behrens, T.R., Clack, L., & Alprin, L. Mathematics curriculum supported by computer-assisted instruction. *American Annals of the Deaf*, 1969, *114*(5), 889–892.

Berthold, H.C., & Sachs, R.H. Education of the minimally brain damaged child by computer and by teacher. *Programmed Learning and Educational Technology*, 1974, *11*(3), 121–124.

Cartwright, G.P. *Costs of CAI for special education teacher training: Three perspectives*. Paper presented at the International Learning Technology Congress and Exposition on Applied Learning for Human Resource Development, Washington, D.C., July 1976. (ERIC Document Reproduction Service No. ED 127 911)

Chiang, A. *Demonstration of the use of computer-assisted instruction with handicapped children. Final Report*. Arlington, Va.: RMC Research Corp., 1978. (ERIC Document Reproduction Service No. ED 166 913)

Ciarcia, S. Mind over matter: Add biofeedback input to your computer. *Byte*, 1979, *4*(6), 49–58.

Ciarcia, S. Computerize a home. *Byte*, 1980, *5*(1), 28–54.

Colby, K.M. The rationale for computer-based treatment of language difficulties in nonspeaking autistic children. *Journal of Autism and Childhood Schizophrenia*, 1973, *3*(3), 254–260.

Craig, J. New tools for a new era. *Creative Computing*, 1980, *6*(3), 50–57.

Culbertson, L.B. CAI-beneficial teaching tool at Texas School for the Deaf. *American Annals of the Deaf*, 1974, *119*(1), 34–40.

Dugdale, S., & Vogel, P. Computer-based instruction for hearing-impaired children in the classroom. *American Annals of the Deaf*, 1978, *123*(6), 730–743.

Education of the handicapped today. *American Education*, 1976, *12*(5), 6–8.

Elfner, E. *Reading curriculum development project final report*. Wakulla County Board of Public Instruction, Crawfordville, Fla., 1973. (ERIC Document Reproduction Service No. ED 081 152)

Evans, R., & Simkins, K. Computer-assisted instruction for the blind. *Education of the Visually Handicapped*, 1973, *4*(3), 83–85.

Fletcher, J.D. *Computer-assisted instruction for the deaf*. Paper presented at the American Educational Research Association Annual Meeting. Chicago, April 1974. (ERIC Document Reproduction Service No. ED 089 680)

Fletcher, J.D., & Suppes, P. *Computer-assisted instruction in mathematics and language arts for the deaf. Final report*. Washington, D.C.: Bureau of Education for the Handicapped, 1973. (ERIC Document Reproduction Service No. ED 084 871)

Galbraith, G. An interactive computer system for teaching language skills to deaf children. *American Annals of the Deaf*, 1978, *123*(6), 706–711.

Geoffrion, L.D., & Bergeron, P.D. *Initial reading through computer animation*. Paper presented at the Annual Meeting of the American Educational Research Association, New York, April 1977. (ERIC Document Reproduction Service No. ED 138 929)

Gibson, C.F., & Nolan, R.L. Managing the four stages of EDP growth. *Harvard Business Review*, 1974, *52*(1), 76–88.

Hallworth, H.J., & Brebner, A. *CAI for the developmentally handicapped: Nine years of progress*. Paper published in the proceedings of the Association for the Development of Computer-Based Instructional Systems, Washington, D.C., April 1980.

Jamison, D., Suppes, P., & Wells, S. The effectiveness of alternative instructional media: A survey. *Review of Educational Research*, 1974, *44*(1), 1–67.

Jaquiss, R.S. *Microprocessor computer system uses in education (or, you can do it if you try)*. Paper published in the proceedings of the Second West Coast Computer Faire, San Jose, California, March 1978.

Jones, J.V. *Computer-assisted instruction and the education of the hearing impaired*. Unpublished master's thesis, Utah State University, 1978.

Knutsen, J.M., & Prochnow, R.R. *Computer-assisted instruction for vocational rehabilitation of the mentally retarded*. University of Texas at Austin, Texas, 1970. (ERIC Document Reproduction Service No. ED 044 039)

Lance, W.D. Technology and media for exceptional learners: Looking ahead. *Exceptional Children*, 1977, *44*, 92–97.

Linthicum, S. Technical training for severely disabled: A model. *Rehabilitation Literature*, 1977, *38*, 373–375.

Luyben, P.D., & Brown, B.R. *The effects of pictures on the acquisition of a sight vocabulary in rural EMR children*. Tallahassee, Fla.: Florida State University, 1973. (ERIC Document Reproduction Service No. ED 974 752)

Myers, T. *The DAVID concept: Interactive video for the future.* Unpublished manuscript, 1979.

Nelon, E.M. *An evaluation of computer-assisted vocabulary instruction with mentally retarded children.* Research report No. 7322. Syracuse City School District, Syracuse, N.Y., 1972. (ERIC Document Reproduction Service No. ED 090 964)

Nelson, P.J., & Cossalter, J.G. *The potential of microcomputers for the physically handicapped.* Paper published in the proceedings of the First West Coast Faire, San Francisco, Calif., 1977.

Norris, W.C. Via technology to a new era in education. *Phi Delta Kappan*, 1977, *58*(6), 451–453.

Overby, C.M. Will technology change work-living patterns? *Journal of Rehabilitation*, 1973, *39*(6), 18–19, 41.

Overby, C.M. *Some human factors issues in bringing jobs to confined persons.* Paper published in the proceedings of the Annual Convention of the American Psychological Association, Washington, D.C., 1976. (ERIC Document Reproduction Service No. ED 137 674)

Propp, G., Nugent, G., Stone, C., & Nugent, R. *Videodisc: An instructional tool for the hearing impaired.* Media Development Project for the Hearing Impaired, University of Nebraska, Lincoln, Neb., 1980.

Rathe, G.H. Computer-assisted instruction: Exciting new tool for teaching the deaf. *American Annals of the Deaf*, 1969, *114*(5), 884–888. (a)

Rathe, G.H. Computer-assisted instruction and its potential for teaching deaf students. *American Annals of the Deaf*, 1969, *114*(5), 880–883. (b)

Rosenkranz, C.I. *COMP (computerized operational materials prescription).* Gillett, Wisc.: Cooperative Educational Service Agency 3, 1974. (ERIC Document Reproduction Service No. ED 094 539)

St. Aubin, R. *Evaluation of CAI as used by various handicaps.* South Metropolitan Association for Low-Incidence Handicapped, Chicago, 1975. (ERIC Document Reproduction Service No. ED 136 775)

Sandals, L.N. Computers assist handicapped children with learning problems. *Education Manitoba*, 1974, *1*(2), 11–12.

Sandals, L.N. *Computer-assisted applications for learning with special needs children.* Paper presented at the meeting of the American Educational Research Association, 1979. (ERIC Document Reproduction Service No. ED 173 983)

Saunders, F.A., Hill, W.A., & Easley, T.A. Development of a PLATO-based curriculum for tactile speech recognition. *Journal of Educational Technology Systems*, 1978, *7*(1), 19–27.

Scully, T. *Microcomputer communication for the handicapped.* Paper published in the proceedings of the Second West Coast Computer Faire, San Jose, Calif., March 1978.

Simpson, C.A. *Alphabetical versus graphotactic CRT page layout of letters for a versatile portable speech prosthesis.* Paper published in the proceedings of the Fifth West Coast Computer Faire, San Francisco, Calif., March 1980.

Skinner, B.F. The science of learning and the art of teaching. *Harvard Educational Review*, 1954, *24*, 86–97.

Stuckless, E.R. Planning for individualized instruction of deaf students at NTID. *American Annals of the Deaf*, 1969, *114*(5), 868–873.

Thorkildsen, R., Bickel, W.K., & Williams, J.G. A microcomputer/videodisc CAI system for the moderately mentally retarded. *Journal of Special Education Technology*, 1979, *2*(3), 45–51.

Von Feldt, J.R. A national survey of the use of computer-assisted instruction in schools for the deaf. *Journal of Educational Technology Systems*, 1978, 7(1), 29–38.

Watson, P.G. Utilization of the computer with deaf learners. *Educational Technology*, 1978, *18*(4), 47–49.

Withrow, F.B. Educational technology for the handicapped learner. In F.B. Withrow & C.J. Nygren (Eds.), *Language, materials, and curriculum management for the handicapped learner.* Columbus, Ohio: Charles E. Merrill, 1976.

Withrow, M.S. Computer animation and language instruction. *American Annals of the Deaf*, 1978, *123*(6), 723–725.

Zawolkow, G. *Computer education for the deaf in the San Francisco Bay Area.* Paper published in the proceedings of the Association of Computer-Based Instructional Systems, San Diego, Calif., March 1979.

EXERCISES

1. Explain how programming could foster in children the following qualities:

   - developing logical thinking and problem solving;
   - using strategies and variables;
   - gaining information about symmetry, design, angles, geometric forms;
   - learning to develop and test one's own theories;
   - developing the ability to take independent action;
   - improving the ability to sustain interest in a project;
   - increasing self-esteem;
   - achieving greater self-knowledge about personal ways of exploring.

2. Contact organizations using computers to aid the physically handicapped, and report your findings. Start with The Johns Hopkins University Applied Physics Lab or the IEEE Technical Committee on Computing and the Handicapped.

3. The Kurzweil Reading Machine aids the blind by converting ordinary printed material into spoken words. Find out how the machine works and record the reactions of some users.

4. Examine some of the problems in trying to adapt computers for use by handicapped people. What are some of the rewards of success?

5. Discuss whether educators should take the lead in developing CAI materials for the mentally retarded.

6. The computer will increase our ability to mainstream handicapped children. Discuss.

7. Conventional programs for exceptional students cannot compete with 6 hours a day and 18 hours on the weekend of on-line computer time in an upper-middle-class home.

Glossary

Acoustic Coupler A device attached to a computer terminal to send and receive information via telephone lines. It is a part of one kind of modem. (See Modem.)

Algorithm A set of instructions for solving a problem. (See Flowchart.)

ASCII American Standard Code for Information Interchange. Binary codes to represent certain characters, such as alphabet numerals, that have been accepted as standard by the computer industry.

Backup Duplicate copies of data files and programs to be used if the originals are lost or destroyed.

BASIC Beginners All-Purpose Symbolic Instruction Code. The most popular high-level programming language available for microcomputers.

Binary Code A numeric coding system using only the digits zero and one to represent data.

Bit Binary Digit. The smallest unit of digital information. (See Byte.)

Bubble Memory A device for storing large amounts of data in a small space. Composed of tiny magnetic pockets or bubbles created in thin semiconductive chips.

Bug An error. A hardware bug is an equipment malfunction or design error. A software bug is a programming error in syntax or logic.

Bus A physical connection of parallel wires providing a communication line along which data can be sent.

Byte The basic unit of information in a computer, usually consisting of a sequence of eight binary bits. Each byte has the capacity to store one character of information. (See Bit.)

Canned Program Preprogrammed software; a complete, ready-to-use program, usually stored on cassette or diskette.

Chip A thin slice of silicon, usually about a quarter-inch square, that contains various types of electronic circuitry. (See IC.)

COBOL Common Business-Oriented Language. A high-level programming language used in data processing applications.

Courseware Software designed for educational applications.

CPU Central Processing Unit. The "brain" of the computer, controlling what the computer does. Consists of the arithmetic/logic unit, the control unit, and main memory.

CRT Cathode Ray Tube. Similar in appearance to a television screen; a computer output device. (See Terminal.)

Cursor Small lighted rectangle on the screen of a video terminal or microcomputer that indicates the location where the next character will appear on the screen.

Daisy Wheel Printer A printer that has a wheel mechanism with characters on the perimeter of the wheel. Provides letter-quality type.

Debugging Detecting and removing program errors.

Diskette A small, flexible disk with a magnetic surface for recording data and programs. Often referred to as a "floppy" disk.

DOS Disk Operating System. A program that controls the interaction of the computer processor with its disk drives.

Dot Matrix A method by which video terminals and certain printers form characters as a pattern of dots, rather than solid lines.

Dumb Terminal A term used to describe a terminal used only to transmit and receive data with no independent processing capabilities.

EPROM Erasable Programming ROM. A read-only memory that can be erased either by an electrical signal or by ultraviolet light. (See RAM, ROM, and PROM.)

Execute To cause the computer to carry out the set of instructions in a program.

Firmware Software stored in ROM that can only be read, not written onto nor erased.

Floppy Disk (See Diskette.)

Flowchart A diagramatic representation of the solution to a problem. (See Algorithm.)

FORTRAN Formula Translator. A science-oriented high-level language.

GIGO Garbage in, garbage out. Implies that incorrect input results in invalid output.

Hard Copy Computer output on paper.

Hardware The physical parts of a computer system.

High-Level Languages Programming languages that use commands close to the English language.

Hollerith Coding system used to represent characters in a punched card.

IC Integrated Circuit. A solid-state device containing hundreds or thousands of circuits.

Ink Jet Printer A fast, high-quality printer in which a high-speed stream of electrically-charged ink droplets are deflected by a magnetic field.

Intelligent Terminal Terminal with a limited ability to process data without being connected to a large computer.

Interface The connecting device between a computer and peripheral device, such as a printer, allowing the two to communicate.

Kilo Symbol for approximately 1000 (actually, 2^{10} or 1024). Abbreviated "K."

Letter Quality Refers to a type of print or printer in which characters are fully formed (like typewriter characters), as opposed to dot matrix.

Line Printer A printer that prints an entire line of type simultaneously, rather than one character at a time.

LSI Large Scale Integration. Refers to an integrated circuit (IC) with more than 1000 logic gates.

Mainframe The CPU of a particularly large, powerful computer.

MODEM A contraction of MOdulator-DEModulator. A telecommunications device that allows computers to transmit data over telephone lines. (See Acoustic Coupler.)

Monitor A video display unit that uses a cathode ray tube to display information. (See CRT.)

Pascal A high-level programming language named after the mathematician Blaise Pascal. Particularly well-adapted to structured programming techniques.

Program A series of computer-language instructions to cause the computer to perform a certain task. (See Software.)

PROM Programmable Read-Only Memory. (See ROM.)

RAM Random Access Memory. Internal memory that can be written into or read from.

ROM Read-Only Memory. A form of memory that cannot be written onto and so protects data held in it.

RPG Report Program Generator. A high-level programming language commonly used for business data processing applications.

Run The command used to cause the computer to carry out the set of instructions in a program.

Scroll A feature of certain video display units that allows text on the screen to be moved up or down for viewing.

Software Programs written for computer systems. Hardware needs software to function.

Syntax The grammatical rules outlining how instructions should be written.

Telecommunications Information sent over the telephone lines.

Terminal A device used for communicating with a computer. Usually consists of a CRT screen and a keyboard.

Text Editor Program allowing efficient text manipulation using a computer or a word processor. Includes additions, deletions, and revisions.

Time-Sharing A system that allows two or more users to access the same computer simultaneously.

Turn-Key A computer system ready to perform all necessary tasks as soon as it is turned on.

Word Processing The process of recording, manipulating, editing, and storing textual data.

Index